Federal Wealth Transfer Taxes

BLACK LETTER OUTLINES

Federal Wealth Transfer Taxes

by **Kevin M. Yamamoto**
Professor of Law
South Texas College of Law

Samuel A. Donaldson
Associate Dean
Professor of Law
University of Washington School of Law

SECOND EDITION

WEST.
A Thomson Reuters business

Mat #41144149

Black Letter Series and Black Letter Series design appearing on the front cover are trademarks registered in the U.S. Patent and Trademark Office.

COPYRIGHT © 2006 West, a Thomson business
© 2011 Thomson Reuters
    610 Opperman Drive
    St. Paul, MN 55123
    1–800–313–9378

Printed in the United States of America

ISBN: 978–0–314–27533–2

Dedication

To my wife and son.
KMY

To Kelly.
SAD

Preface

This "Black Letter" is designed to help a law student recognize and understand the basic principles and issues of law covered in a law school course. It can be used both as a study aid when preparing for classes and as a review of the subject matter when studying for an examination.

Each "Black Letter" is written by experienced law school teachers who are recognized national authorities on the subject covered.

The law is succinctly stated by the authors of this "Black Letter." In addition, the exceptions to the rules are stated in the text. The rules and exceptions have purposely been condensed to facilitate quick and easy recollection. For an in-depth study of a point of law, citations to major student texts are given. In addition, a Text Correlation Chart provides a convenient means of relating material contained in the Black Letter to appropriate sections of the casebook the student is using in his or her law school course.

If the subject covered by this text is a code or code-related course, the code section or rule is set forth and discussed wherever applicable.

FORMAT

The format of this "Black Letter" is specially designed for review. (1) **Text.** First, it is recommended that the entire text be studied and, if deemed necessary, supplemented by the student texts cited. (2) **Capsule Summary.** The Capsule Summary is an abbreviated review of the subject matter which can be used both before and after studying the main body of the text. The headings in the Capsule

Summary follow the main text of the "Black Letter." (3) **Table of Contents.** The Table of Contents is in outline form to help you organize the details of the subject and the Summary of Contents gives you a final overview of the materials. (4) **Practice Examination.** The Practice Examination in Appendix B gives you the opportunity to test yourself with the type of questions asked on an exam and compare your answer with a model answer.

In addition, a number of other features are included to help you understand the subject matter and prepare for examinations:

Perspective: In this feature, the authors discuss their approach to the topic, the approach used in preparing the materials, and any tips on studying for and writing examinations.

Analysis: This feature, at the beginning of each section, is designed to give a quick summary of a particular section to help you recall the subject matter and to help you determine which areas need the most extensive review.

Examples: This feature is designed to illustrate, through fact situations, the law just stated. This, we believe, should help you analytically approach a question on the examination.

Glossary: This feature is designed to refamiliarize you with the meaning of a particular legal term. We believe that the recognition of words of art used in an examination helps you to better analyze the question. In addition, when writing an examination you should know the precise definition of a word of art you intend to use.

We believe that the materials in this "Black Letter" will facilitate your study of a law school course and assure success in writing examinations not only for the course but for the bar examination. We wish you success.

THE PUBLISHER

Summary of Contents

■ CHAPTER I: THE FEDERAL ESTATE TAX

■ CHAPTER II: GIFT TAX

■ CHAPTER III: GENERATION SKIPPING TRANSFER TAX

A. INTRODUCTION.

B. TERMINOLOGY.

Table of Contents

■ CHAPTER III: GENERATION SKIPPING TRANSFER TAX

APPENDICESAPPENDICES
App.

Capsule Summary

■ I. THE FEDERAL ESTATE TAX

A. THE GROSS ESTATE

IRC § 2031(a) defines the gross estate as the date-of-death value of all property specifically described in IRC §§ 2031–2044. Generally, the gross estate contains not only those assets and interests actually owned by the decedent at death (conceptually, the "actual gross estate") but also certain assets and interests owned by another individual or entity over which the decedent has certain powers, incidents of ownership, or other rights (conceptually, the "artificial gross estate").

1. Property Held at Death

Logically enough, the actual gross estate includes property held by the decedent at death, including certain property the decedent may not be able to transfer at death because of state law constraints.

a) Property in Which the Decedent Had an Interest [IRC § 2033]

The gross estate generally consists of assets owned by the decedent at death. Specifically, IRC § 2033 requires inclusion of "all property to the extent of the interest therein of the decedent at the time of death."

(1) Amount Included in Gross Estate

The value of any property interest included in the decedent's gross estate is its "fair market value," defined as "the price at which the property would change hands between a willing buyer and a willing seller, neither being under any compulsion to buy or sell and both having reasonable knowledge of relevant facts." [Reg. § 20.2031–1(b)]

(2) Application of State Law

Whether a decedent "owned" property for federal estate tax purposes is a question of state law. If the state's highest court has interpreted state law, the Internal Revenue Service is bound by that decision in examining an estate or gift tax return.

(3) Relationship of Gross Estate to Probate Estate or Taxable Income

To the extent IRC § 2033 requires inclusion of any interest in property that the decedent held at death, the gross estate is a significantly broader concept than the probate estate. Furthermore, inclusion in the gross estate is not conditioned upon the underlying property being subject to federal income tax.

b) Dower or Curtesy Interests [IRC § 2034]

IRC § 2034 requires inclusion of a decedent's dower or curtesy interests, the rights to a decedent's property conferred to the decedent's surviving spouse under state law.

2. Re–Inclusion Provisions

In some cases, a decedent may continue to have so much control or influence over property previously transferred by the decedent that the property should be included in the decedent's gross estate, even though the property was not legally owned by the decedent at the date of death. Congress has identified four transactions that raise this problem.

a) Transfers With a Retained Life Estate [IRC § 2036]

(1) Elements

In order for IRC § 2036(a) to cause inclusion in the decedent's gross estate of property gratuitously transferred by the decedent, a three-part test must be met: the decedent must have transferred property while retaining a prescribed interest for a prescribed period.

(2) Grantor as Trustee

The retained power to choose among beneficiaries, even if such power is exercisable only in the capacity of a trustee, will generally trigger inclusion under IRC § 2036(a). The grantor-trustee's power to choose must have some effect on the enjoyment of the income earned from the trust property. If the grantor-trustee's power does not affect the enjoyment of the income, IRC § 2036(a) will not apply. Often, this problem is solved by naming an independent trustee. But IRC § 2036(a) will still apply even with an independent trustee if the grantor retains the power to replace the trustee and the class of permissible successors includes the grantor or a party related or subordinate to the grantor.

(3) The Sale Exception

By its own terms, IRC § 2036(a) applies only to property gratuitously transferred by the decedent and not property transfers resulting from a "bona fide sale for an adequate and full consideration in money or money's worth." Sometimes the question is not whether the sale was bona fide but whether the purchaser paid full consideration for the property. There is a split of authority where the decedent sells a remainder interest in property but retains a life estate. Some courts have concluded that the sale exception to IRC § 2036(a) applies if the consideration received by the decedent equals the value of the remainder interest. Other courts conclude that the decedent must receive consideration equal to the value of the property transferred.

(4) Retained Voting Rights as a Prescribed Interest

Where the decedent gratuitously transfers stock in a "controlled corporation" but retains the right to vote the transferred shares, whether directly or indirectly, the decedent is considered to have retained the enjoyment of the transferred stock. Generally, a corporation is "controlled" if the decedent owned or had the right to vote stock possessing at least 20% of the total combined voting power of all classes of stock at any time following the gratuitous transfer (or, if longer, the three-year period ending on the decedent's death).

(5) Reciprocal Trust Doctrine

In a reciprocal trust arrangement, a transferor (T1) agrees to create a trust that gives a life estate to the other transferor (T2) and the remainder to the beneficiaries of T2. In exchange, T2 creates a similar trust for T1 and T1's beneficiaries. The Supreme Court has held that where two trusts are "interrelated, and that the arrangement, to the extent of mutual value, leaves the settlors in approximately the same economic position as they would have been in had they created trusts naming themselves as life beneficiaries," a transferor will be treated as the grantor of the trust created for the benefit of the transferor and the transferor's beneficiaries, meaning IRC § 2036(a) will apply.

b) Transfers Taking Effect at Death [IRC § 2037]

(1) Elements

Inclusion under IRC § 2037 results when both the survivorship test (IRC § 2037(a)(1)) and the reversion test (IRC § 2037(a)(2)) are met. In order to meet the survivorship test, a beneficiary's possession or enjoyment of the property at issue must be obtainable only by surviving the decedent. The reversion test is met if the decedent retained a reversionary interest in the subject property and the value of the reversion immediately before the decedent's death exceeded 5% of the value of the subject property. If IRC § 2037(a) applies, the amount includible is the value of all property subject to the decedent's reversionary interest.

(2) Survivorship

The survivorship test requires that a beneficiary be able to take only by surviving the decedent. If the beneficiary can take ownership by any other means, such as the exercise of a general power of appointment, the survivorship test is not met.

(3) Reversionary Interests

The reversion test is met when the decedent retained a reversion, whether expressly or by implication or by operation of law. Thus, it is not necessary for the instrument of transfer to explicitly refer to the decedent's reversion. If the decedent's reversion affects only the rights to income from the transferred property, however, the reversion test is not met.

c) Revocable Transfers [IRC § 2038]

If a transferor retains a power to revoke or materially change the wealth transfer, then the transferor still has sufficient control over the transferred property such that it is fair to say the transferor still "owns" the property at death.

(1) Power to Revoke

Inclusion under IRC § 2038 occurs when the transferor has the power to revoke or terminate a transfer even where that power can only be exercised with the consent of another.

(2) Power to Alter or Amend

IRC § 2038 is not limited to situations where the transferor holds a power to revoke the wealth transfer; inclusion under IRC § 2038 is also triggered by powers to alter or amend a transfer of property, even if the transfer is otherwise irrevocable. The capacity in which a power to alter or amend a trust is of no consequence. Thus, if the transferor holds a power to alter or amend in a fiduciary capacity (as trustee of a trust, for instance), IRC § 2038(a)(1) still applies. Where the grantor of a trust also wants to serve as trustee, the trustee's discretion to distribute income or principal to beneficiaries should be limited to an ascertainable standard related to the maintenance, education, support, or health of a beneficiary. When a trustee's discretion is so limited, the trustee is seen as having merely a ministerial power and not a discretionary power to alter or amend the original transfer (which would cause inclusion under IRC § 2038) or a power to control beneficial enjoyment of trust property (which would cause inclusion under IRC § 2036).

(3) Interrelationship with IRC § 2036

Because both IRC §§ 2036 and 2038 look to retained powers over gratuitously transferred property, it should come as no surprise that inclusion of the same property may be required by both Code sections. Where that happens, of course, the value of the property is only included in the gross estate once.

d) Certain Transfers Within Three Years of Death [IRC § 2035]

One popular misconception about the federal estate tax is that all gifts within three years of death are included in the gross estate. This used to be the rule, but not since 1982.

(1) The General Rule

Now, only two types of gifts within three years of death are pulled back into the gross estate under IRC § 2035(a). The first is a decedent's gift of a life insurance policy on the decedent's life within three years of death. The second is a gift of an interest in property that would have caused inclusion under IRC §§ 2036 through 2038 if the decedent had held onto the interest until death.

(2) Gift Tax Paid on Gifts Made Within Three Years of Death

IRC § 2035(b) requires inclusion in the gross estate of any federal gift tax paid by the decedent attributable to gifts made within three years of death. Thus, in the case of near-death gifts, the benefit deriving from the tax-exclusive nature of the federal gift tax is lost.

e) Consideration Paid by the Recipient [IRC § 2043]

It is worth noting that IRC §§ 2035–2038 only apply to gratuitous lifetime transfers. If the recipient(s) give(s) adequate consideration for the received property, none of these "re-inclusion" provisions apply. Equally important of note, the recipient(s) must give full consideration to avoid application of IRC §§ 2035–2038. Under IRC § 2043(a), if the recipient gives something less than full consideration in exchange for the transferred property, the decedent's gross estate will include the entire value of the transferred property minus the consideration received.

3. Special Rules for Certain Assets

The concept of "ownership" in the context of certain assets is sufficiently complex to warrant separate attention. Here, Congress has identified five types of "special" assets that require separate rules for inclusion in the gross estate.

a) Annuities [IRC § 2039]

An annuity is a contractual arrangement whereby one party agrees to make a series of payments to the other party. In the typical annuity arrangement, an individual pays a premium to a corporation (usually, but not necessarily, a life insurance company) and the corporation agrees to make quarterly or monthly payments to the individual, either for a term of years or, more commonly, for the individual's life.

(1) The General Rule

IRC § 2039 requires inclusion of the value of any payment(s) made to a beneficiary made by reason of surviving the decedent if such payment is made pursuant to an annuity contract under which the decedent received payments or had a right to receive payments for any of the "prescribed periods" described in IRC § 2036. In order for IRC § 2039 to apply to an annuity, one or more payments must be made to someone by reason of surviving the decedent (i.e., the annuity must pay survivorship benefits). Note that IRC § 2039 is also broad enough to capture any survivor benefits paid under retirement or pension plans.

(2) Income Tax Aspects

Annuities are an investment, and like any investment, a taxpayer has a basis in the right to future payments. When a taxpayer receives an annuity payment, there is an issue as to how much of the payment represents a return of the taxpayer's basis. Under IRC § 72, annuitants are generally allowed to amortize their basis in the annuity contract over the expected payment period. Consequently, each annuity payment usually consists of a combination of income and a non-taxable return of capital.

b) Jointly–Owned Property [IRC § 2040]

(1) The General Rule

Generally, a decedent's estate includes the entire value of any property held as joint tenants with rights of survivorship except to the extent the estate can show that consideration for the property was furnished by a co-tenant. [IRC § 2040(a)]

(2) Joint Interests of Husbands and Wives

IRC § 2040(b) provides an absolute rule: exactly one-half of property held by the decedent and the decedent's spouse as joint tenants with rights of survivorship is included in the decedent's gross estate. It does not matter whether the account was created with community funds or separate property, and the amount of consideration furnished by the decedent is likewise irrelevant.

(3) Income Tax Aspects

A beneficiary's basis in property acquired from a decedent is "stepped up" (or down) to the property's fair market value as of the date of the decedent's death. Where the surviving joint tenant assumes ownership over the whole property because of the co-tenant's death, the step-up (or down) in basis is limited to that portion of the property that was included in the decedent's gross estate.

c) **Property Subject to a General Power of Appointment [IRC § 2041]**

Where the decedent holds a power to appoint trust income or corpus among a designated class of beneficiaries including the decedent (or the decedent's estate or creditors), the decedent in effect holds ownership-type rights in the trust property. IRC § 2041 realizes that a wealth transfer occurs if the decedent dies holding a general power of appointment or exercises such a power in a manner consistent with the re-inclusion provisions in IRC §§ 2036–2038.

(1) **General Powers of Appointment Held at Death**

a. **The General Rule**

Formally, IRC § 2041(a)(1) requires inclusion of property subject to a "general power of appointment" held by the decedent at death. A general power of appointment is any power of appointment over property that is exercisable in favor of the decedent, the decedent's estate, or the creditor's of the decedent's estate.

b. **Exceptions to Treatment as a General Powers of Appointment**

There are three situations where holding a general power of appointment at death will not cause inclusion in the gross estate.

i) **Power Limited to an Ascertainable Standard**

The first situation is where the decedent's discretion in appointing the trust property is limited by an "ascertainable standard" related to the maintenance, education, support, or health of a permissible appointee.

ii) **Power Must be Exercised in Conjunction with Creator of Power**

The second situation is where the power can only be exercised jointly by the decedent and the person who created the power.

iii) Substantial Adverse Interests

The third situation is where the power can only be exercised jointly by the decedent and a third party with a "substantial adverse interest" in the exercise of the power in the decedent's favor.

c. Other Issues

Unless one of the exceptions noted above applies, gross estate inclusion of property subject to a general power of appointment results no matter whether the decedent exercised the power and even where the power expires at the decedent's death. Moreover, under the last sentence of IRC § 2041(a)(2), the decedent is assumed to hold a general power of appointment at death even if the exercise of that power was subject to the condition precedent of giving advance notice.

(2) Exercise or Release of a General Power of Appointment

a. The General Rule

In addition to including property subject to a general power of appointment held at the decedent's death, IRC § 2041(a)(2) requires inclusion in the gross estate where the decedent exercised or released a general power of appointment in a manner that, if it had been a direct transfer of property by the decedent, would result in gross estate inclusion under any of the re-inclusion provisions (IRC §§ 2035–2038).

b. Lapse

The lapse of a general power of appointment is treated as the release of a general power of appointment to the extent that the value of the property which could have been appointed by the exercise of the power exceeds the greater of $5,000 or 5% of the value of the assets from which the exercise of the lapsed power could have been satisfied.

d) Life Insurance [IRC § 2042]

(1) The General Rule

The death benefits from a life insurance policy are included in the gross estate of the insured in two situations: (1) where the death benefits are payable to the insured's estate; or (2) where the insured has any of the "incidents of ownership" over the policy.

(2) Strategies to Avoid Inclusion

Where an individual with a substantial estate has any of the incidents of ownership in a policy on his or her life, that individual may seek to avoid the application of IRC § 2042 by transferring such incidents of ownership to another. This solution is feasible assuming the individual survives for three years following the transfer. If the individual does not so survive, the death benefit will still be included in the decedent's gross estate under IRC § 2035(a). Another common strategy is for the insured to transfer all ownership rights in the policy to an irrevocable trust. If the insured lives for three years following the transfer of the policy, the death benefits will not be included in the insured's gross estate.

(3) Insurance Policies on Another's Life

IRC § 2042 is limited to policies insuring the decedent's life. Policies owned by the decedent that insure the lives of others are included in the decedent's gross estate under IRC § 2033, for the decedent controls how the ownership of such policies will pass at the decedent's death.

e) Certain Property for Which the Marital Deduction Was Previously Allowed [IRC § 2044]

To make sure Uncle Sam eventually gets an estate tax bite on property previously transferred to a surviving spouse, IRC § 2044 requires inclusion of any property not already included under IRC §§ 2033–2042 for which another decedent validly claimed a marital deduction. The effect of this rule is to require inclusion of property for which either a "QTIP election" under IRC § 2056(b)(7) was made upon the death of the first spouse or a "spousal charitable remainder trust" under IRC § 2056(b)(8) was claimed.

f) Disclaimers [IRC § 2046]

Any person making a "qualified disclaimer" of an interest in property is treated as if the interest was never transferred to that person at all. Disclaimers for the estate tax are treated the same as in the gift tax, and are covered therein.

4. Valuation Issues

In some situations, the use of fair market value produces inappropriate results. Accordingly, there are special rules to take into account necessary deviations from the fair market value standard.

a) Alternate Valuation Date [IRC § 2032]

(1) General Rule

Although the general rule is that assets included in the gross estate must be valued as of the date of death, the executor of the estate may, under IRC § 2032, elect to value all of the included assets as of the date six months after the decedent's death.

(2) Conditions for Application

To be eligible for the election, use of the alternate valuation date must result in both a reduced gross estate and a reduced estate tax and generation-skipping tax liability, although there are few situations where an election would be helpful if it did not have that effect.

(3) Post–Death Dispositions of Gross Estate Assets

If the decedent's personal representative makes an IRC § 2032 election and any of the property included in the decedent's gross estate is sold, distributed, or otherwise disposed of prior to the alternate valuation date, such property must be valued as of the date of the sale, distribution, or disposition.

(4) Valuation Changes Due to the "Mere Lapse of Time"

To the extent the reduction in the value of an asset included in the gross estate is attributable merely to the passage of time, the asset must be valued as of the date of the decedent's death. Assets whose values are affected merely by the lapse of time include patents, estates for the life of a person other than the decedent, remainders, and reversions.

(5) Effect on Estate Tax Deductions

Use of the alternate valuation date may have a corollary effect on the deductions available in computing the taxable estate.

b) Qualified Real Property [IRC § 2032A]

Under IRC § 2032A, so-called "qualified real property" (generally, land used for farming or for the operation of any other trade or business) will qualify for valuation based on its "actual use" instead of its "highest and best use."

(1) Qualified Real Property

To claim the benefit of IRC § 2032A, three requirements must be met. First, the decedent had to be a citizen or resident of the United States at the time of death. Second, the personal representative must make an irrevocable election on the federal estate tax return to apply IRC § 2032A. Finally, the property to be valued under IRC § 2032A must be "qualified real property." In order to be qualified real property, no less than eight requirements must be met. For ease of reference, seven of these eight requirements can be placed into three groups.

a. The "Property" Requirements

First, the real property must be located in the United States. Second, the real property must pass from the decedent to a "qualified heir."

b. The "Value" Requirements

First, at least 50% of the "adjusted value" of the decedent's gross estate must consist of property (real or personal) which both was used for a "qualified use" by the decedent or a member of the decedent's family on the date of the decedent's death and passes to a qualified heir. Second, at least 25% of the adjusted value of the decedent's gross estate must consist of real property (not including personal property) that passes to a qualified heir and which meets the "use" requirements described below.

c. The "Use" Requirements

First, the property must have been used for a qualified use by the decedent on the date of death. Second, for periods totaling at least five of the eight years prior to the decedent's death, the real property must have been owned and put to a qualified use by the decedent or a member of the decedent's family. Third, for periods totaling at least five of the eight years prior to the decedent's death, the decedent or a member of the decedent's family must have materially participated in the farm or other family business.

(2) Limitation on Aggregate Reduction in Value

The maximum reduction in value that can result by application of IRC § 2032A to qualified real property is $750,000. But that figure is adjusted for inflation in multiples of $10,000. In 2011, for example, the limitation was $1,020,000.

(3) Dispositions and Failure to Continue Qualified Use

a. Generally

An "additional estate tax" is imposed if, within ten years of the decedent's death (or before the qualified heir's death within that time) (the "probation period"), the qualified heir either disposes of any interest in qualified real property or ceases to use the qualified real property for the qualified use.

b. Amount of Additional Estate Tax

The amount of the additional estate tax is, very generally, the difference in estate tax liability attributable to the qualified real property having been valued under IRC § 2032A instead of its highest and best use.

c. Lack of Material Participation Deemed a Nonqualified Use

If, during any eight-year period ending within the probation period, none of the decedent, the qualified heir, or a family member of the decedent or the qualified heir participated materially in the farm or business operation related to the qualified real property for periods totaling at least five years, the qualified real property is treated as no longer being used for the qualified use.

c) Premiums and Discounts

Because the fair market value standard refers to what a hypothetical buyer would pay for the decedent's interest in property, some adjustments to the value of an asset included in the gross estate are appropriate, especially where the decedent's interest has special powers or leverage over the interests of others or, conversely, where the decedent's interest is comparatively weaker to other interests in the same asset.

(1) Control Premium

Where the decedent's interest is a controlling interest in a business or some other asset, a willing buyer might indeed pay a premium on top of the liquidation value of the interest.

(2) Minority Interest Discount

The minority interest discount reflects the inability both to compel a sale, distribution, or other disposition of the underlying asset and to control its management.

(3) Marketability Discount

Where an interest cannot be readily sold because of practical obstacles to sale, a limited market of buyers, or because of restrictions on the owner's ability to transfer the interest, valuation experts will apply the marketability discount to reflect the fact that a willing buyer will consider the costs and delay involved in selling the subject property in deciding the appropriate value of the subject interest.

(4) Fractional Interest Discount

The fractional interest discount reflects the fact that a willing buyer will not pay liquidation value for an undivided interest in an asset because of the costs to partition the property or sever the interest, not to mention the general inconveniences that are part of co-ownership.

(5) Blockage Discount

An adjustment is often made to the liquidation value of property (usually marketable securities) to reflect the fact that the trading volume in the applicable market may not be large enough to absorb the sale of the large block at issue.

(6) Other Discounts

Although the above-mentioned discounts are most common, others can come into play, including the capital gains discount, the key person discount, and the litigation discount.

(7) Combinations of Premiums and Discounts

Premiums and discounts are layered and taken in a serial fashion; they are not cumulative.

d) Special Valuation Rules [§§ 2701–2704]

Introduced in 1990, Chapter 14 of the Code consists of four Code sections introducing a number of special valuation rules designed to eliminate the use of certain "estate freeze" techniques which Congress found abusive to the federal wealth transfer tax system.

(1) Transfers of Interests in Certain Corporations and Partnerships [IRC § 2701]

IRC § 2701 values a transferred interest in property as the full value of the subject property (by valuing the retained interest at zero). It applies when two conditions are met. First, the taxpayer must transfer a "subordinate equity interest" in a partnership or corporation to or for the benefit of a member of the taxpayer's family in a younger generation. Second, immediately after the transfer, the taxpayer or a member of the taxpayer's family in an older generation must hold an "applicable retained interest."

(2) Transfers of Interests in Trusts [IRC § 2702]

IRC § 2702 imposes another zero-value rule to neutralize the benefit of certain trust arrangements where the grantor attempts to make a gift of a remainder interest at an actuarially-reduced value. Where it applies, IRC § 2702 values the grantor's retained interest at zero, meaning that the grantor is deemed to make a gift of the entire value of the property transferred to the trust at the time of the transfer to the trust.

(3) Certain Rights and Restrictions Disregarded [IRC § 2703]

IRC § 2703 requires property to be valued without regard to any option, agreement, or other right to buy or use property. It also requires property to be valued without regard to any restriction on the right to sell or use property.

(4) Treatment of Certain Lapsing Rights and Restrictions [IRC § 2704]

IRC § 2704 contains two sets of rules for measuring the value of transferred interests in a corporation or partnership. The first set of rules considers the effect of lapsing rights, and the second set of rules pertains to the effect of certain restrictions on liquidation of the entity.

B. DEDUCTIONS

Once the value of the gross estate is determined, the focus shifts to the five available deductions.

1. Certain Expenses and Debts [§ 2053]

Four types of expenses are deductible under IRC § 2053.

a) Funeral Expenses

Funeral expenses actually paid by the estate are deductible in determining the taxable estate.

b) Administration Expenses

Amounts deductible as administration expenses under IRC § 2053(a)(2) are those expenses "actually and necessarily incurred . . . in the collection of assets, payment of debts, and distribution of property to the persons entitled to it."

(1) Personal Representative Commissions

Commissions actually paid or reasonably expected to be paid to the decedent's personal representative (another term for executor) are generally deductible as administration expenses.

(2) Attorney's Fees

Estates can claim a deduction for an attorney's fees that are actually paid or are reasonably expected to be paid.

(3) Miscellaneous Administration Expenses

Other deductible administration expenses common to many estates include court costs, accountant's fees, appraiser's fees, maintenance expenses, and storage costs.

(4) Administration Expenses Related to Non–Probate Property

Expenses incurred in connection with administering a trust established during the decedent's lifetime are also deductible, as are other administration expenses related to other non-probate assets.

(5) Income Tax Crossover

If an expense is deductible for both estate tax and income tax purposes, the expense generally can only be claimed on the estate tax return unless the estate waives the right to claim a deduction under IRC § 2053, in which case the expense may be claimed on the income tax return.

c) Claims Against the Estate

IRC § 2053(a)(3) allows a deduction for enforceable claims against the estate, and IRC § 2053(b) offers a corollary deduction for claims against non-probate assets included in the gross estate. Only personal obligations of the decedent in existence at the date of death are deductible under this rule.

d) Unpaid Mortgages

If the estate is liable for the amount of any mortgage or other debt encumbering property included in the gross estate, then the proper approach is to include the full fair market value of the property in the gross estate and then deduct the full amount of any unpaid mortgage or other debt attributable to such property.

2. Casualty Losses During Estate Administration [IRC § 2054]

If property included in the gross estate is damaged or lost because of "fires, storms, shipwrecks, or other casualties, or from theft" during the time the estate is administered, the resulting losses may be deducted from the gross estate, but only to the extent such losses are not compensated for by insurance or any other means.

3. Transfers to Charities [IRC § 2055]

Testamentary transfers to certain public, religious, charitable, scientific, literary, and educational organizations (collectively, "charities") qualify for the IRC § 2055 charitable deduction.

a) Charities

Only those transfers to organizations specifically identified in IRC § 2055(a) qualify for the charitable deduction.

(1) Organizations That Qualify as Charities

A deductible bequest is one made to any of the five types of organizations identified in IRC § 2055(a).

a. Governments

Transfers to or for the use of the federal government, a state, a political subdivision of a state, or a municipality will qualify for the deduction, assuming the governmental beneficiary uses the transfer "for exclusively public purposes."

b. Certain Nonprofit Organizations

Transfers to or for the use of any corporation or association "organized and operated exclusively for religious, charitable, scientific, literary, or educational purposes, including the encouragement of art, or to foster national or international amateur sports competition . . . , and the prevention of cruelty to children or animals" may also qualify for the deduction.

c. Trusts and Certain Fraternal Organizations

Transfers to trustees and lodges can qualify for the deduction, but "only if such contributions or gifts are to be used . . . exclusively for religious, charitable, scientific, literary, or educational purposes, or for the prevention of cruelty to children or animals."

d. Veterans' Organizations

Transfers to or for the use of any Veterans' organization incorporated under federal law are eligible for the deduction.

(2) Indefinite Charitable Bequests

Indefinite charitable bequests qualify for the deduction provided either the testamentary instrument or local law restricts the class of permissible recipients to organizations that are charities within the meaning of IRC § 2055(a).

b) Split–Interest Transfers

Where a bequest is split between a charity and another, non-charitable beneficiary (typically, an individual), complicated valuation issues can arise.

(1) General Rule

If property is to be enjoyed by both a charity and another, non-charitable beneficiary, the charitable deduction is generally disallowed.

(2) Exceptions

There are four situations where a split-interest transfer will be deductible under IRC § 2055.

a. Transfers Described in IRC § 170(f)(3)(B)

Split-interest transfers of property described in IRC § 170(f)(3)(B) remain eligible for the IRC § 2055 deduction. IRC § 170(f)(3)(B) lists three types of transfers. The first type of transfer is the contribution of a remainder interest in a personal residence or farm. The second type of transfer is the contribution of an undivided portion of the decedent's entire interest in property. The third type of transfer is a qualified conservation contribution of property.

b. Charitable Remainder Trusts

Perhaps the most significant exception to the deduction disallowance for split-interest transfers is the charitable remainder trust.

i) Charitable Remainder Annuity Trusts (CRATs)

Under a charitable remainder annuity trust (or "CRAT"), the non-charitable beneficiary receives a fixed annuity amount paid at least annually.

ii) Charitable Remainder Unitrusts (CRUTs)

Under a charitable remainder unitrust (or "CRUT"), the non-charitable beneficiary receives a fixed percentage of the net fair market value of the trust assets, as determined annually.

iii) Net Income Makeup Charitable Remainder Unitrusts (NIMCRUTs)

Under a net income makeup charitable remainder unitrust (or "NIMCRUT"), a CRUT can pay the trust's income to the non-charitable beneficiary where the amount of income is less than the amount normally required to be paid (a fixed percentage of the value of the trust's assets). Then, in later years, when the trust's income exceeds the amount required to be paid to the non-charitable beneficiary, the excess income is paid to the non-charitable beneficiary to make up for the amount that should have been paid in the earlier year when trust income was less than the required distribution amount.

iv) Powers of Appointment in a Charitable Remainder Trust

No one should hold a power to consume, invade, or appropriate the property of a charitable remainder trust for the benefit of any individual, including the non-charitable beneficiary. The existence of such a power violates the requirements for a valid charitable remainder trust and, thus, jeopardizes the IRC § 2055 deduction. But if such a power goes unexercised and is completely terminated prior to the date the decedent's estate is required to file the estate tax return, the termination shall be treated as a valid disclaimer of the power under IRC § 2518.

v) Charitable Remainder Trusts and the Alternate Valuation Date

In applying the alternate valuation date, contingencies that occur after death (like the death of the annuity or unitrust beneficiary) are disregarded in valuing the proper amount of the IRC § 2055 deduction.

c. Charitable Lead Trusts

Under a charitable lead trust, the annual payments are made to the charitable organization with the remainder passing to one or more non-charitable beneficiaries. All other requirements applicable to charitable remainder trusts also apply to charitable lead trusts.

d. Pooled Income Funds

In a pooled income fund, two or more donors agree to contribute property to a single fund administered by the charity. The fund will pay an income interest to one or more persons and, at the end of the term, the remainder will pass to the charity.

4. Marital Bequests [IRC § 2056]

Since the early 1980s decedents (or at least their estates) have enjoyed an unlimited marital deduction. Thus, if a decedent leaves his or her entire estate to the surviving spouse, the taxable estate will be zero, since the gross estate will be reduced by an offsetting marital deduction.

a) The Terminable Interest Rule

(1) Generally

The terminable interest rule states that no marital deduction is allowed where, due to the lapse of time or on the occurrence (or failure to occur) of an event or contingency, the interest in property passing from the decedent to the surviving spouse will terminate, causing the interest to pass to another (for less than an adequate and full consideration in money or money's worth) who may possess or enjoy the property after the termination of the surviving spouse's interest.

(2) Exceptions

There are four exceptions to the terminable interest rule.

a. Surviving Spouse Holds a General Power of Appointment

The first exception applies where the surviving spouse holds a general power of appointment over the transferred property.

b. Life Insurance or Annuities with a General Power of Appointment

The second exception is for life insurance or annuity payments to be paid in two or more installments where the surviving spouse is given a general power of appointment over the payments.

c. Charitable Remainder Trusts

The third exception is for a trust that meets the definition of a charitable remainder trust and names the surviving spouse as the non-charitable beneficiary. Here, the trust gives a lifetime annuity or unitrust interest to the surviving spouse and the remainder to charity.

d. Qualified Terminable Interest Property (QTIP)

The final exception is for trusts or other property transfers that give the surviving spouse a "qualifying income interest" for life and where the personal representative of the decedent elects on the estate tax return to treat the trust property as qualified terminable interest property (or "QTIP," for short). A qualifying income interest has three components: the surviving spouse is entitled to all of the income from the property for life; such income is payable at least annually; and no one (not even the surviving spouse) holds a power to appoint any portion of the property to anyone but the surviving spouse. Upon the death of the surviving spouse, IRC § 2044 requires inclusion of the remaining QTIP trust property in the surviving spouse's gross estate.

i) Effect of Contingencies

If the surviving spouse's right to income is limited to a term of years or subject to termination upon the occurrence of a contingency (like remarriage), the spouse does not hold a qualifying income interest, meaning the decedent's estate may not make a QTIP election. However, if the surviving spouse's income interest is contingent on the personal representative making the QTIP election, the spouse's interest will not fail to be a qualified income interest solely because of such contingency.

ii) Repayment of Estate Tax Due on QTIP Remainder

The personal representative can seek reimbursement from the beneficiaries of the QTIP trust to the extent the surviving spouse's estate must pay estate tax attributable to the inclusion of the QTIP trust assets in the gross estate. [IRC § 2207A(a)]

iii) Lifetime Dispositions of QTIP Interest

If the surviving spouse disposes of any portion of the qualifying income interest, the surviving spouse will be treated for federal gift tax purposes as having transferred all interests in the qualified terminable interest property except for the qualifying income interest. [IRC § 2519]

iv) Practical Considerations

A QTIP trust is a common technique for substantial estates where the first spouse to die wants to leave his or her estate for the benefit of the surviving spouse but is hesitant to make an outright bequest of property to the surviving spouse for fear of losing control over the disposition of the property at the surviving spouse's death.

(3) Interests Conditioned on Survival

To accommodate survivorship clauses, a bequest to a surviving spouse that terminates if the surviving spouse fails to survive the decedent for a period of up to six months will not violate the terminable interest rule if the surviving spouse actually survives the required period and the bequest does not terminate.

(4) The Tainted Asset Rule

Where the interest passing to the surviving spouse may be satisfied out of a group of assets which includes an asset that would be nondeductible if it passed from the decedent to the surviving spouse (a "tainted asset"), the amount of the marital deduction is reduced by the value of the tainted asset.

(5) The Executor Purchase Rule

No marital deduction is allowed where a terminable interest is, at the direction of the decedent, to be acquired by the personal representative for the surviving spouse.

b) Credit Shelter Trusts

With proper planning, married couples can fully utilize the applicable exclusion amount of the first spouse to die without substantively affecting the general dispositive scheme of leaving everything to the surviving spouse. Typically, such planning involves the use of a "credit shelter trust," where the estate of the first spouse to die is apportioned between two beneficiaries: that portion of the estate equal to the then-remaining exemption amount is allocated to the credit shelter trust and the balance passes to the marital deduction share (either outright to the surviving spouse or to a QTIP trust). The credit shelter trust typically provides the surviving spouse with access to income or principal as needed for the surviving spouse's maintenance, education, support, or health.

c)   Interests That Pass to the Surviving Spouse

The marital deduction is available only where an interest in property passes to the surviving spouse from the decedent. There are seven ways for an interest in property to pass from the decedent: (1) a bequest or devise from the decedent; (2) an inheritance from the decedent; (3) a dower, curtesy, or other statutory interest taken as the surviving spouse; (4) any lifetime transfer from the decedent; (5) taking property held with the decedent as joint tenants with rights of survivorship; (6) taking property pursuant to the exercise or non-exercise of a power of appointment held by the decedent; and (7) receiving the death benefit from a policy of insurance on the decedent's life.

5.   State Death Taxes [IRC § 2058]

Just as individuals can deduct state income taxes on the federal income tax return, an estate may deduct "state death taxes" (estate, inheritance, legacy, or succession taxes) actually paid to any state (or the District of Columbia) attributable to property included in the gross estate.

6.   The Former Deduction for Qualified Family–Owned Business Interests [IRC § 2057]

Prior to 2004, there was a fifth deduction for certain family-owned business interests under IRC § 2057. Originally an exclusion provision, special relief for family-owned business interests was introduced in 1997. The next year, the exclusion was converted to a deduction. Both the credit and the deduction proved to be remarkably complex.

C.   COMPUTING TAX LIABILITY

Having computed the taxable estate, one can then proceed to determine the liability for estate tax.

1. **Tentative Tax Liability [IRC § 2001]**

The estate's tentative tax liability is determined with reference to the rate table in IRC § 2001(c). The taxable estate is added to the "adjusted taxable gifts" (taxable gifts made in 1977 or later that are not subject to "re-inclusion" in the gross estate under IRC §§ 2035–2038). This sum is then applied to the rate table. The resulting tax is then reduced by any federal gift tax that would have been payable on gifts made in 1977 or later using the rate tables in effect at the decedent's death, regardless of whether such gifts are re-included in the gross estate.

2. **Credits**

The tentative estate tax computed under IRC § 2001(c)(1) is reduced by six credits.

a) **The Unified Credit [IRC § 2010]**

Every estate is entitled to the "applicable credit amount" set forth in IRC § 2010(c). The applicable credit amount is equal to the tentative tax under IRC § 2001(c) on the "applicable exclusion amount." The applicable exclusion amount is the sum of the "basic exclusion amount" and, in the case of a surviving spouse, the "deceased spousal unused exclusion amount." The basic exclusion is $5 million. Without regard to the deceased spousal unused exclusion amount, in effect, the first $5 million of the taxable estate for decedents dying is exempt from tax.

The "deceased spousal unused exclusion amount" is generally equal to that portion of the first spouse to die's basic exclusion amount that was not used by the first spouse. Effectively, then, any unused exclusion carries over to the surviving spouse for both estate tax and gift tax purposes, but only if the proper election is made on the first spouse's estate tax return.

b) **State Death Taxes [IRC § 2011]**

Congress phased-out the credit for state death taxes paid beginning in 2002. The credit disappeared altogether in 2005, when IRC § 2058 offered a deduction for state death taxes paid.

c) **Tax on Pre–1977 Gifts [IRC § 2012]**

The addition of adjusted taxable gifts in the determination of tentative tax liability requires that any gift tax previously payable on adjusted taxable gifts be accounted for in the computation of estate tax liability, else the decedent will be taxed a second time on the lifetime gift. For gifts made after 1976, the correction is contained in the computation of tentative tax liability, for the amount of any gift tax payable on gifts made in 1977 or later is subtracted from the tax computed under the IRC § 2001(c) rate table. Subtracting that amount from tentative tax liability is the functional equivalent of crediting the gift tax payable against the tentative tax liability.

d)   Tax on Prior Transfers [IRC § 2013]

Where a decedent's will makes a substantial bequest to a person who dies shortly after the decedent, there is a risk that the same assets will be subject to two rounds of estate tax very close in time. In those situations, IRC § 2013 offers a credit for tax previously paid by another on property included in the decedent's gross estate. The credit applies if the transferor died within ten years before or within two years after the decedent and if the decedent acquired the property from the transferor.

e)   Other Credit Provisions [IRC §§ 2014, 2015, 2016]

The other credit provisions have limited application. Two of these three statutes pertain to death taxes paid to other countries. Under IRC § 2014, there is a nonrefundable credit for foreign death taxes paid on property included in the gross estate but situated outside the United States. IRC § 2015 permits a credit for foreign death taxes attributable to remainder interests included in the gross estate. If an estate paid death taxes to a foreign country and subsequently claimed the IRC § 2014 foreign death tax credit, IRC § 2016 requires the personal representative to notify the Service if the estate recovers all or a portion of such tax at a later date.

3.   **Liability for Payment**

Under IRC § 6018(a), an estate must file an estate tax return (Form 706) only if the gross estate exceeds the applicable exclusion amount under IRC § 2010(c). For example, the estate of a decedent dying in 2011 must file a Form 706 if the decedent's gross estate exceeds $5 million. If the decedent has made lifetime taxable gifts, however, the filing threshold is reduced by the amount of such gifts. Any federal estate tax payable is due nine months after the decedent's death.

■ II. GIFT TAX

A. INTRODUCTION

The gift tax (Chapter 12) is designed as a backstop for the federal estate tax. If no tax on lifetime gift transfers existed, individuals could avoid payment of the estate tax simply by gifting away their property any time before death (optimally, for them, the moment before death) to avoid inclusion of assets in their gross estates.

B. IMPOSITION OF GIFT TAX [IRC § 2501]

Under IRC § 2501(a)(1), the gift tax is imposed on all "transfers of property by gift" made during the calendar year, regardless if made by a resident or non-resident of the United States.

1. Exceptions

Even if there is a "transfer of property by gift" certain transactions are not taxable under Chapter 12.

a) Transfers of Intangibles by Non–Citizens or Non–Residents [IRC § 2501(a)(2)]

Transfers of intangible property (i.e., stocks and bonds) by non-resident, non-citizens of the United States are not subject to the gift tax.

b) Transfers to Political Organizations [IRC § 2501(a)(4)]

No gift tax is due on transfers to any party, committee, fund, or other organization that accepts contributions or spends money to influence the election or selection of any individual to any Federal, State or local public office.

c) Services

Although not expressly stated in the Code, services are excluded from gift taxation.

2. "Property"

The gift tax covers all types of property, tangible and intangible, real and personal.

a) Contingent Interests

If the donor transfers a contingent interest in property the contingency never has to be fulfilled in order for the gift to be complete; the gift tax considers the moment of transfer and no further.

b) Reversionary Interest Incapable of Being Valued

If the property is subject to a reversionary interest to the donor on the occurrence of a contingency and the contingency cannot be valued, the reversionary interest will be disregarded and the donor will be treated as transferring the entire property interest.

3. "Transfer"

The general rule defining a "transfer" for the gift tax is found in IRC § 2511. However, several Code sections included in Chapter 12, and two that are not in Chapter 12, also find a "transfer" in situations where the transferor does not have an interest in the property transferred.

a) Transfers in General [IRC § 2511]

The most basic example of a transfer subject to the gift tax is a direct transfer from one person to another. But other less obvious direct transfers are also covered, such as forgiving a debt, assigning a judgment, or paying benefits from an insurance policy.

b) "Dominion and Control"

(1) General Rule

If a donor maintains dominion and control over the property there will be no "transfer" for IRC § 2511 to apply. The power of the donor can be either to change who can take the property (not just solely when) or the express or implied ability to take back the property. So long as the donor can manipulate who receives the property, there is no transfer, and if there is no transfer, the gift tax will not apply.

(2) Control Over Timing is Not Retained Dominion or Control

A completed gift transfer occurs if the donor merely has the power over when an individual may take enjoyment of the property, not if they will be able to enjoy the property at all.

(3) Checks

When a donor gives a check as a gift, the transfer does not occur until the check is cashed or negotiated for value to a third person.

(4) Exceptions

In certain instances a donor may have continued dominion and control over the gifted property, but because that control is not unfettered, the transfer is deemed complete.

a. Control Exercisable With Another Having Substantial Adverse Interest

If the donor's ability to exercise dominion and control over the property is held in conjunction with a person having a substantial adverse interest to the property's disposition, the donor will be treated as making a completed transfer.

b. Control Limited by Ascertainable Standard

A transfer will also be treated as complete to the extent the donor's power is limited by a fixed and ascertainable standard. Nevertheless, to the extent the donor's power allows the donor to reclaim the property, then the interest will be treated as an incomplete transfer.

(5) Estate Tax Crossover

If a donor maintains enough dominion and control over the property to render the gift tax inapplicable for want of a transfer, and if the donor dies while still possessing such control over the property, IRC §§ 2036, 2038 or both may apply to include the property into the donor's gross estate.

4. "By gift"

a) General Rule § 2512(b)

Under IRC § 2512(b), a "gift" occurs when property is transferred for less than "adequate and full consideration in money or money's worth." By primarily considering the adequacy of any consideration received, this test looks at objective facts rather than the more difficult-to-determine subjective motivations of the donor (e.g., for determining if a gift exists for IRC § 102(a)).

(1) Measuring Adequate and Full Consideration

a. Generally

If the consideration received by the transferor is not capable of being valued in terms of dollars and cents, it is "wholly disregarded" when determining whether a gift occurs under IRC § 2512(b).

b. Income Tax Crossover

The release of marital rights is treated as consideration to support the sale of property. Accordingly, because there is a deemed sale, the property received by the transferee has a fair market value basis and not a transferred basis under IRC § 1015.

(2) Payment of Gift Tax by Donee

The payment of the gift tax by the donee may be treated as offsetting consideration.

a. Prior Agreement by Donee to Pay Tax

If the donee agreed prior to the transfer to pay the gift tax, such payment is treated as offsetting consideration.

b. No Prior Agreement for Donee to Pay Gift Tax

There is no reduction in the amount of gift where the donee is either forced to pay the gift tax by operation of law, or does so voluntarily with no prior agreement.

c. Estate Tax Crossover

Under IRC § 2035(b), any gift tax paid, by the donor or any one else, on gifts made during the three years prior to the decedent's death is included in the decedent's gross estate.

d. Payment of Gift Tax by Donee (Income Tax Crossover)

If the donee pays the gift tax, that amount is included in the amount realized by the donor under IRC § 1001(b). This means if the gift tax paid by the donee is greater than the adjusted basis of the donor's transferred property, the donor realizes and recognizes gain. Additionally, the donee may have a basis in the property equal to the gift tax paid.

(3) "By Gift" (Income Tax Crossover)

Unlike the gift tax, donative intent is required for finding a "gift" for the income tax.

(4) Marital Transfers

Marital rights are not treated as consideration for either the gift or estate taxes. But several exceptions counteract this general rule.

a. Property Settlements Under IRC § 2516

The transfer is deemed "made for a full and adequate consideration in money or money's worth" under IRC § 2516 if the transfer is either in settlement of the spouses' marital or property rights or provides support for the minor children of the marriage. The agreement must be in writing and made within a three-year period of the divorce decree beginning on the date one year before such agreement is entered into.

b. Support Rights

Transfers made in exchange for the release of support rights or for the current support of a former spouse or any of the couple's children are treated as made for full consideration.

c. Judicial Decree

Property transferred by judicial decree pursuant to a divorce is not founded on a "promise or agreement" and therefore does not need to be supported by consideration to avoid gift treatment.

b) Exceptions to the General Rule

There are three exceptions to the general rule that a gift is the amount by which the fair market value of the property transferred is greater than any consideration received by the transferor.

(1) Transfers Made in Satisfaction of Support Obligations

If payments made by the donor on the behalf of the donee are in satisfaction of the donor's support obligations, those payments are not considered gift transfers.

(2) Qualified Transfers by Donor to Donee [IRC § 2503(e)]

For gift tax purposes, any "qualified transfer" is not treated as a "transfer of property by gift" for the gift tax. There are two types of "qualified transfers": one for the payment of tuition to an educational institution, and the other for medical care payments made directly to a medical provider.

a. Education Payments

Tuition payments are treated as a "qualified transfer" only if made directly to the educational institution. Payments for books, supplies, or room and board are not excluded under IRC § 2503(e) and may constitute a gift.

b. Medical Payments

Any payments for expenses, not reimbursed by the donee's insurance, resulting from the diagnosis, cure or prevention of disease, as well as for transportation to receive such care constitute a "qualified transfer," as do payments for qualified long-term care services or medical insurance.

c. Income Tax Crossover

The amounts spent for tuition or medical care can still apply when determining support for dependency under IRC § 152(a), can still qualify for the IRC § 213(a) deduction, and can still be excluded from gross income for the income tax under IRC § 102(a) as a gift.

(3) Transfers Made in "Ordinary Course of Business" [Reg. § 25.2512–8]

Transactions completed in the "ordinary course of business" are considered made for adequate and full consideration in money or money's worth. This permits bad bargains, loss leaders and the like to escape gift taxation.

C. OTHER "TRANSFERS"

Several Code sections in Chapter 12 (as well as two outside of Chapter 12) either create a transfer where one may not exist or modify the "transfer" requirement in order to determine if the gift tax is applicable on the transaction.

1. Powers of Appointment [IRC § 2514]

IRC § 2514 covers certain powers of appointment. If the power was created after October 21, 1942, the exercise, release or lapse of the power is treated as a "transfer" of property.

a) Treatment of Post–1942 General Powers of Appointment

The exercise, release, and (sometimes) the lapse of a general power of appointment is deemed a "transfer of property."

(1) General Powers of Appointment

The definition of a general power of appointment in IRC § 2514(c) tracks the estate tax definition in IRC § 2041(b)(1). The primary difference from the estate tax is that the power must be held by the "decedent," while under the gift tax provisions the power must be held by the "possessor."

(2) Lapse

A lapse of a general power of appointment is treated as a release of that power (and thus as a transfer) only to the extent that the amount subject to withdrawal exceeds the greater of $5,000 or 5% of the value of the assets controlled by the power. This means that a donor may give a donee the right to withdraw at least $5,000 per year without having the withdrawal treated as a transfer by the donee under IRC § 2514. The term "five by five power" is used to describe a general power of appointment that can be exercised only to the extent of the greater of $5,000 or 5% of the value of the property subject to the power. Limiting the power holder's interest to a five by five power ensures that the power holder will not make a gift to the other trust beneficiaries when the power lapses without exercise.

(3) Exceptions for Disclaimers Under IRC § 2518

A qualified disclaimer under IRC § 2518 is not treated as a "release" of a power under IRC § 2514.

b) Treatment of Pre–1942 Powers

For powers of appointment created before October 21, 1942, only the actual exercise of the power (and not the release or lapse of the power) creates a "transfer of property."

c) Treatment of Non–General Powers of Appointment

Unless the power holder also has an interest in the property, no transfer of property usually occurs upon the exercise or release of a non-general power of appointment.

2. Disclaimers [IRC § 2518]

IRC § 2518 provides that any person making a "qualified disclaimer" of an interest in property is treated as if the interest was never transferred to that person at all. In order for a disclaimer to be "qualified," the disclaimer must be in writing, it must be irrevocable and unqualified, and it must generally be delivered to either the transferor, the legal representative of the transfer, or the legal titleholder of the property interest transferred within nine months of the date of transfer. The disclaimer is valid only if there has been no acceptance or use of the disclaimed interest, and the interest must pass without the direction of the disclaimant and may only go to the surviving spouse of the decedent or a person other than the individual disclaiming the interest.

a) When the Period Begins for a Qualified Disclaimer

Generally, unless the interest passes to a minor, the nine-month period starts when the interest to be disclaimed is created. For those under twenty-one, the period starts on their twenty-first birthday.

(1) Inter Vivos Gift Transfers

In the case of inter vivos gifts, the period starts when there is a completed gift for Federal gift tax purposes.

(2) Testamentary Transfers

For transfers made at death (e.g., bequests), the nine-month period starts on the date of decedent's death. For interests in property created during the decedent's lifetime (i.e., a trust) and later included in the decedent's gross estate, the date of the transfer (i.e., the creation of the trust) is the controlling date, not the decedent's death.

(3) Powers of Appointment

For general powers of appointment, the period starts to run upon receipt of the power. If an interest in property passes by the exercise, release, or lapse of a general power, the individual receiving the property has nine months from the exercise, release or lapse of the power to disclaim the property. For non-general powers of appointment the power holder and all other possible power holders must disclaim within nine months of the original transfer that created the power.

(4) Joint Interests in Property

Joint interests in property are treated as transferred in two parts. One-half of the property transfers at the time of the initial transfer and one-half of the property transfers when the joint tenant dies.

b) No Acceptance of Benefits

In order to have an effective disclaimer, the disclaimant cannot accept any of the property nor any benefits from the interest in the property. Acceptance is defined as "an affirmative act which is consistent with ownership of the interest in property."

3. Dispositions of Certain Life Estates [IRC § 2519]

IRC § 2519 is the gift tax complement to IRC § 2044 in the estate tax and one or the other, but not both, will apply to all qualifying income interests for which an election was made. IRC § 2519 provides that if the donee spouse disposes of any portion of a qualifying income interest, a constructive transfer of all the interests in property other than the income interest (normally the remainder of a trust) occurs.

4.   Gifts by Husband and Wife to a Third Party [IRC § 2513]

In community property states, a gift made by a husband or wife of community property is treated as a gift of a one-half interest by the husband, and a one-half interest by the wife. IRC § 2513 allows for the same result on transfers by spouses in separate property states if they so elect to "split gifts." There are three requirements to split gifts. First, the gift must be made during the couple's marriage. Second, each spouse must be either a citizen or resident of the United States at the time of the gift. Finally, both spouses must consent to the election to split gifts.

a)   Spousal Consent

Both spouses must consent to the election each year they decide to split gifts. Once they do decide to consent, the consent applies to all gifts made by either spouse during the entire year. The couple cannot specify which transfers they want to split.

b)   Exceptions

(1)   Interests Incapable of Valuation

If the gift is made in trust and the corpus may be invaded by one of the spouses making it impossible to determine the value of the remainder, the gift may not be split.

(2)   Spouse Maintains a General Power of Appointment Over the Transferred Property

If the donor spouse transfers a piece of property but grants the non-donor spouse a general power of appointment over such property, the gift may not be split.

c)   Estate Tax Crossover

Couples cannot split gifts for purposes of the estate tax. This means the entire amount of any gift transfer (not just one-half) will go into computing the estate tax (part of the "adjusted taxable gifts" made during the decedent's lifetime) even if the gifts were split for purposes of the gift tax when the gift was made.

5. Payments of Generation–Skipping Transfer Tax on Direct Skips [IRC § 2515]

Any generation-skipping transfer tax paid by the transferor results in an additional gift. Therefore, the transferor is essentially treated as giving two gifts, one for the initial transfer and another for the payment of the generation-skipping transfer tax.

6. Below–Market Gift Loans [IRC § 7872]

In certain circumstances, the interest-free use of money is considered a transfer of property. Two transfers are created under IRC § 7872. First, an imputed amount is transferred from the lender to the borrower. Second, an interest payment is imputed passing from the borrower to the lender.

a) Elements of IRC § 7872

(1) "Below–Market Loan"

Demand loans qualify as below-market loans if the interest rate is less than the applicable federal rate. The applicable federal rate is the Federal short-term rate for the year in question. Term loans are considered below market if the amount loaned exceeds the discounted present value of all payments due under the loan.

(2) "To Which this Section Applies"

In order for IRC § 7872 to apply, the below-market loan must be one "to which this section [IRC § 7872] applies." "Gift loans" (those where the "foregoing of interest is in the nature of a gift") are included in the types of loans to which IRC § 7872 applies.

b) Gift Tax Consequences of the Application of IRC § 7872

The imputed transfer amount for below-market gift loans depends on whether the loan is a demand or term loan.

(1) Gift Demand Loans

For gift demand loans, the transfer from lender to borrower and again from borrower to lender is the same and is the amount of "foregone interest." The foregone interest is the amount of interest due using the applicable Federal rate less any interest payable on the loan.

(2) Gift Term Loans

a. Imputed Gift Transfer

Under IRC § 7872(b)(1), the deemed gift transfer equals the amount loaned less the present value of all payments required under the loan.

b. Imputed Interest Payment

Just as for gift demand loans, the amount of foregone interest is the deemed interest payment from borrower to lender.

D. SPECIAL VALUATION RULES

1. Transfers of Interests in Certain Corporations and Partnerships [IRC § 2701]

a) Background

IRC § 2701 thwarts the "preferred interest freeze," where the taxpayer retains a limited and preferred interest in a corporation or partnership while transferring to a family member a common interest that will receive most all of the entity's future growth. In this way the shareholder can maintain control, while transferring appreciating property at a low gift tax value.

b) Application of IRC § 2701

IRC § 2701 applies when two conditions are met. First, the taxpayer must transfer a common interest (formally, a "subordinate equity interest") in a partnership or corporation to or for the benefit of a member of the taxpayer's family in a younger generation. [IRC § 2701(a)(1); Reg. § 25.2701–3(a)(2)(iii)] Second, immediately after the transfer, the taxpayer or a member of the taxpayer's family in an older generation must hold a preferred interest (called an "applicable retained interest"). [IRC §§ 2701(a)(1)(B); 2701(b)(1)]

c) Consequences of IRC § 2701

When it applies, IRC § 2701 requires that the computation of the value of the gifted common interest be determined by valuing the retained preferred interest at zero (the "zero-value rule"). [IRC § 2701(a)(3)(A); Reg. § 25.2701–1(a)(2)] In effect, then, a gift of the common interest is valued as though it was a gift of both the common and preferred interests.

d) Exceptions

There are a number of specific exceptions to the application of IRC § 2701. Where one of these exceptions applies, the zero value rule does not come into play. First and foremost, the zero value rule does not apply if the retained preferred interest represents a right to a "qualified payment." [IRC § 2701(a)(3)(A)] A right to a qualified payment is a right to a dividend on cumulative preferred stock payable on a periodic basis to the extent the amount of the dividend is determined at a fixed rate or bears a fixed relationship to a specified market rate. [IRC § 2701(c)(3)] Thus, if the entity pays a market rate dividend on the preferred interest, Congress will forego application of the zero value rule because there is assurance that dividends will be paid to the transferor and thus become part of the transferor's gross estate to the extent not consumed before death. The zero value rule also does not apply to interests for which market quotations are readily available, [IRC § 2701(a)(2)(A)] nor to proportionate transfers, such as where the transferor gifts a portion of his or her common interest and the same portion of his or her preferred interest. [IRC § 2701(a)(2)(C)]

2. **Special Rules for Valuing Transfers of Interests in Trust to Family Members [IRC § 2702]**

a) Background

If applicable, IRC § 2702 determines whether any transfer made to a member of the transferor's family will be treated as a "gift." It can also give a zero value to any retained interests of the transferor in order to increase the amount of any gift transfer.

b) Application of IRC § 2702

For the application of IRC § 2702 there must be: 1) a "transfer" in trust, 2) of an "interest," 3) to a "member of the transferor's family," 4) by "gift," and 5) an interest in the trust must be "retained by the transferor" or "any applicable family member."

(1) Specific Elements

a. Transfers in Trust

As used in IRC § 2702, the word "transfer" includes transfers to either new or existing trusts and assignments of an interest in an existing trust. A transfer may also be imputed where two or more family members make a joint purchase of term interests in property. However, the exercise, release or lapse of a non-general power of appointment or a qualified disclaimer under IRC § 2518 of an interest is not considered a "transfer" for purposes of IRC § 2702.

b. "Interest"

i) General Rule

Generally, "interests" are interests in property, but the term also includes powers over trust property that would cause the transfer to be an incomplete gift under Chapter 12.

ii) Treatment of Transfers of a Portion in Trust [IRC § 2702(d)]

If a specified portion of the income or remainder interest is transferred in trust, only such portion will be taken into account when applying IRC § 2702.

c. To a "Member of the Transferor's Family"

This includes the transferor's spouse, ancestors and lineal descendants of transferor or transferor's spouse, brothers and sisters, and the spouses of any of these individuals. It does not include more remote relationships, such as the transferor's aunts, uncles, nieces or nephews.

d.   Transfer is "By Gift"

The transfer must be a completed gift.

e.   "Retained by" the Transferor or Applicable Family Member

The same individual must hold an interest both before and after the transfer in trust.

f.   "Applicable Family Member"

An "applicable family member" is different than a "member of the transferor's family." Applicable family members include only the transferor's spouse as well as the ancestors and their spouses of either the transferor or the transferor's spouse. The lineal descendants of the transferor or the transferor's spouse are not included.

(2) Exceptions

a.   Incomplete Gifts [IRC § 2702(a)(3)(A)(i)]

If no portion of the gift is complete to an applicable family member, IRC § 2702 will not apply to the transfer. Consideration received by the transferor is not considered in determining whether a gift is incomplete.

b.   Personal Residence Trusts

If the proper requirements are followed, an individual may retain a term interest in a personal residence while giving the remainder interest to a member of the transferor's family without triggering IRC § 2702.

i)   Basic Personal Residence Trust

The corpus of a basic personal residence trust must consist only of the personal residence of the term interest holder, and only the transferor, transferor's spouse, or transferor's dependents may occupy the residence during the trust term. The most restrictive aspect of a basic personal residence trust relates to eligible trust assets: only the personal residence itself can be owned by the trust, not any of the household furnishings.

ii) Qualified Personal Residence Trust

A qualified personal residence trust (QPRT) is also restricted to the personal residence of the transferor and has the same restrictions on who may live in the home. However, a QPRT may also hold cash in the amount necessary to pay expenses, mortgages, or improvements to be incurred within the next six months. The residence may also be sold, so long as the proceeds are reinvested into another residence within two years of the sale.

c.   Regulatory Exceptions

IRC § 2702(a)(3)(A)(iii) states that exceptions may be made to the application of IRC § 2702 "to the extent that regulations provide that such transfer is not inconsistent with the purposes of this section."

i) Charitable Transfers [Reg. § 25.2702–1(c)(3)–(5)]

The regulations exclude charitable remainder trusts, pooled income funds, and charitable lead trusts from the application of IRC § 2702.

ii) Assignments of Certain Remainder Interests When the Retained Interest is Under the Control of an Independent Trustee [Reg. § 25.2702–1(c)(6)]

IRC § 2702 does not apply if the interest retained by the transferor or applicable family member is the receipt of trust income under the sole discretion of an independent trustee.

iii) Certain Transfers Made Pursuant to IRC § 2516

Under the regulations, so long as the transferor's spouse holds all the remaining interests in the trust, IRC § 2702 will not apply to any transfers subject to IRC § 2516 made before a divorce is final.

iv) Certain Transfers by Surviving Spouse of Property Received in a Qualified Domestic Trust (QDOT) [Reg. § 25.2702–1(c)(8)]

The regulations provide IRC § 2702 does not apply when a non-citizen surviving spouse transfers an interest in a qualified domestic trust (QDOT) under IRC § 2056A.

(3) Valuation

Valuation under IRC § 2702 depends on the type of interest being valued. "Qualified interests" are valued under the normal valuation rules for the gift tax under IRC § 7520. Non-qualified interests are valued at zero.

a. Qualified Interests under IRC § 2702(b)

There are three types of "qualified interests."

i) Qualified Annuity Interests [IRC § 2702(b)(1)]

A qualified annuity interest arises in the context of a popular estate planning technique commonly known as a GRAT (grantor-retained annuity trust). A GRAT is an irrevocable trust where the grantor retains the right to receive not less than once per year either a stated dollar amount or a fixed percentage of the initial fair market value of the property transferred to the trust.

ii) Qualified Unitrust Interests

A qualified unitrust interest arises when the grantor maintains a fixed percentage of the fair market value of the trust determined annually (instead of a fixed dollar amount or a fixed percentage of the initial value with the qualified annuity interest).

iii) Qualified Remainder Interests

A qualified remainder interest is a non-contingent remainder interest where all of the term interests are either qualified annuity interests or qualified unitrust interests.

(4) Reduction in Taxable Gifts of Subsequent Transfer of a Retained Interest

If the retained interest is later transferred, the amount of taxable gifts is reduced by the lesser of: 1) the amount of increase in the taxable gifts due to the application of IRC § 2702 on the initial transfer, or 2) the increase in the amount of taxable gifts (or gross estate) due to the subsequent transfer of the interest.

(5) Application of IRC § 2702 to Chapter 13 (Generation–Skipping Tax)

IRC § 2702 does not apply to the generation-skipping tax of Chapter 13

E. "TAXABLE GIFTS" [IRC § 2503(a)]

The term "taxable gifts" refers to the total amount of gifts made during the taxable year minus any gift tax deductions allowable.

1. The Annual Exclusion [IRC § 2503(b)]

Under IRC § 2503(b)(1) the first $10,000 of gifts (except for gifts of future interests) are excluded from "taxable gifts" under IRC § 2503(a). After 1998, the $10,000 exclusion amount is indexed for inflation in $1,000 increments. As of 2011, the exclusion amount is $13,000.

a) Application of IRC § 2503(b)

(1) Identification of the Donee

IRC § 2503(b) allows an exclusion for a "gift . . . made to any person by the donor." Under IRC § 7701(a)(1) "person" includes people, trusts, estates, partnerships and corporations. This means gifts to entities may qualify for the exclusion, but the courts have made it difficult to receive an exclusion for such transfers.

a. Trusts

The regulations provide that in a gift transfer of property through a trust, the donees are the beneficiaries of the trust and not the trustee or trust itself.

b. Partnerships

On gift transfers to partnerships, the donees are the individual partners.

c. Joint Interests in Property

Each co-owner is a donee when a donor gifts property to two or more persons, no matter whether the gift is made as tenants in common, joint tenants with rights of survivorship, or tenants by the entirety.

d. Corporations

The individual shareholders are the donees on gift transfers to corporations, but the donor may not claim an annual exclusion for a transfer to a corporation because it is treated as the transfer of a future interest.

e. Charities, Public or Political Organizations

Transfers to other organizations are generally treated as a gift to the entity as a whole since there are no easily identifiable beneficiaries, shareholders, or partners.

b) Present and Future Interests

(1) Future Interests

IRC § 2503(b) allows for an exclusion of gifts "other than gifts of future interests in property." Examples of future interests are remainder interests in trust (vested or contingent), a trustee's unfettered discretion to distribute income from a trust (since the property may never be distributed, creating valuation difficulties), and other instances where circumstances prevent the income of the trust from being valued.

(2) Present Interests

The Regulations define a present interest in property as the "unrestricted right to the immediate use, possession, or enjoyment of property or the income from property."

a. Exceptions

i) Power to Invade Corpus for the Income Interest Holder [IRC § 2503(b)(1) (second sentence)]

Where the trustee has the power to give the corpus of the trust only to the income beneficiary, the trustee's power is disregarded, allowing for the interest to be valued and the annual exclusion to be applied.

ii) Lump Sum Payments to Qualified Tuition Plans

Certain gift transfers to qualified tuition programs are treated as present interests in property even though the property is used to pay future education expenses.

b. *Crummey* Powers

Where the beneficiaries of a trust do not have a present interest in the property transferred to the trust, no annual exclusion is available. But if the beneficiaries hold a general power of appointment over some portion of amounts transferred to the trust, gifts to trusts can qualify for the annual exclusion because the beneficiaries have the present right to access such property through exercise of the general power of appointment. Practitioners refer to these general powers of appointment as "*Crummey* powers," after the Ninth Circuit case that upheld their validity.

i) Cross-over Issues

Crummey powers may have both estate and gift tax consequences to the holder of the power.

(3) Gift Tax Consequences

Under IRC § 2514(e) a "lapse" of a general power of appointment will be treated as a "release" to the extent the lapsed *Crummey* power exceeds the greater of $5,000 or 5% of the value of the assets from which the power could be satisfied. The amount treated as "lapsed" is deemed a transfer to the beneficiaries of the trust, which itself is likely a gift to the other beneficiaries.

(4) Estate Tax Consequences

IRC § 2041 will also apply to the *Crummey* withdrawal power if the power holder dies while possessing the right to withdraw funds. If there is a lapse, the amount treated as lapsed (if the power holder receives an income interest in the trust) would constitute a release of a power and such property would be includable in the power holder's gross estate under IRC § 2036. The amount to be included would be the percentage of corpus that has lapsed, which would accumulate over time.

(5) Avoidance of Gift and Estate Tax Consequences

To avoid these results *Crummey* powers can be limited to the greater of $5,000 or 5% of the trust corpus, even though the maximum annual exclusion amount under IRC § 2503(b) is $13,000 in 2011. Another way to avoid these results is to use a "hanging power."

c) Transfers to Minors

Certain transfers under IRC § 2503(c) create present interests in property eligible for the annual exclusion. IRC § 2503(c) applies when the property and income from the property (1) may be expended by, or for the benefit of, the donee before reaching age 21, and (2) the amount not distributed will either pass to the donee upon reaching 21 or, should the donee die before, be distributed to the donee's estate or by a general power of appointment of the donee.

d) Other Issues

(1) Application to the Generation–Skipping Tax (Chapter 13)

Gifts under the annual exclusion amount are given a zero inclusion ratio for the generation-skipping transfer tax.

(2) Gift Tax Returns

No gift tax return is required to be filed if all gifts made are under the annual exclusion amount.

2. Deductions

a) Gift Tax Deduction for Charitable and Similar Gifts [IRC § 2522]

The charitable deduction is very similar under both the estate and gift tax. The primary difference is that inter vivos gifts made to charities may also be deducted for purposes of the donor's Federal income tax liability, while this is not allowed for testamentary gifts of the same nature.

(1) Disallowance of Deductions [IRC § 2522(c)]

a. Gifts to Disallowed Organizations or Trusts [IRC § 2522(c)(1)]

Gifts to certain organizations or trusts are disallowed a charitable deduction.

b. Split Interest Gifts [IRC § 2522(c)(2)]

Gift transfers divided in time between charities and noncharities are either restricted in amount or disallowed under IRC § 2522(c)(2). The analysis here is comparable to the analysis applicable to split-interest gifts under the federal estate tax.

(2) Amount of Deduction

If a full interest in property is transferred to a qualifying charity, a deduction is allowed for the full fair market value of the property transferred. If a partial interest in property is transferred, and the requirements of IRC § 2522(c) are met, the partial interest is valued under IRC § 7520.

(3) Filing of Gift Tax Return

No gift tax return is required to be filed if the donor's only gifts consist of gifts made to charities that are fully deductible.

b) Gifts to Spouses [IRC § 2523]

The gift tax marital deduction under IRC § 2523 and the estate tax marital deduction under IRC § 2056 are very similar in language and scope.

(1) Terminable Interests [IRC § 2523(b)]

When a portion of the transferred property passes to any person other than the donee spouse (including the donor) after the donee spouse's interest, or when the donor retains the power to appoint such an interest, no marital deduction is allowed unless an exception applies.

a. Donor Retains Interest or Third–Party Acquires Interest [IRC § 2523(b)(1)]

A donor's retained interest in the property can be a terminable interest. This is not present in the estate tax terminable interest rule, since that provision covers transfers from a decedent rather than a donor.

b. Retained Powers of the Donor [IRC § 2523(b)(2)]

Under IRC § 2523(b)(2) a terminable interest is created if the donor retains a power to appoint the property after the complete termination of the donee spouse's interest.

c. Exceptions to the Terminable Interest Rule

There are several exceptions to the terminable interest rule. If an exception is found, a marital deduction from the taxable gifts may still be allowed even though the interest transferred to the donee spouse is a terminable interest.

   i) Life Estate with Power of Appointment in Donee Spouse [IRC § 2523(e)]

   This non-elective exception is permitted when the donee spouse has a life estate interest in the property and has the sole power to transfer the interest to whomever the donee spouse should choose.

   ii) Transfer of Qualified Terminable Interest Property (QTIP) [IRC § 2523(f)]

   For this exception to apply to the property 1) the donor spouse must transfer property, 2) the donee spouse must possess a qualifying income interest for life in the property, and 3) the donor must elect to have the exception apply. The primary difference between the gift and estate tax QTIP exceptions is that the donor must elect to have the gift tax section apply, whereas the executor makes the election for estate tax purposes.

   iii) Joint Interests Held Between Donor and Donee Spouse [IRC § 2523(d)]

   If a donor spouse transfers a piece of property to the donee spouse as a joint tenant, the interest is a terminable interest, but transfers made in joint tenancy or tenancy by the entirety are still allowed a gift tax deduction.

(2) Spouse not a U.S. Citizen [IRC § 2523(i)]

No marital deduction is allowed when the donor's spouse is not a citizen of the United States. While the deduction is disallowed, the annual exclusion is increased from a base of $10,000 to $100,000 for transfers to the non-citizen spouse, an amount that is adjusted for inflation.

(3) Gift Tax Return [IRC § 6019(a)(2)]

A gift tax return is not required to be filed for any gift receiving a marital deduction, unless a QTIP election is made during the year.

c) Extent of Deductions [IRC § 2524]

IRC § 2524 limits any gift tax deductions to the amount of gifts made after any exclusions. This prohibits the improper offset of deductions against gifts that do not qualify for either the charitable or marital deduction.

F. COMPUTATION OF THE GIFT TAX [IRC § 2502]

Computing the gift tax is a two-step process. First, a "tentative tax" is computed on all taxable gifts made by the donor after June 6, 1932, including those taxable gifts made during the current year. Next, a "tentative tax" is computed using taxable gifts made after June 6, 1932, but does not include gifts made during the current year (called taxable gifts made during "preceding calendar periods"). This amount is then subtracted from the first tentative tax (which includes the amount of gifts in the current year) to arrive at the gift tax liability for the current year.

1. "Taxable Gifts for Preceding Calendar Periods" [IRC § 2504]

The amount of taxable gifts for preceding calendar periods is figured using the law as it existed at that time. This means that items that are not taxable under current law, but were taxable at an earlier time, are still included, and vice-versa.

2. Unified Credit Against Gift Tax [IRC § 2505]

The amount of the gift tax credit after 2010 is the tentative tax under IRC § 2001(c) on the applicable exclusion amount, which is at least $5 million, or $1,730,800. The result of this credit is that until a donor's total amount of lifetime taxable gifts exceeds at least $5 million there is no tax liability. The amount of the credit is reduced by the amount of credit utilized in any preceding calendar period. The credit amount may be increased by the unused portion of applicable credit carried over from a deceased spouse.

G. PROCEDURAL RULES

1. Who Must File

A gift tax return must be filed each calendar year an individual makes "any transfer by gift" unless the transfer falls into one of three categories. First, no return is required for transfers excluded under the annual exclusion or under IRC § 2503(e) (for certain transfers for medical or educational expenses). Second, transfers deductible under the gift tax marital deduction do not need to be reported. Third, no return is required for deductible charitable contributions under IRC § 2522, so long as the entire interest was deductible (only of present interests in property) or it was a qualified conservation contribution of an easement.

2. Date Return Due

A gift tax return may be filed as early as January 1, but no later than April 15, of the year following the transfer. A six month extension to file can be obtained.

3. Payment of Gift Tax and Liens

Generally, payment of the gift tax by the donor occurs when the gift tax return is due "without regard to any extension of time for filing the return." If the gift tax is not paid, there is ten-year lien starting on the date the gifts were made on all property subject to the gift tax for such calendar year.

H. CARRYOVER BASIS RULES STARTING IN 2010

At the election of the executor, decedents dying in 2010 may take advantage of the estate and generation-skipping transfer tax repeal in that year. If so, instead of receiving an automatic step-up in basis under IRC § 1014, a carryover basis regime will come into effect. The basis of the acquired property is the lower of the decedent's basis or the fair market value at the time of the decedent's death. This basis rule is augmented by allowable increases to the acquired property's basis of $1.3 million, with an additional $3 million increase for certain property acquired by a surviving spouse.

1. Property Acquired from a Decedent [IRC § 1022(e)]

Property acquired from a decedent subject to the carryover basis rule includes both property acquired by bequest, devise or inheritance, and the property acquired by the decedent's estate from the decedent. Also included is property received from a trust that the decedent could alter, amend, revoke, or terminate.

2. Additional Basis Increase

To offset the loss of the fair market value basis rule, IRC § 1022 allows for a limited increase of the decedent's basis in property up to a maximum of the property's fair market value. Increases are allowed to all property "owned" by the decedent up to a total increase for all property of $1.3 million, with an additional $3 million in increases allowed for property acquired by a surviving spouse.

a) "Property to Which this Subsection Applies"

The general rule is that the property must be "owned" by the decedent at the time of death, but not be received by gift within three years of death (unless from a spouse).

(1) Property Owned by Decedent at Death

IRC § 1022 provides limited guidance for the determination of when items are, and are not, owned by the decedent at death. For example, the statute does not provide for an exact definition of when something is "owned," but it does provide for when certain items are to be included or excluded from the definition.

(2) Property Not Allowed a Basis Increase

No basis increase is allowed for any property received as a gift (in whole or in part) or purchased for less than full consideration, by the decedent within three years of death. Also, certain stock held by the decedent does not qualify for the basis increase.

b) Basic Basis Increase

Unless adjusted higher, the executor of the decedent's estate may increase the decedent's basis by an aggregate of $1.3 million, but the basis of property cannot be increased beyond the property's fair market value at the time of the decedent's death.

c) Additional Basis Increase for Property Acquired by Surviving Spouse

The basis of "qualified spousal property" may be increased by an additional $3 million aggregate adjustment. Therefore, if the surviving spouse receives all of the decedent's property the basis could be increased, before any upward adjustments, by a total of $4.3 million. "Qualified spousal property" includes outright property transfers to a surviving spouse and all qualified terminable interest property.

■ III. GENERATION SKIPPING TAXATION

A. INTRODUCTION

Chapter 13 of Subtitle B (covering estate and gift taxes) establishes the generation-skipping transfer ("GST") tax. The primary rationale behind the GST tax is not to generate revenue, but to ensure that transfer taxes are applied uniformly regardless of whether a transfer was made to the next succeeding generation or made in such a way to skip generations.

B. TERMINOLOGY

1. Introduction

Three types of generation-skipping transfers exist: a direct skip, a taxable termination, and a taxable distribution. For the most part these require a "skip person" to receive an "interest in property" under Chapter 13. A skip person can either be a natural person or a trust. To establish who is a skip person (or, conversely, a "non-skip person") one must establish the identity of the "transferor" of the property. For transfers in trust, one must determine who has an "interest in property," which requires a finding of a "trust" and the "generational assignment" of individuals.

2. Transferor

a) General Rule

In the case of the estate tax, the transferor is the decedent. For property "subject to" the gift tax, the transferor is the donor.

b) Treatment of Split Gifts Under IRC § 2513 [IRC § 2652(a)(2)]

When a married couple elects to treat a transfer of property as a split gift, they can also treat it as a split gift for the purposes of Chapter 13.

c) Reverse QTIP Election [IRC § 2652(a)(3)]

The "cost" of making a QTIP election is deferred taxation of the property. Without any exception to the general rule, there would always be a new transferor created for any qualified terminable interest property since the property is later "subject to" either the estate or gift tax. This would result in the loss of any GST exemption amount granted to the trust by the transferring spouse. The election under IRC § 2652(a)(3) solves this dilemma by treating the property for purposes of Chapter 13 "as if the election to be treated as qualified terminable interest property had not been made."

3. **"Interest"**

a) General Rule

There are three different types of Chapter 13 interests in property held in trust. The first type includes individuals, trusts, corporations, and the like, who have a present right to receive income or corpus from the trust. The second includes those individuals or entities other than charities, which are permissible current recipients of the trust's income or corpus. The third type includes charities treated as having an interest in trust even though they do not have any present right to trust income, so long as the trust is either a charitable remainder annuity trust (CRAT), charitable remainder unitrust (CRUT) or pooled income fund.

b) Disregarded Interests [IRC § 2652(c)(2), (3)]

Interests, in two situations, may be disregarded in determining the presence of a generation-skipping transfer. First, an interest is disregarded if it is created primarily to postpone or avoid the generation-skipping tax. Second, disbursements of trust assets used to satisfy support obligations in a discretionary manner, or pursuant to laws equivalent to the Uniform Gifts to Minors Act, are not treated as giving the individuals whose support obligations are satisfied a Chapter 13 interest in property held in trust.

c) Disclaimed Interests [IRC § 2654(c)]

If a qualified disclaimer is made pursuant to IRC § 2518, the interest is treated as if it never existed for Chapter 13 purposes.

4. Generational Assignments [IRC § 2651]

The classification of an individual or trust as a skip person or a non-skip person depends on their generational assignment. Generational assignments are determined by comparing the individual receiving the interest with the Chapter 13 "transferor."

a) Lineal Descendants of the Transferor's Grandparent [IRC § 2651(b)]

(1) General Rule

If an individual is a lineal descendant of the transferor's grandparent, his or her generational assignment is calculated by comparing the number of generations between the grandparent and such individual to the number one (the generations between the transferor's grandparent and the transferor).

(2) Spouses

The transferor's spouse is assigned to the same generation as the transferor.

(3) Adoption and Step–Children

Lineal descendants related by adoption or with only one parent in common ("half-blood") are treated as whole-blood descendants.

b) Non–Lineal Descendants of the Transferor's Grandparent [IRC § 2651(d)]

Individuals who are not lineal descendants of the transferor's grandparent are given generational assignments based on set age ranges.

c) Special Rules

(1) Predeceased Parent Rule [IRC § 2651(e)]

An individual is moved up to the generational level of his or her predeceased parent if (1) the individual is the descendant of the transferor's parent, (2) the parent died before the transfer was subject to the estate or gift tax, and (3) the individual is a lineal descendant of the transferor (i.e., child, grandchild, etc.), unless the transferor has no living descendants.

(2) Individuals Assigned to More than One Generation [IRC § 2651(f)(1)]

Any individual who is assigned to more than one generation after applying the rules is assigned to the youngest possible generation level.

(3) Generational Assignments of Entities

Except for transfers to charitable or governmental entities (which are deemed to have the same generational assignment of the transferor), transfers to entities are treated as transfers to the individuals holding the entities' beneficial interests and the above rules are then applied to find each individual's generational assignment.

d) Multiple Skips [IRC § 2653(a)]

The generational assignment of the transferor changes if there is (1) a generation-skipping transfer of property, and (2) immediately after such transfer the property is held in trust. In such a case, the transferor is deemed to be only one generational level above the person with the highest generational level possessing a Chapter 13 interest in the trust immediately after transfer.

5. "Trust" and "Trustee"

a) "Trust" [IRC § 2652(b)(1), (3)]

(1) General Rule

In order for a generation-skipping transfer to be either a taxable termination or taxable distribution (two of the three types of generation-skipping transfers), the property must be held in trust.

(2) Multiple Trusts [IRC § 2654(b)]

A single trust can be treated as separate trusts for the purposes of Chapter 13 if there is more than one transferor or where the beneficiaries have separate and independent portions for the entire term of the trust.

b) "Trustee" [IRC § 2652(b)(2)]

The trustee of a true trust is the person so designated by local law.

6. Skip Person and Non–Skip Person [IRC § 2613]

All generation-skipping transfers require a transfer or distribution, either directly or indirectly, to a "skip person." A "skip person" is a Chapter 13 term used to designate when a generation is skipped. Skip persons can either be "natural persons" (individuals), or trusts. Any individual or trust that is not a skip person is classified as a "non-skip person."

a) Individuals (a.k.a. "Natural Persons") [IRC § 2613(a)(1)]

Skip persons have a generational assignment (*see supra* III. B. 4. of the capsule summary) two or more generations below that of the transferor.

b) Trusts [IRC § 2613(a)(2)]

A trust is a skip person when all of the current Chapter 13 interests in the trust are held by skip persons. Also, if no one has a current Chapter 13 interest in the trust, a trust is deemed a skip person if no distributions, including upon termination of the trust, can ever be made to a non-skip person.

c) Treatment of Entities

When a transfer to an entity is involved, the generational levels of the individual beneficial interest holders control in determining whether the transfer is made to skip persons. However, charitable organizations, charitable trusts, and governmental entities are considered non-skip persons since they are given the same generational assignment as the transferor.

C. GENERATION SKIPPING TRANSFERS

The next step is to determine if a "generation-skipping" transfer has occurred.

1. Defining Generation–Skipping Transfers

a) Direct Skips

A direct skip is a transfer of a Chapter 13 interest to a skip person that is subject to the estate or gift tax.

(1) Elements of a Direct Skip

    a.   Interest Transferred to a Skip Person

        i)   General Rule

For a direct skip an "interest" must be transferred to a skip person.

        ii)   Anti–Look–Through Rule for Transfers to Trusts [IRC § 2612(c)(2)]

The general rule for entities is that they are first pierced to determine the generation assignment of those with a beneficial interest in the entity. However, if the transfer is to a trust and subject to the gift or estate tax, the look-through rule does not apply.

    b.   Subject to Estate or Gift Tax

In order to have a direct skip, the transfer must be "subject to" either the estate or the gift tax. This does not necessarily mean that a tax liability must be imposed or that any tax becomes due. Technically, it is enough that the transferred property be included in the decedent's gross estate or be treated as a transfer of property by gift.

(2) Generational Assignment After Direct Skip in Trust [IRC § 2653(a)]

The generational assignments of individuals with a Chapter 13 interest in trust change to one below the transferor if (1) a generation-skipping transfer of property exists, and (2) immediately after such transfer the property is held in trust.

(3) Exceptions and Exclusions

There are various general exclusions to all generation-skipping transfers, and the predeceased parent rule also applies.

    b)   Taxable Terminations [IRC § 2612(a)]

A taxable termination is present when there is (1) a termination, (2) of an "interest in property," (3) held in trust, (4) unless, immediately after the termination, a non-skip person has a Chapter 13 interest in the trust or no future distributions (including those on termination of the trust) may be made to a skip person. A fifth element from the Regulations requires that no federal estate or gift tax can exist on the termination of the trust.

(1) Elements of a Taxable Termination

    a. "Termination"

        "Death, lapse of time, release of power, or otherwise" satisfies the termination requirement.

        i) Simultaneous Terminations

            The termination of more than one interest in a single trust results in only one taxable termination generation-skipping transfer.

        ii) Partial Terminations [IRC § 2612(a)(2)]

            If a Chapter 13 interest held in trust by a lineal descendant of the transferor is terminated by death and trust assets are distributed out of the trust to a skip person, a taxable termination is present for that portion of the property so distributed.

    b. Interests in Property Held in Trust

        When determining possession of a Chapter 13 interest, apply the look-through rules of IRC § 2651(f)(2).

    c. Trusts

        "Trusts" for Chapter 13 purposes include formal as well as nonexplicit trusts.

    d. Not Subject to Estate or Gift Tax

        The regulations provide that a taxable termination cannot occur if the transfer is subject to estate tax or gift tax.

    e. "Unless" Rules

        In two instances, the termination of interests in property not subject to estate or gift tax does not result in a taxable termination: (1) when, immediately after the termination, a non-skip person has a Chapter 13 interest in the trust; or (2) if no one has a Chapter 13 interest in the trust, and after the termination, no distributions can be ever made to skip persons.

(2) Exclusion and Exceptions

Various exclusions and exceptions apply where a taxable termination will not trigger imposition of generation-skipping transfer tax.

c) Taxable Distributions [IRC § 2612(b)]

By definition, a taxable distribution only occurs when a direct skip or taxable termination is not present. The additional requirements of a taxable distribution are simple—there must be a distribution from a trust (which includes non-explicit trusts) to a skip person.

(1) Elements of a Taxable Distribution

Any distribution from a trust qualifies as a taxable distribution, no matter whether it is required or discretionary (i.e., under a power of appointment), and no matter whether it is paid from the income (current or accumulated) or corpus of the trust.

(2) Trust's Payment of GST Tax on a Taxable Distribution

If the trust pays the tax on a taxable distribution generation-skipping transfer, the payment is treated as a second taxable distribution.

(3) Exclusions and Exceptions

Various exceptions and exclusions apply that render taxable distributions non-taxable.

2. Excluded Transfers

The GST tax will not necessarily apply, even if a generation-skipping transfer is present under IRC § 2611(a). Several exclusions or exceptions must be considered.

a) Indirect Payments of Medical or Educational Expenses [IRC § 2611(b)(1)]

Transfers which would not be treated as taxable gifts under IRC § 2503(e) if made by the transferor directly are not generation-skipping transfers.

b) Property Previously Subject to the GST Tax [IRC § 2611(b)(2)]

A transfer is not treated as a generation-skipping transfer to the extent it involves property previously subject to a GST tax, the previous transferee had the same or lower generational assignment as the current transferee, and the effect of the transfer is not avoidance of the GST tax.

c) Multiple Skips

Skips over multiple generations are not subject to more than one GST tax.

d) Trusts Created Before the GST Effective Date

The effective date for the GST tax is October 23, 1986. Therefore, trusts created on or after this date are subjected to the GST tax on generation-skipping transfers. The effective date is expanded to cover trusts created after September 25, 1985, that are subject to the gift tax upon creation.

(1) Irrevocable Trusts Created Before September 26, 1985

a. General Rule

The GST tax does not apply to any taxable distributions from, or taxable terminations of, irrevocable trusts created before September 26, 1985. Interestingly, any trust in existence on September 25, 1985, is treated as an "irrevocable trust" for purposes of this rule.

b. Trust or Trust Assets Not Treated as an Irrevocable Trust

If the trust's property is includable in the transferor's gross estate under IRC §§ 2038 or 2042 and the settlor of the trust dies after September 25, 1985, then Chapter 13 applies.

(2) Continuous Mental Incompetence of Transferor from October 22, 1986

Certain transfers are not subject to the GST tax if the settlor of the trust suffered under a mental disability at all times from October 22, 1986, until the settlor's death. Excludable transfers are (1) direct skips caused by the settlor's death, and (2) testamentary transfers from trusts included in the individual's gross estate (e.g., where the individual had the right to income from the trust).

(3) Revocable Trusts and Wills of Decedent's Dying Before 1987

Chapter 13 excludes generation-skipping transfers from revocable trusts or wills created before October 22, 1986, if the trust was not amended after October 22, 1986, the trust received no additions after such date, and the decedent died before January 1, 1987.

(4) "Gallo" Amendment

Before 1990, direct skips to the transferor's grandchildren up to $2 million were excluded transfers.

D. COMPUTATION OF THE GENERATION SKIPPING TRANSFER TAX

The Chapter 13 GST tax is computed by multiplying the "taxable amount" by the "applicable rate."

1. Taxable Amount

To determine the taxable amount, one must first identify the type of generation-skipping transfer that occurred. The appropriate taxable amount is then ascertained by applying the appropriate statute.

a) Direct Skip [IRC § 2623]

(1) Taxable Amount

The taxable amount for a direct skip generation-skipping transfer is the value of the property received by the transferee less any consideration paid by the transferee.

(2) Method and Time of Valuation

The time and method of valuation for the taxable amount of a direct skip is controlled by the type of transfer.

a. Inter Vivos Gift

The value of a direct skip made by gift directly or through a trust is the fair market value of the property determined at the time of the transfer.

b. Testamentary Transfer

Property included in the transferor's gross estate subject to a testamentary direct skip is valued at the same time and in the same manner as under the estate tax.

c. Estate Tax Inclusion Period

If a transfer is a direct skip but the property would be includible in the transferor's gross estate after the transfer, it is subject to the estate tax inclusion period ("ETIP").

b) Taxable Termination [IRC § 2622]

(1) Taxable Amount

The taxable amount for taxable termination generation-skipping transfers includes all property involved in the taxable termination. Since the tax liability in a taxable termination is borne by the trust this means the taxable amount includes amounts that will be used to pay the GST tax.

(2) Method and Time of Valuation

The method of valuation for a taxable termination is the fair market value of the property, no exceptions. Generally, the valuation date is the termination of the trust.

c) Taxable Distributions [IRC § 2621]

(1) Taxable Amount

The taxable amount for a taxable distribution is the value of the property received by the transferee reduced by any expenses incurred "by the transferee in connection with the determination, collection, or refund" of any GST tax imposed on the distribution.

(2) Method and Time of Valuation

The only allowable valuation method for a taxable distribution is the property's fair market value at the time of distribution.

d) Tax Inclusive v. Tax Exclusive

Chapter 13 contains both tax inclusive and tax exclusive transfers. Taxable terminations and taxable distributions are tax inclusive transfers. The tax liability for each is paid from the amount used to compute the tax. Testamentary direct skips are tax exclusive transfers; no amount of tax is due from the property transferred.

2. Applicable Rate

The applicable rate is the product of the "maximum Federal estate tax rate" multiplied by the "inclusion ratio."

a) Maximum Estate Tax Rate [IRC § 2641(b)]

The maximum Federal estate tax rate is the highest marginal rate provided for by IRC § 2001(c) at the time the generation-skipping transfer occurs.

b) Inclusion Ratio

(1) General Rule

In general, the inclusion ratio is computed by subtracting the applicable fraction from the number 1. The applicable fraction is computed by taking the amount of GST exemption allocated (if any) to the transaction or trust, divided by the value of the property received (for direct skips or taxable distributions) or the value of the trust (for taxable terminations), less any federal or state tax paid and charitable deductions allowed on the property.

a. Exception to General Rule for Inclusion Ratio: Zero Inclusion Ratio for Direct Skips of Transfers Excluded from Gift Tax Under IRC § 2503(b)

Where a nontaxable gift transfer results in a direct skip, the transfer, in whole or in part, receives a zero inclusion ratio, even if no GST exemption has been allocated. Direct skip transfers made by a trust have additional requirements to qualify for the automatic zero inclusion ratio. These additional requirements prevent the automatic zero inclusion ratio from shielding subsequent generation-skipping transfers from the trust. Absent these requirements, remote beneficiaries with *Crummey* powers could permanently shield transfers to trusts from the GST tax.

(2) Applicable Fraction

Unless a special rule applies, the applicable fraction is computed by dividing the GST exemption allocated to the transfer (in the case of a direct skip) or trust (in the case of all other generation-skipping transfers) by the value of the property. The value of the property is reduced by certain federal estate or state death taxes and any charitable deductions allowed under IRC §§ 2055 or 2522 attributable to the property. This fraction is then put into decimal form and rounded to the nearest one-thousandth (.001). The applicable fraction is then subtracted from 1 to compute the inclusion ratio.

a. The Numerator of the Applicable Fraction

The numerator of the applicable fraction is generally the amount of GST exemption allocated to the trust or the transferred property (for direct skips not in trust).

i) Who is Allowed to Allocate the GST Exemption [IRC § 2631(a)]

(1) General Rule

The allocation of the GST exemption can be applied to inter vivos transfers by the donor or to testamentary transfers by the individual's executor. For transfers to a trust with more than one transferor, the trust is split into separate portions and the GST exemption for any one transferor will only serve to reduce the tax on his or her specific portion of the trust.

(2) Marital Planning and the GST Exemption

Married couples have the advantage of utilizing two GST exemption amounts, one for the husband and another for the wife. The GST exemption does not transfer, so spouses may only use their GST exemption for those amounts for which they are deemed the transferor. Two techniques help married couples maximize their respective GST exemptions: the split-gift for Chapter 13 purposes and the reverse QTIP election.

ii) GST Exemption Amount [IRC § 2631(c)]

Since 2004, the GST exemption amount equals the estate tax applicable exclusion amount provided by IRC § 2010(c).

iii) Allocation of GST Exemption

Since the GST exemption lowers the tax rate for generation-skipping transfers, and is not unlimited, prudent use of the GST exemption is important.

(1) Inter Vivos Transfers

(a) Direct Skips

The GST exemption amount may be allocated either by default or specific election. The specific election may be made at any time before the federal estate tax return is due, but in most cases will not have the same effect as a timely election.

i) Deemed Allocations for Inter Vivos Direct Skips [IRC § 2632(b)]

Any remaining GST exemption (called the "unused portion" in the Code) automatically creates a zero inclusion ratio on all inter vivos direct skips.

ii) Transferor's Election to Allocate GST Exemption

A transferor must affirmatively elect out of the automatic allocation of GST exemption to inter vivos direct skips.

iii) Estate Tax Inclusion Period

If a transfer is a direct skip but the property would be includible in the transferor's gross estate after the transfer, it is subject to the estate tax inclusion period ("ETIP").

(b) Transfers, Not Direct Skips, to a Trust

GST exemption may be allocated to a trust created after 2001 in three different ways. First, certain trusts receive an automatic allocation if the transferor does not elect out. Second, the transferor may make a specific GST exemption allocation to the trust. Third, under certain specific circumstances a transferor may retroactively make an allocation of GST exemption to trusts.

(2) Testamentary Transfers

Any unused GST exemption at T's death may be used to protect testamentary or inter vivos transfers made by the decedent from the GST tax. The effective date for an elective GST allocation depends on whether the transfer is allocated to property included in the decedent's gross estate and transferred at death and/or whether it is allocated to an inter vivos transfer. If the executor fails to make a timely allocation of the GST exemption then the unused GST exemption is used automatically in order to minimize the GST tax consequences.

b. The Denominator of the Applicable Fraction

The denominator of the applicable fraction is the value of the property less the sum of any applicable federal estate and state death taxes and any charitable deductions. Federal estate or state death taxes paid, as well as any charitable deductions under IRC §§ 2055 or 2522, reduce the value of the property when computing the denominator of the applicable fraction. These reductions only apply to property transferred to trusts, since a direct skip cannot be subject to either of the allowable reductions.

(3) Exceptions to the General Rules for Computing the Applicable Fraction and Inclusion Ratio

For certain trusts or after certain events, the applicable fraction is redetermined to accurately reflect the original use of the GST exemption.

a. Charitable Lead Annuity Trust [IRC § 2642(e)]

A taxpayer may deduct the present value of the charitable lead interest from his or her federal estate and gift taxes when the lead interest is a guaranteed annuity (e.g., the charity receives $10,000 from the trust each year). This allows for leveraging of the exemption amount when the trust assets generate a higher rate of return than the factor used in computing the present value of the charitable assets. To prevent this type of leveraging, both the numerator and denominator of the applicable fraction are determined when the lead charitable annuity interest terminates.

b. Estate Tax Inclusion Period [IRC § 2642(f)]

Property transferred by an inter vivos transfer that is includible in the transferor's gross estate immediately after the transfer is subject to the estate tax inclusion period ("ETIP"). The ETIP is the period starting with the transfer of property includible in the transferor's gross estate and ending at the earlier of one of three events: (1) when the property is no longer potentially includible in the transferor's gross estate; (2) when the property is subject to a generation-skipping transfer (but only for such portion of the property); or (3) when the transferor dies. The application of the ETIP affects three aspects of the computation of the GST tax. First, any allocation of the GST exemption is not effective until the close of the ETIP. Second, IRC § 2642(f)(2) determines the value of the property. Third, direct skip transfers are treated as occurring at the close of the ETIP.

c. Trust Consolidation [Reg. § 26.2642–4(a)(2)]

If a transferor creates separate trusts that the transferor then wants to consolidate, a new applicable fraction must be computed for the consolidated trust.

d. Additional Transfers of Property or GST Exemption to a Trust [IRC § 2642(d)]

The applicable fraction is recomputed if additional property or GST exemption is allocated to an existing trust.

e. Pour–Over Trusts [IRC § 2653(b)(2)]

If the property is transferred to another trust (a "pour-over trust"), a portion of the transferring trust's GST exemption is allocated to the pour-over trust. This is done regardless of whether the transferring and pour-over have the same transferor. However, if the trusts do have the same transferor, the applicable fraction of the pour-over trust must be recomputed since there has been an additional transfer of property and GST exemption to a trust.

f. **Recomputation of Applicable Fraction After Taxable Terminations [IRC § 2653(b)(1)]**

If a trust is assigned GST exemption and either a taxable termination occurs or the trust does not terminate and the transferor remains the same after the taxable termination, the applicable fraction is recomputed to reflect a "proper adjustment."

g. **Qualified Severance [IRC § 2642(a)(3)]**

Trusts severed in a "qualified severance" are treated as separate trusts for purposes of Chapter 13. A severance is qualified if the division is allowed under the governing instrument or local law, the trust is divided on a fractional basis, and, in the aggregate, the new trusts provide for the same succession of interests in benefits as the severed trust.

h. **Recapture of Estate Tax Savings from Special Use Valuation [Reg. § 26.2642–4(a)(4)]**

The applicable fraction computed using property valued under IRC § 2032A must be recomputed upon a recapture of the IRC § 2032A benefit.

3. Credit for State Death Taxes [IRC § 2604]

Before 2005, GST tax due could be reduced by up to five percent of the GST tax liability for payment of state tax due on generation-skipping transfers. The credit is no longer available under current law.

E. COLLATERAL ISSUES

1. Effect on Adjusted Basis of Property

The recipient of gifted property may increase his or her adjusted basis (but not over the fair market value of the property) for the portion of the GST tax imposed on the appreciation of the property. The basis increase for GST tax paid does not apply to direct skip testamentary transfers. If property is transferred at death to a trust that is later the subject of a taxable distribution, the property's basis may be increased in the same manner as property transferred by gift. Two different rules apply to determine the adjustments to basis allowed for the GST tax paid on property transferred in a taxable termination occurring upon the death of an individual, one for trusts with inclusion ratios of "1" and another for trusts with inclusion ratios less than "1."

2. Generation–Skipping Procedural Rules

No specific rules in the Code establish who must file, what return must be filed, or when any required return must be filed to account for any generation-skipping transfer. Responsibility and return requirements for the GST tax depends on which generation-skipping transfer occurred.

a) Direct Skip

Unless the transfer is from a trust, any GST tax due on direct skips must be paid by the transferor. For non-trust direct skips, the transferor is liable to pay the GST tax. For transfers from a trust, the tax liability is on the trustee of the trust. For inter vivos direct skips, Form 709 (pertaining to gift and generation-skipping transfers) must be filed before April 15 of the year following the transfer, unless an extension of time is granted. Direct skips following an individual's death must be reported on Form 706 (estate tax return).

b) Taxable Termination

The trustee of a trust assumes liability for the GST tax on any taxable terminations. The trustee must file a return for taxable termination generation-skipping transfers by the 15th day of the fourth month after the close of the taxable year of the trust, unless an extension is granted.

c) Taxable Distributions

The transferee is liable for any GST tax on taxable distributions. Initially, the trustee must file an informational Form 706–GS(D) for the trust and provide a copy of Form 706–GS(D–1) to each distributee. The transferee must fill out and file the form received by the 15th day of the fourth month after the close of the taxable year of the taxable distribution.

Perspective

■ ANALYSIS

A. **An Introduction to Federal Wealth Transfer Taxes**
    1.   The Federal Estate Tax
    2.   The Federal Gift Tax
    3.   The Federal Generation–Skipping Transfer Tax
B. **Computing Liability for Federal Estate and Gift Taxes: A Unified System?**
    1.   Computing the Transfer Tax Due
    2.   Planning Techniques with the Unified Credit
C. **History of Federal Wealth Transfer Taxes**
D. **The Future of Federal Wealth Transfer Taxes**
E. **Review Questions**

A. AN INTRODUCTION TO FEDERAL WEALTH TRANSFER TAXES

The federal wealth transfer tax regime consists of three separate taxes: (1) the federal estate tax; (2) the federal gift tax; and (3) the federal generation-skipping transfer tax. All three taxes are excises imposed on the gratuitous transfer of wealth by individuals. Accordingly, they are generally imposed on the transferor and/or the transferor's estate. This is different from an inheritance tax, where the recipients of gratuitous wealth transfers pay an excise on the receipt of wealth. It is also distinct from an income tax imposed on an annual or other regular basis. Wealth transfer taxes are imposed only upon the occasion of a gratuitous transfer.

Modern political rhetoric uses the term "death tax" to refer to the federal estate tax (and, sometimes, the federal gift tax and the federal generation-skipping transfer tax). To the extent a death tax, by its name, is imposed upon the death of an individual, it is inaccurate to refer to any of the federal wealth transfer taxes as a death tax. Although some wealth transfers occur upon the death of an individual, triggering the estate tax, there is no tax imposed upon one's death.

The federal wealth transfer taxes focus on the types of interests that constitute "ownership" and the types of property transfers that are, in substance, transfers of wealth. The federal wealth transfer tax regime cares little about "detached and disinterested generosity" or other subjective motives of the decedent or donor. In this regard, one can gain a solid familiarity with federal wealth transfer taxes without any prior study of federal income tax laws, and, likewise, one with a mastery of fundamental income tax concepts must expect to learn an entirely new analytical framework.

1. The Federal Estate Tax

The federal estate tax captures wealth transfers that occur at death. It is measured by determining a decedent's "gross estate" and then subtracting up to five deductions to arrive at the "taxable estate." The "taxable estate" is then applied to a simple tax table to compute the tentative tax liability. Credits are then subtracted from the tentative tax to reach the final tax liability. Any tax due must be paid no later than nine months following the decedent's death. Because the estate tax is an excise imposed upon the transfer of wealth at death, the decedent's estate is primarily liable for payment of the tax.

2. The Federal Gift Tax

The federal gift tax was originally designed as a back-stop to the federal estate tax. Without a federal gift tax, the federal estate tax would be easy to avoid: in the moments before death, an individual with a taxable estate would simply give all of his or her assets to the intended beneficiaries, dying with nothing. In effect, an estate tax would only be imposed on individuals that died suddenly or who could not give everything away prior to death. Because the federal gift tax exists in part to enforce the federal estate tax's excise on wealth transfers, the two taxes bear close resemblance. The federal estate and gift taxes are "unified" in the sense that they share the same rate table for tax computations. Beyond that, however, the taxes are "similar," but not so "unified." Because the gift tax applies to lifetime wealth transfers, the donor is primarily liable for payment of the tax.

The legislative changes of the early 21st century have changed the underlying premise of the federal gift tax. From 2001 to 2010 the federal estate tax was phased-out, but the federal gift tax continued. The continuation of the federal gift tax in light of the federal estate tax's demise suggests that there is a broader purpose to the gift tax than simply policing the estate tax. Perhaps the federal gift tax is also a vehicle for enforcing the federal income tax. Affluent individuals in the highest income tax brackets might have an incentive to transfer substantial sums of income-producing wealth to family members in lower tax brackets in an effort to reduce income tax liability while keeping the wealth "all in the family." An excise tax on the transfer of substantial wealth might discourage this practice. Although there is the common law doctrine of "assignment of income" to thwart abusive shifts of income to individuals in lower tax brackets, perhaps this doctrine alone is not a sufficient defense. In any event, it is clear that the gift tax was originally a derivative of the estate tax, so understanding the mechanics of the gift tax requires a crude understanding of the estate tax. Accordingly, this text discusses the gift tax after the estate tax.

3. The Federal Generation–Skipping Transfer Tax

The federal generation-skipping transfer tax is similarly designed to enforce the federal estate tax. Affluent families could easily avoid multiple layers of transfer taxes by locking up wealth in trusts designed to last in perpetuity. While the Rule Against Perpetuities would force the termination of these trusts at some point in the future, a number of states have repealed the Rule. Trusts subject to the laws of these states can, apparently, last forever.

Example: Two families, the Hatfields and the McCoys, each have $100 million in wealth all currently in the hands of the first generation. The Hatfields take no action and the McCoys lock away their wealth into a perpetual trust. The after-tax wealth of the two families will be dramatically different, assuming a flat transfer tax rate of 50% and ignoring any applicable exemptions and deductions:

The Hatfields		The McCoys	
Original wealth	= $100,000,000	Original wealth	= $100,000,000
Tax at 1st gen. death	= $ 50,000,000	Tax at formation of trust	= $ 50,000,000
Tax at 2nd gen. death	= $ 25,000,000	Tax at 1st gen. death	= $ 0
Tax at 3rd gen. death	= $ 12,500,000	Tax at 2nd gen. death	= $ 0
Total remaining	= **$ 12,500,000**	Tax at 3rd gen. death	= $ 0
		Total remaining	= **$ 50,000,000**

This example ignores the fact that the assets of each family are likely to appreciate in value over time, but the proportionate difference in estate sizes between the two families remains the same even if we assume a modest 3.6% annual growth rate such that the after-tax value of the assets doubles at each 20–year generation:

The Hatfields		The McCoys	
Original wealth	= $100,000,000	Original wealth	= $100,000,000
Wealth at 1st gen. death	= $200,000,000	Tax at formation of trust	= $ 50,000,000
Tax at 1st gen. death	= $100,000,000	Wealth at 1st gen. death	= $100,000,000
Wealth at 2nd gen. death	= $200,000,000	Tax at 1st gen. death	= $ 0
Tax at 2nd gen. death	= $100,000,000	Wealth at 2nd gen. death	= $200,000,000
Wealth at 3rd gen. death	= $200,000,000	Tax at 2nd gen. death	= $ 0
Tax at 3rd gen. death	= $100,000,000	Wealth at 3rd gen. death	= $400,000,000
Total remaining	= **$100,000,000**	Tax at 3rd gen. death	= $ 0
		Total remaining	= **$400,000,000**

Congress thought these results unduly benefited families like the McCoys, so it imposed a separate tax on so-called "generation-skipping transfers." The goal is to discourage affluent families from locking away wealth and thus avoiding federal estate tax at each generation. The tax is imposed upon the receipt of wealth by a person two or more generations below the transferor, whether such transfer occurs directly or through a trust created by the transferor.

B. COMPUTING LIABILITY FOR FEDERAL ESTATE AND GIFT TAXES: A UNIFIED SYSTEM?

Both the federal estate tax and the federal gift tax utilize the tax tables set forth in § 2001(c) of the Internal Revenue Code of 1986, as amended (the "Code") (throughout this text, all references to "IRC § " are references to the Code). In addition, the federal estate tax is computed with reference to prior taxable gifts made during the decedent's lifetime. One "**unified credit**" amount is applied to the tax liability computed under this tax table. The unified credit amount is equal to the tax on a specified sum, often referred to as the "**exemption amount.**" Every United States citizen or resident is entitled to transfer (whether while alive or at death) an amount equal to the exemption amount without payment of any federal wealth transfer tax. The exemption is not elective.

1. Computing the Transfer Tax Due

After 2010, the unified credit amount is equal to the tax imposed under IRC § 2001(c) on a taxable estate totaling $5 million. [IRC § 2010(c)] The "exemption amount" is therefore $5 million, and the "unified credit" is $1,730,800. In effect, then, individuals may transfer a total of $5 million during life and/or at death before becoming liable for payment of tax. If an individual dying in 2011 made total lifetime "taxable gifts" of exactly $5 million (which, as explained in Chapter II, is not necessarily equal to the total value of all gift transfers made during life), then any amount in the individual's taxable estate would trigger liability for federal estate taxes. Likewise, if an individual dying in 2011 made total lifetime taxable gifts of $4.5 million, then the estate would be liable for federal estate taxes only to the extent that the taxable estate exceeded $500,000. It is helpful to think of the unified credit and the corresponding exemption amount as a single exemption amount available during life and, to the extent not fully utilized during life, at death.

It is a common misperception that the exemption amount is used twice—both during life and at death. But in fact, the exemption amount is available only once. The following examples illustrate this point. In each example, the transferor (Dan) has total wealth of $10 million, and all applicable deductions are ignored. For simplicity, all computations assume a unified credit equal to the tax imposed on $5 million and a flat transfer tax rate of 35%.

Example (1): Dan dies having made no taxable gifts. Dan's federal estate tax liability is $1.75 million:

Tax on $10 million taxable estate	=	$3,500,000
Less Unified Credit	=	($1,750,000)
Total estate tax liability	=	**$1,750,000**

Example (2): Shortly before death, Dan gives away all of his wealth by making a taxable gift of $7,407,407 and paying $842,592 in federal gift tax (gift tax of $2,592,592 less the IRC § 2505 credit on $5 million or $1,750,000). As will be explained in Chapter I the federal gift tax paid by Dan will be included in his gross estate at death because the gift tax was paid within three years of his death. [IRC § 2035(b)] This will trigger liability for federal estate tax, but the combined gift and estate tax liability will be the same as in Example (1):

Tax on taxable gift	=	$ 2,592,592
Less Unified Credit	=	($ 1,750,000)
Total gift tax liability	=	$ 842,592
Taxable Estate	=	$ 2,592,592
Plus Adjusted Taxable Gifts	=	$ 7,407,407
Total Amount Subject to Tax	=	$10,000,000
Tax on $10 million	=	$ 3,500,000
Less Unified Credit	=	($ 1,750,000)
Less Prior Gift Tax Paid	=	($ 842,592)
Total Estate Tax Liability	=	$ 907,408
Total gift and estate tax paid	=	$ 1,750,000

Example (3): Dan transfers $3 million by gift. Dan dies more than three years later, owning the remaining $7 million. Here, too, the total transfer tax liability is the same as in Examples (1) and (2):

Tax on $3 million taxable gift	=	$ 1,050,000
Less Gift Tax Credit	=	($ 1,050,000)
Total gift tax liability	=	$ 0
Taxable Estate	=	$ 7,000,000
Plus Adjusted Taxable Gifts	=	$ 3,000,000
Total Amount Subject to Tax	=	$10,000,000
Tax on $10 million	=	$ 3,500,000
Less Unified Credit	=	($ 1,750,000)
Less Prior Gift Tax	=	($ 0)
Total Estate Tax Liability	=	$ 1,750,000
Total gift and estate tax paid	=	$ 1,750,000

Notice that the full unified credit amount is used here; it is not reduced by virtue of the $3 million gift. We need to apply the full credit amount here because the tax on $10 million was computed with reference to D's taxable *and lifetime taxable gifts.* If we do not take the full credit amount in this step, we effectively tax what was the tax-free portion of the gift at death.

2. Planning Techniques with the Unified Credit

In each of the above examples, the total wealth transfer tax imposed on Dan and/or his estate is the same: $1,750,000. Of course, this does not mean that Dan would have no preference as between paying tax during life or paying tax at death. Generally, one should defer the payment of tax as long as possible. This would lead one to favor hoarding wealth until death. But following a taxable gift, all appreciation on the gifted property will not be subject to further tax for the transferor. In the last example above, all subsequent appreciation in value on the $3 million taxable gift was not subject to estate tax at Dan's death. In this particular example, that advantage was not very significant because death soon followed the gift. But if Dan had lived for several years following the gift, the advantage would be much more significant, perhaps enough to warrant the early payment of tax attendant with making a taxable gift. As this discussion illustrates, the decision of whether to make a lifetime taxable gift in excess of the exemption amount and incur liability for federal gift tax depends upon a number of factors that will vary from one transferor to the next.

Those willing to make lifetime gifts should give assets likely to appreciate in value. All post-transfer appreciation on gifted property escapes further federal wealth transfer taxation, thus leveraging the value of the initial gift. There is an income tax drawback to gifting appreciated property, for the recipient of the gift will take the property with a basis for federal income tax purposes equal to the basis of the property in the client's hands. Generally, however, a 15% capital gains tax at disposition is better than a substantially higher federal transfer tax (currently 35%) that would be imposed on the appreciated value of the gifted property.

Example (1): In 2011, Ernie made his only lifetime taxable gift: a gift of marketable securities worth $5,000,000 to his best friend, Bert. Ernie's income tax basis in the securities at the time of the gift was $4,000,000. Because the applicable exclusion amount in 2011 was $5,000,000, Ernie paid no federal gift tax on the transfer. In the years following the gift, the value of the marketable securities doubled to $8,000,000. When Ernie dies in 2020, no additional transfer tax is owed. If Bert sells the securities after Ernie's death for $8,000,000 cash, Bert will realize and recognize a long-term capital gain of $4,000,000 because Bert took Ernie's basis in the gifted securities. [IRC § 1015(a)] Under current law, that $4,000,000 long-term capital gain would be taxed at 15%, triggering a $600,000 tax liability (15% * $4,000,000) and leaving Bert with $7,400,000 cash after all taxes.

Example (2): Same facts as Example (1), except that Ernie does not make the gift to Bert but instead bequeaths the marketable securities to Bert in his will. Assuming the stocks are still worth $8,000,000 at his death, and assuming an applicable exemption amount of $5,000,000, Ernie's estate would pay federal estate tax of $1,050,000 ($2,780,800 tax on a $8 million estate under IRC § 2001(c) less $1,730,800 unified credit on an exemption amount of $5,000,000). That leaves Bert with a net bequest of $6,950,000 ($8 million less the $1,050,000 tax). Bert would take these stocks with a fair market value basis of $6,950,000 under IRC § 1014(a). Accordingly, Bert's immediate sale of the gifted stocks would trigger no income tax gain or loss, leaving Bert with $6,950,000 cash after all taxes, or $450,000 worse than under Example (1).

C. HISTORY OF FEDERAL WEALTH TRANSFER TAXES

The modern federal wealth transfer tax regime traces back to the Revenue Act of 1916. It contained an estate tax with many features of today's system. With an exemption amount of $50,000 (estimated to be over $11 million in terms of today's wealth), estate tax rates started at 1% and climbed to 10% on estates over $5 million (adjusted for inflation, this equates to over $1 billion in today's wealth). As the United States entered World War I, Congress raised these rates. At war's end, however, Congress increased the rates further and introduced the federal gift tax in 1924.

Increased rates were the central theme behind most reforms for the next two decades. By the late 1940s, the maximum estate and gift tax rate reached 77%, as Congress viewed the transfer tax system as a key to income redistribution. It was not until 1976 that the exemption amounts for federal estate and gift taxes were unified.

Beginning in 1981, Congress chipped away at the estate tax. The maximum tax rate dropped from 70% to 50%, and the increase in the exemption amount to

$600,000 significantly narrowed the focus of the taxes. By 1997, Congress increased the exemption amount again and provided for additional increases to reach $1 million by 2006.

D. THE FUTURE OF FEDERAL WEALTH TRANSFER TAXES

In 2001, Congress placed the federal estate tax on death row. The Economic Growth and Tax Relief Reconciliation Act of 2001 set forth both scheduled increases to the exemption amount and a scheduled reduction in the maximum tax rate applicable to estates. Under the 2001 Act, the estate tax was to be repealed altogether in 2010. Although the universal consensus of estate planners was that outright repeal would never come to pass, 2010 indeed started without a federal estate tax. In December, 2010, however, Congress passed the Tax Relief, Unemployment Insurance Reauthorization and Job Creation Act of 2010. Part of that legislation revived the federal estate and generation-skipping transfer taxes, retroactive to the start of 2010, though it introduced a $5 million exemption for estate and generation-skipping transfer tax purposes and a 35% top rate for estate and gift taxes. In 2011, the gift tax exclusion amount similarly grew to $5 million, and the generation-skipping transfer tax applied with a 35% rate. Curiously, however, the provisions of the 2010 Act expire, as do the provisions of the 2001 Act, come 2013. Unless Congress takes some action in the near future, the applicable exclusion amount will revert to $1 million (although adjusted to some extent for inflation) and the maximum transfer tax rate will return to 55%. Whether Congress makes the increased exemption amount and lower tax rate permanent depends largely upon the same forces that will shape the 2012 presidential election. There is even a chance that the wealth transfer taxes could be repealed altogether, as the $5 million exemption substantially reduces the number of taxpayers subject to (and, thus, the amount of revenue collected from) the federal wealth transfer taxes. Accordingly, the long-term future of the federal wealth transfer tax regime is anyone's guess.

That is not very comforting for affluent individuals seeking certainty in their estate plans. To no one's surprise, many estate planning decisions are tax-motivated; if the taxes disappear, many of the strategies implemented by clients (thought by no means all of them) will become unnecessary. But on the other hand, if Congress makes no changes and we see reduced exemptions and higher tax rates, these strategies will have much greater significance. Some clients might wish to wait until the start of 2013 to see in what form the estate tax still exists. But most should not wait. The careful practitioner will consult regularly with the client as the future of the estate tax becomes increasingly clear. Certainly clients should avoid irrevocable strategies that will become undesirable should the tax be completely repealed. Fortunately, most traditional estate planning strategies have non-tax benefits that make them worthwhile even if there is no transfer tax at death.

E. REVIEW QUESTIONS

1.   Politics aside, is it inaccurate to refer to the "federal death tax?" Explain your answer.

2.   In 2005, a national newspaper reported that "[b]eginning in 2006, the unified credit for estates will be $2 million." Is this statement entirely correct? Explain your answer.

3.   Flanders owns three parcels of real estate: Blackacre, Whiteacre, and Redacre. Each is worth $5 million. Flanders is contemplating a gift of one of these parcels to his son, Rod. Flanders acquired Blackacre several years ago for $100,000. Because Blackacre is located in a major metropolitan area, Flanders reasonably expects that its value will continue to grow over time. The same cannot be said of Redacre. Flanders bought it five years ago for $5.3 million, but the recent addition of a factory on adjoining acreage has made the property far less suitable for development. Flanders recently purchased Whiteacre for $5 million. While Flanders hopes the property will appreciate like Blackacre has, it is too early to know whether neighboring development will occur and, if so, how it will affect the value of Whiteacre. How would you advise Flanders with respect to his proposed gift to Rod?

CHAPTER I

The Federal Estate Tax

■ ANALYSIS

b) Qualified Real Property [IRC § 2032A]
    (1) Qualified Real Property
        (a) The "Property" Requirements
        (b) The "Value" Requirements
        (c) The "Use" Requirements
    (2) Limitation on Aggregate Reduction in Value
    (3) Dispositions and Failure to Continue Qualified Use
        (a) Generally
        (b) Amount of Additional Estate Tax
        (c) Lack of Material Participation Deemed a Nonqualified Use

c) Premiums and Discounts
    (1) Control Premium
    (2) Minority Interest Discount
    (3) Marketability Discount
    (4) Fractional Interest Discount
    (5) Blockage Discount
    (6) Other Discounts
    (7) Combinations of Premiums and Discounts

d) Certain Rights and Restrictions Disregarded [IRC § 2703]

B. Deductions

1. Certain Expenses and Debts [§ 2053]
    a) Funeral Expenses
    b) Administration Expenses
        (1) Personal Representative Commissions
        (2) Attorney's Fees
        (3) Miscellaneous Administration Expenses
        (4) Administration Expenses Related to Non–Probate Property
        (5) Income Tax Crossover
    c) Claims Against the Estate
    d) Unpaid Mortgages

2. Casualty Losses During Estate Administration [IRC § 2054]

3. Transfers to Charities [IRC § 2055]
    a) Charities
        (1) Organizations That Qualify as Charities
            (a) Governments
            (b) Certain Nonprofit Organizations
            (c) Trusts and Certain Fraternal Organizations
            (d) Veterans' Organizations
        (2) Indefinite Charitable Bequests

As indicated in the Perspective, the federal **estate tax** is an excise tax imposed on the transfer of wealth at death. It is generally determined by computing a "taxable estate" for every decedent. The taxable estate is defined as the gross estate less certain deductions. IRC § 2051.

A. The Gross Estate

IRC § 2031(a) defines the **gross estate** as the date-of-death value of all property specifically described in IRC §§ 2031–2044. Generally, the gross estate contains not only those assets and interests actually owned by the decedent at death (conceptually, the "actual gross estate") but also certain assets and interests owned by another individual or entity over which the decedent has certain powers, incidents of ownership, or other rights (conceptually, the "artificial gross estate"). This part begins with a discussion of the actual gross estate (IRC §§ 2033 and 2034) and then considers inclusion of the artificial gross estate (IRC §§ 2035–2038, and 2043). Finally, there is discussion of special inclusion and valuation rules for certain assets (IRC §§ 2039–2042, and 2044).

1. Property Held at Death

Logically enough, the actual gross estate includes property held by the decedent at death, including certain property the decedent may not be able to transfer at death because of state law constraints.

a) Property in Which the Decedent Had an Interest [IRC § 2033]

The gross estate generally consists of assets owned by the decedent at death. Specifically, IRC § 2033 requires inclusion of "all property to the extent of the interest therein of the decedent at the time of death." Necessarily, then, inclusion under IRC § 2033 is a two-part test. First, the decedent must own an interest in property immediately prior to death. It is not necessary that the decedent hold the underlying *res* of a property interest, just that the decedent own an *interest* in the property. [*Smith v. Shaughnessy*, 318 U.S. 176, 63 S.Ct. 545, 87 L.Ed. 690 (1943)]

Example (1):   The value of a remainder interest in a trust held by the decedent at death would be included in the gross estate.

Example (2):   On the other hand, the proceeds from a wrongful death action would not be included in the gross estate because the right to commence such an action arises *at* or immediately *after* the decedent's death, not immediately *before* death. [*Connecticut Bank & Trust Co. v. United States*, 465 F.2d 760 (2d Cir. 1972); Rev. Rul. 75–127, 1975–1 C.B. 297]

Example (3):   To the extent a lawsuit is filed seeking damages for the decedent's "pre-mortem" pain and suffering, however, the Service believes inclusion is required. [Rev. Rul. 75–127, 1975–1 C.B. 297]

Second, the decedent must have held the right to transfer that interest at death. If an asset simply disappears at death, it is generally not included in the gross estate.

Example: Gomer creates a trust that gives Xavier the right to income for Xavier's life and a remainder to Denise if Denise is living at Xavier's death. If Denise is not then living, the remainder passes to Yancy or Yancy's estate. If Denise dies while Xavier is still alive, Denise's gross estate will not include the value of the contingent remainder, since Denise has no power to transfer the contingent remainder at her death. Likewise, Xavier's gross estate will not include the value of the life estate because it expires at Xavier's death. But notice that if Yancy dies while both Denise and Xavier are still living, Yancy's gross estate *will* include the value of Yancy's contingent remainder because Yancy's contingent remainder does not die with Yancy; Yancy can designate who will succeed to Yancy's interest in the contingent remainder.

Consistent with this rule, lump-sum Social Security death benefits payable to the decedent's spouse are not included in the decedent's gross estate because the decedent lacks any power to designate the individual(s) who shall take the benefits. [Rev. Rul. 67–277, 1967–2 C.B. 322]

Likewise, the gross estate includes the value of a promissory note payable to the order of the decedent, even if the decedent's will provides for forgiveness of the balance of the note. [Reg. § 20.2033–1(b)] If the promissory note itself contained a clause that forgave repayment in the event of decedent's death, no inclusion in the decedent's gross estate occurs because the decedent has nothing to transfer at death. [*Estate of Moss v. Commissioner*, 74 T.C. 1239 (1980)]

In the case of a married couple living in a community property state, the gross estate of the first spouse to die will include one-half of the value of the community property. This is because the deceased spouse only has an interest in one-half of any asset held as community property. The result does not change merely because formal title in any community property asset rests with only one spouse.

Example: Fred and Wilma reside in Arizona, a community property state. Title to their personal residence is in Wilma's name only. Fred dies before Wilma. Fred's gross estate includes his one-half interest in the personal residence even though Wilma alone has formal title to the residence.

(1) Amount Included in Gross Estate

The value of any property interest included in the decedent's gross estate is its "**fair market value**," defined as "the price at which the property would change hands between a willing buyer and a willing seller, neither being under any compulsion to buy or sell and both having reasonable knowledge of relevant facts." [Reg. § 20.2031–1(b)] The determination of fair market value is a question of fact. [*Messing v. Commissioner*, 48 T.C. 502, 512 (1967); *McGuire v. Commissioner*, 44 T.C. 801, 812 (1965)] As indicated above, assets included in the gross estate are valued at the date of the decedent's death. Conceptually, it is helpful to think of the gross estate as a snapshot of the decedent's assets taken as of the moment of death.

Example: The decedent held marketable securities. On the day before the decedent's death, the fair market value of the securities was $10,000. On the date of the decedent's death, the fair market value of the securities was $20,000. On the day after the decedent's death, the fair market value of the securities was $5,000. With very limited exceptions discussed briefly elsewhere in this Section, the value of the securities included in the decedent's gross estate is $20,000.

This rule assumes the decedent's death does not affect the value of the asset included in the gross estate. As a general rule, the value reported on an estate tax return is not adjusted to account for events occurring after the decedent's death unless these events were known or reasonably foreseeable at the time of death. [*Estate of Spruill v. Commissioner*, 88 T.C. 1197 (1987)]

Example: Dorothy's gross estate includes stock in a publicly-traded corporation. The fair market value of the stock on the date of Dorothy's death is $10,000. Three months following Dorothy's death, the corporation's directors agree to sell the company to a competitor, causing the value of the shares held by Dorothy's estate to soar to $50,000. Although the value of the shares ultimately received by the beneficiaries of Dorothy's estate will be considerably higher, the amount properly reportable on Dorothy's estate tax return with respect to the shares will be $10,000.

(2) Application of State Law

Whether a decedent "owned" property for federal estate tax purposes is a question of state law. If the state's highest court has interpreted state law, the Internal Revenue Service is bound by that decision in examining an estate or gift tax return. [*Commissioner v. Estate of Bosch*, 387 U.S. 456, 87 S.Ct. 1776, 18 L.Ed.2d 886 (1967)] The Service is not bound by any lower court interpretation of state law unless it was a party to the underlying proceeding. Nonetheless, the Service has ruled that it will follow a lower court's interpretation if that decision made a binding determination of the decedent's interest in the property at issue. [Rev. Rul. 73–142, 1973–1 C.B. 405]

(3) Relationship of Gross Estate to Probate Estate or Taxable Income

To the extent IRC § 2033 requires inclusion of any interest in property that the decedent held at death, the gross estate is a significantly broader concept than the probate estate. While most assets subject to probate will be included in the gross estate, the gross estate also includes the decedent's interest in **non-probate assets** like life insurance policies and retirement plan benefits (although many non-probate assets are subject to special rules discussed below). Furthermore, inclusion in the gross estate is not conditioned upon the underlying property being subject to federal income tax. Thus, municipal bonds are included in a decedent's gross estate even though the interest paid on such bonds is exempt from federal income taxation. [Reg. § 20.2033–1(a); Rev. Rul. 81–63, 1981–1 C.B. 455]

b) **Dower or Curtesy Interests [IRC § 2034]**

IRC § 2034 requires inclusion of a decedent's **dower** or **curtesy** interests, the rights to a decedent's property conferred to the decedent's surviving spouse under state law. Although the decedent has no power to transfer property subject to these rights (thus leaving such property outside the scope of IRC § 2033), such property is still included in the gross estate. Inclusion is justified on the grounds that the surviving spouse's interest in the property is fully consummated upon the death of the decedent, as is the case when the decedent's estate formally conveys property to the spouse. Since direct property transfers to the surviving spouse are subject to federal estate tax, indirect property transfers arising by operation of state law should be so subject as well.

As mentioned above, IRC § 2033 requires inclusion of the decedent's one-half share of community property. IRC § 2034 does not change this result, nor does it affect the result in any way because community property rights vest at creation, not at death. IRC § 2034 is aimed at dower-type rights that vest at death and are dependent upon the continuation of the marriage until death.

2. Re–Inclusion Provisions

While the "snapshot" metaphor is helpful in understanding the basic rules of inclusion and valuation, it is not wholly accurate by itself. In some cases, a decedent may continue to have so much control or influence over property previously transferred by the decedent that the property should be included in the decedent's gross estate, even though the property was not legally owned by the decedent at the date of death. Congress has identified four transactions that raise this problem: (1) transfers with a retained life estate (IRC § 2036); (2) transfers taking effect at death (IRC § 2037); (3) revocable transfers (IRC § 2038); and (4) certain transfers within three years of the decedent's death (IRC § 2035). Collectively, these are sometimes referred to as the "**re-inclusion**" provisions, because each of these sections involves the inclusion in the gross estate of property previously transferred by the decedent.

a) Transfers With a Retained Life Estate [IRC § 2036]

Though many find the general rule of IRC § 2036(a) elusive, it is relatively easy to understand once the reader breaks the rule down into its component parts.

(1) Elements

In order for IRC § 2036(a) to cause inclusion in the decedent's gross estate of property gratuitously transferred by the decedent, a three-part test must be met: the decedent must have transferred property while retaining a prescribed interest for a prescribed period.

The prescribed interests are:

- the <u>right to income</u> from the transferred property;

- the <u>right to possession</u> of the transferred property;

- the <u>right to enjoyment</u> of the transferred property;

- the <u>right to designate who shall receive the income</u> from the transferred property;

- the <u>right to designate who shall receive possession</u> of the transferred property; or

- the <u>right to designate who shall receive enjoyment</u> of the transferred property.

The prescribed periods are:

- for the decedent's <u>life</u>;

- for a <u>period not ascertainable without reference to the decedent's death</u>; or

- for a <u>period which does not in fact end before the decedent's death</u>.

Example (1):   Donald transfers property to an irrevocable trust. The trust instrument gives Donald the right to income from the trust property for Donald's life. At his death, the trust will terminate and the remainder will pass to the beneficiaries identified in the trust instrument. By retaining one of the most important rights associated with property, the right to income from the property, no wealth transfer really occurs until Donald's death. Since this looks the same as a testamentary transfer, IRC § 2036(a) requires inclusion of the trust property in Donald's gross estate. This is because Donald retained a prescribed interest (the right to income from the property) for a prescribed period (his life).

Example (2):   Lenore transfers her personal residence to an irrevocable trust and retains the right to occupy the home until her death. At her death, the trust will terminate and the remainder (the home) will pass to the beneficiaries designated in the trust instrument. Lenore's gross estate includes the value of the residence as of the date of her death because she retained a prescribed interest (the right to enjoyment of the home) for a prescribed period (her life).

Example (3): Myrtle transfers property to an irrevocable trust. At Myrtle's death, the trust will terminate and the remainder will pass in equal shares to Myrtle's children, Jay and Kay. The trust instrument gives Myrtle the power to allocate the trust's annual income between Jay and Kay in her sole discretion. If Myrtle dies survived by Jay and Kay, her gross estate will include the value of the property transferred to the trust because Myrtle retained a prescribed interest (the power to control enjoyment of the income from the transferred property) for a prescribed period (her life).

Example (4): Harold transfers property to an irrevocable trust, retaining the right to receive income from the trust property until one month prior to his death. The income that accrues in the month prior to Harold's death is to be paid to Harold's daughter, Dee, or to Dee's estate if she is not then living. At Harold's death, the then-remaining trust property shall pass to Dee or Dee's estate. The value of the trust property will be included in Harold's gross estate at his death because Harold holds a prescribed interest (the right to income) for a prescribed period (a period not ascertainable without reference to Harold's death).

Example (5): Melba transfers property to an irrevocable trust, retaining the right to receive income from the trust property annually for a term of ten years. After the expiration of the ten-year term, the trust's income will accumulate and be added to the trust's principal. At Melba's death, the then-remaining trust property shall pass to Janet or Janet's estate. Melba dies six years into the ten-year term. Because Melba retained a prescribed interest (the right to income) for a prescribed period (a period that did not end prior to her death), IRC § 2036(a) requires inclusion of all trust property in Melba's gross estate.

The amount included in the gross estate under IRC § 2036(a) is limited "to the extent of any interest therein" held by the decedent at the time of death. Thus, if the decedent retained the right to only one-half of the income for life from a prior gift to a trust, only one-half of the value of the trust principal will be included in the decedent's gross estate. [Reg. § 20.2036–1(c)(1)(i)]

A decedent will be considered to have held a prescribed interest in transferred property if the use, possession, enjoyment, or right to income from the property is to be applied to discharge a legal obligation of the decedent. [Reg. § 20.2036–1(b)(2)] In addition, if the transferor retains a prescribed interest that does not affect another's prior income interest in the same property, the amount included in the gross estate under IRC § 2036(a) is the value of the transferred property less the value of such outstanding income interest. [Reg. § 20.2036–1(c)(1)(i)]

Example: Alex transfers property to an irrevocable trust. The trust instrument provides that income from trust property shall be paid annually to Zack for Zack's life, then to Alex for Alex's life if Alex is then living. Upon the death of both Zack and Alex, the remaining trust property shall be distributed to Monty or Monty's estate. Alex dies survived by Zack. Although Alex retained an interest in the transferred property's income for life, the amount included in Alex's gross estate is equal to the value of the trust property less the value of Zack's income interest as of the date of Alex's death.

The decedent's prescribed interest need not be expressly reserved in the written instrument of transfer. The course of action between the decedent and the transferee(s) may indicate a retained interest that can cause inclusion under IRC § 2036(a).

Example: Peggy conveys her personal residence to her niece, Luanne. The deed purports to be absolute, and there is no written arrangement indicating Peggy's retention of any interest in the house. Nonetheless, Peggy continues to occupy the residence until her death. Peggy's continued occupancy of the home implies the existence of an arrangement of retained enjoyment by Peggy, so Peggy's gross estate includes the value of the home. [Rev. Rul. 78–409, 1978–2 C.B. 234]

(2) Grantor as Trustee

One acting in the capacity of a trustee often has some discretion in deciding both how much a beneficiary receives and when a distribution will be made to that beneficiary. In that sense, a trustee holds one of the prescribed interests: the power to designate who shall enjoy the trust property. If taken literally, IRC § 2036(a) would require inclusion of any trust property where the decedent served as both grantor and trustee. In practice, however, inclusion can be avoided with proper planning.

It is certainly true that the retained power to choose among beneficiaries, even if such power is exercisable only in the capacity of a trustee, will generally trigger inclusion under IRC § 2036(a). [Reg. § 20.2036–1(b)(3)(ii)] The grantor-trustee's power to choose must have some effect on the enjoyment of the income earned from the trust property. [Reg. § 20.2036–1(b)(3)] If the grantor-trustee's power does not affect the enjoyment of the income, IRC § 2036(a) will not apply (though most likely IRC § 2038 will apply, as explained below). Often, this problem is solved by naming an independent trustee. But IRC § 2036(a) will still apply even with an independent trustee if the grantor retains the power to replace the trustee and the class of permissible successors includes the grantor or a party related or subordinate to the grantor. [Rev. Rul. 95–58, 1995–2 C.B. 191]

Example (1): Sharpay creates an irrevocable trust that gives Gabriella or Gabriella's estate the right to income for Sharpay's life. Upon Sharpay's death, the trust will terminate and the remainder will pass to Troy or Troy's estate. The trust instrument names Sharpay as the trustee, and it gives the trustee the power to invade corpus at any time for the benefit of Troy. Although Sharpay's power is exercisable only in her capacity as trustee, she has effectively retained the power to designate who will enjoy the trust property and the income therefrom (either Gabriella or Troy). Thus, IRC § 2036(a) applies and the value of the entire trust corpus will be included in Sharpay's gross estate.

Example (2): Same as Example (1), except that instead of having the power to invade corpus for Troy, the trust instrument gives Sharpay (as trustee) the power to accumulate income and add it to corpus. Here again, Sharpay effectively holds the power to decide whether the income will be paid to Gabriella or added to the amount that Troy will take. Accordingly, the result is the same: the value of the trust property will be included in her gross estate. [*United States v. O'Malley*, 383 U.S. 627, 86 S.Ct. 1123, 16 L.Ed.2d 145 (1966)]

Example (3): Same as Example (1), except that instead of having the power to invade corpus for Troy, the trust instrument gives Sharpay (as trustee) the power to invade corpus for the benefit of Gabriella. Although Sharpay holds the power to decide who ultimately enjoys the trust property, IRC § 2036(a) does not apply in this example because Sharpay's power has no effect on the enjoyment of the income earned on the property. No matter whether Sharpay exercises the power, Gabriella or Gabriella's estate will enjoy the income from the property contributed to the trust. Accordingly, no portion of the trust property is included in Sharpay's gross estate under IRC § 2036(a). However, the amount will be included under IRC § 2038. [Reg. § 20.2036–1(b)(3)]

Example (4): Same as above, except that the trust instrument names Ryan as the trustee and the trust instrument gives the trustee no power to invade corpus or accumulate income. No portion of the trust property will be included in Sharpay's gross estate unless the trust instrument gives Sharpay the power to substitute herself or a related or subordinate party as trustee. [Reg. § 20.2036–1(b)(3); Rev. Rul. 95–58, 1995–2 C.B. 191]

Where the grantor of a trust insists on serving as trustee, the trustee's discretion to distribute income or principal to beneficiaries should be limited to an ascertainable standard related to the maintenance, education, support, or health of a beneficiary. When a trustee's discretion is so limited, the trustee is seen as having merely a ministerial power and not a discretionary power to control beneficial enjoyment of trust property. [*Jennings v. Smith*, 161 F.2d 74 (2d Cir. 1947)]

(3) The Sale Exception

By its own terms, IRC § 2036(a) applies only to property gratuitously transferred by the decedent and not property transfers resulting from a "bona fide sale for an adequate and full consideration in money or money's worth." The exception for sale transfers makes sense on two levels. First, in a bona fide sale transaction there is no transfer of wealth, so no federal wealth transfer tax should apply. Second, if sale transactions could trigger IRC § 2036(a), there would be potential for double-inclusion: inclusion of the transferred property under IRC § 2036(a) and inclusion of the remaining sale proceeds under IRC § 2033.

In determining whether property was gifted or sold for an adequate and full consideration in money or money's worth, special attention must be given the facts surrounding the transfer. Two superficially identical transactions may have opposite results once the surrounding facts are known.

Example (1):   Old Mother Hubbard sold her personal residence to her son, Elron, for its fair market value. Elron paid the purchase price in cash. On the same day, Elron agreed to lease the residence to Mother at fair rental value. Because Old Mother Hubbard's transfer of the residence was for an adequate and full consideration in money or money's worth, IRC § 2036(a) will not apply and the value of the residence will not be included in her gross estate.

Example (2):   Same as the prior example, except that Elron paid for the residence by giving Mother a promissory note with a principal amount equal to the fair market value of the property. The note required monthly payments of principal and interest. Mother routinely forgave the principal payments when they became due. In addition, the rent payable to Elron under the lease agreement just happened to match the amount of interest Elron was required to pay Mother under the promissory note. With these additional facts, the transaction should be treated as a disguised gift by Mother, for it appears that Mother did not expect to receive any consideration from Elron for the home. Furthermore, the lease arrangement appears to disguise Mother's retained right to occupy the home, for the rent she owes is offset by the interest due to her under the note. Accordingly, the full fair market value of the residence should be included in Mother's gross estate at her death. [*Estate of Maxwell v. Commissioner*, 3 F.3d 591 (2d Cir. 1993)]

Sometimes the question is not whether the sale was bona fide but whether the purchaser paid *full* consideration for the property. There is a split of authority, for instance, where the decedent sells a remainder interest in property but retains a life estate. Some courts have concluded that the sale exception to IRC § 2036(a) applies if the consideration received by the decedent equals the value of the remainder interest. [*D'Ambrosio v. Commissioner*, 101 F.3d 309 (3d Cir. 1996); *Wheeler v. United States*, 116 F.3d 749 (5th Cir. 1997); *Estate of Magnin v. Commissioner*, 184 F.3d 1074 (9th Cir. 1999)] Other courts conclude that the decedent must receive consideration equal to the value of the property transferred. [*Gradow v. United States*, 897 F.2d 516 (Fed. Cir. 1990); *Estate of Gregory v. Commissioner*, 39 T.C. 1012 (1963)]

Example: Peter transfers $200,000 to an irrevocable trust. The trust agreement requires all of the trust income to be paid to Peter for life. Upon Peter's death, the remainder will pass to Meg (or to her estate if she is not then living). At the formation of the trust, the value of Meg's vested remainder interest is $50,000. If Meg pays $50,000 cash to Peter in exchange for her vested remainder interest, some courts will conclude that she has paid Peter an adequate and full consideration, meaning that no portion of the value of the trust corpus will be included in Peter's gross estate. [*See, e.g., D'Ambrosio v. Commissioner*, 101 F.3d 309 (3d Cir. 1996).] Other courts would require Meg to pay Peter $200,000 if Peter is to avoid inclusion of the trust property in his gross estate. [*See, e.g., Gradow v. United States*, 897 F.2d 516 (Fed. Cir. 1990).]

(4) Retained Voting Rights as a Prescribed Interest

Where the decedent gratuitously transfers stock in a "controlled corporation" but retains the right to vote the transferred shares, whether directly or indirectly, the decedent is considered to have retained the enjoyment of the transferred stock. [IRC § 2036(b)(1)] Generally, a corporation is "controlled" if the decedent owned or had the right to vote stock possessing at least 20% of the total combined voting power of all classes of stock at any time following the gratuitous transfer (or, if longer, the three-year period ending on the decedent's death). [IRC § 2036(b)(2)] In determining the number of shares owned by the decedent during this testing period, the attribution rules of IRC § 318 are applied, meaning that the decedent will be treated as owning shares formally owned by certain family members and other entities in which the decedent and/or certain family members have majority interests.

Example (1): As of the beginning of Year 1, Uncle Pennybags owned 50% of the voting common stock of Boardwalk Corporation. At the beginning of Year 2, Uncle Pennybags gave half of his Boardwalk shares (a 25% voting interest) to Andy but retained the right to vote those shares until Uncle Pennybags' death. Uncle Pennybags died in Year 3. Uncle Pennybags' gross estate includes not only the shares he retained but also the shares gifted to Andy in Year 2. This is because Boardwalk Corporation is a "controlled corporation" (Uncle Pennybags owned at least 20% of the total voting power in the corporation after the transfer) and Uncle Pennybags retained the right to vote the gifted shares. [IRC § 2036(a), (b)(1)–(2)]

Example (2): Same as Example (1), except that Uncle Pennybags did not retain the right to vote the shares gifted to Andy. Even though Boardwalk is still a "controlled" corporation after the transfer, IRC § 2036(b)(1) would not apply and the gifted shares would not be included in Uncle Pennybags' gross estate.

Example (3): Same as Example (1), except that Uncle Pennybags also owned all of Boardwalk's nonvoting common stock, and that the gift to Andy in Year 2 consisted of the nonvoting common stock. By giving nonvoting shares, Uncle Pennybags could not retain the voting rights in the gifted stock. Accordingly, neither IRC § 2036(b)(1) nor IRC § 2036(a) applies, so no portion of the gifted shares will be included in Uncle Pennybags' gross estate. [Prop. Reg. § 20.2036–2(a)]

Example (4): Same as the original facts, except that Uncle Pennybags owned 30% of the voting common stock of Boardwalk in Year 1 and gave half of that stock (a 15% voting interest) to Andy in Year 2, subject to Uncle Pennybags' retention of the right to vote the gifted shares. Even if Andy is unrelated to Uncle Pennybags, the value of the gifted shares will be included in Uncle Pennybags' gross estate. Although Uncle Pennybags does not have at least 20% of the total voting power of Boardwalk at any time after the gift, he did have such control in the three-year period prior to his death. Consequently, IRC § 2036(b)(1) triggers the application of IRC § 2036(a).

The retention of voting rights triggers application of IRC § 2036(b)(1) even where the decedent *indirectly* transfers stock yet retains the right to vote the transferred shares. This happens where, for instance, the decedent transfers cash to a trust in which the decedent serves as trustee, followed by the trust's purchase of shares in the controlled corporation using the contributed cash. As trustee, the decedent holds the right to vote the shares. Substantively, then, this transaction is the same as if the decedent purchased the shares and contributed them directly to the trust while retaining the right to vote the shares. As a result, Proposed Regulations subject the indirect transfer to re-inclusion under IRC § 2036. [Prop. Reg. § 20.2036–2(e)(2)]

(5) Reciprocal Trust Doctrine

Since IRC § 2036(a) comes into play only where the decedent retains an interest in property transferred by the decedent, a transferor might be tempted to conspire with another transferor to defeat inclusion by forming reciprocal trusts. In a reciprocal trust arrangement, a transferor (T1) agrees to create a trust that gives a life estate to the other transferor (T2) and the remainder to the beneficiaries of T2. In exchange, T2 creates a similar trust for T1 and T1's beneficiaries. The Supreme Court has held that where two trusts are "interrelated, and that the arrangement, to the extent of mutual value, leaves the settlors in approximately the same economic position as they would have been in had they created trusts naming themselves as life beneficiaries," a transferor will be treated as the grantor of the trust created for the benefit of the transferor and the transferor's beneficiaries, meaning IRC § 2036(a) will apply. [*United States v. Estate of Grace*, 395 U.S. 316, 324, 89 S.Ct. 1730, 1735, 23 L.Ed.2d 332, 338 (1969)] This is the so-called **reciprocal trust doctrine**.

> *Example:* Romeo transfers $1 million to an irrevocable trust that provides a lifetime income interest to Juliet and the remainder to Juliet's family. At or around the same time, Juliet transfers $1 million to a separate irrevocable trust that provides a lifetime income interest to Romeo and the remainder to Romeo's family. Under the reciprocal trust doctrine, Romeo will be treated as the grantor of the trust created by Juliet, and Juliet will be treated as the grantor of the trust created by Romeo. Consequently, when the transferors die (by poison or otherwise), IRC § 2036(a) will apply and each of their gross estates will include the value of the property held by the trust he or she was deemed to create.

b) Transfers Taking Effect at Death [IRC § 2037]

Despite its title, IRC § 2037 really applies to **reversions** retained by the decedent from a lifetime transfer of property. Since a retained reversion can cause a previous transfer to take effect at the decedent's death, inclusion is appropriate even though the decedent may not have any retained possession or enjoyment of the property.

(1) Elements

Inclusion under IRC § 2037 results when both the survivorship test (IRC § 2037(a)(1)) and the reversion test (IRC § 2037(a)(2)) are met. In order to meet the survivorship test, a beneficiary's possession or enjoyment of the property at issue must be obtainable only by surviving the decedent. The reversion test is met if the decedent retained a reversionary interest in the subject property and the value of the reversion immediately before the decedent's death exceeded five percent of the value of the subject property. If IRC § 2037(a) applies, the amount includible is the value of all property subject to the decedent's reversionary interest.

Example (1): Amy creates an irrevocable trust providing income to Todd for Todd's life and, at Todd's death, the remainder to Chris if Chris is then living. If Chris is not then living, the remainder is to be paid to Amy or Amy's estate. Although Amy retains a reversion, neither Todd's income interest nor Chris' contingent remainder interest is conditioned upon surviving Amy. Todd receives the income for life regardless of whether Amy dies, and Chris' ability to take depends upon his surviving Todd, not Amy. Thus, neither interest meets the survivorship test. Accordingly, IRC § 2037(a) does not apply. [Reg. § 20.2037–1(e), ex. (1)] The value of Amy's contingent remainder, however, is included in her gross estate under IRC § 2033.

Example (2): George creates an irrevocable trust that requires the income to be accumulated for George's life. At his death, the principal and the accumulated income is to be paid in equal shares to George's then living children. If none of George's children are then living, the principal and accumulated income will instead be paid to Robert or Robert's estate. Although the contingent remainder interests of George's living children meet the survivorship test (a child can only take by surviving George), IRC § 2037(a) does not apply because the reversion test is not met. George did not retain a reversion in the trust property. [Reg. § 20.2037–1(e), ex. (2)]

Example (3): Ryan creates an irrevocable trust providing income to Ben for Ben's life, then the remainder to Ryan if Ryan is then living. If Ryan is not living at Ben's death, the remainder instead passes to Cathy or Cathy's estate. Although Ryan has no interest in the income from the trust property or any right to possession or enjoyment of the property, Ryan retains a contingent interest in the remainder. Because the recipient of the remainder is unknown until the death of Ryan or Ben, there is effectively no transfer of the remainder until either Ryan or Ben dies. If Ryan dies before Ben, therefore, IRC § 2037(a) requires inclusion of a portion of the trust property in Ryan's gross estate. The amount included in Ryan's gross estate is the excess of the fair market value of the transferred property as of Ryan's death over the present value of Ben's continuing income interest. The value of Ben's income interest is not included in Ryan's gross estate because it flunks the survivorship test: Ben need not survive Ryan in order to take the income interest. But the value of Cathy's contingent remainder interest is included in Ryan's gross estate. Cathy's contingent remainder meets the survivorship test (Cathy or Cathy's estate can only take if Ryan has died) and the reversion test (assuming the value of Ryan's reversion was equal to at least five percent of the value of the trust property). [Reg. § 20.2037–1(e), ex. (3)]

(2) Survivorship

The survivorship test requires that a beneficiary be able to take *only* by surviving the decedent. If the beneficiary can take ownership by any other means, such as the exercise of a general power of appointment, the survivorship test is not met. [IRC § 2037(b)]

Example: Groucho creates an irrevocable trust that pays income to Chico for life and the remainder to Groucho if

Groucho is then living. If Groucho is not then living, the remainder will be paid to Harpo or Harpo's estate. The trust instrument also gives Chico a power to appoint all or any portion of the trust property to anyone Chico chooses during his lifetime. Because Chico could appoint the trust property to Harpo during Chico's lifetime, it is not necessary for Harpo to survive Groucho in order to obtain ownership of the property. Thus, no matter whether Chico in fact exercises this power in favor of Harpo, the survivorship test is not met. So if Groucho predeceases Chico and Harpo, IRC § 2037(a) will not apply to include the value of Harpo's contingent remainder in Groucho's gross estate. [Reg. § 20.2037–1(e), ex. (6)]

(3) Reversionary Interests

The reversion test is met when the decedent retained a reversion, whether expressly or by implication or by operation of law. Thus, it is not necessary for the instrument of transfer to explicitly refer to the decedent's reversion. [Reg. § 20.2037–1(c)(2)] If the decedent's reversion affects only the rights to income from the transferred property, however, the reversion test is not met. [IRC § 2037(b); Reg. § 20.2037–1(c)(2)]

Example: Shelly creates an irrevocable trust that pays income to Robin for Robin's life, then income to Shelly if she is then living. If Shelly is not then living (or upon the death of Shelly), the trust shall terminate and the remainder shall be paid to Erin or Erin's estate. Shelly's reversion relates only to the income interest. Accordingly, the reversion test is not met so IRC § 2037 does not apply. Of course, Shelly's retained right to income might implicate IRC § 2036.

Under IRC § 2037(b)(2), the transferor's power to allocate the property between two or more beneficiaries is treated as a reversionary interest. This makes sense because the power to choose the appointee of property is akin to ownership of the property.

Example: Ralph creates an irrevocable trust that pays income to Alice for her life and the remainder to either Ed or

Trixie, to be chosen by Ralph either during his lifetime or in his will. If Ralph fails to appoint the remainder by the time Alice dies, the remainder will be paid in equal shares to Ed and Trixie (or their estates if they do not survive Alice). Ralph's power to appoint the remainder as between Ed or Trixie is treated as a reversionary interest, so the reversion test is met. In addition, the survivorship test is met because Ed and Trixie must survive Ralph to know if there will be an interest to take. Assuming the value of Ralph's "reversion" exceeds five percent of the value of the trust property, the value of the remainder interest must be included in Ralph's gross estate under IRC § 2037.

As mentioned above, IRC § 2037 does not apply if the value of the decedent's reversionary interest does not, because of the contingencies affecting the likelihood of occurrence, exceed five percent of the value of the transferred property immediately before the decedent's death. In determining whether the value of the reversion exceeds this five percent threshold, the value of the reversion is compared to the value of the transferred property, including those interests not dependent upon surviving the decedent. [Reg. § 20.2037–1(c)(4)] The value of the reversion is computed with reference to mortality tables and actuarial principles set forth in the Regulations to IRC § 2031. [IRC § 2037(b); Reg. § 20.2037–1(c)(3)]

c) Revocable Transfers [IRC § 2038]

If a transferor retains a power to revoke or materially change the wealth transfer, then the transferor still has sufficient control over the transferred property such that it is fair to say the transferor still "owns" the property at death. This uncontroversial concept is codified in IRC § 2038. Formally, IRC § 2038(a)(1) requires inclusion of an interest in property previously transferred by the decedent as a gift if, at the decedent's death, enjoyment of that interest was subject to a power held by the decedent to alter, amend, revoke, or terminate. The decedent is deemed to have held such a power at death even if the exercise of the power is subject to a requirement of giving notice and even if a waiting period is imposed between the exercise of such a power and its effectiveness. [IRC § 2038(b)]

Example: Veronica creates a trust that pays income to Archie for Archie's life. When Archie dies, the trust terminates and the remainder passes to Reggie or Reggie's estate. Veronica names Jughead (an unrelated individual) as trustee but she retains the power to revoke the trust while she is alive. In order to exercise this revocation power, the trust instrument requires Veronica to give Jughead notice at least three months before the intended revocation date. If Veronica dies without ever having given notice, one could argue that she lacks the power to revoke at her death because of the required three-month waiting period between the giving of notice and the effective date of revocation. Nonetheless, IRC § 2038(b) instructs us to ignore the required waiting period. Accordingly, if Veronica dies before Archie, the value of the trust property is included in Veronica's gross estate less three months of income.

(1) Power to Revoke

Inclusion under IRC § 2038 occurs when the transferor has the power to revoke or terminate a transfer even where that power can only be exercised with the consent of another. This rule is not taken to ridiculous extremes, however. For instance, just because applicable state law might permit a transferor to join the beneficiaries and the trustee of an irrevocable trust in seeking the revocation or premature termination of the trust, the transferor's estate need not include the value of the trust property. [*Helvering v. Helmholz*, 296 U.S. 93, 56 S.Ct. 68, 80 L.Ed. 76 (1935); Reg. § 20.2038–1(a)(2)]

Example: Richie creates a trust that pays income to Joanie for Joanie's life. At Joanie's death, the trust terminates and the remainder is paid to Potsie or Potsie's estate. The trust instrument allows Richie to revoke the trust with the consent of Joanie. Although Joanie is "adverse" to Richie in the sense that she would likely never consent to revocation because it would impair her income interest, the value of the trust property will be included in Richie's gross estate under IRC § 2038 if he dies before Joanie.

IRC § 2038 does not require inclusion where the decedent's power to revoke is contingent on some event that has not in fact occurred prior to death. This is because IRC § 2038 considers only whether the decedent had the power to revoke at the moment of death. Of course, if the decedent held a contingent power to designate the beneficial enjoyment of property at death, inclusion will be required under IRC § 2036 even though IRC § 2038 will not apply. This is because IRC § 2036 *does* consider whether the power was held during one of the prescribed periods and asks whether the contingency could have occurred during that period. [*Estate of Farrel v. United States*, 553 F.2d 637 (Ct.Cl. 1977); Reg. § 20.2036–1(b)(3)(iii)]

(2) Power to Alter or Amend

IRC § 2038 is not limited to situations where the transferor holds a power to revoke the wealth transfer; inclusion under IRC § 2038 is also triggered by powers to alter or amend a transfer of property, even if the transfer is otherwise irrevocable.

Example: Don transfers property to an irrevocable trust that requires income to be paid to Roger for Don's life. Upon Don's death, the remainder of the trust estate is to be distributed to Peggy or Peggy's estate. The trust instrument gives Don the power to name a new remainder beneficiary. If Don dies never having executed this power, Don's gross estate nonetheless includes the value of Peggy's remainder interest (here, the entire value of the trust property, because the income interest has expired at Don's death) because it was subject to Don's power of alteration.

The capacity in which a power to alter or amend a trust is of no consequence. Thus, if the transferor holds a power to alter or amend in a fiduciary capacity (as trustee of a trust, for instance), IRC § 2038(a)(1) still applies. Moreover, even if the grantor is not the named trustee of a trust, the grantor still risks inclusion under IRC § 2038(a)(1) if the grantor retains the power to substitute himself or herself as trustee, provided the trustee has some power to alter or amend the beneficial enjoyment of the trust property. [Reg. § 20.2038–1(a)(3)]

Where the grantor of a trust also wants to serve as trustee, the trustee's discretion to distribute income or principal to beneficiaries should be limited to an ascertainable standard related to the maintenance, education, support, or health of a beneficiary. When a trustee's discretion is so limited, the trustee is seen as having merely a ministerial power and not a discretionary power to alter or amend the original transfer (which would cause inclusion under IRC § 2038) or a power to control beneficial enjoyment of trust property (which would cause inclusion under IRC § 2036). [*Jennings v. Smith*, 161 F.2d 74 (2d Cir. 1947)]

Even the mere power to alter the *timing* of a beneficiary's interest is enough to trigger the application of IRC § 2038(a) if all other requirements are met. For instance, where the decedent created a trust that paid income to a non-dependent beneficiary for a term of years before distributing the corpus to that same beneficiary (or that beneficiary's estate), the decedent's retained power (as trustee) to accumulate trust income and add it to corpus was enough to cause inclusion of the trust property in the decedent's gross estate under IRC § 2038(a) because the decedent died during the trust term with a power to control the timing of when the beneficiary would receive the income (either currently or upon termination of the trust term). [*Lober v. United States*, 346 U.S. 335, 74 S.Ct. 98, 98 L.Ed. 15 (1953)] Likewise, where the decedent retained a power to invade the corpus of a trust for the benefit of the term income beneficiary who was also the remainder beneficiary of the trust, the value of the remainder interest will be included in the decedent's gross estate because of the decedent's power to alter the timing in which the principal is distributed to the beneficiary. [Rev. Rul. 70–513, 1970–2 C.B. 194]

Where the decedent dies holding mere administrative powers with respect to transferred property, IRC § 2038(a) should not apply. Thus, if the decedent served as trustee of a trust she created and, as trustee, held the power to invest trust assets and allocate receipts between income and principal, these powers alone should not cause inclusion under IRC § 2038(a).

(3) Interrelationship with IRC § 2036

Because both IRC §§ 2036 and 2038 look to retained powers over gratuitously transferred property, it should come as no surprise that inclusion of the same property may be required by both Code sections. Where that happens, of course, the value of the property is only included in the gross estate once.

Example (1):   Ann creates an irrevocable trust that pays income to Bob or Bob's estate for Ann's life. At Ann's death, the trust will terminate and the remainder will be paid to Claire or Claire's estate. In addition, Ann, as trustee of the trust, holds the power to invade the principal of the trust for the benefit of Dick. Ann's power to invade the corpus of the trust renders Bob's income interest and Claire's remainder interest vulnerable to Ann's power, so if Ann dies holding this power to "alter" the transfer, the trust assets will be included in Ann's gross estate under IRC § 2038. In addition, IRC § 2036 would apply because of Ann's retained power to control enjoyment of the trust assets for a period measured by her life. Although both IRC §§ 2036 and 2038 require inclusion in Ann's gross estate, the trust property will be included only once.

Example (2):   Same general facts as Example (1), except that Ann's power as trustee is to substitute Dick for Claire as the remainder beneficiary. Under IRC § 2038, Ann still holds a power to "alter" the enjoyment of the remainder interest so the value of the remainder interest (which will be the value of the entire trust property since Bob's income interest expires at Ann's death) will be included in her gross estate. But IRC § 2036 would not apply because Ann's power does not affect enjoyment of the income received by Bob or Bob's estate during Ann's lifetime. If the transferor's retained interest does not affect the right to income from the transferred property, IRC § 2036(a) does not apply. [Reg. § 20.2036-1(b)(3)] Although IRC §§ 2036 and 2038 reach opposite results, the value of the remainder interest is included in Ann's gross estate, for inclusion is required if any one Code provision supports it.

Example (3):   Same general facts as Example (1), except that Ann names Eddie, an unrelated individual, as the trustee of the trust. Eddie thus holds the power to invade the corpus for the benefit of Dick. Since Ann has retained neither a power to alter, amend, revoke, or terminate the trust nor retained a power to control beneficial enjoyment of the trust property, neither IRC § 2036 nor IRC § 2038 applies. No portion of the trust property will be included in Ann's gross estate.

Example (4): Fran creates a trust that pays income to Gilligan for Gilligan's life, followed by the remainder to Hal or Hal's estate. Fran names an independent trustee but specifically reserves the right to order the trustee to return all trust property to Fran. Because of Fran's power to revoke the trust, IRC § 2038 applies, so the trust property must be included in Fran's gross estate even though she may never exercise this power. Inclusion would also be required under IRC § 2036(a) because of Fran's retained power to determine who shall possess or enjoy the trust property. The value of the trust property is only included in Fran's gross estate once even though two Code provisions independently require inclusion.

d) Certain Transfers Within Three Years of Death [IRC § 2035]

One popular misconception about the federal estate tax is that all gifts within three years of death are included in the gross estate. This used to be the rule, but not since 1982.

(1) The General Rule

Now, only two types of gifts within three years of death are pulled back into the gross estate under IRC § 2035(a). The first is a decedent's gift of a life insurance policy on the decedent's life within three years of death. The particulars of life insurance policies are discussed later in this Section.

The second is a gift of an interest in property that would have caused inclusion under IRC §§ 2036 through 2038 if the decedent had held onto the interest until death. This second type is difficult to grasp, but an example will help.

Example: Diane creates an irrevocable trust that pays income to Diane for life and gives the remainder at Diane's death to Jack or Jack's estate. After the transfer, Diane realizes that IRC § 2036(a) will cause inclusion of the entire trust corpus in her gross estate at her death because she transferred property and retained a prescribed interest (the right to income) for a prescribed period (for life). To avoid this result, Diane gives her income interest to Patty. When Diane dies, she no longer has the prescribed interest that would cause inclusion under IRC § 2036. Under IRC § 2035(a), however, if Diane's gift of the income interest occurs within three years of her death, the value of the entire trust corpus will still be included in her gross estate.

As the above example shows, IRC § 2035(a) is now designed primarily to prevent easy avoidance of the other "re-inclusion" provisions. But, again, this is pretty much all it is supposed to prevent. This concept is important enough to merit yet another restatement of the rule: if a decedent transfers property in the three years prior to death, the value of the property (including the post-gift appreciation in that property's value) will *not* be included in the decedent's gross estate unless the transfer consists of a life insurance policy or an interest described in IRC §§ 2036 through 2038.

Example (1): Two years prior to Ziggy's death, Ziggy gave $50,000 cash to Yolanda. No portion of this gift will be included in Ziggy's gross estate (although any gift tax paid on this gift will be included in the gross estate under IRC § 2035(b), as discussed below).

Example (2): Ten years prior to his death, Xavier purchased a life insurance policy on his life for $10,000. Two years before his death, Xavier gave the policy to Wanda. Had Xavier owned the policy at his death, the benefit payable under the policy would have been included in his gross estate under IRC § 2042. Accordingly, Xavier's gross estate includes the amount of the death benefit payable to Wanda under the life insurance policy. [IRC § 2035(a)]

Example (3): Same facts as above, except that Wanda sells the policy to Victor three months before Xavier's death. Xavier's gross estate still includes the amount of the death benefit payable to Victor under the policy, even though Xavier did not give the policy to Victor. [Rev. Rul. 72–282, 1972–1 C.B. 306]

While gifts made within three years of death are included in the gross estate under the conditions explained above, IRC § 2035(c)(1) provides that *all* gifts made within three years are considered to be part of the decedent's gross estate for certain purposes apart from computing estate tax liability. For instance, the decedent's gross estate is deemed to include all gifts made within three years of death for purposes of determining whether the estate can avail itself of the benefit of capital gain treatment under IRC § 303 for certain stock redemption transactions or whether the estate may elect to the special use valuation rules for certain real property under IRC § 2032A. Inclusion of all gifts made within three years of death for these purposes serves to help the estate qualify for special benefits, so IRC § 2035(c)(1) is seen as a taxpayer-friendly rule.

Example: Two years prior to his death, Ichiro gave $50,000 cash to Cher. The cash gift is not included in Ichiro's gross estate for purposes of computing estate tax liability, but it is considered part of his gross estate in determining whether his estate can make use of the benefits provided in IRC §§ 303 and 2032A.

(2) Gift Tax Paid on Gifts Made Within Three Years of Death

Because the dollars used to pay federal gift tax on a gift of property are tax-exclusive (meaning they are not themselves subject to federal gift tax), a decedent nearing death might decide to give away assets near death to pay less total tax. Assuming a flat estate and gift tax rate of 50%, therefore, a decedent might give away two-thirds of his or her estate and use the remaining one-third of the estate to pay the corresponding federal gift tax. If the decedent dies having made no gift, the entire estate is subject to federal estate tax and half of it (not just one-third) is lost to tax. Congress foresaw this strategy and thwarted it with IRC § 2035(b). It requires inclusion in the gross estate of any federal gift tax paid by the decedent attributable to gifts made within three years of death. Thus, in the case of near-death gifts, the benefit deriving from the tax-exclusive nature of the federal gift tax is lost. Of course, the benefit is very much available for those transfers made more than three years prior to death.

It is important to note that because IRC § 2035 refers to the three-year period as "ending on the date of the decedent's death," one counts the date of death in determining whether a gift was made within the three-year period. Thus, where the decedent made a taxable gift on April 1 of Year 1 and died on April 1 of Year 4, the gift tax paid with respect to the April 1, Year 1, gift is *not* included in the decedent's gross estate because the three-year period ran from April 2, Year 1, to April 1, Year 4. [Tech. Adv. Mem. 200432016 (March 10, 2004)] Note, too, that IRC § 2035(b) does not require inclusion of all gift tax paid within three years of death, just that gift tax paid on *gifts made* within three years of death.

e) Consideration Paid by the Recipient [IRC § 2043]

It is worth noting that IRC §§ 2035–2038 only apply to gratuitous lifetime transfers. If the recipient(s) give(s) adequate consideration for the received property, none of these "re-inclusion" provisions apply. Equally important of note, the recipient(s) must give *full* consideration to avoid application of IRC §§ 2035–2038. Some mistakenly believe that if, for example, a recipient pays the decedent 75% of the value of the property received in a transaction described in IRC §§ 2035–2038 then only 25% of the value of the property at death will be included in the decedent's gross estate. Under IRC § 2043(a), however, if the recipient gives something less than full consideration in exchange for the transferred property, the decedent's gross estate will include the entire value of the transferred property minus the consideration received. In other words, the partial consideration rule of IRC § 2043 requires *all* of the post-transfer appreciation in value to be included in the decedent's gross estate.

Example: Ten years before his death, Hikaru purchased an insurance policy on his life. Two years before his death, when the value of the policy was $50,000, Hikaru sold the policy to Pavel for $20,000. At Hikaru's death, Pavel received a $300,000 benefit from the policy. Had Hikaru held the policy until his death, IRC § 2042(1) would have included the $300,000 death benefit in his gross estate. By making a partial gift of the policy to Pavel within three years of death, IRC § 2035(a) applies. Because Pavel furnished $20,000 of consideration, Hikaru's gross estate includes $280,000 (the $300,000 death benefit less the $20,000 consideration furnished by Pavel). [IRC §§ 2035(a); 2043(a)]

As discussed at I. A. 2. a) (3), there is a split of authority as to whether a transferee furnishes full consideration by paying the decedent an amount equal to the fair market value of the interest received. Some courts have held that sufficient to avoid IRC § 2043, while others have held that the transferee must pay to the decedent an amount equal to the full fair market value of the property transferred, even if that amount exceeds the value of the transferee's interest in the subject property. Although the courts have examined this question only in the context of applying IRC § 2036(a), the same analysis would likely apply for purposes of the other "re-inclusion" provisions, IRC §§ 2035, 2037, and 2038.

3. Special Rules for Certain Assets

The chief concept in the federal estate tax is "ownership." If a decedent "owns" property, it is included in the gross estate (i.e., under IRC § 2033). Thus, as shown above, where a decedent continues to have ownership-type rights in property previously gifted to another, the property is included in the gross estate. The concept of "ownership" in the context of certain assets is sufficiently complex to warrant separate attention. Here, Congress has identified five types of "special" assets that require separate rules for inclusion in the gross estate: (1) annuities (IRC § 2039); (2) jointly-owned property (IRC § 2040); (3) property subject to a general power of appointment (IRC § 2041); (4) life insurance (IRC § 2042); and (5) certain property for which the marital deduction was previously allowed (IRC § 2044).

a) Annuities [IRC § 2039]

An **annuity** is a contractual arrangement whereby one party agrees to make a series of payments to the other party. In the typical annuity arrangement, an individual pays a premium to a corporation (usually, but not necessarily, a life insurance company) and the corporation agrees to make quarterly or monthly payments to the individual, either for a term of years or, more commonly, for the individual's life. If the annuity payments end at the individual's death, there is no wealth transfer at death. In such cases, therefore, the gross estate includes nothing attributable to the annuity contract. But if payments continue after the individual's death, there is clearly a wealth transfer. Absent some express provision, however, it would be difficult to apply any of the inclusion rules covered thus far to cause inclusion of any amount attributable to the annuity arrangement. Inclusion under IRC § 2033 would be improper because the right to the post-death payments did not belong to the decedent. IRC § 2036 would not apply because merely naming a beneficiary to take the payments after death does not rise to the level of a completed gift required to trigger the re-inclusion rules. IRC § 2037 would not apply because the decedent has no reversion. And IRC § 2038 would not apply because there is no completed gift to the beneficiary over which the decedent would have retained a power to control. Thus, IRC § 2039 steps in to fill the gap.

(1) **The General Rule**

A comparative newcomer to the federal estate tax (it was enacted in 1954), IRC § 2039 requires inclusion of the value of any payment(s) made to a beneficiary made by reason of surviving the decedent if such payment is made pursuant to an annuity contract under which the decedent received payments or had a right to receive payments for any of the "prescribed periods" described in IRC § 2036. Under this rule, no inclusion results if annuity payments cease at the death of the decedent (because there is no wealth transfer at death). In order for IRC § 2039 to apply to an annuity, one or more payments must be made to someone by reason of surviving the decedent (i.e., the annuity must pay survivorship benefits). Note that IRC § 2039 is also broad enough to capture any survivor benefits paid under retirement or pension plans.

Example: Daisy purchases a joint and survivor annuity which entitles Daisy to receive fixed monthly payments for life. Upon Daisy's death, the same monthly payments continue to be paid to Lily for Lily's life. If Daisy dies survived by Lily, the entire present value of the remaining payments is included in Daisy's gross estate. If Lily predeceases Daisy, there is no inclusion in Daisy's gross estate because no payments will be made after Daisy's death.

If the decedent paid all of the consideration to obtain the annuity, full inclusion of the payments to the survivor results. If the decedent paid only part of the consideration, only that proportion of the annuity payments equal to the proportion of consideration furnished by the decedent is included. [IRC § 2039(b)] Thus, if a decedent uses community funds to purchase an annuity, only one-half of the value of the survivorship benefits will be included in the gross estate. For purposes of applying IRC § 2039(b), amounts paid by the decedent's employer are treated as if paid by the decedent directly.

Example (1):   Daisy and Rose each supplied one-half of the consideration required to purchase a joint and survivor annuity which entitles Daisy to receive fixed monthly payments for life, followed by monthly payments to Rose for Rose's life. If Daisy dies survived by Rose, one-half of the value of the remaining payments to Rose is included in Daisy's gross estate. [Reg. § 20.2039–1(c), ex. (1)]

Example (2):   Same facts as above, except that Daisy's one-half share of the consideration is paid by Daisy's employer as compensation. The result is unchanged because consideration paid by Daisy's employer is treated as consideration paid directly by Daisy.

(2)   Income Tax Aspects

Annuities are an investment, and like any investment, a taxpayer has a basis in the right to future payments. When a taxpayer receives an annuity payment, there is an issue as to how much of the payment represents a return of the taxpayer's basis. Under IRC § 72, annuitants are generally allowed to amortize their basis in the annuity contract over the expected payment period. Consequently, each annuity payment usually consists of a combination of income and a non-taxable return of capital.

Example (1):   Myrtle buys an annuity contract for $1,000 in Year 1. The contract provides that Myrtle will begin receiving annual payments of $500 for ten years beginning in Year 11. Because Myrtle will apportion her $1,000 basis over the ten-year payout period, $400 of the first $500 payment she receives in Year 11 will be included in gross income and $100 will be excluded as a return of capital. [IRC § 72(a), (b)(1)]

Example (2):   Same facts as above, except that Myrtle will receive annual payments of $500 beginning in Year 11 and lasting until her death. Myrtle will apportion her $1,000 basis over her remaining life expectancy. [IRC § 72(b)(1), (c)(3)(A)] Thus, for instance, if Myrtle's life expectancy beginning in Year 11 is for 20 years, $450 of each payment will be included in gross income and $50 will be excluded as a recovery of her basis. If Myrtle dies prematurely, the unrecovered basis will be deductible for federal income tax purposes. [IRC § 72(b)(3)] If she outlives her life expectancy, her annuity payments will be fully taxable once she has recovered her original basis. [IRC § 72(b)(2)]

Under IRC § 691(d)(1), survivor benefits paid to a decedent's beneficiary under an annuity contract are treated as "income in respect of a decedent," or "IRD." Under IRC § 1014(c), IRD does not get a stepped-up basis upon the decedent's death. Thus, when the benefits are paid to the survivor, the survivor will have gross income to the extent the decedent would have had gross income under the annuity rules in IRC § 72 discussed above.

b) Jointly–Owned Property [IRC § 2040]

Where two individuals own property as "**joint tenants with rights of survivorship**," there is certainly some wealth transfer when one tenant dies and the surviving tenant claims complete ownership over the property. One might assume that if there are two tenants, one-half of the value of the property should be included in the deceased tenant's gross estate. But if the decedent furnished all of the consideration to acquire the property, the fair result would be to include the entire value of the property in the decedent's gross estate. IRC § 2040(a) works precisely this way.

(1) The General Rule

Generally, a decedent's estate includes the *entire* value of any property held as joint tenants with rights of survivorship except to the extent the estate can show that consideration for the property was furnished by a co-tenant. [IRC § 2040(a)] This general rule can be expressed in formula form:

$$\frac{\text{consideration paid by decedent}}{\text{total consideration}} * \text{value of joint property} = \text{amount included}$$

Thus, if each of two tenants contributes the same amount to purchase the jointly-owned property, only one-half of the value of the property will be included in the gross estate of the first co-tenant to die. If all of the co-tenants received the property without having to give any consideration (for example, they received it by gift), then the amount included in the deceased co-tenant's gross estate is computed by dividing the value of property by the number of co-tenants.

Example (1):   Felix and Oscar own a bank account as joint tenants with rights of survivorship. Felix made all of the deposits to the account. If Felix dies before Oscar, the entire value of the account as of the date of Felix's death will be included in Felix's gross estate. If Oscar dies before Felix, no portion of the account's value will be included in Oscar's gross estate.

Example (2):   Same facts as Example (1), except that Felix furnished 60% of the account funds and Oscar supplied 40% of the account funds. If Felix dies before Oscar, 60% of the value of the account as of the date of Felix's death will be included in Felix's gross estate. If Oscar dies before Felix, 40% of the account's value will be included in Oscar's gross estate.

Example (3):   Same facts as Example (1), except that neither Felix nor Oscar ever made a deposit to the account. When Benny Factor opened the account, he named Felix and Oscar as the co-tenants as a gift. If Felix dies before Oscar, one-half of the value of the account as of the date of Felix's death will be included in Felix's gross estate. If Oscar dies before Felix, one-half of the account's value will be included in Oscar's gross estate.

In measuring the amount of consideration furnished by a decedent's co-tenant, IRC § 2040(a) requires one to ignore any consideration that the co-tenant originally acquired by gift from the decedent. However, a co-tenant's contribution of income from previously gifted property is treated as consideration furnished by the co-tenant. [Reg. § 20.2040–1(c)(5)]

Example (1):   Daisy gave $5,000 cash to her cousin, Bo. Bo immediately deposited the cash into a bank account naming Bo and Daisy as joint tenants with rights of survivorship. Although Bo was the tenant that formally deposited the check into the joint bank account, those funds were acquired by gift from Daisy. Thus, if Daisy dies before Bo, and assuming no other contributions to the joint account, the entire value of the account will be included in Daisy's gross estate.

Example (2): Same facts as above, except that Bo first deposited the $5,000 cash into a separate bank account in his name. The account earned $2,500 in interest and thus grew to $7,500, at which time Bo re-titled the account to name Bo and Daisy as joint tenants with rights of survivorship. If Daisy dies before Bo, and assuming no other contributions to the joint account, only two-thirds of the value of the account will be included in Daisy's gross estate. This is because the $2,500 of interest is treated as a contribution by Bo. [Reg. § 20.2040–1(c)(5)]

IRC § 2040(a) does not apply to other forms of co-ownership like tenancies in common. Only joint tenancies with rights of survivorship (and, subject to a major exception discussed below, tenancies by the entirety) are valued and included under the rules of IRC § 2040(a). [Reg. § 20.2040–1(b)] This is not to say that other forms of co-ownership escape inclusion; on the contrary, a decedent's interest as a tenant in common is included in the gross estate under IRC § 2033. But the value of such an interest is not determined by the proportionate consideration rule of IRC § 2040(a). Instead, the value of a decedent's tenancy in common interest would be based upon the normal "willing buyer, willing seller" test for fair market value.

(2) Joint Interests of Husbands and Wives

Where the two co-tenants are married to each other, notions of relative consideration supplied by the co-tenants fly out the window. IRC § 2040(b) provides an absolute rule: exactly one-half of property held by the decedent and the decedent's spouse as joint tenants with rights of survivorship is included in the decedent's gross estate. It does not matter whether the account was created with community funds or separate property, and the amount of consideration furnished by the decedent is likewise irrelevant.

The absolute rule in IRC § 2040(b) applies to joint tenancies with rights of survivorship where the spouses are the only joint tenants. It also applies to property held by spouses as tenants by the entirety. A tenancy by the entirety is essentially a form of joint tenancy with rights of survivorship but exists only between spouses. While a normal joint tenancy can be severed by either joint tenant, a tenancy by the entirety may be severed only with the consent of both spouses. Although there is a distinction between these two forms of co-ownership between spouses, they are treated the same under IRC § 2040(b).

(3) Income Tax Aspects

A beneficiary's basis in property acquired from a decedent is "stepped up" (or down) to the property's fair market value as of the date of the decedent's death. [IRC § 1014(a)(1)] Since property generally appreciates in value, this is known as a "stepped-up basis"; however, the basis can also decrease if the property depreciates in value. Where the surviving joint tenant assumes ownership over the whole property because of the co-tenant's death, the step-up (or down) in basis is limited to that portion of the property that was included in the decedent's gross estate. [IRC § 1014(b)(9)]

Example (1): Thelma and Louise held property as joint tenants with rights of survivorship. Each of them paid $5,000 to acquire the property ($10,000 total cost). When the property was worth $30,000, Thelma died and Louise became sole owner of the property by operation of law. Since Thelma's gross estate includes $15,000 (one-half of the value of the property), Louise's income tax basis in the property is $20,000 ($15,000 from Thelma's half of the property under IRC § 1014(a) plus the $5,000 cost basis from her own half).

Example (2): Same facts as Example (1), except that Thelma supplied the entire $10,000 consideration paid to acquire the property. Since Thelma's gross estate includes the entire $30,000 value of the property as of the date of her death, Louise's income tax basis in the property is $30,000 under IRC § 1014(a). [IRC § 1014(b)(9)]

c) **Property Subject to a General Power of Appointment [IRC § 2041]**

Throughout the long history of property law, a "**power of appointment**" over property has never been considered an interest in the subject property. Thus, if a decedent holds a power to distribute trust income or principal among a designated class of beneficiaries not including the decedent, the decedent has no interest in the trust property. Nothing would be included in the decedent's gross estate under IRC § 2033, nor under IRC § 2036, assuming the decedent did not create the trust (since the decedent would have made no transfer).

But where the decedent held at the moment of death a power to appoint trust income or corpus among a designated class of beneficiaries *including* the decedent (or the decedent's estate or creditors), the decedent in effect held ownership-type rights in the trust property. This is because the decedent could have appointed the entire trust property to himself or herself. So if a decedent dies holding this power (and does not exercise the power completely in his or her favor prior to death), the decedent effectively chooses to let the property pass to the default beneficiary or beneficiaries named in the trust instrument. IRC § 2041 realizes that a wealth transfer occurs at the decedent's death under these circumstances.

(1) General Powers of Appointment Held at Death

    (a) General Rule

        Formally, IRC § 2041(a) requires inclusion of property subject to a "**general power of appointment**" held by the decedent at death. A general power of appointment is any power of appointment over property that is exercisable in favor of the decedent, the decedent's estate, or the creditor's of the decedent's estate. [IRC § 2041(b)(1)] IRC § 2041 contains two sets of rules: one set applicable to general powers of appointment created on or before October 21, 1942, and another set applicable to general powers of appointment created after that date. Given virtually all general powers of appointment in existence today were created after this date, this discussion does not consider the first set of rules applicable to powers created on or before October 21, 1942 (often referred to imprecisely as "pre–1942 powers").

        Example (1):   Grover creates a trust that pays income to Bobby for Bobby's life. At Bobby's death, the trust terminates and the remainder will be distributed to Candice or Candice's estate. Danica, the trustee, holds a power to appoint all or any portion of the trust property to Bobby during his life. Assuming Bobby is not one of Danica's creditors nor Danica's dependent, Danica does not hold a general power of appointment. Accordingly, if Danica dies survived by Bobby, no portion of the trust property will be included in Danica's gross estate.

Example (2):   Same facts as Example (1), except that Danica holds a power to appoint all or any portion of the trust property to anyone. Because Danica is a permissible appointee under this power, Danica holds a general power of appointment. If Danica dies survived by Bobby, the entire value of the trust property will be included in her gross estate under IRC § 2041(a).

Example (3):   Same facts as Example (1), except that Danica holds a power to appoint all or any portion of the trust property to anyone other than herself. Because Danica's creditors are permissible appointees under this power, Danica holds a general power of appointment. If Danica dies survived by Bobby, the entire value of the trust property will be included in her gross estate under IRC § 2041(a).

(b) Exceptions

There are three situations where holding a general power of appointment at death will *not* cause inclusion in the gross estate. If the power is either: (1) limited by an ascertainable standard related to maintenance, education, support, or health of a permissible appointee; (2) exercisable only in conjunction with the creator of the power; or (3) exercisable only in conjunction with someone holding a "substantial adverse interest," the power is not a general power of appointment.

i)   Power Limited to an Ascertainable Standard

The first situation is where the decedent's discretion in appointing the trust property is limited by an "**ascertain-**

able standard" related to the maintenance, education, support, or health of a permissible appointee. [IRC § 2041(b)(1)(A)]

Example: A testamentary trust created by Demetra's spouse provides that Demetra is to receive income annually for life. At Demetra's death, any remaining trust property will pass to Bob or Bob's estate. The trust instrument also gives Demetra the power to withdraw all or any portion of the trust corpus as needed for her reasonable maintenance, education, support, or health. Demetra serves as the sole trustee of this trust. Although Demetra holds the power to appoint trust property to herself, no portion of the trust property will be included in her gross estate under IRC § 2041(a) when she dies because her exercise of the power is limited by an ascertainable standard. Thus, she does not hold a general power of appointment.

ii)   **Power Exercisable in Conjunction with Creator**

The second situation is where the power can only be exercised jointly by the decedent and the person who created the power. [IRC § 2041(b)(1)(C)(i)]

Example: Gus creates a trust that pays income to Dixie for Dixie's life. At Dixie's death, the trust property will be distributed to Bonnie or Bonnie's estate. Dixie is named as trustee of the trust. The trust instrument gives the grantor (Gus) and the trustee (Dixie) the power appoint all or any portion of the trust corpus to Dixie during her life. This power is exercisable only with the consent of both the grantor and the trustee. Although Dixie holds a power to appoint property to herself, the value of the trust property will not be included in her gross estate under IRC § 2041(a) because it is exercisable only in conjunction with Gus, the creator of the power. Consequently, she does not hold a general power of appointment.

iii) Substantial Adverse Interests

The third situation is where the power can only be exercised jointly by the decedent and a third party with a "substantial adverse interest" in the exercise of the power in the decedent's favor. [IRC § 2041(b)(1)(C)(ii)] If the decedent's power is exercisable only in conjunction with a third party, but that third party does not have a "substantial adverse interest" in the exercise of the power in the decedent's favor, then, assuming the third party is a permissible appointee of the property, the decedent is considered to have a general power of appointment only as to an equitable portion of the subject property. [IRC § 2041(b)(1)(C)(iii)] If, for instance, the decedent is one of two power-holders, then one-half of the value of the subject property is included in the decedent's gross estate. But if the decedent is one of three power-holders, only one-third of the value of the subject property is included in the decedent's gross estate.

Logically, then, where the decedent was not the only power-holder, one must determine whether the other power-holder(s) had a "substantial adverse interest" in the exercise of the power in favor of the decedent. One who would take the property by default if the power goes unexercised is adverse to the exercise of the power in favor of the decedent. Likewise, a co-holder of the power has an adverse interest where that co-holder may alone hold the power after the death of the decedent to exercise the power in favor of himself or herself. [Reg. § 20.2041–3(c)(2)] The Regulations provide that an adverse interest is "substantial" if "its value in relation to the total value of the property subject to the power is not insignificant." [*Id.*]

Example (1):   Greg creates a trust that gives Diane the right to income until Diane's death. Following Diane's death, the trust will terminate and the remainder will be distributed to Barry or Barry's estate. The trust instrument gives Diane and Barry the power to appoint all or any portion of the trust property to Diane during her life. Although Diane has the power to appoint the trust property to herself, she needs the consent of Barry to do so. Barry, the taker in default of appointment, is adverse to the exercise of the power in Diane's favor since the exercise of the power will reduce the amount he will take as the remainder beneficiary. Furthermore, Barry's adverse interest is substantial because it relates to the whole value of the trust property. Consequently, Diane does not hold a general power of appointment because her co-power-holder, Barry, has a substantial adverse interest. No portion of the trust property will be included in Diane's gross estate under IRC § 2041(a). [Reg. § 20.2041–3(c)(2), ex. (1)]

Example (2): Same facts as Example (1), except that the trust instrument gives Diane and Charlotte the power to appoint all or any portion of the trust property to Diane during her life. Although Diane needs Charlotte's consent to power to appoint the trust property to herself, Charlotte has no interest in the trust and thus is not adverse to exercise of the power in favor of Diane. As a result, Diane holds a general power of appointment at her death, meaning the entire value of the trust property will be included in Diane's gross estate under IRC § 2041(a).

Example (3): Same facts as Example (1), except that the trust instrument gives Diane and Charlotte the power to appoint all or any portion of the trust property to anyone during the life of Diane. Diane can exercise this power only with the consent of Charlotte. Although Charlotte is a permissible appointee under this power, that fact alone does not make Charlotte adverse to the exercise of the power in Diane's favor. [Reg. § 20.2041–3(c)(2)] After all, Diane might consent to the appointment of half of the trust property to Charlotte in exchange for Charlotte's consent to appoint the other half of the trust property to Diane. Consequently, if Diane dies before Charlotte, Diane is considered to hold a general power of appointment at her death as to one-half of the trust property, meaning one-half of the value of the trust property will be included in Diane's gross estate under IRC § 2041(a). Likewise, if Charlotte dies before Diane, Charlotte's gross estate will include one-half of the value of the trust property under IRC § 2041(a), for Charlotte is considered to hold a general power of appointment over one-half of the property, too.

(c) Other Issues

Unless one of the exceptions noted above applies, gross estate inclusion of property subject to a general power of appointment results no matter whether the decedent exercised the power and even where the power expires at the decedent's death. Inclusion is required even where the decedent-power holder was legally incapable of exercising the power in the decedent's favor. [*Estate of Alperstein v. Commissioner*, 613 F.2d 1213 (2d Cir. 1979)] Moreover, under the last sentence of IRC § 2041(a)(2), the decedent is assumed to hold a general power of appointment at death even if the exercise of that power was subject to the condition precedent of giving advance notice.

Note that a decedent does not even have to be aware that he or she holds a general power of appointment for inclusion to result. As a result, careful practitioners always ask clients whether they are serving or have agreed to serve as trustees or fiduciaries with respect to property held in trust purportedly for the benefit of others. If so, the practitioner should review the trust document to determine whether inclusion under IRC § 2041 could result.

(2) Exercise or Release of a General Power of Appointment

(a) General Rule

In addition to including property subject to a general power of appointment held at the decedent's death, IRC § 2041(a)(2) requires inclusion in the gross estate where the decedent exercised or **released** a general power of appointment in a manner that, if it had been a direct transfer of property by the decedent, would result in gross estate inclusion under any of the re-inclusion provisions (IRC §§ 2035–2038).

> *Example:* A testamentary trust created by Donald's spouse provides that Donald is to receive income annually for life. At Donald's death, any remaining trust property will pass to Benny or Benny's estate. The trust instrument also gives Donald the discretion to withdraw all or any portion of the trust corpus at any time. Donald serves as trustee. Because Donald has the power to appoint trust property to himself, Donald's power is a general power of appointment. Donald validly executes a document releasing Donald's general power of appointment. As a consequence, Donald is no longer able to access the trust corpus, meaning Benny will take the remainder at Donald's death. At Donald's death, the entire trust corpus is included in his gross estate under IRC § 2041(a)(2), just as IRC § 2036 would have required inclusion if Donald had owned the trust assets directly because of the retained right to income. In effect, IRC § 2041(a)(2) treats Donald's release of a general power of appointment as a transfer of the property subject to the general power of appointment. [*de Oliveira v. United States*, 767 F.2d 1344 (9th Cir. 1985)]

(b) Lapses Treated as Releases

The **lapse** of a general power of appointment is treated as the release of a general power of appointment to the extent that the value of the property which could have been appointed by the exercise of the power exceeds the greater of $5,000 or 5% of the value of the assets from which the exercise of the lapsed power could have been satisfied. [IRC § 2041(b)(2)]

Example (1):   Dominic held a non-cumulative power to withdraw $12,000 annually from a trust created by Ginger in January of Year 1. The trust instrument requires the trustee to pay income to Dominic for life and, at Dominic's death, distribute the remainder to Randy or Randy's estate. At all times relevant in this example, the trust assets have a value of $70,000. Dominic allowed his withdrawal power to lapse in each of Years 1 through 4 and then died in July of Year 5. In each of Years 1 through 4, Dominic's lapse is treated as a release of $7,000, which equals the amount he was entitled to withdraw ($12,000) minus the greater of $5,000 or 5% of the value of the trust assets (5% * $70,000 = $3,500). [IRC § 2041(b)(2)} Because each year's $7,000 release would be includible in Dominic's gross estate under IRC § 2036 if he were treated as transferring the released amount to the trust each year (retaining the right to income from each such transfer), IRC § 2041(a)(2) requires inclusion of these released amounts in Dominic's gross estate. In addition, Dominic's gross estate includes the entire $12,000 he was entitled to withdraw up to the moment of his death in Year 5. Consequently, the total amount included in Dominic's gross estate on these facts is $40,000 ($7,000 from each of Years 1 through 4 as having lapsed under IRC § 2041(b)(2) plus $12,000 from Year 5 under IRC § 2041(a)(2)).

Example (2):   Same facts as Example (1), except that the trust assets at all times relevant to this example have a value of $200,000. In each of Years 1 through 4, Dominic's lapse is treated as a release of $2,000, which equals the amount he was entitled to withdraw ($12,000) minus the greater of $5,000 or 5% of the value of the trust assets (5% * $200,000 = $10,000). [IRC § 2041(b)(2)] Because each year's $2,000 release would be includible in Dominic's gross estate under IRC

§ 2036 if he were treated as transferring the released amount to the trust each year (retaining the right to income from each such transfer), IRC § 2041(a)(2) requires inclusion of these released amounts in Dominic's gross estate. In addition, Dominic's gross estate includes the entire $12,000 he was entitled to withdraw up to the moment of his death in Year 5. Consequently, the total amount included in Dominic's gross estate on these facts is $20,000 ($2,000 from each of Years 1 through 4 under IRC § 2041(b)(2) plus $12,000 from Year 5 under IRC § 2041(a)(2)).

Example (3):   Same facts as Example (1), except that the trust assets at all times relevant to this example have a value of $250,000. In each of Years 1 through 4, Dominic's lapse is not treated as a release to any extent. This is because the amount he was entitled to withdraw ($12,000) does not exceed the greater of $5,000 or 5% of the value of the trust assets (5% * $250,000 = $12,500). Accordingly, there is no inclusion in Dominic's gross estate under IRC § 2041(b)(2). However, Dominic's gross estate still includes the $12,000 he was entitled to withdraw up to the moment of his death in Year 5. Thus, the total amount included in Dominic's gross estate on these facts is $12,000 (nothing from the lapse in each of Years 1 through 4, but $12,000 from Year 5 under IRC § 2041(a)(2)).

Example (4):   Same facts as Example (1), except that Dominic's power to withdraw is exercisable only in the months of January, February, and March. Dominic allowed his withdrawal power to lapse in each of Years 1 through 5. In each of these years, then, Dominic's lapse is treated as a release of $7,000, which equals the amount he was entitled to withdraw ($12,000) minus the greater of $5,000 or 5% of the value of the trust assets (5%

* $70,000 = $3,500). [IRC § 2041(b)(2)] Because each year's $7,000 release would be includible in Dominic's gross estate under IRC § 2036 if he were treated as transferring the released amount to the trust each year (retaining the right to income from each such transfer), IRC § 2041(a)(2) requires inclusion of these released amounts in Dominic's gross estate. No amount is included under IRC § 2041(a)(2) for year 5, however, because Dominic did not die holding a general power of appointment over the trust property. Thus, the total amount included in Dominic's gross estate on these facts is $35,000 ($7,000 from each of Years 1 through 5 under IRC § 2041(b)(2)).

Example (5): Same facts as Example (1), except that while the value of the trust assets in Years 1 through 4 remained at $70,000, the value of the trust property in the days before Dominic's death surged to $100,000. As previously explained, Dominic's lapse in each of Years 1 through 4 is treated as a release of $7,000. [IRC § 2041(b)(2)] That amounts to 10% of the value of the trust property in each of those years. Over the course of four years, then, Dominic is considered to have released a total of 40% of the value of the trust. Thus, IRC § 2041(a)(2) requires inclusion of 40% of the value of the trust assets as of the date of death (here, $40,000) in Dominic's gross estate. In addition, Dominic's gross estate includes the entire $12,000 he was entitled to withdraw up to the moment of his death in Year 5. Consequently, the total amount included in Dominic's gross estate on these facts is $52,000 ($40,000 under IRC § 2041(b)(2) plus $12,000 under IRC § 2041(a)(2)). [Reg. § 20.2041–3(d)(4)]

d) Life Insurance [IRC § 2042]

Very often, there will be one or more insurance policies on the life of the decedent. To the extent the decedent controls the disposition of the death benefits payable under the life insurance policies, it is fair to subject those benefits to federal estate tax. IRC § 2042 identifies those situations where the decedent has such control.

(1) General Rule

The death benefits from a life insurance policy are included in the gross estate of the insured in two situations: (1) where the death benefits are payable to the insured's estate [IRC § 2042(1)]; or (2) where the insured has *any* of the "**incidents of ownership**" over the policy. [IRC § 2042(2)] The emphasis in the last sentence is not hyperbole. Regulations confirm that if the insured holds any of the following rights with respect to the policy, the death benefits are includible: the power to change the beneficiary; the power to surrender or cancel the policy; the power to assign the policy; the power to revoke a prior assignment of the policy; the power to pledge the policy to creditors; the power to borrow against the policy; or the power to change the beneficial enjoyment of a policy owned by a trust. [Reg. § 20.2042–1(c)] As if that is not enough, the Regulations state that this list is not exhaustive of the various incidents of ownership that will trigger inclusion.

Inclusion results even where the decedent has no practical ability to exercise any of the powers associated with incidents of ownership. Thus, proceeds from flight insurance purchased by the decedent immediately prior to a plane crash are included in the decedent's gross estate even though there was really no way the decedent could exercise the power to change beneficiaries or assign the policy to others. [*Commissioner v. Estate of Noel*, 380 U.S. 678, 85 S.Ct. 1238, 14 L.Ed.2d 159 (1965)]

A decedent does not have incidents of ownership in an insurance policy if the decedent's powers with respect to the policy are held merely in a fiduciary capacity such that the decedent cannot personally benefit from their exercise, provided the decedent did not directly transfer the policy or the consideration used for purchasing the policy to the trust in which the decedent serves as trustee. [Rev. Rul. 84–179, 1984–2 C.B. 195]

Example: David purchased an insurance policy on his life several years ago. More than three years prior to his death, David transferred all incidents of ownership in the policy to Alice. Alice died, bequeathing the policy to a trust and naming David as the trustee. The terms of the trust require income to be paid to Barb for her life. At Barb's death, the trust will terminate and the remainder will be paid to Corwin or Corwin's estate. In his fiduciary capacity as trustee, David has the power to surrender the policy and to borrow against the policy, all for the benefit of Barb and Corwin. When David dies, the death benefit from the insurance policy will not be included in his gross estate because David did not directly transfer the policy to the trust and the powers he held over the policy were exercisable only in a fiduciary capacity and not for his own benefit.

Where community property funds of the decedent and his or her spouse are used to acquire a policy on the life of the decedent, only one-half of the death benefit is included in the decedent's gross estate. [Reg. § 20.2042–1(c)(5)] This is true even if the terms of the policy give only the decedent (and not the spouse) the power to change beneficiaries or assign ownership of the policy. The "one-half" rule also applies where the proceeds are paid entirely to the decedent's estate. [Reg. § 20.2042–1(b)(2)]

A corporation's ownership of a policy on the life of a decedent-shareholder will not be imputed to the decedent where the proceeds are payable to the corporation. [Reg. § 20.2042–1(c)(6)] This is true no matter whether the decedent-shareholder held a controlling interest in the corporation's stock. If the proceeds are payable to the decedent's estate or to beneficiaries of the decedent's estate, however, the corporation's incidents of ownership *will* be imputed to the decedent-shareholder if he or she held a controlling interest in the corporation's shares. [*Id.*]

Example: At the time of his death, Bill, a widower, held 70% of the stock in XYZ Corporation. Unrelated individuals held the remaining XYZ shares. XYZ held an insurance policy on Bill's life that paid a lump sum death benefit in equal shares to Bill's children. Because Bill held a controlling interest in XYZ and the proceeds were payable to the beneficiaries of Bill's estate, the entire lump sum death benefit payable to Bill's children will be included in Bill's gross estate. If the death benefit had been payable to the corporation, no portion of the death benefit would have been included in Bill's gross estate.

(2) Strategies to Avoid Inclusion

Where an individual with a substantial estate has any of the incidents of ownership in a policy on his or her life, that individual may seek to avoid the application of IRC § 2042 by transferring such incidents of ownership to another. This solution is feasible assuming the individual survives for three years following the transfer. If the individual does not so survive, the death benefit will still be included in the decedent's gross estate, not under IRC § 2042 but under IRC § 2035(a). [*See supra* I. A. 2. d) (1)] Inclusion under IRC § 2035(a) is mitigated to some extent if the transferee makes premium payments with respect to the policy following the transfer but before the decedent's death.

Example: Irene purchased an insurance policy on her life in Year 1 and named Ricky as the beneficiary. In each of Years 1 through 8, Irene paid the $10,000 annual premium to keep the policy in force. At the beginning of Year 9, Irene transferred the policy to Ricky. Ricky paid the $10,000 annual premiums in Year 9 and Year 10. Irene died at the end of Year 10, and the $200,000 death benefit was paid to Ricky. The premiums paid by Ricky are akin to improvements made to the transferred property. Accordingly, Irene's gross estate will include only $160,000 of the $200,000 death benefit (80% of the total) because she furnished 80% of the consideration (in the form of premium payments) while Ricky furnished the remaining 20%. [*Silverman v. Commissioner*, 521 F.2d 574 (2d Cir. 1975)]

Another common strategy is for the insured to transfer all ownership rights in the policy to an irrevocable trust. The trust is also named as the beneficiary of the policy. The trust instrument can then provide for the disposition of the proceeds upon the death of the insured. If the insured lives for three years following the transfer of the policy, the death benefits will not be included in the insured's gross estate. If, however, the insured dies within three years of the transfer of the policy to the trust, the death benefit will still be included in the decedent's gross estate under IRC § 2035(a). If the insurance policy is originally purchased by the trust (i.e., the insured transfers cash to the trust that can be used by the trustee to pay the initial premium), there is no need for the insured to survive for three years, for the policy itself was never transferred to the trust by the insured and thus IRC § 2035(a) would not apply.

Example: Earl owns an insurance policy on his own life that will pay a death benefit to Earl's designated beneficiary, Wanda. Hoping to avoid inclusion of the death benefit in his gross estate under IRC § 2042(2), Earl creates an irrevocable trust with an independent trustee. The trust instrument names Wanda and Wanda's estate as the beneficiary. Earl funds the trust by transferring ownership of the life insurance policy to the trustee. The trustee then changes the designated beneficiary to the trust. If Earl dies within three years of this gift transfer, the entire death benefit will be included in Earl's gross estate under IRC § 2035(a). But if Earl dies more than three years following the transfer of the policy to the trust, no portion of the death benefit will be included in Earl's gross estate. In either case, the death benefit will still be distributed, ultimately, to Wanda or Wanda's estate.

(3) Insurance Policies on Another's Life

IRC § 2042 is limited to policies insuring the decedent's life. Policies owned by the decedent that insure the lives of others are included in the decedent's gross estate under IRC § 2033, for the decedent controls how the ownership of such policies will pass at the decedent's death. Where a policy on the life of another is included in the gross estate, the amount reported is the replacement cost of the policy (how much it would cost the decedent to purchase an identical policy on the insured's life at the time of death). [Reg. § 20.2031–8(a)]

e) **Certain Property for Which the Marital Deduction Was Previously Allowed [IRC § 2044]**

As discussed later in this Chapter, the purpose of the marital deduction is to *defer* taxation until the death of the surviving spouse. The marital deduction is not a permanent *forgiveness* of tax. To make sure Uncle Sam eventually gets an estate tax bite on property previously transferred to a surviving spouse, IRC § 2044 requires inclusion of any property not already included under IRC §§ 2033–2042 for which another decedent validly claimed a marital deduction. The upcoming discussion of the marital deduction will show that the effect of this rule is to require inclusion of property for which either a "QTIP election" under IRC § 2056(b)(7) was made upon the death of the first spouse or a "spousal charitable remainder trust" under IRC § 2056(b)(8) was claimed.

f) Disclaimers [IRC § 2046]

Disclaiming interests in property can have estate tax ramifications. IRC § 2518 provides rules applicable to "qualified disclaimers." IRC § 2046 defers to IRC § 2518 for the effect of a qualified disclaimer for estate tax purposes. Qualified disclaimers are covered in II. C. 2.

4. Valuation Issues

Generally, assets included in the gross estate must be valued according to their "fair market values" at the date of the decedent's death. Regulations define fair market value as "the price at which the property would change hands between a willing buyer and a willing seller, neither under any compulsion to buy or to sell, and both having reasonable knowledge of relevant facts." [Reg. § 20.2031–1(b)] In some situations, the use of fair market value produces inappropriate results, as where the value of the asset included in the gross estate has declined significantly following the decedent's death but before estate tax has been paid. Moreover, because the fair market value standard requires reference to a hypothetical buyer and a hypothetical seller, an asset like real estate may be valued much higher than the decedent's actual use of the property. Special Code provisions, IRC §§ 2032 and 2032A, address both of these defects with the fair market value standard. Even where these special rules do not apply, determining the fair market value of an asset can be difficult. Various discounts and premiums adjust the liquidation value of an asset, not to mention the special valuation rules in Chapter 14 of the Code (IRC §§ 2701–2704).

a) Alternate Valuation Date [IRC § 2032]

(1) General Rule

Although the general rule is that assets included in the gross estate must be valued as of the date of death, the executor of the estate may, under IRC § 2032, elect to value all of the included assets as of the date six months after the decedent's death. [IRC § 2032(a)(2)] The **alternate valuation date** election is helpful when assets have declined in value shortly after the decedent's death.

(2) Conditions for Application

To be eligible for the election, use of the alternate valuation date must result in a decrease in both the value of the gross estate and the sum of the estate and generation-skipping transfer (GST) taxes. [IRC § 2032(c)] Only the GST tax payable by reason of the decedent's death with respect to the property includible in the decedent's gross estate is considered. [Reg. 20.2032–1(b)(1)] The election may not be claimed if the estate tax return is filed more than one year after the filing deadline. [IRC § 2032(d)(2)]

Example (1):   Caesar, who made no lifetime taxable gifts, died on March 15, Year 1 (when the applicable exclusion amount was $5 million). His gross estate consisted of a residence worth $1.5 million and publicly-traded stock worth $4 million. As of September 15, Year 1, the value of the residence had grown to $1.8 million, but the value of the publicly-traded stock had fallen to $3.4 million. Caesar's personal representative may elect to use the alternate valuation date because the gross estate has declined from $5.5 million at the date of death to $5.2 million as of the alternate valuation date and because the reduced gross estate will result in a reduced liability for federal estate tax.

Example (2):   Same facts as Example (1), except that the value of the publicly-traded stock at the date of Caesar's death was $2.5 million and its value as of September 15, Year 1, was $2.1 million. Although the total value of the gross estate has declined from $4 million to $3.9 million, Caesar's personal representative may not make the alternate valuation date election because the election would not reduce the estate's liability for federal estate tax. Because of the $5 million applicable exclusion amount, Caesar's estate has no liability for federal estate tax even with the date-of-death values. [IRC § 2010; *see infra* I. C.

2. a)] The election would therefore have no effect on the amount of estate tax owed.

(3) Post–Death Dispositions of Gross Estate Assets

If the decedent's personal representative makes an IRC § 2032 election and any of the property included in the decedent's gross estate is sold, distributed, or otherwise disposed of prior to the alternate valuation date, such property must be valued as of the date of the sale, distribution, or disposition. [IRC § 2032(a)(1)] For purposes of this rule, nonrecognition transactions including like-kind exchanges (IRC § 1031) and transfers of appreciated property in exchange for a controlling interest in a corporation (IRC § 351) do not qualify as dispositions. [Reg. § 20.2032–1(c)(1)]

Example: Brutus, who made no lifetime taxable gifts, died on May 1, Year 1 (when the applicable exclusion amount was $5 million). His gross estate consisted of a residence worth $500,000 and a parcel of investment real property worth $6 million. On June 1, Year 1, Brutus' personal representative sold the residence to an unrelated buyer for $520,000. On August 1, Year 1, the personal representative exchanged the investment real property for a parcel of farmland owned by an unrelated party in a nonrecognition transaction under IRC § 1031. As of November 1, Year 1 (the alternate valuation date), the value of the exchanged farmland was $5.8 million. If the personal representative elects to use the alternate valuation date, the personal residence will be valued as of the date of the June sale (i.e., $520,000). The investment real property will be valued at the $5.8 million value of the farmland as of the alternate valuation date.

(4) Valuation Changes Due to "Mere Lapse of Time"

To the extent the reduction in the value of an asset included in the gross estate is attributable merely to the passage of time, the asset must be valued as of the date of the decedent's death. [IRC § 2032(a)(3)] Assets whose values are affected merely by the lapse of time include patents, estates for the life of a person other than the decedent, remainders, and reversions. [Reg. § 20.2032–1(f)] If the value of an asset is affected by both the mere lapse of time and some other factor, however, an adjustment may be made for such other factor but not for the mere lapse of time.

Example (1):   Cassius, who died on February 1, Year 1, has a gross estate that includes a patent on a particular device used in gardening. As of the date of death, the patent had exactly ten years remaining in its useful life and a value of $100,000. As of August 1, Year 1 (the alternate valuation date), the patent had a value of $95,000, simply because the patent at that point had only 9.5 years remaining in its useful life. If Cassius' personal representative elects to use the alternate valuation date, the patent must be valued at $100,000.

Example (2):   Same facts as Example (1), except that the value of the patent as of August 1, Year 1, had slipped to $80,000, not only because the patent had only 9.5 years remaining but also because the market for gardening had withered. If Cassius' personal representative elects to use the alternate valuation date, the patent must be valued at $84,211, obtained by dividing $80,000 by 0.95 (the ratio of the remaining life of the patent at the alternate valuation date to the remaining life of the patent at the date of Cassius' death). [Reg. § 20.2032–1(f)(2)]

(5)   **Effect on Estate Tax Deductions**

Use of the alternate valuation date may have a corollary effect on the deductions available in computing the taxable estate. [IRC § 2032(b)] If, for instance, an item in the gross estate loses value because of a casualty that occurred during the six-month period following the decedent's death, the personal representative may not claim both a reduced value under IRC § 2032 and a casualty loss deduction under IRC § 2054 if use of the alternate valuation date has the same effect as the allowance of the casualty loss deduction. [Reg. § 20.2032–1(g)]

b)   **Qualified Real Property [IRC § 2032A]**

Because the definition of fair market value refers to a hypothetical willing buyer and willing seller, the fair market value of real property is determined with reference to its "highest and best use." [H.R. Rep. No. 1380, 94th Cong., 2d Sess. 3, 21 (1976)] For certain property, especially farmland, valuation at the "highest and best use" will result in a much larger amount of tax than would be the case if the property were valued at its "actual use." The land used for farming could be made more valuable by converting it to a shopping center or subdividing it into residential parcels. Congress wanted to encourage the use of real property for family farming operations and other family businesses, so it enacted IRC § 2032A in 1976. Under IRC § 2032A, so-called "qualified real property" (generally, land used for farming or for the operation of any other trade or business) will qualify for valuation based on its "actual use" instead of its "highest and best use." This is also known as "**special use valuation**."

(1) **Qualified Real Property**

To claim the benefit of IRC § 2032A, three requirements must be met. First, the decedent had to be a citizen or resident of the United States at the time of death. [IRC § 2032A(a)(1)(A)] Second, the personal representative must make an irrevocable election on the federal estate tax return to apply IRC § 2032A. [IRC § 2032A(a)(1)(B), (d)(1)] Finally, the property to be valued under IRC § 2032A must be "qualified real property." It is easy to determine whether the first two requirements are met, but determining whether a parcel of land is qualified real property can prove difficult.

In order to be **qualified real property**, no less than eight require-ments must be met. For ease of reference, seven of these eight requirements can be placed into three groups: the "property" requirements, the "value" requirements, and the "use" require-ments. The exception to this grouping is the requirement that all persons with an interest in the real property must sign an agreement consenting to the application of certain recapture rules that come into play if some non-qualifying use of the property is made. [IRC § 2032A(a)(1)(B), (b)(1)(D), (d)(2)] The recapture rules and the uses that will trigger those rules are discussed below.

(a) **The "Property" Requirements**

There are two requirements in this group. First, the real property must be located in the United States. [IRC § 2032A(b)(1)] Second, the real property must pass from the decedent to a "qualified heir". [*Id.*] A **qualified heir** is any member of the decedent's "family" who received the property from the decedent. The term also includes one who receives the property from a qualified heir, provided the recipient is a member of the qualified heir's family. [IRC § 2032A(e)(1)]

> *Example:* The decedent, Al, transferred a parcel of farmland to his son, Bud. Some time later, Bud transferred the same property to his sister, Kelly. Kelly is a qualified heir. Although she did not receive the property from the decedent, she received it from a qualified heir (Bud) and she is a member of Bud's family.

Although an individual's family is defined to include only a prescribed class of persons, the definition is quite broad. It includes an individual's ancestors (e.g., parents and grandparents), his or her lineal descendants (e.g., children and grandchildren) and their spouses (e.g., sons- and daughters-in-law), the lineal descendants of an individual's parents (e.g., siblings, nieces, and nephews) and their spouses (nieces- and nephews-in-law, assuming there is such a thing), his or her spouse, and the lineal descendants of an individual's spouse (e.g., step-children and step-grandchildren) and their spouses (step-children-in-law!). [IRC § 2032A(e)(2)] Given this expansive definition, it is no surprise that this definition also treats adopted children as blood children. [*Id.*]

(b) The "Value" Requirements

There are also two requirements in this group, though they are a bit more complicated because of the many conjunctive elements in each requirement. These two requirements are the "50% test" under IRC § 2032A(b)(1)(A) and the "25% test" under IRC § 2032A(b)(1)(B).

For the 50% test, at least 50% of the "adjusted value" of the decedent's gross estate must consist of property (real or personal) which *both* was used for a "qualified use" by the decedent or a member of the decedent's family on the date of the decedent's death *and* passes to a qualified heir. [IRC § 2032A(b)(1)(A)] The adjusted value of the gross estate, generally, is the equity value of the assets included in the gross estate (i.e., the fair market value of the included assets reduced by the amount unpaid mortgages on, or any other debt in respect of, those assets). [IRC § 2032A(b)(3)(A)] A **qualified use** is a use of the property for farming or business purposes. [IRC § 2032A(b)(2)] The statute includes unsurprising definitions for "farm" and "farming purposes," but no definition for "business purposes." [IRC § 2032A(e)(4), (e)(5)]

For the 25% test, at least 25% of the adjusted value of the decedent's gross estate must consist of real property (not including personal property) that passes to a qualified heir and which meets the "use" requirements described below. [IRC § 2032A(b)(1)(B)]

> *Example:* Dennis' gross estate consists of Greenacre, a parcel of farmland used by Dennis in the active business of farming worth $2 million, various farm equipment worth $1 million, and Whiteacre, a parcel of undeveloped real property held for investment worth $3 million. Dennis devised Greenacre and bequeathed the farming equipment to his daughter, Jill. He devised Whiteacre to his son, Jack. Greenacre might be qualified real property, for the "value" requirements are met. The adjusted value of Dennis' gross estate is equal to its fair market value because there is no indebtedness on these facts. The 50% test is met because exactly half of the adjusted value of Dennis' gross estate ($6 million total) consists of property used in the farming business (Greenacre and the farming equipment, worth $3 million), and such property passed to a qualified heir (Jill). Furthermore, the 25% test is met because the adjusted value of Greenacre is 40% of the total adjusted value of Dennis' gross estate. Whiteacre, incidentally, is not qualified real property. Although it passes to a qualified heir (Jack), Whiteacre is held for investment purposes, which is not a qualified use. [IRC § 2032A(b)(2)]

(c) The "Use" Requirements

There are three requirements in this group. First, the property must have been used for a qualified use by the decedent on the date of death. [IRC § 2032A(b)(1)] Again, a qualified use is a use of the property for farming or business purposes. [IRC § 2032A(b)(2)]

Second, for periods totaling at least five of the eight years prior to the decedent's death, the real property must have been owned and put to a qualified use by the decedent or a member of the decedent's family. [IRC § 2032A(b)(1)(C)(i)]

Third, for periods totaling at least five of the eight years prior to the decedent's death, the decedent or a member of the decedent's family must have materially participated in the farm or other family business. [IRC § 2032A(b)(1)(C)(ii)] This requirement effectively ensures that the benefit of special-use valuation is limited to those farms and businesses that are actively operated by a family.

(2) Limitation on Aggregate Reduction in Value

The Code provides that the maximum reduction in value that can result by application of IRC § 2032A to qualified real property is $750,000. [IRC § 2032A(a)(2)] But that figure is adjusted for inflation in multiples of $10,000. [IRC § 2032A(a)(3)] In 2011, for example, the limitation was $1,020,000.

Example (1): Della died holding qualified real property used as farmland. As farmland, the property was worth $1 million at Della's death. At its highest and best use, however, the property was worth $2 million when Della died. Instead of valuing the qualified real property at $2 million, Della's personal representative may value it at $1,250,000 (the difference between the $2 million value at its highest and best use and the $750,000 aggregate limitation to IRC § 2032A not adjusted for inflation).

Example (2): Same facts as Example (1), except that the qualified real property's value at its highest and best use was $1.5 million at the time of Della's death. Instead of valuing the qualified real property at $1.5 million, Della's personal representative may value it at $1 million (its value for farm use). The aggregate limitation does not come into play under these revised facts.

(3) Dispositions and Failure to Continue Qualified Use

(a) Generally

An "additional estate tax" is imposed if, within ten years of the decedent's death (or before the qualified heir's death within that time) (the "probation period"), the qualified heir either disposes of any interest in qualified real property or ceases to use the qualified real property for the qualified use. [IRC § 2032A(c)(1)] This additional estate tax is due six months after the date of disposition or change in use, as the case may be. [IRC § 2032A(c)(4)]

(b) Amount of Additional Estate Tax

The amount of the additional estate tax is, very generally, the difference in estate tax liability attributable to the qualified real property having been valued under IRC § 2032A instead of its highest and best use. [IRC § 2032A(c)(2)] In the case of a sale of qualified real property during the probation period, the additional estate tax cannot exceed the difference between the amount realized from the sale and the value of the qualified real property reported on the estate tax return. [IRC § 2032A(c)(2)(A)(ii)]

Example (1): By electing to apply IRC § 2032A, McDonald's estate valued a parcel of qualified real property at its $1.25 million actual use instead of its $2 million value at its highest and best use. The election saved the estate $262,500 in federal estate taxes. Three years after McDonald's death, the qualified heir sold the qualified real property to an unrelated buyer for $1.8 million. The sale of the qualified real property during the probation period triggers an additional estate tax liability of $262,500, the amount of estate tax saved from the application of IRC § 2032A. This additional estate tax is due six months following the sale.

Example (2): Same facts as Example (1), except that the sale price was $1.2 million. Because the additional estate tax cannot exceed the difference between the amount realized from the sale ($1.2 million) and the value of the qualified real property reported on the estate tax return ($1 million), the additional estate tax is limited to $200,000. [IRC § 2032A(c)(2)(A)(ii)]

(c) Lack of Material Participation Deemed a Nonqualified Use

If, during any eight-year period ending within the probation period, none of the decedent, the qualified heir, or a family member of the decedent or the qualified heir participated materially in the farm or business operation related to the qualified real property for periods totaling at least five years, the qualified real property is treated as no longer being used for the qualified use. [IRC § 2032A(c)(6)(B)] As a result, the additional estate tax would be triggered.

Example: For several years prior to her death, Lenore owned and operated a farm. Lenore devised the property to her daughter, Patty, who continued to operate the property as a farm. Exactly two years after Lenore's death, however, Patty stopped participating in the farm and delegated all decisions and oversight of the property to an unrelated person. On the day following the fifth anniversary of Lenore's death, the additional estate tax will be triggered. Although the property is still operated as a farm and Patty has not sold the property, neither Patty nor Lenore nor any other family member have materially participated in the farm operations for at least five years during the eight-year period ending on that date.

c) **Premiums and Discounts**

Because the fair market value standard refers to what a hypothetical buyer would pay for the decedent's interest in property, some adjustments to the value of an asset included in the gross estate are appropriate, especially where the decedent's interest has special powers or leverage over the interests of others or, conversely, where the decedent's interest is comparatively weaker to other interests in the same asset.

In most cases, the pre-adjustment base price is the "liquidation value" of the decedent's interest, generally expressed as the decedent's share of the underlying property to which the interest relates. Thus, if the gross estate includes a 60% interest in a parcel of real property worth $100,000, the liquidation value of the decedent's 60% interest is $60,000. But $60,000 is probably not the price that a willing buyer would pay for the decedent's interest, for the reasons discussed below. In determining what a willing buyer would pay, one must consider the various adjustments that will increase the value of the decedent's interest above its liquidation value (premiums) as well as those adjustments that will reduce the value of the decedent's interest below liquidation value (discounts).

(1) Control Premium

Where the decedent's interest is a controlling interest in a business or some other asset, a willing buyer might indeed pay a premium on top of the liquidation value of the interest. [Reg. § 20.2031–2(e)] For instance, if the subject property is an 80% interest in a closely-held business, a willing buyer might pay more than 80% of the net asset value or income value of the business because the interest also represents unfettered control over the election of officers, the timing and amount of distributions, and all votes of the owners. In such a case, it is proper to apply a **control premium** to the liquidation value of the 80% interest.

Interests held by family members or others under the control of the decedent are not considered in determining whether the decedent holds a controlling interest so as to justify application of a control premium. [Rev. Rul. 93–12, 1993–1 C.B. 202] But aggregation of two separate interests in the same asset or business is proper where both interests are included in the decedent's gross estate. [Rev. Rul. 79–7, 1979–1 C.B. 294]

Example (1): Carla's gross estate includes a 30% interest in Cheers, Inc., a closely-held corporation. Carla's surviving spouse, Nick, likewise holds a 30% interest in the corporation. No control premium should be applied in determining the value of Carla's interest even though the couple together held a 60% interest in the company.

Example (2): At his death, Cliff owned an outright 30% interest in Cheers, Inc., a closely-held corporation. Cliff's gross estate also includes the assets of a revocable living trust that also held a 30% interest in Cheers. In determining fair market value, it is proper to treat these interests as a single 60% interest in the corporation, perhaps justifying application of a control premium.

Where a control premium applies, the proper adjustment depends upon both the degree of control possessed by the decedent and the nature of the underlying property. For instance, the control premium for a 60% interest in a business should be much less than the control premium applicable to an 80% interest, because only the latter has the ability under most state laws to unilaterally compel liquidation, merger, or other extraordinary corporate action (which typically require a vote of at least two-thirds or three-fourths of the corporate stock). But the control premium for a 60% interest in one business will likely be different from the control premium applicable to a 60% interest in another business. Like all of the premiums and discounts discussed herein, the proper adjustment is best determined by qualified valuation experts, not the typical estate planning attorney.

(2) Minority Interest Discount

The **minority interest discount** reflects the inability both to compel a sale, distribution, or other disposition of the underlying asset and to control its management. The minority interest discount is essentially the inverse of the control premium: while a willing buyer is prepared to pay a premium for a controlling interest, a willing buyer will insist on paying less than liquidation value for a non-controlling interest.

As with the control premium, there is no attribution of others' interests to the decedent. In essence, the decedent's interest is valued in isolation, even though the decedent might have indirectly controlled the interests of others in the same asset or enterprise through familial or friendly influence.

Example: Mother owned a 20% interest in X Co., a closely-held corporation. At the time of Mother's death, Mother's child, Son, owned a 35% interest in X Co. In valuing Mother's 20% interest in X Co., the minority interest discount will apply because Son's interest is not attributed to Mother. This would be true even if Son was a minor.

The focus of the minority interest discount is on the decedent's degree of control. Even a block of stock representing a majority equity interest in a corporation is entitled to a minority interest discount if the shares carry no voting rights and thus lack any power to compel a distribution or a sale of substantially all of the corporation's assets. [*Okerlund v. United States*, 365 F.3d 1044 (Fed.Cir. 2004)]

Because valuation is always a question of fact, there is no fixed minority discount amount. A survey of the many cases analyzing the minority interest discount indicates that the typical minority interest discount ranges from 10% to 30%, although there are cases where the final minority interest discount was above or below this range. [*See, e.g., Estate of Berg v. Commissioner*, 976 F.2d 1163 (8th Cir. 1992)]

(3) Marketability Discount

By definition, a readily marketable interest is easily sold by its owner. Shares in Google Corporation, for instance, can be traded on an established securities market at the push of a button. Where an interest cannot be readily sold because of practical obstacles to sale, a limited market of buyers, or because of restrictions on the owner's ability to transfer the interest, the fair market value of the interest is less than its liquidation value. The **marketability discount** reflects the fact that a willing buyer will consider the costs and delay involved in selling the subject property in deciding the appropriate value of the subject interest.

The marketability discount applies to both controlling and minority interests in an asset or business. [*Estate of Trenchard v. Commissioner*, 69 T.C.M. (CCH) 2164 (1995)] As with the minority interest discount, there is no fixed marketability discount amount. Here too, the proper discount requires an extensive inquiry into the facts. Still, one can obtain a sense of the importance of the marketability discount through a review of some of the litigated cases. In many cases, the typical range for a marketability discount will be from 15% to 35%. Logically, the greater the restrictions on (or impediments to) transfer, the higher the discount.

Even where a decedent owns all of the interests in an asset or business entity, a marketability discount may be appropriate. [*Estate of Dougherty v. Commissioner*, 59 T.C.M. (CCH) 772 (1990) (accepting the 25% marketability discount claimed for the decedent's 100% interest in the stock of a holding company that owned nonliquid assets that would prove cumbersome to sell)]

(4) Fractional Interest Discount

Much like a minority interest discount, a **fractional interest discount** reflects the inherent risks of co-ownership of an asset. The fractional interest discount reflects the fact that a willing buyer will not pay liquidation value for an undivided interest in an asset because of the costs to partition the property or sever the interest, not to mention the general inconveniences that are part of co-ownership. While these same risks may be present with respect to property held as joint tenants with rights of survivorship, IRC § 2040 provides specific rules for inclusion and valuation, and courts will not apply a fractional interest discount to the amount required for inclusion under IRC § 2040. [*Estate of Young v. Commissioner*, 110 T.C. 297 (1998); *Estate of Fratini v. Commissioner*, 76 T.C.M. (CCH) 342 (1998)] But assets held by the decedent and another as tenants in common are eligible for a fractional interest discount. Furthermore, a fractional interest discount is appropriate for community property and property held as tenants by the entirety.

(5) Blockage Discount

On some occasions, the size of the subject property included in the gross estate is such that the market will require a discount in the ordinary course. For example, if the decedent owned a significant share of publicly-traded stock and tried to sell the entire block at once, the decedent would not be able to sell each share for the same price. This is because the significant increase in the number of shares available for sale will cause the price per share to drop as the number of shares in the block increases. In the case of stock or other business interests, this is referred to as a **blockage discount**. [Reg. § 20.2031–2(e); Rev. Rul. 83–30, 1983–1 C.B. 224] The typical size of the blockage discount for business interests is smaller than the typical minority interest and marketability discounts; often the discount ranges from about five to ten percent, although thinly-traded interests often score at the upper end of this range.

(6) Other Discounts

Although the above-mentioned discounts are most common, others can come into play. The capital gains discount acknowledges that when the liquidation value of the subject property is substantially greater than its basis, a willing buyer may discount the value of the subject property by the amount of tax that would be paid if the subject property were sold or exchanged. [*Estate of Davis v. Commissioner*, 110 T.C. 530 (1998) (court discounted gifted stock in a closely-held corporation by $9 million for potential built-in gains)]

Courts have recognized and applied a key person discount, often in the range of about 10%, if the decedent was instrumental to the value of the subject business and his or her death will reduce the future earnings potential or goodwill of the business. [*Estate of Furman v. Commissioner*, 75 T.C.M. (CCH) 2206 (1998)]

Courts will also apply a litigation discount when valuing an asset that is or will likely be subject to litigation. The risk of litigation and the likelihood of loss greatly affect the size of the discount, making it useless to describe a typical discount range. [*Estate of Sharp v. Commissioner*, 68 T.C.M. (CCH) 1521 (1994) (court applied a 25% litigation discount because of evidence that the subject property was conveyed to the decedent through undue influence); *Estate of Davis v. Commissioner*, 65 T.C.M. (CCH) 2365 (1993) (court applied a 5% discount for litigation risks in valuing a pending lawsuit alleging securities churning)]

(7) Combinations of Premiums and Discounts

As the foregoing discussion suggests, it is common for several premiums and discounts to apply to the same interest. As the following examples show, premiums and discounts are layered; they are not cumulative.

Example (1):   The decedent's gross estate includes a minority interest in a closely-held business with a liquidation value of $1 million. A detailed valuation analysis by a qualified expert appraiser determines that the decedent's interest should be adjusted by a 20% minority interest discount and a 30% marketability discount. The total discount adjustment is 44%, not 50%:

Liquidation Value of Interest	$1,000,000
Less: 20% minority interest discount	(200,000)
	800,000
Less: 30% marketability discount	(240,000)
Fair Market Value of Interest	$ 560,000

The order in which the discounts are applied does not matter; mathematically, layered discounts will produce the same aggregate discount regardless of order. Note that the results remain the same in Example (1) if the discounts are applied in reverse order [$1 million less $300,000 marketability discount (30%) equals $700,000; $700,000 less $140,000 minority interest discount (20%) equals $560,000, the same answer].

Example (2): The decedent's gross estate includes a controlling interest in a closely-held business with a liquidation value of $1 million. A detailed valuation analysis by a qualified expert appraiser determines that the decedent's interest should be increased by a 25% control premium and decreased by a 30% marketability discount. The total discount adjustment is 12.5%, not 5%:

Liquidation Value of Interest	$1,000,000
Plus: 25% control premium	250,000
	1,250,000
Less: 30% marketability discount	(375,000)
Fair Market Value of Interest	$ 875,000

d) Certain Rights and Restrictions Disregarded [IRC § 2703]

A **buy-sell agreement** is a contractual arrangement between two or more parties that fixes the price at which property may be transferred. Such agreements are most common in the context of closely-held businesses because owners want to restrict the class of eligible co-owners, but they can be utilized for any form of property. Where a person agrees to purchase or sell property at an agreed value, that agreement is often good evidence of the property's value. Not surprisingly, then, estates frequently take the position that property included in the gross estate that is subject to a buy-sell agreement should be valued at the price set forth in the agreement. Where the agreement was negotiated at arms-length between the decedent and the prospective buyer of the property, the value stated in the agreement probably should be respected for estate tax purposes. But where the parties to the agreement are the decedent and the beneficiary, there is a temptation to under-value the property in the agreement in order to limit the value of the property reportable on the estate tax return.

Example: Hillary and her daughter, Chelsea, own all of the shares in Whitewater Corporation. Hillary, Chelsea, and the corporation enter into a buy-sell agreement. The agreement provides that upon the death of one shareholder, the surviving shareholder shall be given the exclusive right to purchase all or any number of the shares of the deceased shareholder for 60 days. To the extent the surviving shareholder does not purchase all of the deceased shareholder's shares, the corporation shall be obligated to redeem the remaining shares of the deceased shareholder. Although an appraisal has determined that the Whitewater stock has a value of $500 per share, the buy-sell agreement sets the purchase and redemption price at $50 per share. If Hillary dies before Chelsea, Hillary's estate might argue that the value of the Whitewater shares includible in Hillary's gross estate should be $50 per share because of the buy-sell agreement.

While common law and the Treasury provided some guidance for identifying and correcting abusive buy-sell agreements, IRC § 2703 provides a more comprehensive litmus test for valuing property subject to such an agreement. Generally, IRC § 2703 requires property to be valued without regard to any option, agreement, or other right to buy or use property. [IRC § 2703(a)(1)] It also requires property to be valued without regard to any restriction on the right to sell or use property. [IRC § 2703(a)(2)]

An option, agreement, right or restriction will not be disregarded under IRC § 2703 if it meets each of three requirements. [Reg. § 25.2703–1(b)(2)] It must: (1) be a bona fide business arrangement; (2) not be a device to transfer property for less than an adequate and full consideration in money or money's worth; and (3) have terms comparable to similar arrangements entered into at arms-length. [IRC § 2703(b)] In effect, these tests attempt to sniff out those buy-sell agreements and other arrangements principally designed to under-value property for transfer tax valuation purposes. Accordingly, if persons who are not members of the decedent's (or transferor's) family own a majority of the interests in the subject property, the three requirements in IRC § 2703(b) are deemed to be satisfied. [Reg. § 25.2703–1(b)(3)]

In determining whether a buy-sell agreement or other option, right, or restriction has terms comparable to those in arms-length dealings, one must consider the expected term of the agreement, the current value of the property, anticipated changes that will occur in the value of the property during the term of the agreement, and the adequacy of any consideration given in exchange for the rights granted under the agreement. [Reg. § 25.2703–1(b)(4)(i)]

B. Deductions

Once the value of the gross estate is determined, the focus shifts to the five available deductions: (1) certain expenses and debts (IRC § 2053); (2) casualty losses during estate administration (IRC § 2054); (3) charitable bequests (IRC § 2055); (4) marital bequests (IRC § 2056); and (5) state death taxes paid (IRC § 2058). Note that only these five deductions will reduce the gross estate. A sixth deduction for qualified family-owned business interests (IRC § 2057) became obsolete in 2004. Subtraction of the applicable deductions from the value of the gross estate yields the **taxable estate** (IRC § 2051), the base for computing estate tax liability. [IRC § 2001(b)]

1. Certain Expenses and Debts [§ 2053]

Four types of expenses are deductible under IRC § 2053: (1) funeral expenses; (2) administration expenses applicable to both probate and non-probate assets; (3) claims against the estate; and (4) unpaid mortgages and other debts on property included in the gross estate at full fair market value. The policy for permitting deduction of these expenses is clear: because the estate tax is an excise on the transfer of wealth, only the decedent's wealth remaining after payment of these debts and expenses is available for transfer to beneficiaries.

Technically, the IRC § 2053 deduction comes in two parts. IRC § 2053(a) authorizes a deduction for expenses and debts related to those assets included in the gross estate and subject to the probate process. IRC § 2053(b) then authorizes a deduction for similar costs related to those assets included in the decedent's gross estate but not subject to the probate process. Examples of non-probate assets that can comprise all or a portion of the decedent's gross estate include life insurance policies, assets held as joint tenants with rights of survivorship, assets held in a revocable living trust, and pension and other retirement benefits.

a) Funeral Expenses

Funeral expenses actually paid by the estate are deductible in determining the taxable estate. [IRC § 2053(a)(1), (b)] Included in the definition of funeral expenses are reasonable costs for a tombstone, monument, mausoleum, or for a burial lot, as well as reasonable costs for future care and upkeep of the same. [Reg. § 20.2053–2] Even transportation costs for the person bringing the body to the place of burial are deductible. [*Id.*]

b) Administration Expenses

Amounts deductible as administration expenses under IRC § 2053(a)(2) are those expenses "actually and necessarily incurred . . . in the collection of assets, payment of debts, and distribution of property to the persons entitled to it." [Reg. § 20.2053–3(a)] If an expense is incurred simply for the personal benefit of beneficiaries but not for the proper settlement of the estate, the expense is not deductible. [*Id.*]

(1) Personal Representative Commissions

Commissions actually paid or reasonably expected to be paid to the decedent's personal representative (another term for executor) are generally deductible as administration expenses. [Reg. § 20.2053–3(b)(1)] No deduction is allowed, however, if the personal representative waives the right to a commission. [*Id.*] If the decedent bequeaths or devises property to the personal representative in lieu of paying a commission, the bequest or devise is not deductible. [Reg. § 20.2053–3(b)(2)]

(2) Attorney's Fees

Estates can claim a deduction for an attorney's fees that are actually paid or are reasonably expected to be paid. [Reg. § 20.2053–3(c)(1)] Attorney's fees incurred in contesting the assessment of a tax deficiency or in ·commencing an action for refund may also be deducted under this rule—even if the return has already been filed—but they should be claimed at the time of the contest or suit. [Reg. § 20.2053–3(c)(2)] But attorney's fees incurred by the beneficiaries in the litigation of their interests in the estate are not deductible by the estate even if the estate reimburses the beneficiaries for these costs, unless the litigation is essential to the proper settlement of the estate. [Reg. § 20.2053–3(c)(3)]

(3) Miscellaneous Administration Expenses

Other deductible administration expenses common to many estates include court costs, accountant's fees, appraiser's fees, maintenance expenses, and costs for storing or maintaining property of the estate if it is impossible to effect immediate distribution to the beneficiaries. [Reg. § 20.2053–3(d)(1)] Selling expenses incurred in paying the decedent's debts or taxes, paying other administration expenses, or to effect a distribution are also deductible. [Reg. § 20.2053–3(d)(2)] Deductible selling expenses include brokerage and auctioneering fees.

The estate can also deduct losses incurred from the bona fide but below-market sale of property included in the gross estate. [Reg. § 20.2053–3(d)(2)] The amount of the loss is measured with reference to the lesser of the value of the property on the applicable valuation date or the value of the property on the date of sale.

Example (1):   Ernie's gross estate includes property worth $500,000 at the applicable valuation date. Eight months after Ernie's death, when the property was still worth $500,000, his personal representative sold the property to an unrelated purchaser at a commercially reasonable auction for only $350,000. The estate can treat the $150,000 difference as a deductible selling expense.

Example (2):   Same facts as Example (1), except that the fair market value of the property at the time of the sale was $400,000. The estate can deduct $50,000 (the difference between the $400,000 fair market value of the property at the time of sale and the $350,000 sale price) as a selling expense.

Example (3):   Same facts as Example (1), except that the fair market value of the property at the time of the sale was $600,000. The estate can deduct $150,000 (the difference between the $500,000 fair market value of the property at the applicable valuation date and the $350,000 sale price) as a selling expense.

(4) Administration Expenses Related to Non–Probate Property

Most administrative expenses relate to assets subject to the probate process. Yet expenses incurred in connection with administering a trust established during the decedent's lifetime are also deductible, as are other administration expenses related to other non-probate assets. [IRC § 2053(b); Reg. § 20.2053–8]

Example: In Year 1, Whitney created a trust that paid income annually to Whitney for her life. The trust instrument named Dionne as trustee and provided that the trust would terminate at Whitney's death, with the remainder passing to Bobby or Bobby's estate. Whitney died in Year 5. The trust assets are included in Whitney's gross estate under IRC § 2036. Three months after Whitney's death, Dionne distributed all but $6,000 in the trust to Bobby. The withheld amount represented Dionne's fee as trustee ($5,000) and an attorney's fee in connection with termination of the trust ($1,000). Both fees are deductible under IRC § 2053. [Reg. § 20.2053–8(d), ex. (1)]

(5) Income Tax Crossover

A decedent's estate is also a taxpayer for federal *income* tax purposes, so of course the estate will have certain expenses that are deductible on the estate's income tax return. If an expense is deductible for *both* estate tax and income tax purposes, the expense generally can only be claimed on the *estate tax* return unless the estate waives the right to claim a deduction under IRC § 2053, in which case the expense may be claimed on the income tax return. [IRC § 642(g); Reg. § 1.642(g)–1] The waiver is made by attaching a statement to the federal estate tax return and is irrevocable once made. [Reg. § 1.642(g)–1] If the estate tax return has already been filed without a waiver statement, a statement may still be filed anytime before the statute of limitations for the taxable year in question has expired. [*Id. See infra* I. C. 3. covering the statute of limitations for assessing additional estate tax liability]

In some cases, the personal representative can elect to allocate certain administrative expenses between the estate's income tax return and the federal estate tax return. This election can be made on an item-by-item basis, and even a single expense can be apportioned between the income tax return and the estate tax return in the discretion of the personal representative. [Reg. § 1.642(g)–2] Estate administration expenses that can be allocated under this rule include: (1) court costs and filing fees; (2) appraisal fees; (3) personal representative commissions and attorney fees; (4) accountant fees; (5) traveling expenses related to estate administration; (6) storage and maintenance expenses; and (7) selling expenses.

Certain expenses, however, cannot be claimed on the estate's income tax return—they may only be deducted (if at all) on the estate tax return because there is no deduction available for income tax purposes. These items include: (1) funeral expenses; (2) personal expenses of decedent paid after death; (3) federal income and gift taxes owed by the decedent; and (4) expenses incurred by decedent with respect to tax-exempt income.

Likewise, some expenses can be deducted only on the estate's federal income tax return. Examples include: (1) state income taxes on income received after the decedent's death (IRC § 164(a)(3)); and (2) property taxes accrued on estate property after the decedent's death (IRC § 164(a)(1)). [IRC § 2053(c)(1)(B)]

Generally speaking, it is a toss-up whether to claim administration expenses on the estate tax return or the income tax return. The estate tax rate is now the same (a flat 35% in 2011) as the highest income tax rate (35% in 2011). And while the estate tax is often due sooner than the income tax for the year in which the expenses are incurred, the combination of federal and state income taxes may render the total income tax bite larger than the total estate tax bite. Of course, if there is no federal estate tax due (either because the estate is sufficiently small or because the estate will utilize other deductions to reduce the taxable estate), the personal representative should claim the expenses on the estate's income tax return.

c) Claims Against the Estate

IRC § 2053(a)(3) allows a deduction for enforceable claims against the estate, and IRC § 2053(b) offers a corollary deduction for claims against non-probate assets included in the gross estate. Examples of non-probate assets include life insurance proceeds, certain inter vivos trusts, and property held as joint tenants with rights of survivorship. Only personal obligations of the decedent in existence at the date of death are deductible under this rule. [Reg. § 20.2053–4] Interest attributable to a claim qualifies, but only that interest that accrued at the time of death is deductible, even if the estate makes use of the alternate valuation date under IRC § 2032.

In determining what qualifies as a "claim" against the estate, IRC § 2053(c)(1)(A) requires that claimant paid full and adequate consideration in money or money's worth. Absent this requirement, a decedent could "promise" all of his or her assets to the beneficiaries and reduce the gross estate to zero, thus eliminating any liability for estate tax.

Example: Morrie promised to bequeath $500,000 to Mitch in exchange for Mitch's comfort and care for the rest of Morrie's life. Mitch provided comfort and care to Morrie, but Morrie's will left no bequest to Mitch. Mitch made a claim for $500,000 against the estate, and the personal representative paid this amount to Mitch. Morrie's estate will not be entitled to deduct the $500,000 payment to Mitch under IRC § 2053, for while the payment settles Mitch's claim against the estate, the claim was not based on Mitch having supplied consideration in money or money's worth to Morrie.

Claims against the estate are deductible only as allowable under the law of the jurisdiction where the estate is being administered (or, in the case of non-probate property, where the estate would be administered, assuming such amounts are paid before the expiration of the statute of limitations). [IRC § 2053(a), (b)] Local laws often require claims against the estate to be filed within a set period of time (usually ranging from three to six months following public notice), although many jurisdictions give the personal representative discretion to pay late claims. Some courts have ruled that the payment of late claims still gives rise to a deduction, under the theory that it is sufficient that the claim existed on the date of death and that the creditor's failure to submit a timely claim should be ignored. [*Propstra v. United States*, 680 F.2d 1248 (9th Cir. 1982)] Other courts have held that the payment of late claims does not give rise to a deduction because technically the claims were no longer "allowable" under applicable law. [*Estate of Hagmann v. Commissioner*, 60 T.C. 465 (1973), *aff'd*, 492 F.2d 796 (5th Cir. 1974)]

To the extent the decedent's liability for a claim (or the amount of the claim) is uncertain as of the date of death, no deduction is allowed until such time as both the decedent's liability and the amount of the claim are determined. [Reg. § 20.2053–1(d)(4)]

Example: Roger died in an automobile accident that seriously injured Charlene. Charlene made a claim against Roger's estate for the damages stemming from the accident. If the amount of the claim is reasonably certain, and if Roger's liability is not contested, the estate can claim a deduction for the amount of the claim. [IRC § 2053(a)(3)] But if either the amount of Charlene's claim or Roger's liability is uncertain, then the estate cannot claim a deduction until both of these matters become certain. [Reg. § 20.2053–1(d)(4)] If the deadline for filing the estate tax return will pass before both Roger's liability and the amount of the claim are determined, the estate should file the return with no deduction and then file an amended return with the deduction once the amount of the claim is established.

d)   Unpaid Mortgages

The proper reporting of the value of encumbered property depends upon the estate's liability for the underlying debt. If the estate is liable for the amount of any mortgage or other debt encumbering property included in the gross estate, then the proper approach is to include the full fair market value of the property in the gross estate and then deduct the full amount of any unpaid mortgage or other debt attributable to such property. [IRC § 2053(a)(4), (b)] If the estate is not liable for the debt, then the gross estate includes only the equity value of the property (the excess of the fair market value of the property over the amount of the debt), with no deduction under IRC § 2053. [Reg. § 20.2053–7]

Example (1):   The decedent's gross estate includes Blackacre, a parcel of real property worth $100,000. At the time of death, the decedent was the debtor on a $20,000 loan secured by Blackacre. Because the decedent's estate is liable for repayment of the loan, the full $100,000 value of Blackacre is included in decedent's gross estate, and the estate may claim a $20,000 deduction for the loan under IRC § 2053(a)(4).

Example (2):   Same facts as Example (1), except that the decedent's friend is the debtor on the $20,000 loan. Under applicable law, the decedent's estate is not liable for repayment of the friend's loan. Accordingly, the decedent's gross estate includes only the $80,000 equity value of Blackacre, with no deduction for the amount of the unpaid loan.

To the extent the estate can claim a deduction for unpaid mortgages or other debts, the estate can also deduct interest attributable to such debts that has accrued at the date of death. [Reg. § 20.2053–7]

2. Casualty Losses During Estate Administration [IRC § 2054]

If property included in the gross estate is damaged or lost because of "fires, storms, shipwrecks, or other casualties, or from theft" during the time the estate is administered, the resulting losses may be deducted from the gross estate, but only to the extent such losses are not compensated for by insurance or any other means. [IRC § 2054] The deduction does not come into play very often since it is limited to casualties and thefts that occur during estate administration. Thefts and casualties that occur after distribution of the property to the beneficiary are not deductible by the estate under IRC § 2054.

If property has lost value for some reason other than a casualty or theft, the personal representative should strongly consider use of the "alternate valuation date" under IRC § 2032 described at I. A. 4. a). Of course, the alternate valuation date election can also be used to value property affected by a casualty or theft during the first six months following the decedent's death. If the estate elects to apply the alternate valuation date, the amount of the casualty or theft loss will be reflected in the reported value of the property. In such a case, the estate cannot claim a double benefit by deducting the loss again under IRC § 2054. [Reg. § 20.2032–1(g)]

Thefts and casualty losses are also deductible for federal income tax purposes. [IRC § 165] An estate may not claim both an income tax deduction and an estate tax deduction for the same casualty or theft loss. [IRC § 642(g); Reg. § 1.642(g)–1] The estate must claim the loss under IRC § 2054 unless it irrevocably waives the right to do so, in which case it may claim the income tax deduction instead.

3. Transfers to Charities [IRC § 2055]

Testamentary transfers to certain public, religious, charitable, scientific, literary, and educational organizations (collectively, "charities") qualify for the IRC § 2055 **charitable deduction**. [IRC § 2055(a)] The amount of the deduction is the value of the property transferred to charity, not to exceed the value of such property required to be included in the gross estate. [IRC § 2055(d)] In effect, a decedent's estate can completely escape liability for federal estate tax by leaving everything to charity.

a) Charities

Only those transfers to organizations specifically identified in IRC § 2055(a) qualify for the charitable deduction. Where the decedent's will does not specify the charity entitled to receive a bequest or devise, a charitable deduction may still be allowed as long as the personal representative's discretion in selecting the charity ensures that only an organization identified in IRC § 2055(a) will receive the testamentary gift. [Rev. Rul. 69–285, 1969–1 C.B. 222]

(1) Organizations That Qualify as Charities

While not every nonprofit organization or tax-exempt organization will qualify as a "charity" for purposes of IRC § 2055(a), organizations that would not generally constitute charities in the colloquial sense can qualify. Bequests to individuals, no matter how needy, are not deductible. Instead, a deductible bequest is one made to any of the five types of organizations identified in IRC § 2055(a). The rationale for the deduction is that these types of organizations all perform services that might otherwise have to be paid for by taxpayers. To the extent these qualifying charities do work that would otherwise have to be performed by the government, Congress is willing to forego the transfer tax dollars otherwise payable on amounts transferred to them.

(a) Governments

Perhaps it is not surprising that Uncle Sam is willing to forego revenues on bequests made to Uncle Sam or one of his close relatives. Transfers to or for the use of the federal government, a state, a political subdivision of a state, or a municipality will qualify for the IRC § 2055 deduction, assuming the governmental beneficiary uses the transfer "for exclusively public purposes." [IRC § 2055(a)(1)]

(b) Certain Nonprofit Organizations

Transfers to or for the use of any corporation or association "organized and operated exclusively for religious, charitable, scientific, literary, or educational purposes, including the encouragement of art, or to foster national or international amateur sports competition . . . , and the prevention of cruelty to children or animals" may also qualify for the IRC § 2055 deduction. [IRC § 2055(a)(2); Reg. § 20.2055–1(a)(2)] This category includes most schools, churches, hospitals, the Red Cross, and similar entities.

There are three additional conditions applicable to these non-profit organizations in order to be qualified recipients of a charitable bequest. First, no part of their net earnings may inure to the benefit of any private shareholder or individual "other than as a legitimate object" of their charitable purposes. [Reg. § 20.2055–1(a)(2)] This means, for instance, that an officer of the charity cannot receive a fixed percentage of the organization's net profits, but may receive a regular salary as compensation for legitimate services performed in the capacity of an officer.

Second, the organizations must not be engaged in lobbying activities or other attempts to "influence legislation." [IRC § 2055(a)(2); Reg. § 20.2055–1(a)(2)] For instance, a bequest to the League of Women Voters would not qualify for the IRC § 2055(a) deduction since the primary purpose of the League is to influence legislation. [*League of Women Voters v. United States*, 180 F.Supp. 379 (Ct.Cl. 1960)]

Finally, the organizations must not participate (or intervene) in any political campaign for or against a candidate for public office. [IRC § 2055(a)(2); Reg. § 20.2055–1(a)(2)] Thus, a bequest to the Vote for Pedro Committee would not be deductible.

(c) **Trusts and Certain Fraternal Organizations**

Transfers to trustees and lodges can qualify for the IRC § 2055 deduction, but "only if such contributions or gifts are to be used . . . exclusively for religious, charitable, scientific, literary, or educational purposes, or for the prevention of cruelty to children or animals." [IRC § 2055(a)(3)] Like the charitable corporations, the trusts and lodges may not be engaged in influencing legislation or participating in a campaign for or against a candidate for public office. [*Id.*, Reg. § 20.2055–1(a)(3)]

Example: Fred's will makes a cash bequest to the Loyal Order of Water Buffaloes, a fraternal society operating under the lodge system, to be added to the lodge's college scholarship fund. Because the bequest requires that the gift be used exclusively for educational purposes, the bequest is deductible under IRC § 2055.

(d) Veterans' Organizations

Transfers to or for the use of any Veterans' organization incorporated under federal law are eligible for the IRC § 2055 deduction, provided that no part of the organization's net earnings inure to the benefit of a private shareholder or individual. [IRC § 2055(a)(4); Reg. § 20.2055–1(a)(4)]

(2) Indefinite Charitable Bequests

In some cases, decedents direct their personal representatives to pay a portion of the estate to one or more charitable organizations selected by the personal representatives. Such indefinite charitable bequests qualify for the IRC § 2055 deduction provided either the testamentary instrument or local law restricts the class of permissible recipients to organizations that are charities within the meaning of IRC § 2055(a). [Rev. Rul. 69–285, 1969–1 C.B. 222] Thus, an indefinite charitable bequest phrased along the lines of "I direct my Personal Representative to pay $100,000 to any charitable organization(s) of his or her choosing, provided that any such organization is an organization described in section 2055 of the Internal Revenue Code of 1986, as amended" should be sufficient.

b) Split–Interest Transfers

Where a bequest is split between a charity and another, non-charitable beneficiary (typically, an individual), complicated valuation issues can arise. Determining the proper amount of the deduction proves even trickier where the charity's interest is contingent or subject to a prior interest of a non-charitable beneficiary. What is the proper amount of the deduction, for instance, where a decedent bequeaths a life estate in income-producing property to an individual followed by a remainder to the charity that vests only if another individual is not then living? Congress, especially sensitive to these issues, enacted significant limitations on the ability to deduct so-called **"split-interest" transfers**.

(1) General Rule

If property is to be enjoyed by both a charity and another, non-charitable beneficiary, the charitable deduction is generally *disallowed*. [IRC § 2055(e)(2)]

Example (1): One of the assets included in Zuzu's gross estate is Blackacre, a parcel of undeveloped real property. Zuzu's will devises a life estate in Blackacre to Janie, with the remainder passing to Charity, an organization described in IRC § 2055(a). Zuzu's estate may not deduct the value of the remainder interest passing to Charity.

Example (2): Same facts as Example (1), except that Zuzu's will devises the remainder to Pete if he is then living. If Pete is not then living, the remainder interest shall pass to Charity. If Zuzu dies with Pete surviving, Zuzu's estate may not deduct the value of the contingent remainder interest passing to Charity.

(2) Exceptions

There are four situations where a split-interest transfer will be deductible under IRC § 2055. Even if one of these situations is present, however, the amount of the deduction is limited to the present value of the interest that passes to the charity.

(a) Transfers Described in IRC § 170(f)(3)(B)

Split-interest transfers of property described in IRC § 170(f)(3)(B) remain eligible for the IRC § 2055 deduction. [IRC § 2055(e)(2)] IRC § 170(f)(3)(B) lists three types of transfers. The first type of transfer is the contribution of a "remainder interest in a personal residence or farm." [IRC § 170(f)(3)(B)(i)] Thus, where the § 2055(a) charity receives a direct remainder interest in a personal residence or farm, a charitable contribution deduction is available.

Example (1): Yoko's gross estate includes Blackacre, a parcel of real property on which her principal residence sat. Yoko's will gives her son, Sean, a life estate in Blackacre, with the remainder to Charity, an organization described in IRC § 2055(a). Yoko's estate can deduct the value of Charity's remainder interest under IRC § 2055.

Example (2): Same facts as Example (1), except that Yoko's vacation home (not her principal residence) sits on Blackacre. Yoko's estate can deduct the value of Charity's remainder interest, for the statute merely requires a contribution of a remainder interest in *a* personal residence, not the contributor's *principal* residence. [Reg. § 20.2055–2(e)(2)(ii)]

Example (3): Same basic facts as Example (1), except that Yoko devises Blackacre to a new trust that gives Sean a right to occupy the home for his life. At Sean's death, the trust will terminate and the remainder will be distributed to Charity. Yoko's estate cannot claim an IRC § 2055 deduction for the value of Charity's remainder interest, because Charity receives a remainder interest in a trust and not a remainder interest in a personal residence or farm. This is because the trustee could sell the residence and invest the proceeds in different assets. [Reg. § 20.2055–2(e)(2)(ii)]

The second type of transfer is the contribution of an *undivided* portion of the decedent's entire interest in property. [IRC § 170(f)(3)(B)(ii)] This means the decedent must leave the charity a fraction or percentage of "each and every substantial interest or right owned by the decedent in such property and must extend over the entire term of the decedent's interest in such property." [Reg. § 20.2055–2(e)(2)(i)]

Example (1): Bill's gross estate includes an apartment building that he owned in fee simple absolute. Bill's will gives Kendra a life estate in the building and the remainder to Charity, an organization described in IRC § 2055(a). Bill's estate cannot deduct the value of Charity's remainder interest because Charity does not received an undivided portion of both the life estate and the remainder interest. [IRC § 2055(e)(2)]

Example (2): Same facts as Example (1), except that Bill's will gives Kendra an 80% tenancy in common interest in the building, leaving the remaining 20%

tenancy in common interest to Charity. Bill's estate can deduct the value of Charity's tenancy in common interest. [IRC §§ 170(f)(3)(B)(ii); 2055(a); Reg. § 20.2055–2(e)(2)(i)]

Example (3):   Same facts as Example (1), except that prior to death, Bill transferred a life estate in the building to Kelly, retaining a reversion. Bill's will bequeaths one-half of the reversion to Kendra and the other half to Charity. Bill's estate cannot deduct the value of Charity's one-half reversionary interest because an interest in the building already passed from Bill to Kelly (the life estate), a non-charitable beneficiary. An undivided portion of Bill's entire interest in the property does not pass to Charity. [Reg. § 20.2055–2(e)(2)(i)]

Example (4):   Same facts as Example (1), except that Bill only owns a twenty-year term interest in the building and dies with fifteen years remaining on the term. His will devises one-half of the remaining term interest to Kendra and the other half to Charity. Bill's estate can deduct the value of Charity's one-half term interest in the building because Bill entire interest in the building at all times was the term interest and he bequeathed Charity an undivided portion of that interest. [Reg. § 20.2055–2(e)(2)(i)]

The third type of transfer is a "qualified conservation contribution" of property. [IRC § 170(f)(3)(B)(iii)] In this context, the term typically refers to the charitable contribution of a remainder interest in real property exclusively for "conservation purposes." [IRC § 170(h)(1)–(2)] Conservation purposes include, among other things, preservation for public outdoor recreation, protection of natural wildlife habitats, preservation of certain open spaces, and the preservation of historic lands and historic structures. [IRC § 170(h)(4)(A)]

(b) Charitable Remainder Trusts

Perhaps the most significant exception to the deduction disallowance for split-interest transfers is the charitable remainder trust. Generally, a **charitable remainder trust** has the following features: [IRC §§ 664; 2055(e)(2)(A)]

First: a fixed amount (or fixed percentage of trust assets) ranging from 5% to 50% of the initial value of the trust's corpus is paid at least annually to the non-charitable beneficiary for his or her life or for a term not to exceed twenty years;

Second: at the end of the trust term, the remainder interest passes to one or more qualified charities;

Third: the present value of the charity's remainder interest (using annuity tables and assumed interest rates computed by the Service under the rules of IRC § 7520) is at least 10% of the value of the property transferred to the trust; and

Fourth: no other payments will be made to any other person.

Example (1): Andy's will bequeaths $100,000 to a new trust that will pay income to Flo for Flo's life. At Flo's death, the trust will terminate and the corpus will be paid to Charity, an organization described in IRC § 2055(a). Based on Flo's life expectancy, the present value of Charity's remainder interest exceeds $10,000. Andy's estate may not claim a deduction for the value of Charity's remainder interest. The trust does not meet the requirements of a charitable remainder trust because Flo is entitled to receive the trust's income and not a fixed amount or a fixed percentage of the value of the trust's assets. [IRC § 664(d)(1)(A)]

Example (2): Same facts as Example (1), except that the trust will pay $3,000 annually to Flo for Flo's life. Andy's estate may not claim a deduction for the value of Charity's remainder interest. The trust does not meet the requirements of a charitable remainder trust, for although Flo is entitled to receive a fixed amount annually, that amount is outside the permissible range of 5% to 50% of the initial fair market value of the trust's assets (in this case, between $5,000 and $50,000).

Example (3): Same facts as Example (1), except that the trust will pay $20,000 annually to Flo for Flo's life. Because of the high annual payment to Flo and her remaining life expectancy, the fair market value of Charity's remainder interest, computed under the principles of IRC § 7520, is $8,000. Andy's estate may not claim a deduction for the value of Charity's remainder interest. The trust does not meet the requirements of a charitable remainder trust, for although Flo is entitled to receive a fixed amount annually that is within the permissible range (in this case, between $5,000 and $50,000), the fair market value of Charity's remainder interest is less than 10% of the value of the property transferred to the trust (here, $10,000).

Example (4): Same facts as Example (1), except that the trust will pay $7,000 annually to Flo for Flo's life. In addition, the trust gives the trustee the power to appoint corpus to Percy, another individual, in the trustee's discretion. Andy's estate may not claim a deduction for the value of Charity's remainder interest. The trust does not meet the requirements of a charitable remainder trust because there is at least one permissible beneficiary beyond Flo and Charity (namely Percy).

Charitable remainder trusts are common estate planning devices, but in most cases, they are created during the donor's life; testamentary charitable remainder trusts are somewhat rare.

i) Charitable Remainder Annuity Trusts (CRATs)

Charitable remainder trusts come in two forms: the "charitable remainder annuity trust" and the "charitable remainder unitrust." Under a **charitable remainder annuity trust** (or "CRAT"), the non-charitable beneficiary receives a fixed annuity amount paid at least annually. [IRC § 664(d)(1)] The amount payable each year to the non-charitable beneficiary of a CRAT does not vary with the increase or decrease in the value of the trust's assets.

Example: Hope's will bequeathed $1 million to a new trust that will pay $70,000 annually to Faith or Faith's estate for a term of 20 years. At the end of the 20–year term, the trust will terminate and the remaining trust property will be distributed to Charity, an organization described in IRC § 2055(a). Because the payment to Faith is a fixed amount equal to seven percent of the trust's initial value and payable annually for a term not in excess of 20 years, Hope's estate will be entitled to an IRC § 2055 deduction in an amount equal to the present value of Charity's remainder interest, provided that the present value is worth at least $100,000 (10% of the $1 million transferred to the trust at formation). This trust is an example of a CRAT.

Computation of the present value of the remainder interest depends primarily upon the assumed rate of growth of the CRAT's assets (determined under IRC § 7520), the length of the trust term, and the number of payments expected to be made during each year of the term. For instance, assuming the IRC § 7520 rate in the month the trust was established was 7.4%, the fair market value of the remainder interest in this Example would be $239,836. Because this figure exceeds 10% of the initial value of the trust's assets at formation, Hope's estate would be entitled to an IRC § 2055 deduction in the amount of $239,836.

ii) Charitable Remainder Unitrusts (CRUTs)

Under a **charitable remainder unitrust** (or "CRUT"), the non-charitable beneficiary receives a fixed percentage of the net fair market value of the trust assets, as determined annually. [IRC § 664(d)(2)] Unlike the CRAT, the amount payable each year to the non-charitable beneficiary of a CRUT will increase or decrease with the value of the trust's assets and undistributed income.

Example: Art's will bequeaths $1 million to a new trust that will pay to Bob or Bob's estate for a term of 20 years an amount equal to 7% of the annual net fair market value of the trust corpus. At the end of the 20–year term, the trust will terminate and the remaining trust property will be distributed to Charity, an organization described in IRC § 2055(a). Because the payment to Bob is a fixed percentage of the annual net fair market value of the trust's assets and payable annually for a term not in excess of 20 years, Art's estate will be entitled to an IRC § 2055 deduction in an amount equal to the present value of Charity's remainder interest, provided that the present value is worth at least $100,000 (10% of the $1 million given to the trust at formation). This trust is an example of a CRUT.

Here, too, computation of the present value of the remainder interest depends primarily upon the assumed rate of growth of the CRUT's assets (determined under IRC § 7520), the length of the trust term, and the number of payments expected to be made during each year of the term. Assuming again that the IRC § 7520 rate in the month the trust was established was 7.4%, the fair market value of the remainder interest in this Example would be $214,892. Because this figure exceeds 10% of the initial value of the trust's assets at formation, Art's estate would be entitled to an IRC § 2055 deduction in the amount of $214,892.

Notice that the value of the remainder interest in this CRUT (and, thus, the amount of the charitable deduction) is less than the value of the remainder interest in the CRAT example, even though most of the basic terms of the two trusts are identical. This is because of the assumption that the trust assets will grow over time, thus increasing the amounts the CRUT will pay to Bob each year.

iii) Net Income Makeup Charitable Remainder Unitrusts (NIMCRUTs)

Some estate planners take advantage of a special rule in IRC § 664(d)(3). This rule permits a CRUT to pay the trust's income to the non-charitable beneficiary where the amount of income is less than the amount normally required to be paid (a fixed percentage of the value of the trust's assets). Then, in later years, when the trust's income exceeds the amount required to be paid to the non-charitable beneficiary, the excess income is paid to the non-charitable beneficiary to make up for the amount that should have been paid in the earlier year when trust income was less than the required distribution amount. A trust with this flexible feature is called a **net income with makeup charitable remainder unitrust** (or "NIMCRUT").

Example: Candy's will bequeaths $1 million to a new trust that will pay to Daisy or Daisy's estate each year for a term of 20 years an amount equal to the lesser of the "unitrust amount" or the "income amount." The unitrust amount equals 7% of the annual net fair market value of the trust corpus. The income amount equals the trust's income for that year. In addition, if the income amount in any given year exceeds the unitrust amount, the trust will pay to Daisy or Daisy's estate that year an amount equal to such excess to the extent that the aggregate of the amounts paid in prior years was less than the aggregate unitrust amounts from such prior years. At the end of the 20–year term, the trust will terminate and the remaining trust property will be distributed to Charity. This trust qualifies as a NIMCRUT, so Candy's estate will be entitled to an IRC § 2055 deduction in an amount equal to the present value of Charity's remainder interest, provided that the present value of that remainder interest is worth at least $100,000 (10% of the $1 million given to the trust at formation).

In the third year of the trust term, the unitrust amount is $80,000 but the income amount is only $60,000. The proper amount payable to Daisy in the third year is $60,000.

In the fourth year of the trust term, the unitrust amount is $85,000 and the income amount is $90,000. The proper amount payable to Daisy in the fourth year is $90,000, which represents the $85,000 unitrust amount plus a $5,000 makeup distribution to partially atone for the $20,000 shortfall in payment from the third year.

In the fifth year of the trust term, the unitrust amount is $90,000 and the income amount is $120,000. The proper amount payable to Daisy in the fifth year is $105,000, consisting of the $90,000 unitrust amount plus a final $15,000 makeup distribution to complete the remaining shortfall from the third year. The undistributed income is added to the corpus of the trust.

iv)   Powers of Appointment in a Charitable Remainder Trust

No one should hold a power to consume, invade, or appropriate the property of a charitable remainder trust for the benefit of any individual, including the non-charitable beneficiary. The existence of such a power violates the requirements for a valid charitable remainder trust and, thus, jeopardizes the IRC § 2055 deduction. [IRC §§ 664(d)(1)(B); 664(d)(2)(B); 2055(e)(2)] But if such a power goes unexercised and is completely terminated prior to the date the decedent's estate is required to file the estate tax return, the termination shall be treated as a valid disclaimer of the power under IRC § 2518. [IRC § 2055(a), flush] That, in turn, means that the power will be deemed to have never existed, allowing the decedent's estate to claim the IRC § 2055 deduction assuming all other requirements are met. If the power goes unexercised because of the power-holder's death, the value of the trust property will be included in the power-holder's gross estate under IRC § 2041(a)(2) if the power constitutes a general power of appointment. [*See supra* I. A. 3. c) for a discussion of IRC § 2041] But the power-holder's estate will be entitled to an offsetting IRC § 2055 deduction, as though the power-holder transferred the property to the charitable remainder trust. [IRC § 2055(b)]

Example: Cubby's will created a CRAT. The trust was to provide Annette with a fixed annuity amount for her life, followed by a remainder to Charity, an organization described in IRC § 2055(a). Cubby's will also gave Annette the power to appoint the trust corpus to anyone she chose. Annette died five months after Cubby, never having exercised her power over the CRAT corpus. Cubby's estate can claim a charitable contribution deduction for the value of Charity's remainder interest. Although Anne's power to invade the trust corpus violates the requirements of a valid CRAT, the power completely terminated before Cubby's estate tax return was due and the power went unexercised. [IRC § 2055(a)] Because the power held by Annette at death was a general power of appointment, Annette's gross estate includes the value of the trust property as of the date of her death. [IRC § 2041(a)(2)] Annette's estate can claim an offsetting IRC § 2055 deduction for the value of the trust property, however. [IRC § 2055(b)]

v) Charitable Remainder Trusts and the Alternate Valuation Date

Where the non-charitable beneficiary of a charitable remainder trust dies within six months following the decedent's death, use of the alternate valuation date under IRC § 2032 could produce a curious result. Since the annuity or unitrust interest is no longer in the picture at the time of the alternate valuation date (six months after the decedent's death), presumably the proper amount of the IRC § 2055 deduction would be the value of the entire trust corpus. In applying the alternate valuation date, however, contingencies that occur after death (like the death of the annuity or unitrust beneficiary) are disregarded in valuing the proper amount of the IRC § 2055 deduction. [IRC § 2032(b)] Consequently, the alternate valuation date election will reflect only a decline in the real value of the trust assets in the six months following death that is not due to the mere lapse of time.

> *Example:* Maude's will created a CRUT. The trust was to provide Ned with a fixed percentage of the annual net fair market value of the trust's assets for his life, followed by a remainder to Charity, an organization described in IRC § 2055(a). Ned died four months after Maude. Maude's estate validly elected to apply the alternate valuation date under IRC § 2032. Maude's estate can claim a charitable contribution deduction under IRC § 2055 only for the value of Charity's remainder interest as of the date of her death (i.e., while Ned was still alive and expected to live out his anticipated life expectancy), with an adjustment only for any decline in value of the trust assets in the six months following Maude's death not due to the mere lapse of time.

(c) **Charitable Lead Trusts**

Although testamentary charitable remainder trusts are somewhat rare, testamentary "charitable lead trusts" are even less common, though still useful for some taxpayers. Under a **charitable lead trust**, the annual payments are made to the charitable organization with the remainder passing to one or more non-charitable beneficiaries. All other requirements applicable to charitable remainder trusts also apply to charitable lead trusts. [IRC § 2055(e)(2)(B)]

> *Example:* Abbott's will bequeaths $1 million to a trust that will pay $70,000 annually to Charity, an organization described in IRC § 2055(a), for a term of 15 years. At the end of the term, the trust will terminate and the remaining trust property will be distributed to Costello or Costello's estate. This is

an example of a charitable lead trust for which a deduction under IRC § 2055 is allowed.

The amount of the deduction is the fair market value of Charity's lead interest. As one would expect, the fair market value of that lead interest will be $760,164, assuming the IRC § 7520 rate in the month the trust was established was 7.4% (the difference between the $1 million transferred to the trust and the value of the remainder interest, determined in the previous CRAT example to be $239,836).

(d) Pooled Income Funds

Even more rare are "pooled income funds." In a **pooled income fund**, two or more donors agree to contribute property to a single fund administered by the charity. The fund will pay an income interest to one or more persons and, at the end of the term, the remainder will pass to the charity. [IRC § 642(c)(5)] Because most donors prefer to select their own fund managers and do not want to pool funds with others, pooled income funds are generally less attractive. Nonetheless, they are an exception to the general rule of disallowance for split-interest transfers. [IRC § 2055(e)(2)(A)]

4. Marital Bequests [IRC § 2056]

Since the early 1980s, decedents (or at least their estates) have enjoyed an unlimited marital deduction. [IRC § 2056(a)] Thus, if a decedent leaves his or her entire estate to the surviving spouse, the taxable estate will be zero, since the gross estate will be reduced by an offsetting marital deduction. Of course, when the surviving spouse dies, any amounts not consumed will be subject to inclusion in the surviving spouse's estate. Accordingly, the marital deduction is considered a *deferral* of estate tax, not a *forgiveness* of estate tax.

a) The Terminable Interest Rule

If the marital deduction was as simple as described above, however, it would be very easy to convert *deferral* of tax into *forgiveness*: the deceased spouse could leave his or her entire estate in trust for the benefit of the surviving spouse and, at the surviving spouse's death, the remainder would pass to those beneficiaries selected by the first deceased spouse. The estate of the first spouse to die would be very small (the marital deduction would offset all but the value of the remainder interest, which could be very small if the trustee is authorized to make generous distributions to the surviving spouse) and would likely pay no estate tax, and nothing would be included in the surviving spouse's gross estate because the surviving spouse has no input as to how the remainder shall pass. IRC § 2056(b)(1) anticipates this strategy and blocks it by the "terminable interest rule."

(1) Generally

The **terminable interest rule** states that if property is placed in trust for the benefit of the surviving spouse and will pass to someone selected by the decedent upon the death of the surviving spouse, *no marital deduction is allowed.* [IRC § 2056(b)(1)] More precisely, no marital deduction is allowed where, due to the lapse of time or on the occurrence (or failure to occur) of an event or contingency, the interest in property passing from the decedent to the surviving spouse will terminate, causing the interest to pass to another (for less than an adequate and full consideration in money or money's worth) who may possess or enjoy the property after the termination of the surviving spouse's interest. [*Id.*] It is helpful to break out the terminable interest rule into its component parts:

Element #1:	due to the lapse of time or on the occurrence (or failure to occur) of an event or contingency,
Element #2:	the interest in property passing from the decedent to the surviving spouse will terminate,
Element #3:	causing the interest to pass to another for less than an adequate and full consideration in money or money's worth
Element #4:	who may possess or enjoy the property after the termination of the surviving spouse's interest.

Example (1): Henry's will leaves his entire estate in trust. The trustee is required to pay the income from the trust property to Henry's spouse, Catherine, for her life. At her death, the trust will terminate and the remainder will be paid to Henry's child, Mary, or to Mary's estate. The terminable interest rule applies because Catherine's interest in the trust assets will terminate at her death and the trust property will pass for no consideration to Mary. [IRC § 2056(b)(1)] Accordingly, Henry's estate cannot claim a marital deduction for any portion of the value of the property passing to the trust. [*Id.*] Upon Catherine's death, no portion of the trust property will be included in her gross estate since she had no power to control the disposition of any of the trust assets.

Example (2): Same facts as Example (1), except that the trustee is required to pay the income from the trust property to Henry's child, Mary, for her life. At Mary's death, the trust will terminate and the remainder will be paid to Henry's spouse, Catherine or to Catherine's estate. The terminable interest rule does not apply on these facts because the interest in property passing from Henry to Catherine (the vested remainder interest in the trust) does not terminate. If Catherine dies before Mary, Catherine has the power to determine who shall receive the vested remainder interest, so the interest is not considered to terminate at Catherine's death.

Example (3): Ulysses' estate included the rights to a patent that had a remaining life of five years. Ulysses' will left the patent to his surviving spouse, Penelope, and his son, Telemachus, as equal tenants in common. Ulysses' estate may claim a marital deduction for the value of Penelope's tenancy in common interest since it is not a terminable interest. Although Penelope's interest will terminate in five years, Telemachus's interest in the patent will expire at the same time, so no one will possess or enjoy the patent once Penelope's interest terminates. [Reg. § 20.2056(b)–1(g) (ex. 6)]

(2) Exceptions

There are four exceptions to the terminable interest rule. Three of these four exceptions are justified on the grounds that the marital deduction property will be subject to tax upon the death of the surviving spouse (thus ensuring a mere *deferral* of tax). The fourth exception is justified on the grounds that the remainder will pass to charity.

(a) Surviving Spouse Holds a General Power of Appointment

The first exception applies where the surviving spouse holds a general power of appointment over the transferred property. [IRC § 2056(b)(5)] There are four elements to this exception:

Element #1:	the surviving spouse is entitled to all of the income from the transferred property for life;
Element #2:	such income is payable at least annually;
Element #3:	the surviving spouse holds a power of appointment over the property that is exercisable in favor of the surviving spouse or the surviving spouse's estate; and
Element #4:	no one else holds a power to appoint the property to anyone other than the surviving spouse.

Because the property subject to the general power of appointment will be included in the surviving spouse's gross estate under IRC § 2041, IRC § 2056(b)(5) ensures that the subject property will ultimately be subject to wealth transfer taxes unless consumed by the surviving spouse. If the surviving spouse exercises the power of appointment in his or her favor before death, the property will be subject to estate tax under IRC § 2033. And if the surviving spouse exercises the power in favor of another prior to death, the appointment will be subject to federal gift tax under IRC § 2514. [*See* II. C. 1.] No matter what the surviving spouse does, then, some form of federal wealth transfer tax will eventually come into play with respect to the property subject to the IRC § 2056(b)(5) exception.

Example (1): Henry's will leaves his entire estate in trust. The trustee is required to pay the income from the trust property to Henry's spouse, Anne, for her life. At her death, the trust will terminate and the remainder will be paid to Henry's child, Elizabeth. In addition, Anne holds a power to appoint the trust corpus during her life to anyone she chooses. The terminable interest rule does not apply because Anne holds a general power of appointment over the trust property. Accordingly, Henry's estate may claim a marital deduction for the value of the property passing to the trust. [IRC § 2056(a), (b)(5)] Upon Anne's death, the then-remaining trust corpus will be included in her gross estate under IRC § 2041, meaning the trust assets will ultimately be subject to estate tax.

Example (2): Same facts as Example (1), except that Anne may only exercise her appointment power in her will (i.e., she holds a testamentary general power of appointment). The result is unchanged: Henry's estate may claim a marital deduction under IRC § 2056(b)(5) and the remaining trust corpus will be included in Anne's gross estate at her death.

(b) Life Insurance or Annuities with a General Power of Appointment

The second exception is for life insurance or annuity payments to be paid in two or more installments where the surviving spouse is given a general power of appointment over the payments. [IRC § 2056(b)(6)] In general, there are four elements to this exception:

Element #1:	the property consists of an interest in life insurance proceeds or annuity payments payable in installments at least annually beginning no later than 13 months following the decedent's death;
Element #2:	amounts are payable only to the surviving spouse during the surviving spouse's lifetime;
Element #3:	the surviving spouse holds a power of appointment over the property that is exercisable in favor of the surviving spouse or the surviving spouse's estate; and
Element #4:	no one else holds a power to appoint the property to anyone other than the surviving spouse.

Of the four exceptions to the terminable interest rule, this is perhaps the least common, although its premise is the same as the first exception: because the property will be included in the surviving spouse's gross estate under IRC § 2041, a deduction for the estate of the deceased spouse is allowed.

Example (1):   Henry's gross estate includes an insurance policy on his life. Henry's spouse, Jane, is the named beneficiary of the death benefit. Under the terms of the life insurance contract, the death benefit will be paid in 20 equal, annual installments, with interest. If Jane dies during this 20–year term, the remaining installments (plus interest) will be paid to Henry's child, Edward, or Edward's estate. The terminable interest rule applies because Jane's interest in the death benefit will terminate at her death and the remaining benefit will pass for no consideration to Edward or his estate. [IRC § 2056(b)(1)] Accordingly, Henry's estate cannot claim a marital deduction for any portion of the death benefit. [*Id.*] Upon Jane's death, no portion of the death benefit will be included in her gross estate since she had no power to control the disposition of the death benefit.

Example (2): Same facts as Example (1), except that Jane also holds a power to appoint all amounts payable under the life insurance contract to anyone Jane chooses. The terminable interest rule does not apply because Jane holds a general power of appointment over the death benefit. [IRC § 2056(b)(6)] Accordingly, Henry's estate may claim a marital deduction for the value of the death benefit. [IRC § 2056(a)] Upon Jane's death, the value of all remaining payments under the life insurance contract will be included in her gross estate under IRC § 2041, meaning that at least a portion of the death benefit will ultimately be subject to estate tax. [*See* I. A. 3. c) for a discussion of IRC § 2041.]

(c) Charitable Remainder Trusts

The third exception is for a trust that meets the definition of a charitable remainder trust and names the surviving spouse as the non-charitable beneficiary. [IRC § 2056(b)(8)] Here, the trust gives a lifetime annuity or unitrust interest to the surviving spouse and the remainder to charity. This exception has only the two elements described *supra* at I. B. 3. b) (2) (b):

Element #1:	the trust satisfies the requirements of a charitable remainder annuity trust or charitable remainder unitrust, as set forth in IRC § 664; and
Element #2:	the surviving spouse is the non-charitable beneficiary of the trust.

This is the one exception that allows for complete forgiveness of estate tax, but that is because the property will ultimately pass to a charitable organization. If an unmarried decedent can reduce his or her taxable estate to zero by leaving everything to charity, a married couple should be allowed to do the same. Technically, the estate of the first spouse to die will claim a marital deduction for the surviving spouse's life interest and a charitable deduction for the remainder interest. Together, these interests equal the value of the property placed in the trust.

Example: Henry's will leaves his entire estate in trust. The trustee is required to pay to Henry's spouse, Katherine, an amount equal to 8% of the initial fair market value of the trust's property annually for her life. At her death, the trust will terminate and the remainder will be paid to Charity, an organization described in IRC § 2055(a). The terminable interest rule does not apply, assuming the trust meets the other requirements of a charitable remainder trust (i.e., that the fair market value of Charity's remainder interest is worth at least 10% of the initial value of the trust property). [*See* I. B. 3. b) (2) (b)] Accordingly, Henry's estate may claim a marital deduction for the value of Katherine's interest as the non-charitable beneficiary. [IRC § 2056(a), (b)(8)] Furthermore, Henry's estate may claim a charitable deduction for the value of Charity's remainder interest. [IRC § 2055(a), (e)(2)(A)] In sum, then, Henry's estate will deduct the full value of the property passing to the trust. Upon Katherine's death, no portion of the trust property will be included in her gross estate, for she lacks the power to control the disposition of any part of the trust corpus or income. The IRC § 2056(b)(8) exception to the terminable interest rule thus achieves a complete *forgiveness* of tax, but only because the property ultimately passes to Charity.

(d) Qualified Terminable Interest Property (QTIP)

The final exception is for trusts or other property transfers that give the surviving spouse a "qualifying income interest" for life and where the personal representative of the decedent elects on the estate tax return to treat the trust property as **qualified terminable interest property** (or "QTIP," for short). [IRC § 2056(b)(7)]

A **qualifying income interest** has three components [IRC § 2056(b)(7)(B)(ii)]:

Element #1:	the surviving spouse is entitled to all of the income from the property for life;
Element #2:	such income is payable at least annually; and
Element #3:	no one (not even the surviving spouse) holds a power to appoint any portion of the property to anyone but the surviving spouse.

Most commonly, transfers of qualified terminable interest property occur in trust. Where all of the requirements are met and the personal representative makes the QTIP election, the estate of the first spouse to die can deduct the entire value of the property transferred to the QTIP trust. [IRC § 2056(a)] This is because the entire qualified terminable interest property is treated as passing to the surviving spouse, not just the qualifying income interest. [IRC § 2056(b)(7)(A)(i)] Upon the death of the surviving spouse, IRC § 2044 requires inclusion of the remaining QTIP trust property in the surviving spouse's gross estate. Thus, once again there is a mere *deferral* of tax and not a complete *forgiveness*.

Example (1): Henry's will leaves his entire estate in trust. The trustee is required to pay the income from the trust property at least annually to Henry's spouse, Joan, for her life. At her death, the trust will terminate and the remainder will be paid to Henry's child, Audrey. The trust instrument allows the trustee to distribute all or any portion of the trust corpus to Joan as needed for her maintenance, education, support, or health. But the trustee cannot make any other distributions to any other individual during Joan's lifetime. Henry's personal representative elects to treat the property transferred to the trust as qualified terminable interest property. Accordingly, Henry's estate may claim a marital deduction for the entire value of the property passing to the trust. [IRC § 2056(a), (b)(7)] Upon Joan's death, the then-remaining trust corpus will be included in her gross estate under IRC § 2044. Absent the inclusion rule of IRC § 2044, there would be no grounds for including the trust assets in Joan's gross estate, for she lacks any power to control the disposition, possession, or enjoyment of the trust assets. [*See* I. A. 3. c) for a discussion of powers of appointment.]

Example (2):   Same facts as Example (1), except that the trustee's power to invade corpus may be exercised for the benefit of Joan or Audrey. Henry's estate may not claim a marital deduction for any portion of the property passing to the trust because of the trustee's power to appoint the property to Audrey, regardless of whether such power is exercised. [IRC § 2056(b)(7)(B)(ii)(II)] This is a terminable interest with no exception. [IRC § 2056(b)(1)] When Joan dies, no portion of the trust property will be included in her gross estate because she lacks any power to control the disposition, possession, or enjoyment of the trust assets. This makes sense, for the value of the trust property has already been taxed to Henry's estate.

i)   Effect of Contingencies

If the surviving spouse's right to income is limited to a term of years or subject to termination upon the occurrence of a contingency (like remarriage), the spouse does not hold a qualifying income interest, meaning the decedent's estate may not make a QTIP election. [Reg. § 20.2056(b)–7(d)(3)(i)] However, if the surviving spouse's income interest is contingent on the personal representative making the QTIP election, the spouse's interest will not fail to be a qualified income interest solely because of such contingency. [*Id.*] This rule gives the decedent's personal representative maximum flexibility in post-mortem estate tax planning.

Example: Clark's will leaves his entire estate in trust. Clark's personal representative is given the discretion to make a QTIP election with respect to all or any portion of the trust. To the extent the personal representative makes the election with respect to trust property, the trustee is required to pay to Clark's wife, Lois, all of the income from that property at least annually. The income from any trust property with respect to which no election is made shall be accumulated and added to the trust's corpus. The trustee also holds a power to distribute trust corpus to Lois as needed for her maintenance, education, support, or health. At Lois' death, the remaining trust property will be distributed in equal shares to Clark's three children, Lex, Zod and Jimmy. The personal representative makes a QTIP election with respect to one-third of the trust property. Accordingly, the income from one-third of the trust's property is payable to Lois at least annually for her life. Clark's estate can claim a marital deduction for the value of one-third of the trust property under IRC § 2056(b)(7) even though Lois' qualifying income interest in one-third of the trust property is contingent on the personal representative making the QTIP election.

ii) Right to Reimbursement for Estate Tax Attributable to QTIP

As previously noted, IRC § 2044 requires the surviving spouse's gross estate to include the value of any property remaining in a QTIP trust established by the first spouse to die. The remainder of the QTIP trust, however, is usually not distributed to the surviving spouse's estate. This creates a hardship for the estate, for it has to pay extra estate tax without access to the trust funds. Accordingly, the personal representative can seek reimbursement from the beneficiaries of the QTIP trust to the extent the surviving spouse's estate must pay estate tax attributable to the inclusion of the QTIP trust assets in the gross estate. [IRC § 2207A(a)]

iii) Lifetime Dispositions of Qualifying Income Interests

If the surviving spouse disposes of any portion of the qualifying income interest, the surviving spouse will be treated for federal gift tax purposes as having transferred all interests in the qualified terminable interest property except for the qualifying income interest. [IRC § 2519; *see infra* II. C. 3.] Absent this rule, the surviving spouse could avoid gross estate inclusion of the qualified terminable interest property under IRC § 2044 because the surviving spouse would not hold the qualifying income interest at death. To the extent this deemed transfer results in the payment of gift tax, the surviving spouse has a right of recovery against the donee for the gift tax attributable to the property deemed transferred. [IRC § 2207A(b)]

Example: Carol's will created a QTIP trust that gave her husband, Mike, a qualifying income interest for life and the remainder (payable at Mike's death) in equal shares to her three daughters. Mike transferred one-half of his qualifying income interest to Alice as a gift at a time when the qualifying income interest was worth $200,000 and the remainder interest in the QTIP trust was worth $300,000 (the total value of the trust property was $500,000). Mike made a gift transfer of $100,000 (one-half of the value of the income interest) to Alice under IRC § 2511 and another gift transfer of $300,000 (the value of the entire trust property less the value of the qualifying income interest) to Alice under IRC § 2519.

iv) Practical Considerations

A QTIP trust is a common technique for substantial estates where the first spouse to die wants to leave his or her estate for the benefit of the surviving spouse but is hesitant to make an outright bequest of property to the surviving spouse for fear of losing control over the disposition of the property at the surviving spouse's death. If the surviving spouse receives property from an outright bequest, the surviving spouse is free to dispose of such property at his or her death however the surviving spouse sees fit—a new paramour, a new spouse, new children, some combination of the foregoing, or something altogether different. By placing the property into a QTIP trust, the decedent spouse can dictate how the remaining trust property should be distributed at the surviving spouse's death. It is most common to see QTIP trusts used for estates where the spouses have children from a prior relationship, but they can be used in any setting.

(3) Interests Conditioned on Survival

It is common for a will to condition a beneficiary's gift on the beneficiary surviving the decedent for a stipulated period of time. These so-called "survivorship" clauses avoid back-to-back probates of the same assets where the decedent and the beneficiary die close in time. A **survivorship clause** applicable to a marital gift technically poses problems with the terminable interest rule, for the surviving spouse's interest will terminate at death and the property will pass to another if the surviving spouse does not outlast the applicable survivorship period. To accommodate survivorship clauses, a bequest to a surviving spouse that terminates if the surviving spouse fails to survive the decedent for a period of up to six months will not violate the terminable interest rule if the surviving spouse actually survives the required period and the bequest does not terminate. [IRC § 2056(b)(3); Reg. § 20.2056(b)–3(a)]

Example (1): Elizabeth's will left a bequest to her spouse, Fred, on the condition that Fred survive for 90 days following Elizabeth's death. If Fred did not so survive Elizabeth, her will provided that the bequest would pass to Lamont or Lamont's estate. Fred was living 90 days after Elizabeth's death and thus received the bequest. Elizabeth's estate may claim a marital deduction for the value of the bequest to Fred since the survivorship exception to the terminable interest rule under IRC § 2056(b)(3) applies.

Example (2): Same facts as Example (1), except that Fred's gift was conditioned on surviving the probate of Elizabeth's estate. The probate of Elizabeth's estate ended five months after Elizabeth's death. Fred was alive at that time, so he received the bequest. Elizabeth's estate may not claim a marital deduction even though Fred survived the required period. This is because the survival period lasted until the end of the probate process, which may or may not occur within six months of Elizabeth's death. Accordingly, Fred held a terminable interest to which the survivorship exception does not apply. The fact that the probate in fact ended within six months of Elizabeth's death does not change this result. [Reg. § 20.2056(b)–3(b);–3(d)(ex. 4)]

(4) The Tainted Asset Rule

Where the interest passing to the surviving spouse may be satisfied out of a group of assets which includes an asset that would be nondeductible if it passed from the decedent to the surviving spouse (a "**tainted asset**"), the amount of the marital deduction is reduced by the value of the tainted asset. [IRC § 2056(b)(2)] In other words, it is presumed the tainted asset will be distributed to the surviving spouse, so its entire value reduces the amount of the marital deduction.

Example: George's gross estate consists of a parcel of land worth $800,000 and a right to the rents of an office building for a term of years, a right reserved by George when he transferred the building to his son, Lionel, as a gift six years before George's death. The right to the rents was worth $200,000 at the date of George's death, bringing the total value of his gross estate to $1 million. George's will leaves one-half of his estate to his wife, Louise, and the other half to Lionel. Under both the will and applicable local law, George's personal representative had the power to assign all or any portion of the right to rents to Louise in satisfaction of this bequest. The right to rents from the building for a term of years is a terminable interest with no exceptions, for Lionel will continue to possess and enjoy the building after the right to the rents terminates. [IRC § 2056(b)(1)] Under the tainted asset rule, therefore, the amount of the marital deduction available to George's estate is $300,000

($500,000 value for one-half of the estate less the value of the $200,000 tainted asset). [IRC § 2056(b)(2)] It does not matter whether all or any portion of the right to rents is in fact paid to Louise. [Reg. § 20.2056(b)–2(d)]

(5) The Executor Purchase Rule

No marital deduction is allowed where a terminable interest is, at the direction of the decedent, to be acquired by the personal representative for the surviving spouse. [IRC § 2056(b)(1)(C)] A deduction is disallowed even where no one will succeed to the surviving spouse's interest upon the death of the surviving spouse. There are no exceptions to this absolute prohibition on the deduction.

Example: Ray's will directs his personal representative to purchase a $200,000 annuity contract for the benefit of Ray's spouse, Debra. The contract will pay a fixed amount annually to Debra for her life. At her death, the annuity contract will end and no further payments will be made to any individual. Ray's estate may not claim a marital deduction for the $200,000 used to purchase the annuity. Furthermore, Ray's estate may not make a QTIP election with respect to the purchased annuity. [Reg. § 20.2056(b)–7(b)(1)(i)]

b) Credit Shelter Trusts

Married couples should not overuse the marital deduction. If spouses with substantial estates execute wills simply leaving all assets to the surviving spouse, there is a risk that the couple will waste the unified credit of the first spouse to die.

Example (1): Ralph and Alice, a married couple, have a $22 million estate and neither has made any taxable gifts. Assume either that the entire estate consists of community property or that each spouse owns exactly half of the value of the couple's assets. Also assume that the applicable exclusion amount in effect at all times relevant is $5 million and the applicable estate tax rate is 35%. Both Ralph's will and Alice's will provide that their estates shall pass to the spouse if the spouse is then living or, if the spouse is not then living, to other individuals. Ralph dies first. Because of the unlimited marital deduction, Ralph's applicable exclusion amount is lost:

Ralph's Estate	
Gross Estate	$11,000,000
Marital Deduction	(11,000,000)
Taxable Estate	0
Exemption	(5,000,000)
Amount Subject to Tax	0
Tax Due:	**0**

When Alice dies, her gross estate will consist of her own $11 million share of the estate plus Ralph's share of the estate, which she received by outright bequest at Ralph's death. But since Alice cannot claim Ralph's unused exemption, the tax owed by Alice's estate will be significant:

Alice's Estate	
Gross Estate	$22,000,000
Marital Deduction	(0)
Taxable Estate	$22,000,000
Exemption	(5,000,000)
Amount Subject to Tax	$17,000,000
Tax Due:	**$ 5,950,000**

The waste of one spouse's exclusion is rescued to some extent by IRC § 2010(c)(2), which provides that in the case of a surviving spouse, the applicable exclusion amount is the sum of the "basic exclusion amount" ($5 million, in these examples) and the "deceased spousal unused exclusion amount." IRC § 2010(c)(4) states that the deceased spousal unused exclusion amount is, generally, an amount equal to what was left of the first spouse's basic exclusion amount. In effect, the executor of the surviving spouse's estate may elect to add the unused exclusion amount of the first spouse to the surviving spouse's own exclusion amount. The **"portability"** of the exclusion amounts between spouses ensures that the exclusion amounts of both spouses can be fully utilized.

Example (2):   Assume the same facts from Example (1), except that Alice's executor elects to add the "deceased spousal unused exclusion amount" to Alice's basic exclusion amount. Because Ralph's estate used no portion of his $5 million exclusion, the deceased spousal unused exclusion amount is $5 million. Alice's gross estate is unchanged, but her executor will add Ralph's unused exclusion ($5 million) to Alice's basic exclusion amount (also $5 million), effectively giving Alice a $10 million exclusion amount:

Alice's Estate	
Gross Estate	$22,000,000
Marital Deduction	(0)
Taxable Estate	$22,000,000
Exemption	(10,000,000)
Amount Subject to Tax	$12,000,000
Tax Due:	**$ 4,200,000**

Although the "portability election" appears to prevent waste of the exclusion amount of the first spouse to die, it is not a perfect remedy. For one thing, under current law the election is only available in 2011 and 2012, and to qualify for the election, the first spouse had to die "after December 31, 2010." [IRC § 2010(c)(4)] There is risk that the portability election may not be permanent. In addition, failure to use the first spouse's exclusion amount at the first spouse's death thwarts the ability to shift future appreciation in the value of assets out of the surviving spouse's gross estate, as discussed below.

Because of these limitations on the benefit of the portability election, estate planners often recommend a different technique that can fully utilize the applicable exclusion amount of the first spouse without substantively affecting the general dispositive scheme of leaving every-thing to the surviving spouse. This technique involves the use of a "credit shelter trust." Under a **credit shelter trust**, the estate of the first spouse to die is apportioned between two beneficiaries: that portion of the estate equal to the then-remaining exemption amount is allocated to the credit shelter trust and the balance passes to the marital deduction share (either outright to the surviving spouse or to a QTIP trust). The credit shelter trust typically provides the surviving spouse with access to income or principal as needed for the surviving spouse's maintenance, education, support, or health. Because the surviving spouse is not guaranteed the right to payments of income at least annually and all of the IRC § 2056(b)(1) elements are present, property passing to the credit shelter trust creates a terminable interest that does not qualify for the marital deduction. That is an acceptable result, since, by definition, the amount passing to the credit shelter trust will not be in excess of the first spouse's remaining exemption amount. Yet the surviving spouse has access to the property held by the credit shelter trust if needed for his or her support. To the extent the property is available to the surviving spouse if needed, the credit shelter trust is functionally similar to an outright bequest of the property to the surviving spouse.

The real benefit from the credit shelter trust technique occurs upon the death of the surviving spouse: because the surviving spouse's interest expires at death and because no marital deduction with respect to the credit shelter trust property was claimed by the estate of the first spouse to die, *no portion of the credit shelter trust estate is included in the surviving spouse's gross estate*, even if the value of the property held in the trust has appreciated substantially in value. Even without appreciation, the credit shelter trust would save the couple in this example a substantial amount of estate tax.

Example (3):   Assume that Ralph and Alice, the same married couple from Example (1), instead execute wills that make provision for a credit shelter trust and an outright marital gift. Each will provides that an amount equal to the decedent's then-remaining applicable exclusion amount will be transferred to a trustee to be held in trust for the benefit of the surviving spouse. The trust will provide the surviving spouse with access to principal and accumulated income as needed for the surviving spouse's maintenance, education, support, and health. At the surviving spouse's death, the trust will terminate and anything remaining in the trust will be distributed to other individuals named in the wills. Any amounts in excess of the deceased spouse's then-remaining applicable exclusion amount would pass outright to the surviving spouse. If the decedent's spouse is not then living, the entire estate will pass to other individuals named in the will. Ralph dies first. Under his will, $5 million (his remaining exemption amount) will pass to the credit shelter trust and the remaining $6 million will pass outright to Alice. The gift to the credit shelter trust will not qualify for the marital deduction because of the terminable interest rule in IRC § 2056(b)(1), but Ralph's estate will still owe no tax thanks to his applicable exclusion amount:

Ralph's Estate

Gross Estate	$11,000,000
Marital Deduction	(6,000,000)
Taxable Estate	$ 5,000,000
Exemption	(5,000,000)
Amount Subject to Tax	0
Tax Due:	**0**

When Alice dies, her gross estate will consist of her own $11 million share of the estate plus the $6 million outright bequest from Ralph. Importantly, however, no portion of the property remaining in the credit shelter trust will be included in Alice's gross estate, for she lacks any power to control the distribution, possession, or enjoyment of this property. This results in a total estate tax liability that is $1.75 million *less* than what was the case in Example (1) when Ralph's exemption was wasted:

Alice's Estate

Gross Estate	$17,000,000
Marital Deduction	(0)
Taxable Estate	$17,000,000
Exemption	(5,000,000)
Amount Subject to Tax	$12,000,000
Tax Due:	**$ 4,200,000**

The credit shelter trust technique is often utilized for married couples with a combined estate in excess of the exemption amount in order to reduce the estate tax bite upon the death of the surviving spouse. As Examples (2) and (3) show, the estate tax savings from the credit shelter trust is the same as the savings from a portability election where the value of the estate does not appreciate between the deaths of the spouses. If the assets do appreciate substantially in value between the deaths of the spouses (i.e., the surviving spouse lives for an extended period of time following the death of the first spouse), however, the potential estate tax savings from the credit shelter trust is much more significant.

Example (4): Our same Ralph and Alice are back, but this time assume that the value of the assets doubles between the time of Ralph's death and Alice's death (a reasonable assumption if Alice outlives Ralph for a number of years). If the couple do not use a credit shelter trust but take advantage of the portability election, they leave some benefit on the table:

Ralph's Estate

Gross Estate	$11,000,000
Marital Deduction	(11,000,000)
Taxable Estate	$ 0
Exemption	(5,000,000)
Amount Subject to Tax	0
Tax Due:	**0**

When Alice dies, her gross estate will consist of her own share of the estate (now worth $22 million by itself) plus Ralph's share of the estate (also now worth $22 million), which she received by outright bequest at Ralph's death. Here is Alice's estate tax bill:

Alice's Estate

Gross Estate	$44,000,000
Marital Deduction	(0)
Taxable Estate	$44,000,000
Exemption	(10,000,000)
Amount Subject to Tax	$34,000,000
Tax Due:	**$11,900,000**

Example (5): If instead Ralph and Alice utilized the credit shelter trust strategy, the estate tax savings would be even more significant. Once again, there is no estate tax due at Ralph's death, though this time his exemption amount is consumed:

Ralph's Estate

Gross Estate	$11,000,000
Marital Deduction	(6,000,000)
Taxable Estate	$ 5,000,000
Exemption	(5,000,000)
Amount Subject to Tax	$ 0
Tax Due:	**$ 0**

When Alice dies, her gross estate will consist of her own share of the estate (now worth $22 million, remember) plus the outright bequest from Ralph (assumed to have doubled to $12 million by Alice's death). Again, no portion of the property remaining in the credit shelter trust (which could be worth $10 million!) will be included in Alice's gross estate, for she lacks any power to control the distribution, possession, or enjoyment of this property. The use of the credit shelter trust thus saves almost $2 million in estate tax under these assumed facts:

Alice's Estate	
Gross Estate	$34,000,000
Marital Deduction	(0)
Taxable Estate	$34,000,000
Exemption	(5,000,000)
Amount Subject to Tax	$29,000,000
Tax Due:	**$10,150,000**

c) Interests That Pass to the Surviving Spouse

The IRC § 2056 deduction is available only where an interest in property passes to the surviving spouse from the decedent. [IRC § 2056(a)] There are seven ways for an interest in property to pass from the decedent: (1) a bequest or devise from the decedent [IRC § 2056(c)(1)]; (2) an inheritance from the decedent [IRC § 2056(c)(2)]; (3) a dower, curtesy, or other statutory interest taken as the surviving spouse [IRC § 2056(c)(3)]; (4) any lifetime transfer from the decedent [IRC § 2056(c)(4)]; (5) taking property held with the decedent as joint tenants with rights of survivorship [IRC § 2056(c)(5)]; (6) taking property pursuant to the exercise or non-exercise of a power of appointment held by the decedent [IRC § 2056(c)(6)]; and (7) receiving the death benefit from a policy of insurance on the decedent's life [IRC § 2056(c)(7)].

In addition, an interest in property passing to the surviving spouse is deductible under IRC § 2056 only to the extent that the value of that interest is included in the decedent's gross estate. [IRC § 2056(a)]

Example: Barney and Betty, a married couple, own their personal residence as joint tenants with rights of survivorship. At Barney's death, Betty receives a fee simple interest in the residence by operation of law as the surviving joint tenant. Because Barney's interest in the residence is deemed to pass to Betty at his death [IRC § 2056(c)(5)], Barney's estate may claim a marital deduction, but the amount of the deduction is limited to one-half of the value of the home because Barney's gross estate includes exactly one-half of the value of the home under IRC § 2040(b).

5. State Death Taxes [IRC § 2058]

Just as individuals can deduct state income taxes on the federal income tax return, an estate may deduct "**state death taxes**" (estate, inheritance, legacy, or succession taxes) actually paid to any state (or the District of Columbia) attributable to property included in the gross estate. [IRC § 2058(a)] Prior to 2005, estates could not claim a deduction for state death taxes paid; instead, they were entitled to a credit for the amount of such taxes paid, computed with reference to a graduated rate table in IRC § 2011(b). [IRC § 2011] Beginning in 2002, however, the amount of the credit was gradually reduced. The otherwise allowable credit was reduced by 25% for decedents dying in 2002, then by 50% for decedents dying in 2003, and then by 75% for decedents dying in 2004. [IRC § 2011(b)(2)] The credit disappeared altogether as of 2005 [IRC § 2011(f)], replaced instead by the IRC § 2058 deduction.

The deduction for state death taxes is unlimited. [IRC § 2058(a)] Under the old IRC § 2011 credit, there was a limitation on the maximum amount of state death taxes creditable against the federal estate tax otherwise due. [IRC § 2011(b)] While there is no such limitation on the IRC § 2058 deduction, the deduction is likely not as valuable to estates as the old IRC § 2011 credit, for while the credit would reduce federal estate tax liability dollar for dollar (a $100 credit would save $100 in estate tax), a deduction only saves tax at the marginal tax rate applicable to the estate, which is 35% under current law (a $100 deduction saves, at most, $35 in estate tax).

As was the case under the old IRC § 2011 credit, the state death taxes must actually be paid, generally within four years of filing the federal estate tax return. [IRC § 2058(b)(1)] Certain exceptions to this deadline apply in cases where the estate has received a notice of deficiency, where the estate has made a claim for refund, and where the estate has received extension of time to pay federal estate tax under IRC §§ 6161 or 6166. [IRC § 2058(b)(2)]

6.   The Former Deduction for Qualified Family–Owned Business Interests [IRC § 2057]

Prior to 2004, there was a fifth deduction for certain family-owned business interests under IRC § 2057. Originally an exclusion provision, special relief for family-owned business interests was introduced in 1997. The next year, the exclusion was converted to a deduction. Both the credit and the deduction proved to be remarkably complex.

Generally, if the personal representative elected to claim the benefit of IRC § 2057, two things happened. First, the estate was allowed a deduction of up to $675,000 for the value of the "qualified family-owned business interests" included in the gross estate. Second, if the estate claimed a full $675,000 deduction, the estate tax was computed as if the applicable exclusion amount (described below) were $625,000 *regardless of the year in which the decedent died.* This is a rather complicated way of saying that the effect of IRC § 2057 was to increase the exemption amount to $1.3 million. Since the exemption amount increased to $1.5 million beginning in 2004, the IRC § 2057 deduction became meaningless.

To qualify for the IRC § 2057 deduction, the estate had to meet several tests. For example, the adjusted value of the qualified family-owned business interests had to equal at least 50% of the value of the decedent's adjusted gross estate. Also, for at least five of the eight years preceding the decedent's death, the decedent or a member of the decedent's family must have owned and materially participated in the business. Further, the interest in the business had to pass to members of the decedent's family or to long-term employees, and the business had to continue operations under the ownership of three or fewer families. To ensure this last requirement was met, the estate was subject to a penalty if there was a prohibited change in the ownership of the entity following the decedent's death. Consequently, IRC § 2057 was really beneficial only where the decedent's children or long-term employees would actively manage the business for at least ten years following the decedent's death.

C. Computing Tax Liability

Having computed the taxable estate, one can then proceed to determine the liability for estate tax. This requires a calculation of "tentative tax liability" using the rate table in IRC § 2001 and then application of various credits to arrive at the final tax liability.

1. Tentative Tax Liability [IRC § 2001]

The estate's **tentative tax liability** is determined with reference to the rate table in IRC § 2001(c). The taxable estate is added to the "**adjusted taxable gifts**" (taxable gifts made in 1977 or later that are not subject to "re-inclusion" in the gross estate under IRC §§ 2035–2038). [IRC § 2001(b)] This sum is then applied to the rate table. The resulting tax is then reduced by any federal gift tax that would have been payable on gifts made in 1977 or later using the tax rates in effect at the date of the decedent's death, regardless of whether such gifts are re-included in the gross estate. [IRC § 2001(b)(2) and (g)]

Example (1): Danica made a taxable gift of $1 million several years prior to her death (but after 1976). No gift tax was payable on this gift, thanks to the unified credit available at that time. Her taxable estate amounted to $5 million. The amount with respect to which the tentative tax liability is computed is $6 million, the sum of the $1 million in adjusted taxable gifts plus the $5 million taxable estate. The tentative tax liability, therefore, is $2,080,800.

Example (2): Same facts as Example (1), except that Danica's taxable gift consisted of a remainder interest in a trust established by Danica and in which she retained an income interest for life. At her death, the $2 million value of the trust assets at Danica's death was included in her gross estate under IRC § 2036(a), which brought her taxable estate to $7 million. Because the $1 million taxable gift is includible in Danica's gross estate, the amount with respect to which the tentative tax liability is computed is $7 million, the sum of the adjusted taxable gifts (zero) plus the $7 million taxable estate. The tentative tax liability, therefore, is $2,430,800.

Example (3): Same facts as Example (1), except that $200,000 of federal gift tax was payable as a result of Danica's $1 million taxable gift. The tentative tax liability is $1,880,800, the excess of the $2,080,800 amount computed under the IRC § 2001(c) rate table over the $200,000 of gift tax payable with respect to the taxable gift.

Note that that federal estate tax rates currently begin at 18% and reach a maximum of 35% beginning in 2011. Like the federal income tax, the federal estate tax is progressive, meaning that the first few dollars in the taxable estate are subject to lower rates than the last few dollars. For example, the first dollar is taxed at 18%, but the one-millionth dollar is taxed at 35%.

Prior to 2003, if the sum of the taxable estate and adjusted taxable gifts exceeded $10 million, the benefit of the lower marginal tax rates was gradually phased-out; once the sum totaled just over $18 million, the tentative estate tax was simply a flat 55% (the maximum marginal estate tax rate prior to 2001). Although the phase-out of the graduated rates no longer happens under current law, the phase-out is scheduled to re-appear in 2013. [P.L. 107–16, § 901(a) (2001) as modified by P.L. 111–312, § 101(a)(1) (2010).]

2. Credits

As is the case with taxpayers and the income tax, estates prefer credits to deductions. A credit actually reduces the estate's tax liability dollar-for-dollar.

A deduction only reduces the tax base applied to the rate table in IRC § 2001. Put another way, the taxable estate of a super-wealthy decedent dying in 2011 would prefer a $1,000 credit to a $1,000 deduction since the credit will reduce the tax liability by $1,000, while the deduction will only reduce the tax liability by about $350 (this is because estates face a maximum 35% marginal tax rate).

The tentative estate tax computed under IRC § 2001(c) is reduced by six credits, but only two have special significance: (1) the unified credit (IRC § 2010); and (2) the credit for tax on prior transfers (IRC § 2013). Two other credit provisions are discussed to a limited extent below. Prior to 2005, the credit for state death taxes (IRC § 2011) was also a significant credit in that it diverted taxes from the federal government to the state governments. Its repeal as of 2005 has affected the revenues of several states that used to impose a tax equal to the maximum amount creditable under IRC § 2011. Finally, IRC § 2012 assures a credit for gift taxes paid on gifts made before 1977, an increasingly unlikely event. It is worth noting that none of the credits against the estate tax are refundable. Where credits exceed tentative tax liability, the estate does not receive a refund. At best, the liability for estate taxes is reduced to zero.

a) The Unified Credit [IRC § 2010]

Every estate is entitled to the "applicable credit amount" set forth in IRC § 2010(c). [IRC § 2010(a)] The applicable credit amount is equal to the IRC § 2001(c) tentative tax that would be imposed on the "applicable exclusion amount." Starting in 2011, computation of the applicable exclusion amount begins with the "basic exclusion amount." The basic exclusion amount is generally $5 million. [IRC § 2010(c)(3)(A)] As explained in I. B. 4. b), surviving spouses may elect to add the "deceased spousal unused exclusion amount" to the basic exclusion amount to arrive at the applicable exemption amount. The deceased spousal unused exclusion amount is generally equal to the remaining portion of the first spouse to die's basic exclusion amount (i.e., the portion of the exclusion that went "unused"). In case the basic exclusion amount in effect at the death of the first spouse is higher than the basic exclusion amount in effect at the death of the surviving spouse, the statute caps the deceased spousal unused exclusion amount to the basic exclusion amount in effect at the surviving spouse's death. [IRC § 2010(c)(4)] In effect, therefore, the highest possible applicable exclusion amount for the estate of a surviving spouse is $10 million (in 2011).

For most estates, however, the applicable exclusion amount will equal the basic exclusion amount. Accordingly, the applicable credit amount is $1,730,800, the IRC § 2001(c) tentative tax on $5 million. In effect, the first $5 million of the taxable estate for decedents dying in those years is exempt from tax. This amount is adjusted for inflation, but only in multiples of $10,000. [IRC § 2010(c)(3)(B)]

Example: Darin died in 2011 without ever having made a taxable gift and having never been married. His taxable estate was $7 million, and his tentative tax liability under IRC § 2001(c) was $2,430,800. Darin's estate will claim a $1,730,800 unified credit under IRC § 2010, reducing the estate tax liability to $700,000. This figure represents the tax on the $2 million excess of the $7 million taxable estate over the $5 million applicable exclusion amount.

Keep in mind that the applicable exclusion amount available at death is reduced by any lifetime taxable gifts. For instance, if an individual dies in 2011 having made a taxable gift of $100,000 in 1995, the taxable gift will be considered an "adjusted taxable gift" and thus will be combined with the taxable estate in computing the tentative tax liability (although the formula works so that the individual will not be taxed twice on the same gift). The bottom-line effect of the lifetime gift is that only $4.9 million of the taxable estate will be protected from estate tax. Although this might seem to discourage the use of lifetime gifts, consider the fact that the property gifted in 1995 may now be worth much more than its 1995 value of $100,000. [*See* III. D. 1. d) for a discussion of the tax-inclusive nature of the estate tax versus the tax-exclusive nature of the gift tax.]

Example: Elisha died in 2011, never having married. In 2000, she made a $200,000 taxable gift. No portion of the taxable gift property was included in Elisha's gross estate. Her taxable estate was $6 million. Elisha's tentative tax liability under IRC § 2001(c) was $2,150,800, the tax on $6.2 million (the sum of the $200,000 adjusted taxable gift plus the $6 million taxable estate). Elisha's estate will claim a $1,730,800 unified credit under IRC § 2010, reducing the estate tax liability to $420,000. This figure represents the tax on the $1.2 million excess of the $6.2 million on which tentative tax liability was computed minus the $5 million applicable exclusion amount. In effect, the lifetime gift utilized $200,000 of Elisha's applicable exclusion amount, leaving only $4.8 million of exemption to cover a $6 million taxable estate.

The unified credit is nonrefundable, for it is limited to the amount of the tax imposed under IRC § 2001. [IRC § 2010(d)] To the extent any portion of the applicable exclusion amount goes unused, it is wasted.

b) State Death Taxes [IRC § 2011]

As explained *supra* at I. B. 5., Congress phased-out the credit for state death taxes paid beginning in 2002. The credit disappeared altogether in 2005, when IRC § 2058 offered a deduction for state death taxes paid.

Historically, most states that imposed death taxes limited the amount of tax to the maximum amount of the IRC § 2011 credit. Thus, an estate's total tax liability was not increased. Effectively, that portion of the federal estate tax equal to the amount of the IRC § 2011 credit was paid to the state. That is why the death tax of most states was referred to as a "pick-up tax"—those states were simply "picking up" the amount of death taxes Congress was willing to credit against the federal tax liability. But the repeal of IRC § 2011 has left many states scrambling to make up for lost revenues. As of 2011, 16 states and the District of Columbia had a stand-alone estate or inheritance tax that survived the repeal of IRC § 2011. Twenty-eight of the other states have a pick-up tax that was effectively abolished when the IRC § 2011 was repealed. These states will either have to implement a stand-alone estate or inheritance tax or take some action to unlink their estate tax from the IRC § 2011 credit.

c) Tax on Pre–1977 Gifts [IRC § 2012]

It is possible for an individual to make a taxable gift and then have the gifted property "re-included" in the gross estate. *See supra* at I. A. 2. a) – d). Re-inclusion of gifted property is acceptable as long as there is some means for correcting the distortion that could occur if the decedent paid federal gift taxes on the prior taxable gifts. Even where gifted property is not re-included in the gross estate, the addition of adjusted taxable gifts in the determination of tentative tax liability requires that any gift tax previously payable on adjusted taxable gifts be accounted for in the computation of estate tax liability, else the decedent will be taxed a second time on the lifetime gift.

For gifts made after 1976, the correction is contained in the computation of tentative tax liability, for the amount of any gift tax payable on gifts made in 1977 or later is subtracted from the tax computed under the IRC § 2001(c) rate table in effect at the time of the decedent's death. [IRC § 2001(b)(2) and (g)] Subtracting that amount from tentative tax liability is the functional equivalent of crediting the gift tax payable against the tentative tax liability.

But for gifts made before 1977, there is no subtraction of gift tax payable under IRC § 2001. Instead, IRC § 2012 offers a nonrefundable credit for gift taxes payable on previously gifted property. Where it applies, IRC § 2012 offers a host of complex rules for determining the amount of gift tax payable with respect to a taxable gift. Generally, the amount of the credit under IRC § 2012 is the amount of gift tax attributable to the decedent's gift of the property in question. But the amount of the credit under IRC § 2012 cannot exceed the amount determined under the following formula [IRC § 2012(a)]:

$$\text{Maximum IRC § 2012 credit} = \frac{\text{value of the gift}}{\text{adjusted gross estate}} * \text{adjusted estate tax liability}$$

In this formula, the "value of the gift" starts as the value of the gifted property as of the date of the gift or the date of death, whichever is less. [IRC § 2012(a)] Adjustments are then made to the extent the gift qualified for the gift tax annual exclusion, the gift tax marital deduction, the gift tax charitable deduction, and the election to split gifts. [IRC § 2012(b)–(c)] The "adjusted gross estate" is the value of the decedent's gross estate less those amounts qualifying for the marital deduction or the charitable deduction. [IRC § 2012(a)] The "adjusted estate tax liability" is the tentative tax liability under IRC § 2001 less the unified credit under IRC § 2010. [IRC § 2012(a)]

Example (1):   In 1970, Felix created a trust and transferred $2 million in assets to the trust. The transfer gave rise to a federal gift tax liability of $320,000, which Felix paid. Felix died in 2011, with a gross estate of $6 million, all of which was left to his best friend, Oscar. At the time of his death, the value of the assets held by the trust created in 1970 was $3 million. Felix's gross estate is $6 million, and his estate has no claim for a marital deduction or charitable deduction on these facts. The amount with respect to which the tentative tax liability is computed is $8 million, the sum of the $2 million in adjusted taxable gifts plus the $6 million taxable estate. The IRC § 2001(c) tax on $8 million is $2,780,800. No reduction is made to this amount for the $320,000 in gift tax paid because Felix's gift occurred before 1977. Thus, the tentative tax liability is $2,780,800. The IRC § 2010 unified credit amount, $1,730,800, is applied against this amount, leaving an "adjusted estate tax liability" of $1,050,000. The IRC § 2012 credit amount is $320,000, the full amount of the gift tax payable on the 1970 gift, for that amount does not exceed the limitation:

$$\text{Max. credit} = \frac{\text{value of gift}}{\text{adjusted GE}} * \$1,050,000$$

$$\text{Max. credit} = \frac{\$2 \text{ million}}{\$6 \text{ million}} * \$1,050,000$$

$$\text{Max. credit} = \$350,000$$

Example (2): Same facts as Example (1), except that Felix's will left one-fourth of his estate to Charity, an organization described in IRC § 2055(a). Felix's gross estate is still $6 million, but his estate may claim a $1.5 million charitable deduction on these facts. The amount with respect to which the tentative tax liability is computed is $6.5 million, the sum of the $2 million in adjusted taxable gifts plus the $4.5 million taxable estate. The IRC § 2001(c) tax on $6.5 million is $2,255,800. No reduction is made to this amount for the $320,000 in gift tax paid because Felix's gift occurred before 1977. Thus, the tentative tax liability is $2,255,800. The IRC § 2010 unified credit amount, $1,730,800, is applied against this amount, leaving an "adjusted estate tax liability" of $525,000. Here, only $233,333 of the $320,000 gift tax payable with respect to the 1970 gift may be credited under IRC § 2012 because of the limitation:

$$\text{Max. credit} = \frac{\text{value of gift}}{\text{adjusted GE}} * \$525,000$$

$$\text{Max. credit} = \frac{\$2 \text{ million}}{\$4.5 \text{ million}} * \$525,000$$

$$\text{Max. credit} = \$233,333$$

So why is there an outright credit for pre–1977 gift tax payable but a functionally equivalent subtraction from tentative tax liability for post–

1976 gifts? The answer stems from the fact that the computation of gift tax payable prior to 1977 did not use the same IRC § 2001(c) rate table. Rather, the tax rates on pre–1977 gifts were 25% less than the estate tax rates. Subtracting gift tax payable on pre–1977 gifts by using the estate tax table in IRC § 2001(c), the method applicable for post–1976 gifts, would over-compensate the decedent's estate for tax payable on those gifts because the actual gift tax liability was less. Accordingly, the IRC § 2012 credit accounts for that difference.

d) Tax on Prior Transfers [IRC § 2013]

Where a decedent's will makes a substantial bequest to a person who dies shortly after the decedent, the "double probate" problem arises. Ultimately, the property will pass to the beneficiary of the decedent's beneficiary, but not until the property goes through two successive estate administrations. The double probate problem can be solved by use of a survivorship clause, which requires the beneficiary to survive the decedent for a stipulated term (90 days, six months) to be eligible to receive the bequest. Just as double probate of an asset can cause undue delay and expense, double deaths can cause two rounds of estate tax very close in time. In those situations, IRC § 2013 offers a credit for tax previously paid by another on property included in the decedent's gross estate.

The IRC § 2013 credit is awarded to the decedent who took the property from another person (referred to as the "transferor"). The credit applies if the transferor died within ten years before or within two years after the decedent and if the decedent acquired the property from the transferor. [IRC § 2013(a)]

Generally, the amount of the credit is computed under the following formula:

$$\text{Maximum IRC § 2013 credit} = \frac{\text{value of property transferred}}{\text{transferor's taxable estate}} * \text{transferor's estate tax}$$

In this formula, "value of property transferred" refers to the amount included in the transferor's gross estate with respect to the transferred property, reduced by any federal or state estate or inheritance taxes payable from such property, the amount of any outstanding indebtedness attached to such property, and any marital deduction allowed with respect to such property. [IRC § 2013(d)] The "transferor's taxable estate" means the transferor's gross estate less any death taxes payable with respect to such property. [IRC § 2013(b)] And the "transferor's estate tax" means the estate tax liability of the transferor's estate, increased by the IRC § 2012 credit allowed for gift tax on pre–1977 gifts and by the amount of any IRC § 2013 credit allowed to the transferor. [IRC § 2013(b)]

Example: Howard died in Year 1 with an estate of $10 million. Howard's will left his entire estate in equal shares to his son, Richie, and daughter, Joanie. After paying a combined $4 million in federal and state estate tax, the estate distributed the remaining $6 million to Richie and Joanie ($3 million each). Joanie died in Year 2. To mitigate the effects of successive estate taxation of the assets originally held by Howard, Joanie's estate will be entitled to a nonrefundable IRC § 2013 credit of up to $2 million, computed as follows:

$$\text{IRC § 2013 credit} = \frac{\text{value of property transferred}}{\text{transferor's taxable estate}} \quad * \text{ transferor's estate tax}$$

$$\text{IRC § 2013 credit} = \frac{\$3 \text{ million}}{\$6 \text{ million}} \quad * \text{ 4 million} = \$2 \text{ million}$$

The full amount of the credit is available where the decedent dies within two years of the transferor's death. As the time between the transferor's death and the decedent's death grows, the harshness of multiple tax exactions lessens. Accordingly, the IRC § 2013 credit is reduced as the time between deaths grows. If the decedent dies within three or four years of the transferor's death, the credit is 80% of the amount otherwise allowed. [IRC § 2013(a)(1)] If the decedent dies within five or six years of the transferor's death, the credit is 60% of the amount otherwise allowed. [IRC § 2013(a)(2)] Likewise, if the decedent dies within seven or eight years of the transferor's death, the credit is 40% of the amount otherwise allowed. [IRC § 2013(a)(3)] And, not surprisingly, if the decedent dies within nine or ten years of the transferor's death, the credit is 20% of the amount otherwise allowed. [IRC § 2013(a)(4)]

Note that a credit is allowed for taxes paid by a transferor that died up to two years *after* the decedent. This two-year provision applies where the property is included in the gross estate of the transferor under the re-inclusion provisions (IRC §§ 2035, 2036, 2037, or 2038).

Example: Gena transferred property to a new irrevocable trust, reserving a life estate in the trust property and giving the remainder to her daughter, Elizabeth, or Elizabeth's estate. Elizabeth died after the trust was established, and the value of the remainder interest in Gena's trust was included in Elizabeth's gross estate under IRC § 2033. Gena died one year after Elizabeth. The trust corpus was included in Gena's gross estate under IRC § 2036(a)(1). Elizabeth's estate will be entitled to the IRC § 2013 credit with respect to taxes paid by Gena's estate attributable to the remainder interest included in Elizabeth's gross estate.

e) Other Credit Provisions [IRC §§ 2014, 2015, 2016]

The other credit provisions have limited application. Two of these three statutes pertain to death taxes paid to other countries. Under IRC § 2014, there is a nonrefundable credit for foreign death taxes paid on property included in the gross estate but situated outside the United States. Logically, this credit is limited to that portion of foreign death taxes paid which is attributable to property included in the United States gross estate. [IRC § 2014(b)(1)] Suppose, for instance, a decedent paid $100,000 in death taxes to Brazil because the decedent held assets situated there, and that $60,000 of that $100,000 Brazilian tax was attributable to property included in the decedent's United States gross estate. In such a case, the decedent's estate may claim an IRC § 2014 credit of $60,000 against the tentative tax liability.

Section 2015 permits a credit for foreign death taxes attributable to remainder interests included in the gross estate. This rare, complicated credit can be illustrated by modifying the previous example. Suppose now that the decedent held a remainder interest in property located in Brazil and, as a result, owed $10,000 in Brazilian death taxes. Brazil's tax laws allow the estate to postpone payment of the $10,000 in Brazilian death taxes until the remainder vests (at which time, the decedent's estate will have funds available to pay the death tax). In addition, the estate filed an election under IRC § 6163 to defer United States estate taxes on the remainder interest included in the decedent's gross estate until six months after the remainder interest "takes effect in actual enjoyment." If the estate pays the $10,000 tax bill to Brazil before the deferred payment date for United States estate taxes allowed in IRC § 6163, the estate can claim a $10,000 credit under IRC § 2015.

Finally, IRC § 2016, while listed as a credit in the Code, is in fact a "recapture" provision related to the credit for foreign death taxes. If an estate paid death taxes to a foreign country and subsequently claimed the IRC § 2014 foreign death tax credit, IRC § 2016 requires the personal representative to notify the Service if the estate recovers all or a portion of such tax at a later date. The Service will then re-compute the estate tax liability by reducing the IRC § 2014 credit as appropriate.

3. Liability for Payment

Under IRC § 6018(a)(1), an estate must file an estate tax return (Form 706) only if the gross estate exceeds the **basic exclusion amount** under IRC § 2010(c). For example, the estate of a decedent dying in 2011 must file a Form 706 if the decedent's gross estate exceeds $5 million. If the decedent has made lifetime taxable gifts, however, the filing threshold is reduced by the amount of such gifts. [IRC § 6018(a)(3)]

Any federal estate tax payable is due nine months after the decedent's death. [IRC §§ 6075(a); 6151] The executor is primarily liable for payment of the tax. [IRC § 2002] Beneficiaries of the estate are secondarily liable if the estate has closed before the estate tax has been paid. [IRC § 6324(a)(2)] Extensions of the nine-month deadline to pay federal estate tax may be granted by the Service upon a showing of reasonable cause. The Service may not extend the deadline for more than ten years. [IRC § 6161(a)(2)(A)]

In addition, an estate can elect an extension of time for payment of estate tax attributable to an unvested remainder or reversionary interest. [IRC § 6163] An estate making such an election gets an automatic deadline extension until six months after the termination of the precedent interest(s) in the property. [IRC § 6163(a)] Upon a showing of reasonable cause, the Service can extend this deadline for up to another three years. [IRC § 6163(b)]

Example: Wilma's estate consists of a substantial remainder interest in a trust created by her friend, Betty. Wilma's estate will receive the remainder interest upon the death of the trust's income beneficiary, Barney. Wilma's estate may elect to postpone the estate tax attributable to this remainder interest until six months after Barney's death. If the estate can show reasonable cause for a longer extension (e.g., a delay in distribution of the remainder attributable to a contest over the dispositive provisions of the trust), the Service may further extend the deadline until three years and six months after Barney's death.

Furthermore, if more than 35% of the value of the decedent's gross estate consists of an interest in a closely-held business, the estate can elect to defer the payment of estate tax attributable to such an interest for up to five years, with such estate tax then payable in equal annual installments over ten years with a minimal amount of interest. [IRC § 6166(a)] In effect, the estate tax attributable to the ownership of a closely-held business can be deferred over a period of 15 years, with no tax payable at all in the first five years.

D. Review Questions

1. Diagnosed with a terminal sinus infection early in Year 1, Sneezy began some aggressive estate planning. Sneezy formed two trusts in Year 1, creatively named "Trust A" and "Trust B." Sneezy contributed property worth $1 million to Trust A, which gave an income interest to Dopey for life and a remainder to Doc. If Doc does not survive Dopey, the remainder is to revert to Sneezy or Sneezy's estate. Assume that the value of Sneezy's contingent remainder interest in Trust A at all times is greater than 5% of the value of the Trust A corpus.

    Sneezy transferred an additional $1 million in assets to Trust B, which gave an income interest to Bashful for life and the remainder to Happy or Happy's estate. Shortly after the formation of Trust B, Happy, flattered but unwilling to accept a gift from Sneezy, purchased the remainder interest for its fair market value ($700,000) immediately after formation of Trust B. Sneezy promptly (still in Year 1) transferred the purchase price proceeds to ACME Insurance Company in exchange for an annuity contract. Under the terms of the annuity contract, Sneezy was to receive fixed payments monthly for life. A lump sum benefit of $500,000 would then be paid to Sneezy's designated beneficiary, Grumpy. When he appointed Grumpy beneficiary, Sneezy renounced any rights to change the identity of the beneficiary.

    If Sneezy dies in Year 2 survived by all other parties named in this question, what will be included in Sneezy's gross estate?

2. Hank and Peggy, residents of a separate property state, have been married for over 20 years. Eighteen years ago, Hank purchased a home in Portland for $100,000. Hank and Peggy owned the house as "joint tenants with rights of survivorship." Five years later, when the home was worth $150,000, Peggy paid for the construction of a swimming pool, deck, and an extra bedroom for the home. The total cost of the improvements was $50,000. In the current year, when the value of the home was $400,000, Peggy died. Based on these facts, how much will be included in Peggy's gross estate?

3. Decedent's will directed the personal representative to transfer Decedent's entire estate (with a date of death value of $3,000,000) to a trust. No other

assets are included in Decedent's gross estate for federal estate tax purposes. Under the terms of the trust, the trustee is to pay $50,000 each year to Decedent's spouse, Spouse, for Spouse's life. If the trust does not have $50,000 of income during any year in which payments to Spouse are required, the trustee is directed to distribute principal to the extent required to satisfy the $50,000 annual distribution obligation. No other payments may be made to Spouse for any reason. Upon Spouse's death, the trust will terminate and the remainder of the trust estate will pass to the American Heart Association, an organization described in §§ 170(c), 2055(a) and 2522(a). The trust makes no provision for any other beneficiary. The value of Spouse's interest in the trust is $900,000, and the value of the American Heart Association's remainder interest is $2,100,000. What is the amount of Decedent's taxable estate?

4. Marcia created a trust on January 1, Year 1. The trust gives her sister, Jan, an income interest for life. Upon Jan's death, the remainder will pass to Marcia's other sister, Cindy, or Cindy's estate. The trust also gives Alice, an individual unrelated to Marcia, Jan, or Cindy, a power to invade income or corpus of the trust up to a total $20,000 each year for the benefit of Jan and/or Cindy. Under the trust instrument, Alice has the discretion to apportion between Jan and Cindy any amounts withdrawn through the exercise of the annual invasion power. The trust only allowed Alice to exercise her annual invasion power during the month of December. At all times from the creation of the trust through the end of Year 3, the value of the trust corpus was $100,000. Alice never exercised her invasion power at any time. In Year 4, the value of the trust corpus grew to $200,000. Alice died in September of Year 4. How much of the trust corpus will be included in Alice's gross estate?

5. Three years prior to D's death, D purchased an annuity contract that will provide monthly payments to D for ten years. The contract provided that if D died before the expiration of the ten-year term, payments would be made to D's spouse, S, for the balance of the term. At the same time, X, D's uncle, created a trust that gives D an income interest for D's life. Upon D's death, the remainder will pass to D's cousin, Z, or to Z's estate if Z is not then living. Seven months prior to D's death, D assigned D's income interest under the trust to S. At the same time, D created a trust that provides an income interest to S for life and a remainder to D's child, C. D named Bank as trustee but retained the power to remove Bank as Trustee and name Trust Company as Bank's successor at any time for any reason. Based only on these facts, what will be included in D's gross estate?

CHAPTER II

Gift Tax

■ ANALYSIS

A. **Introduction**

B. **Imposition of Gift Tax [IRC § 2501]**
   1.   Exceptions
       a)   Transfers of Intangibles by Non–Citizens or Non–Residents [IRC § 2501(a)(2)]
       b)   Transfers to Political Organizations [IRC § 2501(a)(4)]
       c)   Services
   2.   "Property"
       a)   Contingent Interests
       b)   Reversionary Interest Incapable of Being Valued
   3.   "Transfer"
       a)   Transfers in General [IRC § 2511]
       b)   "Dominion and Control"
           (1)   General Rule
           (2)   Control Over Timing is Not Retained Dominion or Control
           (3)   Checks
           (4)   Exceptions
               (a)   Control Exercisable With Another Having Substantial Adverse Interest
               (b)   Control Limited by Ascertainable Standard
           (5)   Estate Tax Crossover

A. Introduction

The **gift tax** is designed as a backstop for the federal estate tax. If no tax on lifetime gift transfers existed, individuals could avoid payment of the estate tax simply by gifting away their property any time before death (optimally, for them, the moment before death) to avoid inclusion of assets in their gross estates. Since the gift tax is an excise tax on the donor's act of making a transfer, it encompasses many of those pre-death transfers.

Since 1976, the gift tax and the estate tax are computationally unified. Gifts made during the lifetime of an individual are totaled and used to increase the marginal rate of estate tax paid after death. However, no double taxation (e.g., once during life, again at death) exists since the amount of gift tax due at the present rates on those transfers is subtracted from the tentative estate tax due. [IRC § 2001(b)(2)] *See supra* discussion at I. C. 1. (estate tax computation).

While the gift and estate taxes are unified, there are advantages and disadvantages (discussed in greater detail in the following sections) to making lifetime gifts to one's heirs instead of passing everything in one's estate. One advantage of the gift tax is that the tax is exclusive (one does not have to pay tax on the value of property used to pay the tax). [*See infra* at III. D. 1. d)] Another advantage, provided by IRC § 2503(b), allows for an exclusion from gift tax for transfers under a certain amount (in 2011 that amount is $13,000), and once the property is transferred, it will eliminate any appreciation in value in that property from one's estate.

The primary disadvantage of the gift tax is that an individual must pay the tax shortly after the gift is made, instead of waiting until death. [IRC § 6151] Another potential disadvantage relates to the transferee's basis in the gifted property. [IRC § 1015(a)] The gifting of appreciated property held by the donor is not completely advantageous under the gift tax, and it may be better to wait until death to make the transfer since the recipient receives a basis in the property at its fair market value at the date of decedent's death. [IRC § 1014(a)] Contrarily, if the donor gifts the appreciated property, the transferee takes the donor's adjusted basis, with a possible increase for a portion of the gift tax paid. [IRC § 1015(a), (d)] This means that, upon the sale or other disposition of the gifted property, the transferee will pay tax on the gain, unless it is excluded by some other Code section (e.g., IRC § 121 Exclusion of gain from the sale of principal residence). However, if property has depreciated in value, waiting until death to transfer the property means all the loss will be eliminated by a fair market value basis under IRC § 1014(a), while some, but not all, of the donor's loss may be maintained if the transfer is by gift. [IRC §§ 1014(a), 1015(a) (after "except that")]

B.   Imposition of Gift Tax [IRC § 2501]

IRC § 2501, found in Chapter 12 of the Internal Revenue Code, imposes the gift tax. Under IRC § 2501(a)(1) the gift tax is imposed on all *transfers of property by gift* made during the calendar year, regardless if made by a resident or non-resident of the United States. Therefore, in order to impose the gift tax, there must be 1) a "transfer," 2) "of property," 3) "by gift." These elements will be taken up below.

1.   Exceptions

As with most rules in the Code, many exceptions exist to the general rule. Even if there is a "transfer of property by gift," certain transactions are not taxable under Chapter 12.

a)   Transfers of Intangibles by Non–Citizens or Non–Residents [IRC § 2501(a)(2)]

Transfers of intangible property (i.e., stocks and bonds) by non-resident, non-citizens of the United States are not subject to the gift tax. [IRC § 2501(a)(2)] This rule encourages foreign investment in United States securities and allows for domestic financial institutions to hold intangible property of non-citizens without it being subject to possible gift taxation. The rule does not apply to individuals who give up their United States citizenship primarily to avoid taxation within ten years from the date of transfer. [IRC § 2501(a)(3)(A)]

b)   Transfers to Political Organizations [IRC § 2501(a)(4)]

No gift tax is due on transfers to any party, committee, fund, or other organization that accepts contributions or spends money to influence the election or selection of any individual to any Federal, State or local public office. Political contributions made directly to an individual are not covered by IRC § 2501(a)(4) and are subject to the gift tax if not excluded under IRC § 2503(b).

c)   Services

Although not expressly stated in the Code, services are excluded from gift taxation. While this can be gleaned from the IRC § 2501(a)(1) application of the gift tax to "transfers of property," in other areas of the Code (like IRC § 102 of the income tax) the term "property" includes both property and services. This is not the case in the gift tax; property means property.

There are two reasons for not taxing services. First, valuation of services is difficult, and it is unclear what services to tax and not tax (how much for babysitting by Grandma?). Second, services do not directly deplete the estate of the service-provider, although they do so indirectly by reducing the time and ability of the donor to create additional wealth for herself.

Example (1): Fred fixes his aunt's car. The parts cost $500 and had the repair been done by a mechanic, the labor would have cost $2,000. The cost of parts is treated as a gift under the gift tax, but Fred's labor is not (although both parts and labor are covered by IRC § 102).

Example (2): Father manages a large mutual fund. On his own time, he manages the stock portfolios of his three adult children. The value of the portfolios has dramatically increased due to Father's expertise. Since Father has provided only services there is no "transfer of property" and no gift tax is due. [*See Commissioner v. Hogle*, 165 F.2d 352 (10th Cir. 1947)]

Example (3): Otto is named executor of his friend's estate, but waives his right to executor fees and provides his services free of charge. If Otto disclaimed the right to fees in a reasonable time after commencing to serve as executor, the fees would be effectively disclaimed and Otto is not considered to be making a gift for the services provided. [*See* Rev. Rul. 66–167, 1966–1 C.B. 20] If services were provided and then disclaimed, there would be income and a gift made. [*See* Rev. Rul. 64–225, 1964–2 C.B. 15]

Example (4): Stephen, a famous author, helps to edit Thomas' first novel. There are no gift tax consequences. However, if Stephen wrote a novel and gave the copyright to Thomas, this would be a gift of property since the copyright is a property interest.

2. "Property"

The gift tax covers all types of property, tangible and intangible, real and personal. [*See* IRC § 2511(a); Reg. § 25.2511–1(a)] The Senate Report on the 1932 internal revenue revisions states the word "property" should be given a broad interpretation and includes "every species of right or interest protected by law and having an exchangeable value." [S. Rep. No. 665, 72d Cong., 1st Sess. (1931)(1939–1 CB (pt. 2) 496, 524)]

a) Contingent Interests

The property interest can be less than one's entire interest in the property or a contingent interest in property. If the donor transfers a contingent interest in property, the contingency never has to be fulfilled; the gift tax considers the moment of transfer and no further.

Example (1): Peter puts stock in trust, income to Peter for life, remainder to Wendy, an unrelated individual. Peter has made a gift of the remainder interest to Wendy. [*See* Reg. § 25.2511–1(e)] However, if Wendy were related, the gift would include the entire trust corpus under IRC § 2702. [*See infra* the discussion of IRC § 2702, at II. D. 2.]

Example (2): Donald has a contingent remainder interest in a trust. Donald only receives the remainder interest if Yolanda is not alive when the life-estate tenant dies. Donald transfers his contingent interest to Daisy. Later that same year the life-tenant dies, and Yolanda is still alive. Donald must still pay gift tax on his transfer of the contingent remainder to Daisy. [*See Goodwin v. McGowan*, 47 F.Supp. 798 (W.D.N.Y. 1942)]

Example (3): Hurlbut transfers 3,000 shares of X stock with a fair market value of $571,000 into an irrevocable trust. The trust income is to be paid to his wife, Anna Nichol for life. Upon her death the stock will revert back to Hurlbut, if living, but if not then it will pass by Anna's will or, if none, to her intestate successors. The remainder interest is therefore contingent upon Anna Nichol surviving Hurlbut. Even though the remainder is contingent and there is no way to know at the time the stocks are transferred to the trust to whom the remainder interest will pass should it vest, there is a completed gift of the life estate and remainder. This is so since Hurlbut has no economic control over the property except for his reversionary interest. [*See Smith v. Shaughnessy*, 318 U.S. 176, 63 S.Ct. 545, 87 L.Ed. 690 (1943)] Since this was a transfer of an interest in trust to a family member,

Hurlbut's interest in property will be valued under IRC § 2702. [*See infra* the discussion of IRC § 2702 at II. D. 2.]

b) Reversionary Interest Incapable of Being Valued

If the property is subject to a reversionary interest to the donor on the occurrence of a contingency and the contingency cannot be valued, the reversionary interest will be disregarded and the donor will be treated as transferring the entire property interest.

Example: At age 55, Meta transfers property to a trust with the income to her daughter, Elisa, and after her death to Elisa's children after they turn 21 years old. If Elisa dies without children, or should all the children die before their 21st birthday, the property reverts back to Meta. Meta has made a gift of the entire property transferred to the trust, less her reversionary interest. However, since the value of grantor's contingent reversionary interest is unascertainable, it has no computable value and nothing may be deducted from the amount of gift. [*See Robinette v. Helvering*, 318 U.S. 184, 63 S.Ct. 540, 87 L.Ed. 700 (1943); Reg. § 25.2511–1(e) (3rd and 4th sentences)]

3. "Transfer"

The general rule defining a "transfer" for the gift tax is found in IRC § 2511. However, several Code sections included in Chapter 12, and two that are not in Chapter 12, also find a "transfer" in situations where the transferor does not have an interest in the property transferred (e.g., IRC § 2514 for powers of appointment and IRC § 2519 for dispositions of certain life estate interests), in situations where Congress felt a transfer existed (IRC § 7872—below market rate interest loans), or due to the relationship between the donor and donee (IRC § 2702—special valuation rules in case of transfers of interests in trusts).

a) Transfers in General [IRC § 2511]

Except for non-resident, non-citizens, IRC § 2511 encompasses all sorts of transfers. The section applies to transfers that are made directly or indirectly, by trust or otherwise (such as transfers to corporations or partnerships).

The most basic example of a transfer subject to the gift tax is a direct transfer from one person to another (e.g., mother gives her son a baseball glove for his birthday). But other less obvious direct transfers are also covered, such as forgiving a debt, assigning a judgment, or paying benefits from an insurance policy. Transfers made in an indirect manner are also covered by the statute, such as the payment of another's debt (rent, credit card bill, etc.).

A transfer is also found where a donor with donative intent (as opposed to a business reason) intends to transfer an interest in property. However, a donative intent is not required to have the gift tax apply. [*See infra* II. B. 4. a)]

b) "Dominion and Control"

(1) General Rule

If a donor maintains dominion and control over the property there will be no "transfer" for IRC § 2511 to apply. The power of the donor can be either to change who can take the property (not just solely when) or the express or implied ability to take back the property. [Reg. § 25.2511–2(b)] So long as the donor can manipulate who receives the property, there is no transfer, and if there is no transfer, the gift is not complete. As discussed in more detail below, if the power can only be used in conjunction with another who possesses a "substantial adverse interest," if the donor's control is subject to a fixed and ascertainable standard, or if there is an actual transfer of property, the donor has sufficiently given up control and the gift will be treated as complete.

Example (1): George creates a trust where he will receive the income for life and at his death can appoint the remainder to whomever he wants. Since George has dominion and control over the remainder interest, no gift has been made. Instead, if George irrevocably assigned the remainder interest of the trust to Erwin, an unrelated individual, there would be a completed gift of only the remainder interest. [*See* Reg. § 25.2511–2(b)]

Example (2): IBM has a plan where the survivors of a deceased employee receive benefits equal to three times the employee's regular annual salary. The benefit is not bargained for and can be terminated at any time by either IBM or the employee, or if the employee leaves the company for any reason other than death. Anthony dies while an employee of IBM and IBM pays benefits pursuant to the plan to his surviving spouse, Joan. Anthony has not made a gift to Joan of the policy since he had no property interest and there was no act by Anthony that constituted a "transfer." His participation in the plan was involuntary and he had no power to select the beneficiaries, or to alter the amount, timing, or benefits of the plan. [*See Estate of DiMarco v. Commissioner*, 87 T.C. 653 (1986)]

Example (3): Harriet creates a trust with income payable to David or Ricky, as selected by the independent trustee, and the remainder to Ozzie. If Harriet has no power to choose or replace the trustee she lacks dominion and control over the property, even though the income interest donee is not known at the time the trust is created. There is, therefore, a completed gift of the entire trust corpus.

Example (4): Dorris creates a trust with income payable to Alice and Bertha as Dorris directs, and the remainder payable to Casey. Dorris also has the power to revoke the trust. Dorris maintains dominion and control of the trust and there is no "transfer."

Example (5): At a later time, Dorris gives up the power to revoke the trust, but retains the power to direct the income to either Alice or Bertha. There is a completed gift to Casey of the remainder, but since Dorris has the power to control who receives the income, there is no gift to Alice or Bertha. [*See Burnet v. Guggenheim*, 288 U.S. 280, 53 S.Ct. 369, 77 L.Ed. 748 (1933)] If Casey is related to Dorris the entire trust corpus could be treated as a gift. [*See infra* the discussion of IRC § 2702, at II. D. 2.]

Example (6): If Dorris distributes the yearly income of the trust to Alice, there is a completed transfer in the calendar year of distribution from Dorris to Alice. [Reg. § 25.2511–2(f)]

(2) Control Over Timing is Not Retained Dominion or Control

A completed gift transfer occurs if the donor merely has the power over *when* an individual may take enjoyment of the property, not *if* they will be able to enjoy the property at all. [Reg. § 25.2511–2(d)]

> *Example:* Dorris creates another trust, this time for the benefit of Emmy. The trust provides for the income of the trust to be distributed to Emmy until she reaches age 40, with the remainder payable to Emmy or her estate. Dorris maintains the right to accumulate the income in the trust instead of distributing it to Emmy. This is a completed gift transfer of the entire trust corpus from Dorris to Emmy since Dorris only has the power to "change the manner or time of enjoyment," not *who* gets the property. [*See* Reg. § 25.2511–2(d)] This transfer is ineligible for the IRC § 2503(b) exclusion since this is not a gift of a present interest. [*See infra* the discussion of IRC § 2503(b), II. E. 1.]
>
> *Estate tax crossover:* If Dorris dies before Emmy turns 40, the trust corpus will be included in her gross estate under IRC § 2038. [*See supra* discussion of IRC § 2038 at I. A. 2. c)]

(3) Checks

When a donor gives a check as a gift, the transfer does not occur until the check is cashed or negotiated for value to a third person. [Rev. Rul. 67–396, 1967–2 C.B. 351] Since the donor has the ability to stop payment on the check until the check is cashed or negotiated, the donor maintains dominion and control over the check.

Generally, a donor "transfers" a check when the donor has no power to change the disposition of the check under local law. The "transfer" is also complete when the check is deposited or presented for payment if "(1) the check was paid by the drawee bank when first presented to the drawee bank for payment; (2) the donor was alive when the check was paid by the drawee bank; (3) the donor intended to make a gift; (4) delivery of the check by the donor was unconditional; and (5) the check was deposited, cashed, or presented in the calendar year for which completed gift treatment is sought and within a reasonable time of issuance." [Rev. Rul. 96–56, 1996–2 C.B. 161]

Example (1):   As a gift, Albert gives John a check from Bank A for $11,000 on December 14, Year 1. On December 31, Year 1, John deposits the check in his own account at Bank B. Bank A honors the check and makes payment to John's account on January 2, Year 2. Under local law a gift of a check is not complete until the check is honored for payment. Since all the requirements of Rev. Rul. 96–56 are met, the $11,000 payment on January 2 relates back to the time when the check was deposited. Albert is deemed to have given John the money on December 31, Year 1. [*See Metzger v. Commissioner*, 38 F.3d 118 (4th Cir. 1994), Rev. Rul. 96–56, 1996–2 C.B. 161]

Example (2):   Same facts as above except that John deposits the check on January 1, Year 2, and the check is honored the next day. Since the check was deposited in Year 2, the transfer is complete in Year 2.

(4) Exceptions

In certain instances a donor may have continued dominion and control over the gifted property, but because that control is not unfettered, the transfer is deemed complete.

(a) Control Exercisable With Another Having Substantial Adverse Interest

If the donor's ability to exercise dominion and control over the property is held in conjunction with a person having a substantial adverse interest to the property's disposition, the donor will be treated as making a completed transfer. [Reg. § 25.2511–2(e)]

Example (1):   Douglas creates a trust that pays income to Nancy for her life and the remainder to Bruce. Nancy and Bruce are unrelated to Douglas. Douglas retains the right to change the income beneficiary, but only with the consent of Nancy. Douglas does not maintain the power to change the remainder. Since Nancy has a substantial adverse interest in the exercise of the power to change the income beneficiary, Douglas has made a completed transfer of the income interest. [Reg. § 25.2511–2(e)] Since Douglas has surrendered control of both the income and remainder interests, Douglas has made a completed transfer of the entire trust corpus.

Example (2):   Same facts as above, but Douglas can also transfer the remainder interest, subject to Nancy's consent. Since Nancy does not have an interest in the remainder, only the income interest is treated as a completed transfer.

Example (3):   Same facts as above, except that Douglas has the right to revoke the trust, but only with Nancy's consent. Nancy's interest should be treated as substantially adverse enough to make this a completed transfer of the entire trust corpus. [*See Camp v. Commissioner*, 195 F.2d 999 (1st Cir. 1952)]

(b)   Control Limited by Ascertainable Standard
A transfer will also be treated as complete to the extent the donor's power is limited by a fixed and ascertainable standard. Nevertheless, to the extent the donor's power allows the donor to reclaim the property, then the interest will be treated as an incomplete transfer.

Example (1):   Bill creates a trust with income payable to Gail or Elaine and the remainder payable to Harry or Harry's estate. Bill retains the power to allocate the income between Gail and Elaine, and to add additional income beneficiaries. There is only a completed gift of the remainder. [Reg. § 25.2511–2(c)]

Example (2):   Same facts as above except that the income of the trust is payable to Gail for her "education, support and maintenance," with any remaining income payable to Elaine. Since the income interest is subject to a fixed and ascertainable standard the entire trust corpus will be treated as a completed transfer even if Bill is the trustee.

Example (3):   Same facts as above except that the income interest is payable to Gail only but Bill has the power to invade the income interest for his own "reasonable support and comfort." The entire trust corpus, less the amount required for Bill's reasonable support and comfort, will be treated as transferred.

(5) Estate Tax Crossover

If a donor maintains enough dominion and control over the property to render the gift tax inapplicable for want of a transfer, and if the donor dies while still possessing such control over the property, IRC §§ 2036, 2038 or both may apply to include the property into the donor's gross estate. [*See supra* the discussion of IRC §§ 2036 and 2038, at I. A. 2. a) and c).]

c) Other Transfers

Several other Code sections create "transfers" for Chapter 12. These sections are covered *infra* in II. C.]

4. "By Gift"

a) General Rule [IRC § 2512(b)]

IRC § 2501(a)(1) imposes a gift tax on "transfers of property by gift." While the statutory wording is not entirely clear, the Supreme Court has stated IRC § 2512(b) defines the element "by gift." Under IRC § 2512(b) a "gift" occurs when property is transferred for less than "adequate and full consideration in money or money's worth." Congress intended this language to encompass all "protean arrangements which the wit of man can devise that are not business transactions within the meaning of ordinary speech." [*Commissioner v. Wemyss*, 324 U.S. 303, 306, 65 S.Ct. 652, 654, 89 L.Ed. 958, 962 (1945)] By primarily considering the adequacy of any consideration received, this test looks at objective facts rather than the more difficult-to-determine subjective motivations of the donor.

Since IRC § 2512(b) does not utilize the subjective motivation of the transferor, donative intent is not required. The Regulations state donative intent is "not an essential element in the application of the gift tax to the transfer." [Reg. § 25.2511–1(g)(1)] However, in order to separate out a transaction that may be in the ordinary course of business, donative intent must be absent. *See infra* discussion II. B. 4. b) (3).

Example (1):   Widow Gimee More receives a sizable income from a trust created by her deceased husband's will. However, the trust income ceases if she remarries. Her boyfriend, William, agrees to transfer stock to Widow More, the value of which would make up for the loss of the trust income. Under the agreement, Widow More promises to marry William and is allowed to keep her marital property and support rights if they divorce. Widow More agrees, William transfers the stock, and they marry. Even if William transfers the stock with no donative intent, he makes a gift to Widow More because the transfer was for less than "adequate and full consideration in money or money's worth," (i.e., the promise of marriage). The fact that the stocks replaced Gimee's trust income does not matter because IRC § 2512(b) requires the consideration to flow directly to the donor (William). [*Commissioner v. Wemyss*, 324 U.S. 303, 65 S.Ct. 652, 89 L.Ed. 958 (1945)]

Example (2):   Spencer transfers $30,000 to his brother, Tyler, on the condition that Tyler give $20,000 to their parents. After the transfers are made, Tyler has made no gift under IRC § 2512(b) since the amount he gave to his parents ($20,000) is offset by the $30,000 he received from Spencer. Spencer, however, gave an indirect gift of $20,000 to his parents, and a direct gift of $10,000 to Tyler. [*See* Reg. § 25.2511–1(h)(2)]

(1) Measuring Adequate and Full Consideration

   (a) Generally

     If the consideration received by the transferor is not capable of being valued in terms of dollars and cents, it is "wholly disregarded" when determining whether a gift occurs under IRC § 2512(b). [Reg. § 25.2512–8] Even if the consideration would support a contract, unless it can be valued, it may not offset the fair market value of the property transferred.

     Example (1):   Merrill and Kinta enter into an ante-nuptial agreement which provides that Merrill will transfer to Kinta $300,000 in return for the release of any marital rights Kinta might acquire during the marriage. Kinta keeps her support rights under the agreement. Merrill transfers the cash into an irrevocable trust, and the two get married the next week. Under IRC § 2043(b)(1) of the estate tax, marital rights are not treated as consideration. Since the estate and gift tax need to be interpreted in light of each other, marital rights will not be treated as consideration for Chapter 12. Therefore, there is a $300,000 gift from Merrill to Kinta. [*See Merrill v. Fahs*, 324 U.S. 308, 65 S.Ct. 655, 89 L.Ed. 963 (1945)]

Note: The *Merrill* case was decided before the marital deduction was allowed under IRC § 2524. Under Rev. Rul. 69–347, a transfer under an ante-nuptial agreement becomes complete on the date of the marriage, since before that time the transferor has dominion and control over the property because the terms of the agreement are not yet satisfied. [Rev. Rul. 69–347, 1969–1 C.B. 227] In the above example, the gift is deemed completed at the time of the marriage so Merrill may receive a marital deduction for the transfer of property.

Example (2):   Brian promised Carnie $20,000 if she lost 100 pounds. Carnie did so, and Brian paid her the money. Carnie's losing weight cannot be considered consideration for the $20,000, since it has no ascertainable value to Brian. Consequently, Brian has made a $20,000 gift to Carnie.

Example (3):   In Year 1, Father promises Son $10,000 if he graduates from college. Son graduates from college in Year 5 and asks for the money promised by Father. Father does not pay and Son sues for payment. Son wins a judgment against Father for $10,000 in Year 6, which Father pays. While Son's graduation from college is consideration to support a contract between Father and Son, it is not consideration in money or money's worth and will not offset the

$10,000 transferred from Father to Son for Father to avoid gift tax consequences. Additionally, since the promise from Father to Son became binding upon Son's graduation from college, the gift of $10,000 is made in Year 5. [*See* Rev. Rul. 79–384, 1979–2 CB 344]

(b) Income Tax Crossover

The release of marital rights is treated as consideration to support the sale of property. [*Farid–Es–Sultaneh v. Commissioner,* 160 F.2d 812 (2d Cir. 1947)] In *Farid,* the release of marital rights was the consideration in exchange for property received. The value of the consideration was the amount realized (IRC § 1001(b)) by the transferor to support the sale of the property. Therefore, because this was considered a sale, the property received by the transferee had a fair market value basis and not a transferred basis under IRC § 1015.

(2) Payment of Gift Tax by Donee

The payment of the gift tax by the donee may be treated as offsetting consideration, depending on whether there was an agreement for the donee to pay any gift tax due on a transfer.

(a) Prior Agreement by Donee to Pay Tax

If the donee agreed prior to the transfer to pay the gift tax, such payment is treated as offsetting consideration.

Since the payment of the gift tax would offset the amount of the gift, which in turn would reduce the amount of gift tax, which in turn would change the amount of the gift, and so on, the Service has promulgated a formula to determine the amount of gift tax due in this situation. [Rev. Rul. 75–72, 1975 C.B. 310]

(b) No Prior Agreement for Donee to Pay Gift Tax

There is no reduction in the amount of gift where the donee is either forced to pay the gift tax by operation of law, or does so voluntarily with no prior agreement. Under IRC § 6324(b), the donee can be held liable for the payment of any gift tax due by the donor up to the fair market value of any gifts received from the donor. Any payment made under IRC § 6324 does not reduce the amount of the gift from donor to donee. [*See Affelder v. Commissioner,* 7 T.C. 1190 (1946); *Moore v. Commissioner,* 146 F.2d 824 (2d Cir. 1945)]

(c) **Estate Tax Crossover**

Under IRC § 2035(b), any gift tax paid on gifts made during the three years prior to the decedent's death is included in the decedent's gross estate. This rule also applies if the donee pays the gift tax. [*See Estate of Sachs v. Commissioner*, 88 T.C. 769 (1987) *aff'd in part and rev'd in part*, 856 F.2d 1158 (8th Cir. 1988)]

(d) **Payment of Gift Tax by Donee (Income Tax Crossover)**

If the donee pays the gift tax, that amount is included in the amount realized by the donor under IRC § 1001(b). [*See Diedrich v. Commissioner*, 457 U.S. 191, 102 S.Ct. 2414, 72 L.Ed.2d 777 (1982)] This means if the gift tax paid by the donee is greater than the adjusted basis of the donor's transferred property, the donor realizes and recognizes gain. Additionally, the donee will have a basis in the property equal to the higher of the gift tax paid or the donor's adjusted basis. [*See* Reg. § 1.1015–4]

(3) **"By Gift" (Income Tax Crossover)**

Unlike the gift tax, donative intent is required for finding a "gift" for the income tax. [*See* IRC § 102(a); *Commissioner v. Duberstein*, 363 U.S. 278, 80 S.Ct. 1190, 4 L.Ed.2d 1218 (1960)] To find a "gift" for income tax purposes, the transferor must give it with "detached and disinterested generosity . . . out of affection, respect, admiration, charity, or like impulses." [*Duberstein*, 363 U.S. at 285, 80 S.Ct. at 1197, 4 L.Ed.2d at 1225 (citations omitted).]

(4) **Marital Transfers**

Marital rights are not treated as consideration for either the gift or estate taxes. [*Merrill v. Fahs*, 324 U.S. 308, 65 S.Ct. 655, 89 L.Ed. 963 (1945)] If property is transferred for the release of marital rights, unless some exception can be found, the transferor spouse will be subject to possible gift tax on the transfer. Fortunately, several exceptions counteract this general rule.

(a) **Property Settlements Under IRC § 2516**

If the elements of IRC § 2516 are met, the transfer is deemed "made for a full and adequate consideration in money or money's worth." [IRC § 2516] The transfer must either be in settlement of the spouses' marital or property rights or provide support for the minor children of the marriage. The agreement must be in writing and made within a three-year period of the divorce decree beginning on the date one year before such agreement is entered into.

Example: Brad and Jennifer sign an agreement in settlement of their marital property rights on March 28, Year 2. A final divorce decree must take place between March 28, Year 1 and March 28, Year 4 for IRC § 2516 to apply.

The agreement need not be submitted to the divorce court in order to qualify under IRC § 2516, but only an official final decree of divorce will be accepted by the Service. [Reg. § 25.2516–1(a)] IRC § 2516 shields only those amounts in settlement of spouses' marital or similar property rights or support for the couple's children. Amounts in excess of those minimum amounts constitute a gift. [*Spruance v. Commissioner*, 60 T.C. 141 (1973), *aff'd* 505 F.2d 731 (3d Cir. 1974)]

Example: Preston and Margaret get divorced. Before the divorce was final they signed a written agreement in which Preston would transfer $1 million of marketable securities to a trust from which Margaret would receive the income for life, with the remainder interest passing at her death to their children from the marriage. Unless the children's remainder interest was bargained for by Margaret in exchange for her marital rights, it will be treated as a gift from Preston to the children. The income interest, however, will be treated as being transferred for full consideration under IRC § 2516, meaning Preston makes no gift to Margaret. [*See Spruance*, 60 T.C. at 151]

(b) Support Rights

Transfers made in exchange for the release of support rights or for the current support of a former spouse or any of the couple's children are treated as made for full consideration. [Rev. Rul. 68–379, 1968–2 C.B. 414] The rationale is that the amounts expended for support during marriage are not treated as a gift, and there is no justification for treating such amounts as gifts solely because the couple is divorced. However, amounts paid in excess of support rights are treated as a gift.

Example: Jimmy gives Roselyn $200,000 in their divorce settlement. The fair market value of Roselyn's support rights is $185,000. The $15,000 transferred over the fair market value of the support rights is not supported by consideration and will be treated as a gift. [Rev. Rul. 68–379, 1968–2 C.B. 414]

(c) Judicial Decree
Property transferred by judicial decree pursuant to a divorce is not founded on a "promise or agreement" and therefore does not need to be supported by consideration to avoid gift treatment. [*Harris v. Commissioner*, 340 U.S. 106, 71 S.Ct. 181, 95 L.Ed. 111 (1950)] This rule applies to agreements, submitted to the court, made in contemplation of divorce that become part of the judicial decree, assuming the court had the ability to modify the agreement. [*Barrett's Estate v. Commissioner*, 56 T.C. 1312 (1971)]

b) **Exceptions to the General Rule**
There are three exceptions to the general rule that a gift is the amount by which the fair market value of the property transferred is greater than any consideration received by the transferor. The first exception involves transfers made in satisfaction of a support obligation. The second exception exists for "qualified transfers" as defined under IRC § 2503(e). The third exception excludes transfers completed in the "ordinary course of business," even if made for less than adequate consideration.

(1) Transfers Made in Satisfaction of Support Obligations
If payments made by the donor on the behalf of the donee are in satisfaction of the donor's support obligations, those payments are not considered gift transfers. While not expressly stated in the Code or Regulations, the Service agrees with this rule. [*See* Rev. Rul 68–379, 1968–2 C.B. 414] This rule is consistent with the estate tax. Under IRC § 2053(a)(3), payments of support rights are deductible for estate tax purposes as a claim against the estate. To the extent the gift tax backstops the estate tax, therefore, it makes sense that payments of support during life are not treated as taxable gifts.

Example (1): Michelle and Lee have lived together many years, but never married. Last year they entered into a formal agreement where Michelle released her support rights under state law in exchange for Lee's MGM stock. Since support rights are treated as consideration (unlike marital property rights under IRC § 2043(b)(1)), no gift is made when the value of the support rights equals the amount of property transferred. Therefore Lee does not make a gift when he transfers the stock to Michelle.

Example (2): Fred gives a new car to his daughter, Pebbles, for her sixteenth birthday. Under the general rule of IRC § 2512(b), Fred is treated as giving a gift to Pebbles of the value of the car since he is not receiving anything in return. However, if under state law this would be considered part of Fred's support obligations to his daughter, the transfer would not be treated as a gift.

(2) Qualified Transfers by Donor to Donee [IRC § 2503(e)]

For gift tax purposes, any "qualified transfer" is not treated as a "transfer of property by gift" for the gift tax. There are two types of "qualified transfers": one for the payment of tuition to an educational institution, and the other for medical care payments made directly to a medical provider. The rationale is to favor these types of transfers and exclude payments that may exceed support obligations or exclude payments on behalf of individuals past the age of majority. To qualify, the payments must be made directly to either the educational institution or medical provider. This requirement eliminates the need to trace funds or disentangle combined assets. Both exclusions are allowed regardless of the relationship between the donor and donee.

(a) Education Payments

Tuition payments are treated as a "qualified transfer" only if made directly to the educational institution. Payments for books, supplies, or room and board are not excluded under IRC § 2503(e), and may constitute a gift. [Reg. § 25.2503–6(b)(2)] However, since there is no degree requirement (e.g., a bachelor's degree), payments for certain travel tours provided by educational institutions may be excludable from the gift tax. Even though payments to qualified tuition programs (i.e., "529 plans" or Coverdell Education Savings Accounts) are for an educational purpose, they are not direct payments of tuition and do not qualify for the exclusion.

> *Example:* Son receives a bill of $20,000 for his law school tuition that he gives to Father to pay. Assuming that Son is past the age of majority and Father does not have any support obligations, this payment would, if not for IRC § 2503(e), be treated as a gift from Father to Son.

(b) Medical Payments

Any payments for expenses, not reimbursed by the donee's insurance, resulting from the diagnosis, cure or prevention of disease, as well as for transportation to receive such care constitute a "qualified transfer," as do payments for qualified long-term care services or medical insurance. Any payments made that are reimbursed by insurance are not excluded and may be treated as a transfer of property by gift. [Reg. § 25.2503–6(b)(3)]

> *Example:* Good Samaritan (GS) comes across Unlucky, who has just been struck by a hit-and-run driver. GS takes Unlucky to a hospital, where she receives treatment for her wounds. GS pays for all the medical care, which amounts to $15,000. Since GS made the payment directly to the hospital, for the treatment of Unlucky's wound, no gift is made from GS to Unlucky under IRC § 2503(e).

(c) Income Tax Crossover

Because IRC § 2503(e)(1) only applies "for purposes of this chapter" (Chapter 12–gift tax), the exclusion does not apply to other areas of the Code. This means that the amounts spent for tuition or medical care can still apply when determining support for dependency under IRC § 152(a), can still qualify for the IRC § 213(a) deduction, and can still be excluded from gross income for the income tax under IRC § 102(a) as a gift.

(3) Transfers Made in "Ordinary Course of Business" [Reg. § 25.2512–8]

Not all exchanges where inadequate consideration is received for the property transferred are treated as "gifts." Transactions completed in the "ordinary course of business" are considered made for adequate and full consideration in money or money's worth. [Reg. § 25.2512–8] This permits bad bargains, loss leaders and the like to escape gift taxation. While the Regulations state that the transactions must be made in the ordinary course of business, qualifying transactions need only be "bona fide, at arm's length, and free from any donative intent." [*Id.*] This is why donative intent is important; if it *is* present then the transaction may be subject to the gift tax.

Example (1):   As part of a shift of management responsibilities due to Senior Executive's pending retirement, Senior sold stock to Junior Executive for less than fair market value. The agreement was bona fide, at arm's length and due to the particular business interest involved, and the discount was not provided with any donative intent. Even though the stock was sold at less than fair market value, there is no gift since the exchange was in the ordinary course of business. [*Estate of Anderson v. Commissioner*, 8 T.C. 706 (1947)]

Example (2):   Bart advertises radios for sale at less than his cost in order to get people to shop at his store, the "Electric Palace." Even though the radios are being transferred to customers at less than full and adequate consideration, since this is part of his ordinary course of business, Bart does not make a gift to his customers of the difference between the fair market value and the price the customers pay.

Example (3):   Jim recently purchased a house as his personal residence for $1 million from Eugenia, but did not get the house inspected before closing. Later, it was determined the house had serious foundation problems which were unknown to either party before the sale and decreased the value of the house by $200,000. Even though this transaction was not in the ordinary course of business (it was for a personal residence), since it was bona fide, made at arm's length and free of donative intent, Jim has not made a gift of $200,000 to Eugenia.

C. Other "Transfers"

Several Code sections in Chapter 12 (as well as two outside of Chapter 12) either create a transfer where one may not exist or modify the "transfer" requirement in order to determine if the gift tax is applicable on the transaction.

1. Powers of Appointment [IRC § 2514]

The rules governing powers of appointment under the gift tax are very similar to the estate tax rules under IRC § 2041. In fact, the interpretive case law and administrative rulings are interchangeable. [*See Sanford v. Commissioner*, 308 U.S. 39, 42, 60 S.Ct. 51, 55, 84 L.Ed. 20, 22 (1939); Rev. Rul. 76–547, 1976–2 C.B. 302]

IRC § 2514 covers certain powers of appointment. If the power was created after October 21, 1942, the exercise, release or lapse of the power is treated as a "transfer" of property. IRC § 2514 signals congressional disagreement with the Supreme Court's ruling that powers of appointment are not property interests. Absent IRC § 2514, the holder of a broad power of appointment could effectively exercise complete control over the property subject to the power without gift tax consequences since the power holder would not possess an interest in the underlying property.

Generally, a power of appointment is the right to designate beneficial interests of property, for example who will enjoy the income from a trust. If the power is only over the administrative aspects of the property (such as where to invest trust property), those rights and duties are not considered "powers of appointment." [Reg. § 25.2514–1(b)(1)] Additionally, the term "power of appointment" does not include powers reserved by a donor to herself (therefore someone other than the donor must hold the powers). [Reg. § 25.2514–1(b)(2)]

Example (1): Phelps creates a trust and names himself as trustee. As trustee, he has the power to distribute the money to anyone he sees fit. By creating the trust Phelps acquired no greater interest in the property than he had before the trust was created, and therefore no power of appointment was created, and IRC § 2514 does not apply. Of course, any transfers of trust income or corpus to any third parties will represent a completed gift by Phelps, but IRC § 2514 is not necessary to make that conclusion.

Example (2): Laurie has the right to income from a trust for life. Laurie has the power to transfer the right to income to Reggie. If Laurie transfers the right to income to Reggie, the general transfer rule of IRC § 2511(a) would apply since Laurie already has a direct interest in the property and IRC § 2514 is not required to create a transfer. [*See* Reg. § 25.2514–3(e)(ex. 1)]

a) Treatment of Post–1942 General Powers of Appointment

Under IRC § 2514(b) general powers of appointment (GPA) are treated as an interest in property. Therefore, the exercise, release, and (sometimes) the lapse of a GPA is deemed a "transfer of property." A transfer by exercise of a GPA is easy to spot, since the property is actually transferred from one person to another. A transfer by release of a GPA is more difficult to spot. A "release" is treated as a transfer because by giving up the GPA, the holder of the GPA effectively transfers the subject property to the default taker. Therefore, a release is treated as if the power holder exercised the power for herself, and then transferred the property to whomever would receive the property in default of the exercise of the GPA.

> *Example:* Ian creates an irrevocable trust naming Ronald as the sole trustee. The trust instrument requires the income and remainder to be payable to Ian's children. Ian also gives Ronald the power to transfer the trust property during the trust term to whomever Ronald chooses, including Ronald. Accordingly, Ronald has a GPA. Unless Ronald makes a proper disclaimer before becoming trustee, a subsequent release of his right to transfer the trust property will be treated as if Ronald transferred the trust corpus to Ian's children. [Reg. § 25.2514–3(e)(ex. 5)]

It is important to note the difference between the estate tax rules for GPAs and the gift tax rules for GPAs. If the estate tax provision on GPAs (IRC § 2041) applies, there is inclusion into the gross estate. *See supra* discussion of IRC § 2041, I. A. 3. c). However, the application of IRC § 2514 merely creates a "transfer of property," not necessarily a gift. Therefore, even after the application of IRC § 2514 one must apply the basic rules discussed above to see if the transfer is taxable under the gift tax. *See supra* discussion of gift transfers, II. B. 3.

> *Example (1):* Same facts as the previous example, except that instead of releasing the GPA, Ronald exercises the power in favor of himself by withdrawing (and keeping) the trust

corpus. IRC § 2514 applies to create a transfer since there has been an "exercise" of a general power of appointment; however, one cannot make a gift to oneself, therefore there is no gift tax on the transfer.

Example (2):   Same as above, except that Ronald exercises his power and places the property into another trust for his children, with the right to add and subtract beneficiaries at a later date. IRC § 2514 applies to create a "transfer of property" since Ronald has exercised a GPA. However, Ronald maintains "dominion and control" over the trust and no taxable transfer exists under IRC § 2501(a). If at a later date Ronald gives up dominion and control it will be treated as a completed gift at that time, or if he maintains control over the property until his death it will be included in his gross estate under IRC § 2041.

(1)   General Powers of Appointment (GPA)

The definition of a GPA in IRC § 2514(c) tracks the estate tax definition in IRC § 2041(b)(1). The primary difference from the estate tax is that the power must be held by the "decedent," while under the gift tax provisions the power must be held by the "possessor." *See supra* discussion of IRC § 2041(b)(1), at I. A. 3. c) (1).

(2)   Lapse

A lapse occurs when the power holder fails to exercise the GPA within the time permitted. Since the power holder could have utilized the power to transfer the property, the failure to do so is substantially the same as making a direct transfer to the default taker. Accordingly, under IRC § 2514(e), a lapse of a GPA is treated as a release, and, if the power is a post–1942 power (one created after 1942), the release is treated as a transfer of property. [IRC § 2514(b), (e)]

However, Congress has made allowances for certain lapses in order to help the donors of moderate sized trusts cope with the possibility that the income from the trust will be insufficient for their needs. [S. Rep. No. 382, 83d Cong., 111th Sess. 4, 7 (1951)] To meet this goal, Congress created an exception to the lapse rule for certain situations where the amount which lapses does not exceed a certain threshold. Under this rule, a lapse is treated as a release of that power (and thus as a transfer) only to the extent that the amount subject to withdrawal exceeds the greater of $5,000 or 5% of the value of the assets controlled by the power. This means that a donor may give a donee the right to withdraw at least $5,000 per year without having the withdrawal treated as a transfer by the donee under IRC § 2514. [IRC § 2514(e)] The term "**5 by 5 power**" is used to describe a GPA that can be exercised only to the extent of the greater of $5,000 or 5% of the value of the property subject to the power. Limiting the power holder's interest to a 5 by 5 power ensures that the power holder will not make a gift to the other trust beneficiaries when the power lapses without exercise.

There are two other nuances regarding lapses. First, if the lapse of the power is caused by a legal disability (such as where the donee is a minor or incompetent), the lapse is not treated as a release of the power. [Reg. § 25.2514–3(c)(4)] Second, the 5 by 5 power applies per beneficiary, not per trust. [Rev. Rul. 85–88, 1985–2 C.B. 202]

Example (1): Larry created an irrevocable trust, giving David the income interest in the trust for life, with the remainder to Ethan or Ethan's estate. David also has the power to withdraw $15,000 from the corpus of the trust each year, but only if the power is exercised in July. If David does not exercise the power, it will lapse to the extent that the amount exceeds the greater of $5,000 or 5% of the value of the trust. If the trust is worth at least $300,000 as of the end of July, the lapse of David's GPA will not be treated as a release of the GPA because the right to withdraw $15,000 does not exceed five percent of the value of the trust (5% of $300,000 is $15,000). If the trust is worth $200,000, the lapse of a $15,000 GPA will be treated as a $5,000 transfer under IRC § 2514 from David to Ethan (5% of $200,000 is $10,000). If the trust is worth $100,000 or less at the time of the lapse, $10,000 will be treated as transferred from David to Ethan. [Reg. § 25.2514–3(c)(4)]

Example (2): Gary created an irrevocable trust with assets less than $100,000, giving Sydney the right to the income of the trust for life, and the remainder to Chris or

Chris' estate. Sydney also held the right to withdraw up to $10,000 from any contribution made by Gary to the trust. This withdrawal power would last only for ten days following a contribution by Gary. Gary made a $10,000 contribution on January 1 and a $10,000 contribution on December 1. Sydney did not exercise her right to withdraw in either instance. During the calendar year, therefore, Sydney had the right to withdraw a total of $20,000. Since the right has lapsed, Sydney is treated as transferring $15,000 to Chris, computed by subtracting the greater of 5% of the value of the trust or $5,000 (here, $5,000) from the $20,000 of the lapsed property ($10,000 from the January transfer; $10,000 from the December transfer). [Rev. Rul. 85–88, 1985–2 C.B. 202]

The treatment of lapses over a period of time is not discussed in the gift tax regulations. Since the amount of the property which lapses and is treated as transferred could be greater than the amount of the corpus of the trust at the time when the power is released or the donee dies, it is thought that the treatment should be the same as in the estate taxation. *See supra* discussion of IRC § 2041, at I. A. 3. c).

(3) Exceptions for Disclaimers Under IRC § 2518
While more fully discussed *infra* at II. C. 2., a qualified disclaimer is not treated as a "release" of a power under IRC § 2514. [Reg. § 25.2514–3(c)(5)] The disclaimer does not have to be of all property interests received. Therefore, the donee may disclaim any general power of appointment while accepting other beneficial interests of the trust. [Reg. § 25.2518–3(a)(1)(i)]

b) **Treatment of Pre–1942 Powers**
For powers of appointment created before October 21, 1942 (a "pre–1942 power"), only the actual exercise of the power (and not the release or lapse of the power) creates a "transfer of property." Furthermore, a pre–1942 power exercisable only in conjunction with another person is *never* treated as a GPA. [IRC § 2514(c)(2)–(3); *see generally supra* discussion of IRC § 2041(b)(1), I. A. 3. c) (1) (b)]

c) **Treatment of Non–General Powers of Appointment**
Powers not exercisable in favor of the power holder, the power holder's estate, the power holder's creditors, or the creditors of the power

holder's estate are not GPAs. They are instead referred to as "non-general" or (somewhat erroneously) "limited" or "special" powers of appointment. Unless the power holder also has an interest in the property, no transfer of property occurs upon the exercise or release of a non-GPA.

This statement does not apply, however, when the power holder has an interest in the property subject to the power. The Service and the Tax Court have held that when such an interest is transferred, it will be treated as a transfer of a property interest under IRC § 2511(a), not IRC § 2514. [*Estate of Regester v. Commissioner*, 83 T.C. 1 (1984); Rev.Rul. 79–327, 1979–2 C.B. 342; Reg. § 25.2514–1(b)(2)] However, where a life estate terminates as a result of the exercise of a non-GPA, an old Court of Claims case states no transfer is created at all since IRC § 2514 does not apply to the transfer, and the life estate was not transferred by the donor, but instead was extinguished "by reason of the power and not by a desire on the part of the income beneficiary to give up the life estate irrespective of the power." [*Self v. United States*, 142 F.Supp. 939, 942 (Ct.Cl. 1956)]

Example (1): Sam creates a trust that provides income to Alice for life. Alice also has the power to appoint the corpus of the trust to Bill, Charley, or David. Since Alice cannot appoint the property to herself, her estate, her creditors or the creditors of her estate, the power is not a GPA. Later, Alice transfers the corpus of the trust in equal shares to Bill and Charley. Since the power was not a GPA, IRC § 2514 does not apply, and therefore the remainder interest is not transferred. But the Service and the Tax Court would deem the life estate a transfer under IRC § 2511(a), making Alice's exercise a completed gift to Bill and Charley. [*Estate of Regester v. Commissioner*, 83 T.C. 1 (1984); Rev.Rul. 79–327, 1979–2 C.B. 342; Reg. § 25.2514–1(b)(2)] However, the Court of Claims would say that there is no taxable transfer under these facts since the transfer is made under a non-GPA and common law would not deem this a transfer. [*Self*, 142 F.Supp. at 942]

Example (2): Same facts as above except that Alice also has the power to dispose the corpus of the trust by her will to anyone, including her estate, if she has not appointed the corpus during her life. If Alice transfers the corpus of the trust during her lifetime, she makes a transfer of the entire corpus of the trust. The transfer of her life estate is a transfer under IRC § 2511, while the transfer of the remainder interest occurs under IRC § 2514 since her GPA is released upon distribution of the property. [Reg. § 25.2514–1(b)(2)]

IRC § 2514(d) is the gift tax counterpart of IRC § 2041(a)(3) and has very limited application. The provision specifies that a transfer occurs when a power (general or non-general) is exercised to create another power, if under local law the new power can be exercised without regard to the creation date of the first power. [IRC § 2514(d); Reg. § 25.2514–3(d)] If not for this rule, property could be passed from generation to generation outside the estate or gift tax and only be possibly subject to the generation-skipping tax of Chapter 13.

2. Disclaimers [IRC § 2518]

IRC § 2518 provides that any person making a "qualified disclaimer" of an interest in property is treated as if the interest was never transferred to that person at all. This section applies to all of subtitle A, which includes the estate, gift and generation skipping transfer taxes. In order for a disclaimer to be "qualified," several elements must be met:

1) the disclaimer must be in writing;

2) it must be irrevocable and unqualified;

3) the written disclaimer must be delivered to either the transferor, the legal representative of the transferor, or the legal titleholder of the property interest transferred within nine months of the date of transfer; or in the case of an interest passing to an individual under the age of twenty-one, within nine months after that individual reaches age twenty-one;

4) there has been no acceptance or use of the disclaimed interest; and

5) the interest must pass without the direction of the disclaimant and may only go to the surviving spouse of the decedent or a person other than the individual disclaiming the interest. [IRC § 2518(b)]

In order to provide some certainty to disclaimers, Congress required that the interest be "irrevocable and unqualified" and in writing. If the section allowed for contingent disclaimers ("I disclaim the property only if Jack disclaims his interest"), difficulties might arise in determining when a disclaimer is present. The written disclaimer must also identify the interest being disclaimed and be signed by the disclaimant. [Reg. § 25.2518–2(b)(1)]

The disclaimer must be received by the proper person before the expiration of the nine-month deadline. The regulations allow for the postmark, not the actual delivery, to meet the delivery date deadline. If the last day of the period falls on a Saturday, Sunday or legal holiday, the date for timely delivery is the following day that is not one of the aforementioned days. [Reg. § 25.2518–2(c)(2)] This nine-month deadline applies not only to the initial recipient of the interest, but also to any individual receiving the property due to a qualified disclaimer.

Example: Transferor dies on January 1 leaving an interest in property to Bill. Bill disclaims the interest in the property exactly nine months later and the property passes to Cathy. If Cathy disclaims the property the next day, her disclaimer is untimely since it is not within nine months of the original transfer. [*See* Reg. § 25.2518–2(c)(5)(Ex. 3)]

a) The Nine–Month Limitation

The timely delivery rule places a premium on knowing when the period commences, as it begins to run on the date the property interest was acquired, not from the time the recipient obtained knowledge of the acquisition. Generally, unless the interest passes to a minor, the nine-month period starts when the interest to be disclaimed is created. [*See* Reg. § 25.2518–2(c)(3)(i)] For those under twenty-one, the period starts on their twenty-first birthday.

(1) Inter Vivos Gift Transfers

In the case of inter-vivos gifts, the period starts when there is a completed gift for Federal gift tax purposes. [Reg. § 25.2518–2(c)(3)(i)]

Example (1): On January 1, Doris creates a trust that pays income to Alice for life and the remainder to Casey. Doris retains the power to revoke the trust. Since Doris has dominion and control over the trust, there is no "transfer." As a result, there is no interest in property for either Alice or Casey to disclaim.

Example (2):   If, on March 1, Doris gives up the power to revoke the trust, there is a completed gift at that time. Alice and Casey have until December 1 (nine months later) to disclaim their respective interests in the property. [Reg. § 25.2518–2(c)(3)(i); *see also* Reg. § 25.2518–2(c)(5)(Ex. 6)]

(2) Testamentary Transfers

For transfers following the decedent's death, the beginning of the nine-month period depends on whether the transfer was made by the decedent at death or whether the decedent had created an interest in property while alive which is included in his or her gross estate. For transfers made at death (e.g., a bequest of a car pursuant to the will), the nine-month period starts on the date of decedent's death. [Reg. § 25.2518–2(c)(3)(i)] For interests in property created during the decedent's lifetime (i.e., a trust) and later included in the decedent's gross estate, the date of the transfer (i.e., the creation of the trust) is the controlling date, not the decedent's death. [*Id.*]

Example: On January 1, Year 1, Doris creates an irrevocable trust with the remainder interest to Casey, but Doris retains the right to income for life. On March 1, Doris dies and the trust corpus is included in Doris' gross estate under IRC § 2036. Casey's remainder interest in the property was created on January 1 and she has nine months from that date to disclaim the interest. The inclusion of the trust corpus into Doris' gross estate has no effect on the time frame for any disclaimer by Casey. [Reg. § 25.2518–2(c)(3)(i)]

(3) Powers of Appointment

Powers of appointment are treated as separate interests in property that may be disclaimed independently from other interests in property. [Reg. § 25.2518–3(a)(1)(iii)] The beginning of the nine-month time period depends on whether the power is a general power of appointment (one exercisable in favor of the power holder, the power holder's estate, the power holder's creditors, or the creditors of the power holder's estate) or a non-general power.

For general powers of appointment, the period starts to run upon receipt of the power. If an interest in property passes by the exercise, release, or lapse of a general power, the individual receiving the property has nine months from the exercise, release or lapse of the power to disclaim the property. [Reg. § 25.2518–2(c)(3)(i)]

Example: On May 13, Year 1, Alex creates an irrevocable trust with the income payable to Bob for life. Bob is given a general power of appointment exercisable at his death over the trust corpus. If Bob fails to exercise the power the corpus will pass to Esther or Esther's estate. Bob dies on June 17, Year 4 and exercises his power in favor of Charlie. If Charlie is twenty-one years or older at the time, Charlie has nine months from June 17, Year 4 to disclaim the trust corpus. [Reg. § 25.2518–2(c)(5)(ex. 2)]

For non-general powers of appointment the power holder and all other possible power holders must disclaim within nine months of the original transfer that created the power.

Example: Same facts as above except Bob's power is a non-general power of appointment to appoint the property to either Chuck or Dan at Bob's death. Assuming they are all age twenty-one or over, if Bob, Chuck, Dan, or Esther want to disclaim an interest in the property they must do so within nine months of May 13, Year 1. [Reg. § 25.2518–2(c)(5)(ex. 1)]

(4) Joint Interests in Property

Joint interests in property are treated as transferred in two parts. One-half of the property transfers at the time of the initial transfer and one-half of the property transfers when the joint tenant dies. [Reg. § 25.2518–2(c)(4)(i)]

Example: On February 1, Year 1, Allen purchased a piece of property with his own funds and named Beatrice as a joint tenant. On January 1, Year 9, Allen dies. Beatrice can disclaim one-half of the property interest within nine months of February 1, Year 1 (the creation of the joint tenancy) and can disclaim the other one-half within nine months of January 1, Year 9 (the date of Allen's death). It does not matter if the property is held as a tenancy by the entirety or that Allen supplied all the consideration for the purchase. [Reg. § 25.2518–2(c)(5)(ex. 7)]

Joint bank accounts receive different treatment since the transferor has the right to take back the account's funds, thereby revoking the transfer. Since the transfer is not complete at the creation of the joint bank account, the nine-month period begins when the co-tenant dies. [Reg. § 25.2518–2(c)(4)(iii)]

b) No Acceptance of Benefits

In order to have an effective disclaimer, the disclaimant cannot accept any of the property nor any benefits from the interest in the property. Acceptance is defined as "an affirmative act which is consistent with ownership of the interest in property." [Reg. § 25.2518–2(d)(1)] Examples are accepting dividends, rent or interest from the property or directing others over the management of the property. It does not include taking mere delivery of title without other acts consistent with ownership.

If the property is capable of being divided into separate distinct portions, a disclaimant may disclaim all of the interest or only a portion of the interest in the property transferred. For this purpose powers are treated as separate interests in property. [IRC § 2518(c)(2)]

Example (1): Gerald gifts Holly 100 shares of Widget Corporation stock. Holly accepts five shares, but sends a written disclaimer to Gerald for the remaining 95 shares within nine months of the transfer. Holly has made an effective disclaimer of the 95 shares. [Reg. § 25.2518–3(a)(1)(ii)]

Example (2): Same facts as above, except that Holly disclaims the income interest in the shares, but retains the remainder interest. Since Holly has not disclaimed an undivided portion of the Widget stock, this is an invalid disclaimer. [Reg. § 25.2518–3(d)(ex. 2)] However, if Holly had received both the income and remainder interests of a trust, it would be a qualified disclaimer if she disclaimed either or both of the interests received. [Reg. § 25.2518–3(d)(ex. 8)]

Example (3): Gilbert receives an income interest from a trust and a testamentary general power of appointment over the trust's corpus. Since powers are treated as separate interests, Gilbert may keep the income interest and disclaim the power over the corpus. [Reg. § 25.2518–

3(d)(ex. 21)] Gilbert may also disclaim a portion of the general power (e.g., retain the power to appoint only 1/3 of the trust corpus), but could not validly disclaim the right to appoint to himself only.

3. Dispositions of Certain Life Estates [IRC § 2519]

IRC § 2519 is the gift tax complement to IRC § 2044 in the estate tax and one or the other, but not both, will apply to all qualifying income interests for which an election was made. IRC § 2519 provides that if the donee spouse disposes of any portion of a qualifying income interest, a constructive transfer of all the interests in property (normally the remainder of a trust) other than the income interest occurs. [IRC § 2519(a)]

This means that on the transfer of a qualifying income interest by the donee-spouse, two transfers are present. First, there is a transfer of the income interest under normal gift tax rules. [i.e., IRC § 2511] Second, the remaining interests in property, other than the qualifying income interest, are constructively transferred under IRC § 2519. Both transfers must be separately analyzed to determine whether the gift tax will apply. It is important to note that even if the donee spouse disposes of only a fraction of the qualifying income interest, the entire remainder interest will be transferred, not just a corresponding fraction. The transfer of only a fraction of the qualifying income interest may also trigger other Code sections like IRC § 2702 (used to determine the amount transferred) and IRC § 2036 (since IRC § 2519 creates a transfer for purposes of *"this chapter and chapter 11"*) to determine the estate tax consequences of the transfer.

Example (1): A testamentary trust created under Donald's will holds Trump stock. The income from the trust is payable at least annually to Donald's wife, Melania, for life. After Melania's death the trust corpus is to pass in equal shares to Donald's children. Donald's executor elects to treat the property as qualified terminable interest property ("QTIP") and the estate receives a marital deduction for the full fair market value of the property under IRC § 2056(a). Several years later when the value of the property is $300,000, and the value of the life estate is $100,000, Melania transfers her income interest in the trust to Carl, her tennis pro. Under IRC § 2511(a), Melania makes a gift of $100,000 (the value of her life estate interest) to Carl. Additionally, IRC § 2519 creates a constructive transfer of the remainder ($200,000, computed by taking the excess of the

$300,000 fair market value of the trust less the qualifying income interest of $100,000) that also will be treated as a gift to Donald's children. While an IRC § 2503(b) annual exclusion is allowed for the transfer of the life estate, none is permitted for the remainder interest since it is a future interest in property. [Reg. § 25.2519–1(g)(ex. 1)]

Example (2): Same facts as above except that Melania sells her life estate to Carl for $100,000. Since the income interest was transferred for full consideration, no gift is made of the transfer of the qualifying life estate interest. [IRC § 2512(b)] However, under IRC § 2519 there is still a transfer of the $200,000 remainder interest that is treated as a gift with no IRC § 2503(b) annual exclusion permitted. [Reg. § 25.2519–1(g)(ex. 2); IRC § 2503(b) discussed *infra* at II. E. 1.]

Example (3): Before Melania transferred the life estate, as an investment decision and as permitted by the trust documents, the trustee of the trust sells the Trump stock and purchases other stock. Selling the stock is not a "disposition" of the qualified income interest for IRC § 2519 purposes, so there is no constructive transfer of the remainder interest. [Reg. § 25.2519–1(f)]

Example (4): Same facts as in the first example, except that instead of making a transfer to her tennis pro, Melania transfers 30% of her life estate to her daughter, Marla. Under general gift tax principles, Melania made a gift transfer to Marla of $30,000 (30% of the $100,000 qualifying income interest). There is also a constructive transfer of the remainder interest under IRC § 2519. Furthermore, since Melania has transferred an interest in trust (her income interest) to a family member (Marla) and retained an interest (the 70% remaining income interest), IRC § 2702 applies. Under IRC § 2702 the value of Melania's remaining income interest is zero, and the total transfer under IRC § 2519 becomes $270,000 (the $300,000 fair market value of the trust less the $30,000 qualifying income interest transferred to Marla). Finally, if Melania does not transfer the rest of her income interest before she dies there will be estate tax consequences under IRC § 2036. Estate tax consequences exist because IRC § 2519 also creates a "transfer" for purposes of chapter 11 (the estate tax) and Melania has the right to the stock for life. The application of IRC § 2036 means that 70% of the trust corpus (the remaining percentage she owns of the life estate) will be included in her gross estate at death (the amount constructively transferred at her death). [Reg. § 25.2519–1(g)(ex. 4)]

IRC § 2207A(b) allows for the donor to recover from the donee any additional gift tax paid due to the application of IRC § 2519. The recoverable amount is equal to the total amount of gift tax payable for the year less the amount due if IRC § 2519 did not apply. [IRC § 2702A(b)(1), (2)]

4. Gifts by Husband and Wife to a Third Party [IRC § 2513]

IRC § 2513 was enacted in 1948 to reduce the tax disparities between married individuals giving gifts in community property states as opposed to separate property states. In community property states a gift made by a husband or wife of community property is treated as a gift of a one-half interest by the husband, and a one-half interest by the wife. IRC § 2513 allows for the same result on transfers by spouses in separate property states if they so elect to "split gifts."

The gift-splitting provision has three requirements. First, the gift must be made during the couple's marriage. Any gift made before marriage cannot be split. If the gift is made while the couple is married, but they divorce (or one spouse later dies in the same calendar year), the gift may be split only if neither spouse (or the surviving spouse) remarries before the end of the calendar year in which the gift occurred. [IRC § 2513(a)(1)] Second, each spouse must be either a citizen or resident of the United States at the time of the gift. [*Id.*; Reg. § 25.2513–1(b)(2)] Finally, both spouses must consent to the election to split gifts. [IRC § 2513(a)(2)]

There are several benefits to gift splitting. First, the IRC § 2503(b) annual exclusion of both spouses can be used, thereby increasing the amount transferred without gift tax liability to $20,000 ($26,000 in 2011 adjusted for inflation) per donee. [IRC § 2503(b)] Second, the IRC § 2505 unified credit of both spouses can be used by each spouse. Finally, since the gift tax rate is imposed on lifetime gifts made by a donor, the lower brackets can be utilized by both spouses. Note, however, that these benefits come at a cost: if the gift is split under IRC § 2513, joint and several liability exists for any gift tax due by either spouse. [IRC § 2513(d)]

Example: Britney and Kevin are married and citizens of the United States. During the current year, Britney gives a gift of $20,000 to Rachel, and Kevin gives a gift of $40,000 to Mike. If Britney and Kevin so consent, the transfers are deemed to be made one-half by each spouse under IRC § 2513(a). Therefore, Britney makes a gift to Rachel of $10,000 and a gift to Mike of $20,000. Likewise, Kevin makes a gift to Rachel of $10,000 and a gift to Mike of $20,000. After the application of the IRC § 2503(b) annual exclusion of $10,000 (unadjusted for inflation), neither Britney nor Kevin makes a taxable gift to Rachel, and each makes only a $10,000 gift to Mike. Britney and Kevin may also use their remaining individual unified credits (if any) under IRC § 2505 to reduce the amount of gift tax due on the gift to Mike.

a) Spousal Consent

Both spouses must consent to the election each year they decide to split gifts. Once they do decide to consent, the consent applies to all gifts made by either spouse during the entire year. The couple cannot specify which transfers they want to split. [IRC § 2513(a)(2)]

The consent must be provided on a gift tax return filed by each spouse. [IRC § 2513(b); Reg. § 25.2513–2(a)(1)] If only one spouse is required to file a return, both spouses may consent on that single gift tax return. [Reg. § 25.2513–2(a)(1)] The consent must be given by the earlier of either: 1) April 15th of the following year, if a timely gift tax return is filed; 2) the time when the gift tax return is filed if no gift tax return was timely filed and it is after April 15th of the following year; or 3) before a notice of deficiency is sent out for the year in question, if no gift tax return is filed. [IRC § 2513(b)(2)]

A revocation of consent may only be made up until April 15th of the year following the transfer. [IRC § 2513(c)(1)] Any consent to split gifts for the prior year given after that date may not be revoked. [IRC § 2513(c)(2)]

b) Exceptions

(1) Interests Incapable of Valuation

If the gift is made in trust and the corpus may be invaded by one of the spouses making it impossible to determine the value of the remainder, the gift may not be split.

Example: Tony transfers $54,000 to an irrevocable trust giving his wife, Maria, the income for her life, remainder to their son, Bernardo. An unrelated trustee also has the power to invade the corpus of the trust for Maria in the trustee's absolute discretion. Normally, the remainder interest given to Bernardo could be split between husband and wife under IRC § 2513. However, since the trustee has absolute discretion to invade the corpus, the various interests of the trust cannot be valued and the gift may not be split as between Tony and his wife. Here, Tony has made a $54,000 total gift to Maria (of the income interest) and to Bernardo (of the remainder). Additionally, since the gift is a terminable interest, no marital deduction is allowed under IRC § 2524 unless the proper elections are made. [*Kass v. Commissioner*, 16 T.C.M. (CCH) 1035 (1957)]

(2) Spouse Granted a General Power of Appointment

If the donor spouse transfers a piece of property but grants the non-donor spouse a general power of appointment over such property, the gift may not be split. [IRC § 2513(a)(1)(penultimate sentence)] Some commentators believe this exception is not required since the GPA would create valuation problems, which would prohibit splitting the gift.

c) Estate Tax Crossover

IRC § 2513 states that gifts are split "for purposes of this chapter" [Chapter 12–Gift Tax]. This means that couples cannot split gifts for purposes of the estate tax, which is in Chapter 11 of the Code. The entire amount of any gift transfer (not just one-half) will go into computing the estate tax (part of the "adjusted taxable gifts" made during the decedent's life time) even if the gifts were split for purposes of the gift tax when the gift was made.

5. Payments of Generation–Skipping Transfer Tax on Direct Skips [IRC § 2515]

The generation-skipping tax ("GST") is imposed on certain transfers that pass over (or "skip") intervening generations. [*See infra* Chapter III. covering the Generation–Skipping Transfer Tax] It is imposed on top of any estate or gift tax due on the transfer. When a transfer of an interest is made directly to a skip person that is subject to the gift tax (called "direct skips" in Chapter 13), the transferor is responsible to pay the gift tax. [IRC § 2603(a)(3)] The additional tax liability paid by the transferor due to the GST results in an additional gift. [IRC § 2515] Therefore, the transferor is essentially treated as giving two gifts, one for the initial transfer and another for the payment of the GST. This makes the transfer tax inclusive (a tax on the amount used to pay the tax) and treats the transaction the same as testamentary direct skips.

Example: T gifts GC, T's grandchild, Blackacre when the property is worth $2 million. T's transfer will be subject to both the gift tax and GST (since this is a direct skip). Assuming an applicable gift and GST tax rate of 35%, the generation-skipping tax is $700,000 (35% of $2 million). The total amount of gifts to GC will be $2.7 million ($2 million for Blackacre, $700,000 from the payment of the GST under IRC § 2515). T's gift tax liability will be $925,800. The total amount of transfer taxes for T from the transfer is $1,625,800, or about 81% of the value of the property transferred.

6. Below–Market Gift Loans [IRC § 7872]

In certain circumstances the interest free use of money is considered a transfer of property. [IRC § 7872] Two transfers are created under IRC § 7872. First, an imputed amount is transferred from the lender to the borrower. [IRC § 7872(a)(1)(A), (b)(1)] Second, an interest payment is imputed passing from the borrower to the lender. [IRC § 7872(a)(1)(B)] Therefore, IRC § 7872 treats the use of money the same as the use of other property (e.g., the rent free use of a house or boat). This was not always the case. [*See, J. Simpson Dean v. Commissioner*, 35 T.C. 1083 (1961) holding the foregone interest was not income to the lender.] The change occurred after the Supreme Court in *Dickman v. Commissioner*, 465 U.S. 330, 104 S.Ct. 1086, 79 L.Ed.2d 343 (1984) held that an interest free loan to a family member resulted in a taxable gift of the unpaid interest. Congress followed up *Dickman* by creating IRC § 7872 statutorily creating a "transfer." IRC § 7872 potentially applies to many different situations, but only gift tax implications will be considered here.

Section 7872 applies to (1) "**below market loans**," (2) "to which this section applies." [IRC § 7872(a)(1), (b)(1)] Both elements are defined below. IRC § 7872 dictates only the amount of transfer, with other Code sections used to determine the tax treatment of each imputed payment.

a) Elements of IRC § 7872

(1) "Below Market Loan"

To determine whether a loan is "below market," there is first a determination of whether it is a demand or term loan. [IRC

§ 7872(e)(1)] **Demand loans** are either "payable in full at any time on the demand of the lender" or are non-transferable and conditioned on the performance of substantial future services by an individual. [IRC § 7872(f)(5)] A **term loan** is a default described as "any loan that is not a demand loan." [IRC § 7872(f)(6)]

Example: On February 1, Year 1, Mother loans Son $20,000 payable in one year. The loan is a term loan since it is not due on the demand of the lender (Mother). [IRC § 7872(f)(6)]

Demand loans qualify as below market loans if the interest rate is less than the applicable federal rate. [IRC § 7872(e)(1)(A)] The applicable federal rate is the Federal short-term rate for the year in question. [IRC § 7872(f)(2)(B)] The Federal short-term rate is the average market yield on outstanding government obligations with three years or less to maturity. [IRC § 1274(d)(1)(A), (C)(i)] Therefore, a comparison of the loan's interest rate to the Federal short-term rate determines whether a demand loan is "below market."

Term loans are considered below market if the amount loaned exceeds the **present value** of all payments due under the loan. [IRC § 7872(e)(1)(B)] The amount loaned is "the amount received by the borrower." [IRC § 7872(f)(4)] The present value of payments is computed by using the appropriate Federal rate for the term of the loan determined under IRC § 1274(d). [IRC § 7872(f)(1)]

Example: On January 1, Mother loans Son $20,000 payable in one year. Son owes $500 of interest at the end of the term when the applicable Federal rate is 10%. The loan qualifies as a term loan since it is not due on the demand of the lender (Mother). [IRC § 7872(f)(6)] The amount loaned is $20,000 (the amount received by Son). [IRC § 7872(f)(4)] The discounted present value of all payments due under the loan ($20,500 due in one year) is $18,594 for a one-year period using the applicable 10% discount rate compounded semi-annually. This loan is considered a "below market loan" since the amount loaned ($20,000) exceeds the present value of all payments due under the loan ($18,594). [IRC § 7872(e)(1)(B)]

(2) "To Which This Section Applies"

In order for IRC § 7872 to apply, the below-market loan must be one "to which this section [IRC § 7872] applies." [IRC § 7872(a)(1), (b)(1)] "Gift loans" are included in the types of loans to which IRC § 7872 applies. [IRC § 7872(c)(1)(A)] A gift loan is any loan where the "foregoing of interest is in the nature of a gift." [IRC § 7872(f)(3)] Therefore, if a lender forgives the interest on a loan out of detached and disinterested generosity, IRC § 7872 will apply, unless an exception applies.

IRC § 7872 will not apply if the total amount of gift loans from one individual to another is less than $10,000 and, therefore, no interest is imputed between the parties. [IRC § 7872(c)(2)(A)] This exclusion is separate from the one under IRC § 2503(b). However, this section does not allow for spouses to each transfer up to the $10,000 limit, since a husband and wife are treated as one person and, as such, the amount loaned is aggregated for both. [IRC § 7872(f)(7)] Moreover, the $10,000 de minimis exception does not apply if the borrower purchases income-producing assets like stocks, bonds, or rental property. [IRC § 7872(c)(2)(B)]

b) Gift Tax Consequences of the Application of IRC § 7872

The imputed transfer amount for below-market gift loans depends on whether the loan is a demand or term loan. However, regardless of the amount, the tax treatment remains the same for the amount deemed transferred from lender to borrower; that amount constitutes a gift. The lender treats the imputed transfers as a gift to the borrower; the borrower is allowed to exclude the imputed amount as a gift under IRC § 102(a). For the borrower, the tax treatment of the imputed interest expense amount from borrower to lender depends on the use of the funds. For example, if the funds were used to purchase a house, the imputed amount may be deductible under IRC § 163. [IRC § 163(a), (h)(2)(D)] The lender treats the imputed amount as interest income. [IRC § 61(a)(4)]

(1) Gift Demand Loans

For gift demand loans, the transfer from lender to borrower and borrower to lender is the same and is the amount of "foregone interest." [IRC § 7872(a)(1)] The time of the transfer occurs on the last day of the calendar year. [IRC § 7872(a)(2)] The foregone interest is the amount of interest due using the applicable Federal rate less any interest payable on the loan. [IRC § 7872(e)(2)] Basically, the amount of foregone interest is what Congress feels should have been paid in interest less the interest due under the agreement.

Example: On January 1, with donative intent, Mother lends $1,000,000 to Son. The loan is payable at the discretion of Mother. The loan has 5% interest (compounded annually) due each year the loan is outstanding. Assume the applicable Federal rate is 10%, compounded semi-annually. IRC § 7872 applies since this is a below-market demand gift loan. [IRC § 7872(a)(1), (e)(1)(A), (f)(5)] The amount of foregone interest for each year the loan is outstanding is $52,500. The forgone interest is determined by first computing the amount of interest due using the applicable Federal rate of 10% compounded semi-annually ($102,500), then subtracting the amount of interest payable ($50,000). The $52,500 represents the amount of gift transfer from Mother to Son. [IRC § 7872(a)(1)(A)] It also represents the deemed interest payment from Son to Mother. [IRC § 7872(a)(1)(B)] The tax implications for Son depend on his utilization of the loan funds.

Unless a tax avoidance purpose exists, the imputed transfer amount from borrower to lender for gift loans of $100,000 or less is limited to the amount of the borrower's net investment income. [IRC § 7872(d)(1)(A), (B), (D)] The net investment income is the excess of the income received on the borrower's investment less the expenses to create that income. [IRC §§ 7872(d)(1)(E)(i), 163(d)(4)(A)] If the borrower's net investment income does not exceed $1,000, it is treated as zero. [IRC § 7872(d)(1)(E)(ii)] This rule does not limit the imputed transfer from lender to borrower, and therefore, does not affect the amount deemed a gift.

(2) Gift Term Loans

(a) Imputed Gift Transfer

The amount of the deemed gift from lender to borrower for below market gift term loans is determined using IRC § 7872(b)(1) as a result of IRC § 7872(d)(2). [IRC § 7872(d)(2)] Under IRC

§ 7872(b)(1), the deemed gift transfer equals the amount loaned less the present value of all payments required under the loan. [IRC § 7872(b)(1)] The gift occurs on the later of the date the loan was made or the first day when IRC § 7872 applies (e.g., when the amount loaned exceeds the $10,000 exception). [IRC § 7872(b)(2)]

Example: With donative intent, Father lends $50,000 to Son for a term of ten years at 0% interest. If the applicable Federal rate is 10% compounded semi-annually, the present value of the loan payments ($50,000 to be paid in ten years) is $18,844. [IRC § 7872(f)(1)] The loan qualifies as a "below-market loan" since the amount loaned ($50,000) exceeds the present value of all payments due under the loan ($18,844). [IRC § 7872(e)(1)(B), (f)(4)] More-over, the loan is one "to which this section applies," since Father's donative intent in foregoing the payment of interest is "in the nature of a gift." [IRC § 7872(c)(1)(A), (f)(3)] Father's deemed gift transfer is determined under IRC § 7872(b)(1), since the loan is a term loan. [IRC § 7872(d)(2), (f)(6)] The deemed gift totals $31,156: the amount loaned ($50,000) less the present value of all payments due under the loan ($18,844). [IRC § 7872(b)(1)] Father is deemed to have transferred $31,156 of the $50,000 loan as a transfer of property by gift. Additionally, under IRC § 102(a) Son does not include any of the deemed transfer in his gross income.

(b) Imputed Interest Payment

Just as for gift demand loans, the amount of foregone interest is the deemed interest payment from borrower to lender. [IRC § 7872(a)(1)(B)] The net investment income limitation also applies to limit the deemed transfer to the borrower's net investment income. [IRC § 7872(d)(1)]

Example: Same facts as above, with the additional fact that Son has $3,000 of net investment income. Gener-ally, the amount of imputed interest from Son (borrower) to Father (lender) is the foregone interest. [IRC § 7872(a)(1)] The foregone interest for the year on $50,000 at 10% interest compounded semi-annually is $5,125. However, unless avoidance of the Federal tax is one of the principal purposes of the loan, the amount of the imputed interest payment is limited to the Son's net investment interest ($3,000). [IRC § 7872(d)(1)(A)] Father will include the $3,000 in his gross income. Son's tax treatment of the $3,000 deemed interest payment depends on his use of the $50,000. [*See, e.g.,* IRC § 163(a)]

D. Special Valuation Rules

1. Special Valuation Rules in Case of Transfers of Certain Interests in Corporations or Partnerships

a) Introduction

Even after a careful reading of IRC § 2701, its purpose and effect can remain elusive. To understand the problem IRC § 2701 addresses, one must first understand the mechanics of the classic preferred interest estate freeze technique. Suppose a taxpayer owns all of the stock in a closely held corporation. The taxpayer wants to transfer a substantial portion of the stock to the taxpayer's child, but there are three obstacles to an outright gift transfer. First, the taxpayer does not want to lose control of the corporation. Second, the taxpayer does not want to lose a substantial portion of the dividend stream flowing from the corporation. And finally, such a large gift would likely result in liability for federal gift tax.

Prior to the enactment of IRC § 2701, a common solution to these obstacles was to effect an income tax-free recapitalization of the stock into two classes: voting preferred stock and nonvoting common stock. [IRC § 368(a)(1)(E)] In addition to carrying all of the voting rights, the preferred stock would feature a fixed liquidation preference equal to the pre-recapitalization value of the corporation's stock and a fixed dividend preference equal to the corporation's pre-recapitalization income stream. The common stock would lack voting rights, but because the preferred stock's rights at liquidation and distribution are frozen, the common stock would receive all future appreciation in the value of the corporation.

Following this recapitalization, the taxpayer would transfer the nonvoting common stock to the child and retain the voting preferred stock. This technique solved the problems of the outright gift: the taxpayer kept control over the corporation by holding all of the voting shares, the fixed dividend preference ensured that the taxpayer would continue to enjoy an income stream at the same level, and the gifted common shares could be transferred at very little value because they lacked voting rights and no present rights to dividends or liquidation proceeds. Meanwhile, all future growth in the corporation was allocated to the common shares. At the taxpayer's death, the gross estate would include only the preferred shares, and that value would be fixed because of the limited and preferred distribution and liquidation rights. All of the post-gift appreciation in the corporation's value was allocable to the common shares that were in the hands of the child.

Despite challenges from the Service, the preferred interest freeze technique worked. Additionally, it worked not only for corporations, but for partnerships as well. It took IRC § 2701 to render the technique ineffective. Where applicable, IRC § 2701 requires that the computation of the value of the gifted common interest be determined by valuing the retained preferred interest at zero (the "zero-value rule"). [IRC § 2701(a)(3)(A); Reg. § 25.2701–1(a)(2)] In effect, then, a gift of the common interest is valued as though it were a gift of both the common and preferred interests. If IRC § 2701 does not apply, the gift transfer is valued under the normal valuation rules.

Example: Petros, an individual, holds all the outstanding common stock of X Corporation (X), with a total fair market value of $1 million. In a tax-free reorganization, Petros transfers his X common stock for 900 shares of preferred stock and 100 shares of common stock. The preferred stock has an annual non-cumulative dividend of $100 per share, and a right to sell the stock back to the corporation (a "put") for $1,000 per share. Assume that the fair market value of the preferred stock is $900,000. Petros transfers the 100 shares of common stock to his daughter, Clarissa. Several years later, Petros dies when the total value of X is $2.5 million.

Without IRC § 2701, the gift and estate tax treatment would be as follows. On the transfer of the common stock to Clarissa, Petros would have a taxable gift of $100,000 ($1 million less the $900,000 fair market value of the preferred stock). On his death, Petros would include the $900,000 of preferred stock in his gross estate under IRC § 2033. The $1.5 million increase in value (which could have been due in part to the corporation never authorizing any dividends to the preferred stock) is not taxed, and therefore, the value is "frozen" at the time of transfer with all the appreciation going to the common stock.

With IRC § 2701 the outcome is very different. Petros' preferred stock (an "applicable retained interest") is valued at zero. Thus, the transfer to Clarissa results in a $1 million taxable gift. On Petros' death, $900,000 is still included in his gross estate, but the estate will receive some relief since the preferred stock has already been taxed under Chapter 12. [IRC § 2701(e)(6); Reg. § 25.2701–5; *see infra.* at II D. 1. i)]

IRC § 2701 is best approached in three steps. First, see if IRC § 2701 applies to the facts. Next, see if any exceptions exist to the application of the rule. Finally, if no exceptions exist, value the property under IRC § 2701.

IRC § 2701 applies when two conditions are met. Under the introductory language of IRC § 2701(a), the taxpayer must transfer an interest (formally, a "subordinate interest") in a partnership or corporation to or for the benefit of a statutorily defined member of the taxpayer's family in a younger generation. [IRC § 2701(a)(1); Reg. § 25.2701–3(a)(2)(iii)] Second, immediately after the transfer, the taxpayer or an applicable family member (a member of the taxpayer's family in an older generation) must hold an "applicable retained interest." [IRC §§ 2701(a)(1)(B); 2701(b)(1)] IRC § 2701 does not apply when market quotations are available for either the retained or transferred interest, if the transferor's retained interest is the same class as the transferred interest, and if the interests are given proportionally. The exceptions are covered in greater detail *infra* at II. D. 1. d). [IRC § 2701(a)(1)(flush), (a)(2)]

b) [Step 1] First Requirement for the Application of IRC § 2701(a): Transfer of Subordinate Equity Interest to a Member of Transferor's Family

(1) "Transfer" Requirement
In order for IRC § 2701 to apply, there must be a "transfer" made by the taxpayer. The transfer may be direct or indirect.

(a) Direct Transfers

The transferor must give up dominion and control of the property to satisfy the transfer requirement. [*See supra*, II. B. 3. b)] Even transfers not considered gift transfers, due to the fact that full and adequate consideration is paid under IRC § 2512(b) for the transferred interest, can still be treated as a "transfer" for IRC § 2701, effectively changing a sale into a gift. [Reg. § 25.2701–1(b)(1)] This prevents avoidance of the zero-value rule by making payments, since the value of the interest given can be nominal.

Example (1): Parent has both preferred and common stock in Corporation X. Parent transfers the common stock outright to Child, while retaining the preferred stock. This is a transfer that is covered by IRC § 2701.

Example (2): Parent has both preferred and common stock in Corporation X with fair market values of $96,000 and $4,000, respectively. Parent sells the common stock to Child for $4,000, while retaining the preferred stock. Although Child paid consideration for the common stock, the sale will be treated as a "transfer" for IRC § 2701. If the zero valuation rules apply, Parent will be treated as making a $96,000 gift to Child ($100,000 transferred less the $4,000 consideration paid). [IRC § 2701(a)(3)(A); Reg. § 25.2701–1(b)(1), –3(b)(4)(iv)]

The exercise, release, or lapse of a power is treated as a "transfer" under IRC § 2701 only when they are treated as transfers under IRC § 2514. [Reg. § 25.2701–1(b)(3)(iii)] Therefore, the exercise, release, or lapse of a post–1942 general power of appointment is treated as a transfer for IRC § 2701.

Example: Parent creates a trust by transferring the common stock from Corporation X discussed above. Parent gives Spouse a non-general power to transfer the common stock to Child. If Spouse exercises the power and transfers the common stock to Child, no transfer will occur for IRC § 2701(a). If instead, Spouse had a general power of appointment, the exercise of the power would be treated as a transfer covered under IRC § 2701.

The disclaimant does not treat any shift of rights occurring due to a qualified disclaimer under IRC § 2518 as a transfer. However, depending on who ultimately receives the interest, IRC § 2701 may apply when valuing the interest from the original transferor. [Reg. § 25.2701–1(b)(3)(ii)]

Example: Grandfather owns all the preferred and common stock of Corporation Y. He transfers the common stock to Parent, while retaining all the preferred stock. Parent makes a qualified disclaimer of the common stock, and as a result the stock goes to Child. Parent is not treated as making a transfer to Child, but IRC § 2701 may apply to value the transfers created by the disclaimer going from Grandfather to Child.

(b)   Indirect Transfers

IRC § 2701 also covers indirect transfers, various transactions where the younger generation receives an interest in the corporation or partnership. Examples of indirect transfers are transfers completed by the application of the attribution rules, and certain contributions to capital or other changes in the capital structure of the corporation or partnership.

i)   Attribution Rules

Equity interests held indirectly through a corporation, partnership, estate, trust, or other entity are attributed to an individual. [IRC § 2701(e)(3)] An individual is treated as owning the stock held by the corporation in proportion to the fair market value of the stock owned by the individual to the total fair market value of all the stock of the corporation. Partnership interests have similar attribution, but the proportion used is the individual's interest in the profits or capital interests in the partnership to the total partnership fair market value of such interests. [Reg. § 25.2701–6(a)]

Example: Parent owns all the common stock of X Corporation (X). Y Corporation (Y) has two classes of stock, preferred and common, both of which are owned by X. Parent has X transfer all the common stock of Y to Child. Since the ownership interests of X are attributed to Parent, the transfer is treated as a transfer by Parent to Child.

ii) Transfers under IRC § 2701(e)(5)

In order to find a transfer under IRC § 2701(e)(5), three elements must be met. First, there must be a contribution to capital, redemption, recapitalization, or other change in the capital structure of a corporation or partnership. Second, the transferor or an applicable family member must receive an applicable retained interest (defined *infra* at II. D. 1. c) (2)) in such entity or, due to the transfer, their interests are increased. Finally, there is no transfer for IRC § 2701 if the transfer leaves the transferor, applicable family members, and members of the transferor's family in substantially identical positions after the transaction. [IRC § 2701(e)(5)]

(I) Contributions to Capital, Redemptions, and Other Changes in the Capital Structure

Neither the Code nor Regulations define a contribution to capital for IRC 2701(e)(5). However, it is thought to include any transfer of money or other property to a corporation or partnership in return for an equity interest in the entity. [STEPHENS, ET AL., FEDERAL ESTATE AND GIFT TAXATION ¶ 19.02[2][a] (8th ed. 2002)] A redemption is a transaction between the entity and shareholder/partner in which the equity interest is surrendered for either cash or property.

Example (1): Parent and Child decide to form X Corporation (X). Parent and Child both transfer cash to X, for which Parent receives preferred stock and Child receives common stock. This is a contribution to capital and is treated as a transfer of common stock from Parent to Child. As discussed above, the consideration paid by Child will not prevent the application of IRC § 2701.

Example (2): Corporation Y (Y) has a total of 1,000 shares outstanding, which are owned 75% by Alice and 25% by Boris, Alice's child. Alice transfers 250 shares of her common stock to Y in exchange for 300 shares of preferred stock, which, due to the nature of the attached rights, is treated as an applicable retained interest. This is a capital structure transaction, and since Alice retains an applicable retained interest, is treated as a transfer of common stock from Alice to Boris. [Reg. § 25.2701–3(d)(ex. 4)]

(II) Qualifying Outcomes to Transferor or Applicable Family Member

Not all contributions to capital or changes to the capital structure are treated as transfers under IRC § 2701(e)(5); the transfer must be one of three specific types of transfers specified in the Regulations. The first type of transfer is what one might expect; as a result of the transaction, the transferor or an applicable family member receives an applicable retained interest in the capital structure transaction. [IRC § 2701(e)(5)(A); Reg. § 2701–1(b)(2)(i)(B)(1)] Applicable retained interests are defined in *infra.* at II. D. 1. c) (2), but the examples below will consist of preferred stock with non-cumulative dividend rights.

Example: The Alice and Boris hypothetical, immediately above, is an example of a transfer where the transferor receives an applicable retained interest in the capital structure transaction. Alice gave up common stock for preferred stock, which was an applicable retained interest. [Reg. § 25.2701–3(d)(ex. 4)]

The second transfer that is treated as indirect is one in which the transferor or an applicable family member holds an applicable retained interest before the capital structure transaction, subsequently surrenders an equity interest that is junior to the applicable retained interest (a "subordinate interest"), and receives property other than an applicable retained interest in return. [IRC § 2701(e)(5)(B); Reg. § 2701–1(b)(2)(i)(B)(2)] This is treated as a transfer since after the termination the subordinate interests are increased by the taxpayer's actions.

Example: Corporation Z is has two shareholders, Parent and Child. Parent holds both preferred and common stock, while Child holds only common stock. If Parent redeems her common stock for cash, the transaction will be treated as a transfer of stock under IRC § 2701 from Parent to Child. [Reg. § 2701–1(b)(2)(i)(B)(2)] After the transaction, Child's interest in Corporation Z increases since there is less stock outstanding after the redemption.

The third type of transfer treated as indirect is one in which the transferor or an applicable family member holds an applicable retained interest before the capital structure transaction, later surrenders an equity interest in the entity (other than a subordinate interest), and the fair market value of the applicable retained interest is increased. [Reg. § 2701–1(b)(2)(i)(B)(3)]

Example: Parent holds two different classes of preferred stock, Class A and B, in a corporation. Child holds common stock in the same corporation. Assume that both the Class A and B are applicable retained interests under IRC § 2701(b)(1)(A). If Parent redeems the Class A stock for cash, this will be treated as a transfer from Parent to Child.

(III) "Substantially Identical" Transfer Exception

There is no indirect transfer created in the case of a capital structure transaction if the interests held by the transferor, the transferor's applicable family members, and members of the transferor's family are substantially identical before and after the transaction. [IRC § 2701(e)(5); Reg. § 25.2701–1(b)(3)(i)] Voting rights are disregarded in determining if the interests are substantially identical. [Reg. § 25.2701–1(b)(3)(i)] The exception for substantially identical interests does not apply to contributions of capital made by the transferor. [IRC § 2701(e)(5)]

Example: Parent holds all the preferred stock in Corporation Alpha, with Child holding all the common stock. In a recapitalization transaction, the preferred stock of the corporation is changed from voting to non-voting stock, but otherwise remains the same. Since the voting rights are disregarded, the holdings of Parent and Child are substantially identical both before and after the recapitalization and no transfer has occurred for IRC § 2701(e)(5).

(2) Interest in Corporation or Partnership

The interest that is transferred (either directly or indirectly) must be an equity interest that possesses a right to the income or capital in either a corporation or partnership. An equity interest is stock in a corporation or any interest as a partner in a partnership. [IRC § 2701(a)(4)(B)(ii)] The transferred interest must be subordinate to other interests (called "senior equity interests") of the entity. [Reg. § 25.2701–3(a)(2)(iii)]

(3) "Member of the Transferor's Family"

In order for IRC § 2701(a) to apply, there must be a "transfer of an interest in a corporation or partnership to (or for the benefit of) a member of the transferor's family." The term "member of the transferor's family" includes only the transferor's spouse, any descendant of the transferor or transferor's spouse, and the spouse of such descendants. [IRC § 2701(e)(1)] In determining such persons, relationships by adoption are treated the same as those by blood. [IRC § 2701(e)(4)] The definition, therefore, includes the transferor's spouse, children, grandchildren, etc., but excludes brothers, sisters, nieces and nephews.

c) **[Step 1] Second Requirement for the Application of IRC § 2701(a): After the Transfer, the Taxpayer or Applicable Family Member Holds an Applicable Retained Interest.**

As stated earlier, the application of IRC § 2701 has two elements. The first, "transfer of an interest in a corporation or partnership to (or for the benefit of) a member of the transferor's family" is discussed above. The second requirement is that the transferor or "applicable family member" must hold an "applicable retained interest" immediately after transfer. Both "applicable family member" and "applicable retained interest" are defined below.

(1) **"Applicable Family Member"**

For IRC § 2701(a), the term "applicable family member" includes the transferor's spouse, any ancestor of the transferor or transferor's spouse, and the spouse of such ancestor. [IRC § 2701(e)(2)] In determining such persons, relationships by adoption are treated the same as those by blood. [IRC § 2701(e)(4)] The definition, therefore, includes the transferor's spouse, parents, grandparents, etc., but excludes brothers, sisters, uncles and aunts. Note that the transferor's spouse can be both a "member of the family" and an "applicable family member."

> *Example:* Widget Corporation has three shareholders, Grandfather, Parent (Grandfather's child) and Grandchild (Parent's adopted child). Grandfather holds all the preferred stock in Widget, while Parent and Grandchild hold the common stock. Parent transfers her common stock to Grandchild. Grandfather is a direct ancestor of Parent and therefore is an "applicable family member." IRC § 2701 will apply to value Parent's common stock since it was made to member of Parent's family (Grandchild) and an applicable family member (Grandfather) had an applicable retained interest (the preferred stock) after the transfer.

(2) "Applicable Retained Interest"

The heart of IRC § 2701 is contained in the definition of what is treated as an "applicable retained interest." Generally, the reason different items are treated as an applicable retained interest is that they are discretionary rights that can be controlled by the transferor or an applicable family member. The Code assumes that this control will be used to maximize the value of the junior equity interest, thereby passing money to a lower generation at no estate tax cost.

An applicable retained interest is any interest in an entity that is either: 1) a distribution right from a controlled entity, or 2) any liquidation, put, call, or conversion right (collectively called "extraordinary payment rights" in the Regulations). [IRC § 2701(b)(1); Reg. § 25.2701–2(b)] It is important to distinguish the two types of applicable retained interests, since the manner in which they are valued is different. [*See* IRC § 2701(b)(3)(A–C)]

(a) Distribution Rights in a Controlled Entity

Generally a distribution right is the right to distributions from an entity with respect to the ownership (equity) interest therein. For a corporation, the right to distributions must be with respect to its stock (i.e., a dividend), and for a partnership, the right to distribution must be made with respect to a partner's interest in the partnership. [IRC § 2701(c)(1)(A)] However, the following are not treated as distribution rights: (1) if the right to distribution is the same or subordinate to the transferred interest, (2) extraordinary payment rights, and (3) guaranteed partnership payments under IRC § 707(c). [IRC § 2701(c)(1)(B)]

Example (1):   Frederick owns two classes of stock in Oreo Corporation (Oreo), preferred stock that has a non-cumulative right to dividends and common stock. Frederick transfers the common stock to his son, Greg. If Oreo is a controlled corporation, Frederick's preferred stock is an applicable retained interest.

Example (2):   Same as above except the preferred stock is subordinate to the rights of the common stock. Frederick's rights will not be treated as a distribution right since they are secondary to the rights of the common stock transferred by Frederick to Greg.

(i) Control

If the transferor does not have the ability to dictate, either alone or with family members, whether the distribution rights of the stock will be satisfied, there is limited freeze possibility and IRC § 2701 will not apply. In finding whether control exists, the ownership interests considered are both the ancestors of the transferor and transferor's spouse **and** any lineal descendants of the parent of the transferor or transferor's spouse. This includes a wide range of people including grandparents, parents, brothers, sisters, nieces and nephews. [IRC § 2701(b)(2)(C); Reg. § 25.2701–2(b)(5)(i)]

For a corporation, control is holding 50 percent or more of the total voting power or the total value of the equity interests in the corporation. Stock that is only allowed to vote on extraordinary measures (liquidations, mergers, etc.) or is subject to a contingency outside the power of the shareholder that has not occurred is not considered in determining control. [IRC § 2701(b)(2)(A); Reg. § 25.2701–2(b)(5)(ii)] Partnerships are "controlled" if either: (1) a partner holds 50 percent or more of the capital or profit interest in the partnership, or (2) any general partner in a limited partnership. [IRC § 2701(b)(2)(B); Reg. § 25.2701–2(b)(5)(iii)]

> *Example:* Corporation P is owned equally by three unrelated shareholders; A, B, and C. The ownership share consists of both preferred and common stock. Since none of the shareholders have 50 percent or greater vote or value of the corporation, the zero-value rule will not apply to any gift transfers they make of their stock.

(b) Extraordinary Payment Rights

Applicable retained interests also include extraordinary payment rights. Extraordinary payment rights include the right to compel the liquidation of the entity, and any put, call, or conversion right, if the exercise or non-exercise affects the value of the transferred subordinate equity interest. However, if the liquidation right, put, call, or conversion right falls into one of two classes, it is not treated as an applicable retained interest. First, rights which are non-discretionary and must be exercised at a specific time and for a specific amount (called "mandatory payment rights" in the Regulations) are not applicable retained interests. [IRC § 2701(c)(2)(A, B); Reg. § 25.2701–2(b)(4)] Neither are nonlapsing rights to convert stock or partnership interests into a fixed number or percentage in the same class as the transferred interest. [IRC § 2701(c)(2)(C); Reg. § 25.2701–2(b)(4)(iv)] The extraordinary payment rights under IRC § 2701 will be treated as if they will not be exercised and valued at zero unless paired with a distribution right. [IRC § 2701(a)(3)]

(c) Liquidation, Put, Call, or Conversion Right

Liquidation Right: The right to compel the liquidation of the entity is an extraordinary payment right. This is more than the right just to participate in any liquidation, which would lack the discretionary element required to force valuation under IRC § 2701. [Reg. § 25.2701–2(b)(4)(ii)] However, if the transferor has sufficient voting power to compel liquidation, the right to participate in liquidation is treated as an extraordinary payment right. [Reg. § 25.2701–2(d)(ex. 3)]

Example (1): Along with applicable family members, Percy owns 60 percent of the voting right in Corporation X. In order to compel liquidation, 80 percent of the vote is required. Percy's right to participate in liquidation of Corporation X is not considered an extraordinary payment right and therefore is not an applicable retained interest. [Reg. § 25.2701–2(d)(ex. 4)]

Example (2): Same as above, except only 60 percent of the vote is required to compel liquidation. Percy's right to participate in liquidation is now an extraordinary payment right, and is an applicable retained interest. [Reg. § 25.2701–2(d)(ex. 3)]

Put: The right of a shareholder to sell his or her interest back to the corporation at a set price (e.g., Class A shares can be sold back to the corporation for $10 minimum). The right may be tied to a specific period of time. A put is given to protect a shareholder from a decrease in the value of the stock.

Call: The right of a shareholder to purchase stock from a corporation at a set price (e.g., the corporation will sell Class A shares to shareholder for $10 maximum). The right may be tied to a specific period of time. Calls include warrants, options, or other rights to acquire additional equity interests. [Reg. § 25.2701–2(b)(2)]

Conversion Right: The right to convert one interest into another interest.

d) [Step 2] Exceptions to IRC § 2701(a)

Situations that lack the discretionary control over the various aspects of the value of an equity interest are excluded from the valuation rules of IRC § 2701(a). Therefore, the zero-value rule does not apply to interests for which market quotations are readily available, if the applicable retained interest is the same class as the transferred interest, and to proportionate transfers, such as where the transferor gifts a portion of his or her common interest and the same portion of his or her preferred interest. [IRC § 2701(a)(2)]

(1) Market Quotations

Since IRC § 2701 was created to value interests that are difficult to value, if either the transferred or applicable retained interest can be valued on an established securities market (e.g., the New York Stock Exchange), IRC § 2701 does not apply. [IRC § 2701(a)(1)(flush), (a)(2)(A); Reg. § 25.2701–1(c)(1, 2)]

(2) Same Class of Stock

Section 2701 does not apply if the applicable retained interest and the transferred interest are identical (or proportional) in rights, disregarding any non-lapsing differences in voting rights. [IRC § 2701(a)(2)(B); Reg. § 25.2701–1(c)(3)]

Example (1): Frederick owns all the preferred and common stock in Oreo Corporation. Frederick transfers 50 percent of his preferred stock to his son Greg. Since the transferred and applicable retained interest are the same class, IRC § 2701 does not apply. [IRC § 2701(a)(2)(B)] There is no estate freezing potential here since Frederick and Greg have the same interests in property.

Example (2): Same as above, except the preferred stock transferred to Greg does not have any voting rights. The voting rights are disregarded and stock is therefore identical and IRC § 2701 does not apply. [Reg. § 25.2701–1(c)(3)]

(3) Proportional Transfers

If the transferor transfers interests in such a way that there is a proportionate reduction in the transferor's interests, the zero-valuation rule does not apply. In computing whether a proportionate reduction is made, the holdings of the transferor and all applicable family members are considered both before and after the transfer. [IRC § 2701(a)(2)(C); Reg. § 25.2701–1(c)(4)] Since the transfer is proportional, there is no potential for freezing the retained interest while passing on the growth in the retained interest and the special valuations rules are not necessary.

Example: Father gives 20% of his interest in the nonvoting common stock of Family Corporation (FC) to Daughter. In the same transaction, Father gives Daughter 20% of his interest in the voting preferred stock in FC. The zero-value rule does not apply to these gifts even though the formal requirements for the application of IRC § 2701 are present; Father has given Daughter a proportionate share of both a subordinate equity interest (the common shares) and a senior equity interest (the preferred shares).

e) **[Step 3] Valuation of Applicable Retained Interests**

If all the elements are met for the application of IRC § 2701, the next step in the analysis is to value the applicable retained interests and transferred interest. Generally, applicable retained interests are valued at zero. This is because the statute assumes the distributions will not be made or the extraordinary rights will not be exercised. The zero valuation rule does not apply where the distribution rights are "qualified payments" and, therefore, outside of the control of the transferor or applicable family member. [IRC § 2701(a)(3)(A, B)] Regardless, if the zero-value rule applies, the transferred interest has a minimum value of 10 percent of the total value of the entity, plus any debt owed to the transferor by the entity. [IRC § 2701(a)(4)]

Example: Mother transfers all of the nonvoting common stock in Family Corporation (FC) to Son, retaining all of the voting preferred stock in FC. An appraisal of the FC shares conducted immediately prior to the gift indicates that the total combined value of the FC stock is $10 million. Because the common stock lacks voting rights and the preferred stock holds substantial distribution and liquidation preferences, the value of the nonvoting common stock is $100,000, and the value of the voting preferred stock is $9,900,000. Since Mother transfers a subordinate equity interest to a member of the family and has an applicable retained interest, IRC § 2701 applies to value the transaction. Assuming the distribution rights are not qualified, Mother will be considered to have made a gift of $10 million to Son, since the preferred shares retained by Mother will be valued at zero.

(1) Qualified Payments

Qualified payments are basically mandatory distribution rights of the shareholder. Since the distributions are non-discretionary, the zero-valuation does not apply. [IRC § 2701(a)(3)(C)] A right to a **qualified payment** is a right to a cumulative dividend on preferred stock payable on a periodic basis to the extent the amount of the dividend is determined at a fixed rate or bears a fixed relationship to a specified market rate. [IRC § 2701(c)(3); Reg. § 25.2701–2(b)(6)] Thus, if the entity pays a market-rate dividend on the preferred interest, Congress will forego application of the zero-value rule because there is assurance that dividends will be paid to the transferor and thus become part of the transferor's gross estate to the extent not consumed before death. If the rate bears a set relationship to a specified market rate interest (e.g., "6 percent above the prime rate"), this will be treated as a fixed rate even though it fluctuates. [IRC § 2701(c)(3)(B)] As discussed in more detail below, a transferor or applicable family member may elect in or out of the treatment of the distribution as a qualified payment. [IRC § 2701(c)(3)(C)]

Example (1): Peter holds all the stock of Dino Corporation (DC). Peter transfers all his non-voting common stock to his daughter, Gabrilla, retaining the DC voting preferred stock that has a cumulative annual dividend of $10. Since Peter controls DC, the right to dividends is an applicable retained interest. [IRC § 2701(b)(1)] However, since the dividend right is cumulative and at a fixed amount, it is a "qualified right" and the preferred stock will not have a zero value. [IRC § 2701(a)(3)(C), (e)(3)(A); Reg. § 25.2701–2(d)(ex. 1)]

Example (2): Same facts as above except that the right to dividends on Peter's preferred stock is non-cumulative. The distribution right is still an applicable retained interest, but is no longer a "qualified right" and will be valued at zero. [IRC § 2701(a)(3)(A), (e)(3)(A)] Note, that if in either example Peter did not control DC, the distribution right would not be an applicable retained interest and the preferred stock would be valued at its fair market value. [IRC § 2701(b)(1)(A); Reg. § 25.2701–2(d)(ex. 2)]

(a) Elections

The transferor or applicable family member may elect to treat distribution rights as qualifying or non-qualifying. [IRC § 2701(c)(3)(C)] The transferor may treat all or a portion of the distribution rights as nonqualifying, although the rights meet the requirements to be considered qualifying payments. [IRC § 2701(c)(3)(C)(i); Reg. § 25.2701–2(c)] This is done primarily to avoid the tax consequences of IRC § 2701(d) (the "lookback" rule discussed *infra* at II. D. 1. h)), which can increase the amount of taxable gifts or taxable estates for payments that were due but not made. It is also possible for the transferor and applicable family members to treat the payments as qualifying payments, regardless of whether they meet the requirements. [IRC § 2701(c)(3)(C)(ii)] Once the election is made, it is irrevocable. [IRC § 2701(c)(3)(C)(iii)]

Example: Same facts as above where Peter's preferred stock had non-cumulative dividend rights. While the stock is non-qualifying, if Peter elects to treat the stock as qualifying, it will not be valued at zero. However, the stock will be subject to the look-back rule of IRC § 2701(d).

(b) Valuation of Qualifying Payments

(i) Solely Distributions Rights

Equity interests with qualifying payment rights not connected to extraordinary payment rights are valued without regard to IRC § 2701. [IRC § 2701(a)(3)(C)]

Example (1):   Parker holds all the stock of Xerxes Corporation (XC) worth a total of $1.5 million. XC is recapitalized, so that there is both preferred and common stock. After the recapitalization, Parker has 1,000 shares of preferred stock with a par value of $1,000 and an annual cumulative dividend of $100 per share, and 1,000 shares of common stock. Assume that the value of the preferred stock is $1 million. Later, Parker transfers all the common stock to his daughter. Since Parker transfers a subordinate equity interest to a member of his family and retains an applicable retained interest, IRC § 2701 applies. However, since the applicable retained interest (the preferred stock) has a cumulative fixed dividend right, it is a qualifying payment. Therefore, the preferred stock is valued at $1 million, and the gift to Parker's daughter is $500,000. [Reg. § 25.2701–1(e)(ex. 1)]

Example (2):   If Parker's right to dividends were noncumulative, the right would not be a qualifying right and valued at zero. This means Parker is treated as transferring $1,500,000 to his daughter. Parker may elect to treat all or a portion of the preferred stock as subject to a qualifying payment to avoid the application of the zero-value rule. [Reg. § 25.2701–1(e)(ex. 2)]

(ii) Qualifying Distribution Rights and Extraordinary Payment Rights

If the transferor's applicable retained interest consists of a distribution right with qualified payments and one or more extraordinary payment rights, the "lower of" rule applies. The extraordinary payment rights are valued as if they were exercised in such a manner that results in the lowest value for all the attached rights. [IRC § 2701(a)(3)(C)]

Example: Xylong Corporation (X) has a total equity value of $1.5 million and has two classes of stock outstanding, all owned by Peggy. One class consists of 1,000 shares of preferred stock with an annual cumulative dividend right of $100 per share, and a right to sell the stock to X (a "put") for $900 per share. Assume that the value of the cumulative annual dividend is $1 million. The other class consists of 1,000 shares of non-voting common stock. Peggy transfers all the common stock to her daughter, Emmy. Here IRC § 2701 applies since Peggy has transferred a junior equity interest to a member of her family and keeps an applicable retained interest. Since the distribution right is cumulative and at a fixed rate, it is a qualifying payment right. Here, the "lower of" rule applies since the preferred stock confers both a qualifying distribution right and an extraordinary payment right (the put). Here, the value of the preferred stock is $900,000 since if Peggy exercised the put it would result in the lowest value ($900,000 v. $1 million). Therefore, the amount of gift to Emmy is $600,000. [Reg. § 25.2701–2(a)(5)(ex.)] If the annual cumulative dividend right was valued at $800,000, the put would be treated as not being exercised and the value of the preferred stock would be $800,000 (the lower of $800,000 or $900,000).

f) Subtraction Method of Valuation

The amount of the gift is computed by using the "subtraction method of valuation." [Reg. § 25.2701–3(a)(1)] Generally, this is done by taking the total fair market value before the transfer of all family-held interest and reducing it by the family-held senior equity interests (which include the applicable retained interests valued under IRC § 2701). The difference is then allocated between the transferred interests and other family-held subordinate equity interests. Finally, any discounts and other appropriate reductions are applied to determine the final value of the gift. The specific steps, covered in a summary fashion, are as follows.

Step 1 (Reg. § 25.2701–3(b)(1)): Value the entire amount of family-held interests. Family-held interests are all those owned by the transferor, applicable family members, and any lineal descendants of the parents of the transferor or the transferor's spouse. [Reg. § 25.2701–2(b)(5)(i)]

Step 2 (Reg. § 25.2701–3(b)(2)): After finding the total value, the senior equity interests and applicable retained interests held by the transferor and applicable family members are determined after the application of IRC § 2701. In subtracting the value of the senior equity interests from the family-held interests, the Regulations isolate the value of the junior interests held by T, applicable family members and members of T's family.

Step 3 (Reg. § 25.2701–3(b)(3)): The remaining value is allocated among the transferred interest, and other subordinate interests held by T, and T's applicable family members.

Step 4 (Reg. § 25.2701–3(b)(4)): Reduce the transferred amount for any minority or similar discount, reductions under IRC § 2702, and any consideration received by the transferor.

g) Minimum Valuation [IRC § 2701(a)(4)]

The transferred interest is subject to a minimum value, and therefore, cannot be treated as zero. All "junior equity interests" have a minimum value of 10 percent of the sum of the total value of all the entities equity interests and the total amount of indebtedness owed by the entity to the transferor and applicable family member. [IRC § 2701(a)(4)(A)] The transferred interest is then given a proportional amount of such minimum value. The rule has limited application, since the applicable retained value is generally zero, which leads to a greater value of the transferred interest than would exist under the minimum valuation rule.

Example: Kermit holds all the stock of Piggy Corporation (PC) worth a total of $1.5 million. PC is recapitalized, creating both preferred and common stock. After the recapitalization, Kermit has 1,000 shares of preferred stock with a par value of $1,500 and an annual cumulative dividend computed at a fixed rate, and 1,000 shares of common stock. Assume that the value of the preferred stock is $1.5 million. Here, IRC § 2701 applies, but the applicable retained interest (the preferred stock) has a cumulative fixed dividend right, so it is a qualifying payment. Instead of valuing the transfer at zero, the minimum valuation rule applies to value the transferred amount at $150,000, 10 percent of the $1.5 million total value of PC.

h) Lookback Rule [IRC § 2701(d)]

Generally applicable retained interests are valued at zero under IRC § 2701. This is not the case for distribution rights (e.g., dividends) that are subject to any qualified payments. In this case, the interest is valued at its fair market value, since the payments are cumulative and at a fixed amount or percentage, thereby taking away any discretion about whether the payments will be made or not. Even though there is a set definition of what is a qualified payment, the transferor and applicable family members may elect in, or out, of treating such rights as qualified.

The lookback rule of IRC § 2701(d) is the statutory check to make sure the promised payments are actually made. If the payments are not made, the Code attempts to approximate the value of the payments plus interest and adds that to either the taxable estate (if computed at the transferor's death) or taxable gift (if computed before transferor's death). In this way, the transferor and applicable family members are kept to the corporate or partnerships obligations of paying off the qualified payments.

i) Adjustments to Estate and Gift Tax [IRC § 2701(e)(6)]

If IRC § 2701 applies to value an interest, unless there is a distribution right with qualified payments, the applicable retained interest is valued at zero. Since the applicable retained interest remains with the transferor, the possibility of the interest being taxed twice is present: once at the time of transfer and again at the transferor's death or subsequent transfer of the interest. Foreseeing this problem, Congress included IRC § 2701(e)(6) to mitigate the possibility of double tax on the same interest.

The relief provision applies when: (1) there is a subsequent transfer or inclusion in the gross estate of the transferor, (2) of an applicable retained interest valued under IRC § 2701(a). In such cases the Code states that the Regulations should provide for "appropriate adjustments" to be made for the estate, gift, and generation-skipping transfer taxes "to reflect the increase in the amount of any prior taxable gift made by the transferor or decedent by such valuation." [IRC § 2701(e)(6)]

The Regulations provide that the amount on which the estate or gift tentative tax is computed is reduced by the "amount of the reduction." The amount of the reduction is the *lesser of*: (1) the amount by which the taxable gifts were increased due to IRC § 2701 on the initial transfers of the subordinate interest to the member of the family, or (2) the "duplicated amount." The duplicated amount is the amount by which the current gift or estate tax value of the applicable retained interest involved in the subsequent transfer exceeds the § 2701 value of the interest at the time of the initial transfer. [Reg. § 25.2701–5(a), (b), (c)]

Example: Petunia holds all the outstanding shares of X Corporation (XC) that consists of both preferred and common stock. There are 1,500 preferred shares which have a $1,000 par value, non-cumulative dividend right of $100 per share, and a put to XC at the demand of the shareholder for par value. There are 1,000 common shares with a fair market value of $500,000. The total value of XC is $2 million.

In Year 1, Petunia transfers the 1,000 shares of common stock to her child, Melissa. Since Melissa is a "member of the family" and transferred a junior interest, while Petunia kept an applicable retained interest, the valuation rules of IRC § 2701(a) apply. [IRC § 2701(a)(1)] Since the preferred stock's distribution rights are not qualified payments, assuming that Petunia does not elect to treat them as such, the preferred stock will have a zero value. [IRC § 2701(a)(3)(A)] Using the subtraction method, the amount treated as transferred to Melissa is $2 million ($2 million family-held interest less zero) and Petunia treats that amount as a taxable gift.

*Example (Gift Transfer
of Applicable Retained
Interest):* Assume that in Year 4, when the value of the preferred stock is $1.4 million, Petunia transfers all 1,500 shares to Melissa. Without any relief, the preferred stock value would be taxed twice, once in Year 1 due to the zero valuation under IRC § 2701, and again in Year 4. Here, IRC § 2701(e)(6) applies since there is a subsequent transfer of the applicable retained interest valued under IRC § 2701(a) (Petunia's preferred stock). Under the Regulations the $1.4 million taxable gift will be reduced by the lesser of: (1) the amount the applicable retained interest was increased under IRC § 2701 (here $1.5 million), or (2) the duplicated amount ($1.4 million). The duplicated amount is the amount of the gift tax value on the transfer of the preferred stock in Year 4 ($1.4 million) less the value of the preferred stock in Year 1 (zero). After applying the reduction, the gift tax on Petunia's transfer will be zero. [Reg. § 25.2701–5(d)(ex. 1)]

*Example (Transfer of
Applicable Retained Interest
at Death):* Instead of making the transfer of preferred stock above, assume that Petunia dies in Year 4 when the value of the preferred stock is $1.5 million. Without any relief, the preferred stock value would be taxed twice, once in Year 1 due to the zero valuation under IRC § 2701, and again in Year 4 since the stock would be included in her gross estate under IRC § 2033. Here, IRC § 2701(e)(6) applies since the applicable retained interest valued under IRC § 2701(a) (Petunia's preferred stock) is included in Petunia's gross estate. Under the Regulations, the $1.5 million increase in Petunia's taxable estate is reduced by $1.5 million. [Reg. § 25.2701–5(d)(ex. 2)]

2. Transfers of Interests in Trust to Family Members [IRC § 2702]

a) Background

IRC § 2702, located in Chapter 14 (Special Valuation Rules) of Subtitle B (Estate and Gift taxes), does more than just value interests, despite its title and placement. If applicable, IRC § 2702 determines whether any transfer made to a member of the transferor's family will be treated as a "gift" or not. It can also give a zero value to any retained interests of the transferor in order to increase the amount of any gift transfer.

IRC § 2702 is a response to several "estate freezing" techniques that would allow individuals with substantial estates to pass assets likely to appreciate significantly in value at little or no transfer tax cost. One common freeze technique was the so-called grantor-retained income trust (GRIT), where the grantor would transfer assets to an irrevocable trust, retaining the right to income for a term of years. The value of the gift would be the present value of the right to the remainder interest, which was often much less than the value of the property contributed to the trust.

Example: Father transfers $100,000 in property to an irrevocable trust he creates for himself and Daughter. He keeps a fifteen-year income interest, with the remainder going to Daughter. If the applicable interest rate for valuation under IRC § 7520 equaled 10%, the gift of the remainder interest to Daughter would be valued at only $23,939. If Father lives fifteen years, Daughter will take the entire trust (valued at over $400,000 provided that there were no withdrawals and the trust assets appreciated at a 10% annual rate) with no further gift (when Father's term of years expires there is no transfer to daughter) or estate (no one died) tax consequences. If Father dies before the fifteen-year term expires, the fair market value of the trust at the time of his death would be included in his gross estate under IRC § 2036. Therefore, without IRC § 2702 Father could transfer appreciating assets eventually worth $400,000, with only gift tax consequences on a $23,939 taxable gift. IRC § 2702 thwarts the estate freeze by valuing the retained interest at zero. So here, Father's retained fifteen-year income interest would be valued at zero, meaning the amount of taxable gift from Father to Daughter would be the full $100,000 transferred in trust.

b) Application of IRC § 2702

The analysis for IRC § 2702 is typical of many sections of the Code. First, see if IRC § 2702 applies to the facts. Next, see if any exceptions exist to the application of the rule. Finally, if no exceptions exist, apply the rule and value the property under IRC § 2702. For the application of IRC § 2702, there must be: 1) a *"transfer"* in trust, 2) of an *"interest,"* 3) to a *"member of the transferor's family,"* 4) by *"gift,"* and 5) an interest in the trust must be *"retained by the transferor"* or *"any applicable family member."* [IRC § 2702(a)(1)]

(1) Specific Elements

(a) Transfers in Trust

As used in IRC § 2702, the word "transfer" includes transfers to either new or existing trusts and assignments of an interest in an existing trust. [Reg. § 25.2702–2(a)(2)] A transfer may also be imputed where two or more family members make a joint purchase of term interests in property. [IRC § 2702(c)(2) (see below)] However, the exercise, release or lapse of a non-general power of appointment or a qualified disclaimer under IRC § 2518 of an interest is not considered a "transfer" for purposes of IRC § 2702. [Reg. § 25.2702–2(a)(2)(i, ii)]

Example: Grandparent holds the income interest to a trust, with Parent, Grandparent's child, holding the remainder interest. Parent transfers his remainder interest to Son. Since Parent assigned an interest in an existing trust, this is a transfer that can trigger application of IRC § 2702. [Reg. § 25.2702–2(a)(2)]

(i) Imputed Transfers in Trust [IRC § 2702(c)]

Another estate freezing technique involves a joint purchase of successive interests in property (e.g., life estates and remainders) between two family members. This accomplishes approximately the same goal as the example at the beginning of this section: no gift exists since the family member purchased the interest in property, albeit at a much lower price, and no estate tax consequences occur because no estate tax provisions provide for inclusion in the transferor's gross estate.

IRC § 2702(c)(1) provides that if two or more family members make a joint purchase of term interests, the individual(s) acquiring the term interests are treated as having acquired the entire property and subsequently transferred the non-term interests to the other person(s). This applies to purchases made in either a single transaction or a series of transactions. [IRC § 2702(c)(2)]

"Term interests" include life interests or interests in property for a term of years. [IRC § 2702(c)(3)] Any series of successive interests in property will be treated as term interests. Term interests do not include fee interests in property (e.g., tenants in common, tenants by the entirety, or joint tenancies). [Reg. § 25.2702–4(a)] Additionally, leasehold interests in property transferred for full and adequate consideration are not treated as "term interests." [Reg. § 25.2702–4(b)]

When IRC § 2702(c)(1) and (c)(2) are applied together, they work to create the requisite "transfer of an interest in trust" required for the application of IRC § 2702(a)(1). IRC § 2702(c)(2) creates a transfer between family members when term interests are purchased. Then IRC § 2702(c)(1) treats those interests as being transferred to a trust.

Example (1): Homer and his child, Bart, make a joint purchase of an apartment building with Homer purchasing a twenty-year term interest in the property, while Bart buys the remainder interest. Since Homer purchased a term interest in property with a family member, under IRC § 2702 he is treated as acquiring the entire property and transferring the remainder interest in trust to Bart for full consideration. Although not yet discussed in this section, Homer's term interest will be valued at zero and the entire value of the building (less Bart's payment) will be treated as a gift to Bart. [Reg. § 25.2702–4(d)(ex. 1)]

Example (2): Marge and her child, Maggie, make a joint purchase of an office building, with each acquiring a 50% undivided interest as tenants in common. Even though this is a joint purchase, made between family members, the interests purchased are not considered term interests and IRC § 2702(c) (and therefore IRC § 2702) does not apply. [Reg. § 25.2702–4(d)(ex. 3)]

(b)   "Interest"

(i)   General Rule

For IRC § 2702, to apply the transferor must make a transfer of an "interest." Generally, "interests" are interest in property, but the term also includes powers over trust property that would cause the transfer to be an incomplete gift under Chapter 12. [Reg. § 25.2702–2(a)(4)]

Example: Tim transfers property to an irrevocable trust, with the income payable at his discretion to either Julie or Jane for ten years and the remainder to Tim's son, Ronald. Since Tim maintains dominion and control over the ten-year income interest, that portion is an incomplete gift. [Reg. § 25.2511–2(c)] However, under IRC § 2702, Tim's power is treated as an "interest" that he has retained over the property. [Reg. § 25.2702–2(a)(4)] This results in the application of IRC § 2702 to the income interest which is subsequently valued at zero. Tim is thus considered to have made a gift to his son of the entire value of the property contributed to the trust. Similarly, if Tim maintained a power to switch the beneficiary of the remainder interest (but not the income interest), the remainder interest would be valued at zero.

(ii)   Treatment of Transfers of a Portion in Trust [IRC § 2702(d)]

If a specified portion of the income or remainder interest is transferred in trust, only such portion will be taken into account when applying IRC § 2702. [IRC § 2702(d)]

Example (1):   Father transferred property to an irrevocable trust, retaining the income interest for life and designating 2/3 of the remainder interest payable to his daughter and the remaining 1/3 to his nephew. Under IRC

§ 2702(d), the transfer will be treated as creating two different trusts, with the IRC § 2702 zero-value rule applying only to the 2/3 portion of the trust for the benefit of his daughter. IRC § 2702 does not apply to the 1/3 portion for the benefit of his nephew since the nephew is not considered a member of Father's family for the purposes of that section. [IRC §§ 2702(e), 2704(c)(2)]

Example (2): Adam creates a trust in which he retains the income interest for his life. The remainder is payable to his son, subject to Adam's retained power to give 1/4 of the remainder interest to his daughter. IRC § 2702 will apply only to the 3/4 remainder interest that is a completed gift. [Reg. § 25.2702–2(d)(ex. 5)]

(c) To a "Member of the Transferor's Family"

"Members of transferor's family" (not to be confused with "applicable family member," defined *infra* at II. D. 2. b) (1) (f)) includes the transferor's spouse, ancestors and lineal descendants of transferor or transferor's spouse, brothers and sisters, and the spouses of any of these individuals. [IRC §§ 2702(e), 2704(c)(2)(A)–(D)] It does not include more remote relationships, such as the transferor's aunts, uncles, nieces or nephews. For IRC § 2702 to apply, only one of the interests need be simultaneously transferred to a member of the transferor's family, not all interests.

Example: Grantor transfers property in trust. The trustee is required to pay the income to Grantor for ten years, then to Grantor's sister for ten years, and then to Grantor's nephew for his life. Grantor's nephew is not a "member of the transferor's family" for the application of IRC § 2702. However, since Grantor's sister is a member of the transferor's family, Grantor's retained income interest may be valued at zero if the other elements of IRC § 2702 apply.

(d) Transfer is "By Gift"

The transfer must be a completed gift. *See supra* discussion of when a gift is complete, II. B. 3. b).

(e) "Retained by" the Transferor or Applicable Family Member

Under IRC § 2702 "retained by" has substantially the same meaning as its common usage: the same individual must hold an interest both before and after the transfer in trust. A wrinkle occurs for purchased term interests (e.g., life estates). Even though the transferor did not hold the interest before transfer (since it was newly purchased), it is treated as "retained by" the transferor if the transferor holds the term interest after the transfer. [Reg. § 25.2702–2(a)(3)]

Since the Regulations define "retained by" with reference to the same individual holding an interest in trust both before and after the transfer, it seems at first as if the phrase "or applicable family member" is superfluous. However, this language applies to transfers of interests from established trusts where an "applicable family member" maintains an interest in the trust both before and after a transfer.

Example (1): Gus holds the income interest in a trust, with Peter, Gus's child, holding the remainder interest. Neither Gus nor Peter created the trust. Peter transfers his remainder interest to his child, Mary. Gus here is an "applicable family member" under IRC § 2701(e)(2)(B) who "retains" an interest both before and after Peter's transfer. IRC § 2702 applies to the transfer and Peter is treated as transferring the full value of the corpus to Mary since under IRC § 2702 Gus' interest is valued at zero.

Example (2): Darrin transfers his separate property to an irrevocable trust. The trust is to pay income to Darrin's spouse, Marta, for her life, with the remainder passing to Darrin's child, Scott. Here there is a transfer of an interest in trust made to members of the transferor family as required under IRC § 2702(a)(1). However, since neither

Darrin nor an applicable family member retained an interest (Marta did not have an interest in the property before transfer), IRC § 2702 does not apply. [Reg. § 25.2702–2(d)(ex. 3)]

(f) "Applicable Family Member"

An "applicable family member" is different than a "member of the transferor's family" as defined above. **Applicable family member**, defined under IRC § 2701(e)(2), includes only the transferor's spouse as well as the ancestors and their spouses of either the transferor or the transferor's spouse. The lineal descendants of the transferor or the transferor's spouse are not included.

> *Example:* John Walton's parents are Zeb and Esther. John and his wife, Olivia, have several children, John Jr. ("John–Boy"), Mary–Ellen, and Jason. John has one brother, Ben. If John Sr. is the transferor, the "applicable family members" include only Olivia (John's wife) and Zeb and Esther (John's ancestors). Neither John's brother Ben nor John Sr.'s children are included. [IRC §§ 2702(a)(1), 2701(e)(2)]

(2) Exceptions

(a) Incomplete Gifts [IRC § 2702(a)(3)(A)(i)]

If no portion of the gift is complete to an applicable family member, IRC § 2702 will not apply to the transfer. [IRC § 2702(a)(3)(A)(i)] Consideration received by the transferor is not considered in determining whether a gift is incomplete. [IRC § 2702(a)(3)(B)]

> *Example (1):* Byron creates an irrevocable trust reserving the right to income for ten years, followed by the remainder passing to his daughter, Cheri. Byron also retains the right to substitute any of his grandchildren for Cheri as the remainder beneficiary. Since Byron has dominion and control over the remainder interest, no portion of the transfer is a completed gift and IRC § 2702 does not apply. [*See* IRC § 2702(a)(3)(A)(i); Reg. § 25.2702–2(d)(ex. 4)]

Example (2):   Helen transfers property to an irrevocable trust, retaining the right to receive income for fifteen years. After fifteen years, the income of the property is to be paid to her spouse, Max, for five years. After that five-year period ends, the trust terminates and the corpus of the trust at the time of termination is to be transferred to Helen's child, Irvin. Helen retains the right to revoke Max's five-year income interest. There is a completed gift of the remainder interest to Irvin, and an incomplete gift of the five-year income interest to Max, since Helen maintains dominion and control (the right to revoke). [Reg. § 25.2511–2(c)] Since the gift transfer is not wholly incomplete, IRC § 2702 applies. Helen's power over the five-year income interest will be treated as a retained interest (therefore valued at zero), and the entire value of the corpus of the trust will be treated as a gift to Irvin.

Example (3):   Father creates a trust, retaining the right to income for ten years, followed by the outright distribution of the remainder to Child. Child pays Father full and adequate cash consideration for the remainder interest. IRC § 2702 applies to this transfer since the gift is not incomplete without regard to the consideration paid. [IRC § 2702(a)(3)(B)]

(b) Personal Residence Trusts

If the proper requirements are followed, an individual may retain a term interest in a personal residence while giving the remainder interest to a member of the transferor's family without triggering IRC § 2702. [IRC § 2702(a)(3)(A)(ii)] Congress probably excludes certain transfers of interests in personal residences because there is less likelihood of manipulation in the transfer of a personal residence as compared to other forms of property.

There are two types of personal residence trusts: a basic personal residence trust and a qualified personal residence trust. The basic personal residence trust is the much more restrictive of the two due to the limits on the type of property the trust may contain. Consequently, most estate planners prefer the qualified personal residence trust.

i) Basic Personal Residence Trusts

The corpus of a basic personal residence trust must consist only of the personal residence of the term interest holder, and only the transferor, transferor's spouse, or transferor's dependents may occupy the residence during the trust term. Up to two residences of the transferor may qualify for inclusion in a personal residence trust. The most restrictive aspect of a basic personal residence trust relates to eligible trust assets: only the personal residence itself can be owned by the trust, not any of the household furnishings. The trust can hold cash only if the money was received for the damage, destruction, or involuntary conversion of the residence, and the money must be reinvested back into the property within two years. The trust documents must also prohibit the sale or transfer of the residence for the duration of the term interest. [Reg. § 25.2702–5(b)]

ii) Qualified Personal Residence Trust

A qualified personal residence trust (QPRT) is also restricted to the personal residence of the transferor and has the same restrictions on who may live in the home. However, a QPRT may also hold cash in the amount necessary to pay expenses, mortgages, or improvements to be incurred within the next six months. The residence may also be sold, so long as the proceeds are reinvested into another residence within two years of the sale. [Reg. § 25.2702–5(c)]

(c) Regulatory Exceptions

IRC § 2702(a)(3)(A)(iii) states that exceptions may be made to the application of IRC § 2702 "to the extent that regulations provide that such transfer is not inconsistent with the purposes of this section." The purpose of IRC § 2702 is to make sure that a transferor cannot artificially reduce the value of a remainder interest gift to a member of the transferor's family by retaining certain trust interests in the trust that reduce the future value of the remainder interest.

i) Charitable Transfers [Reg. § 25.2702–1(c)(3), (4), (5)]

The Regulations exclude charitable remainder trusts, pooled income funds, and charitable lead trusts from the application of IRC § 2702. [Reg. § 25.2702–1(c)(3), (4), (5); *see supra* discussion at I. B. 3. b) (2) (b) for the requirements of these types of trusts].

Example: Grantor transfers property to a pooled income fund, with Grantor retaining an income interest for ten years, then to his child for the child's life, with the remainder to a charity. Under the Regulations, IRC § 2702 does not apply and the amount of the gift is reduced by Grantor's retained term interest. Without the aid of the regulations, Grantor's retained term interest would be valued at zero. Grantor can also receive a charitable deduction for the remainder interest. *See infra* discussion of gift tax charitable deductions [IRC § 2522], II. E. 2. a).

ii) Retained Interest Under the Control of an Independent Trustee [Reg. § 25.2702–1(c)(6)]

IRC § 2702 does not apply if the interest retained by the transferor or applicable family member is the receipt of trust income under the sole discretion of an independent trustee. [Reg. § 25.2702–1(c)(6)]

Example: Greg transfers funds to an irrevocable trust with the income payable to Son for his life, remainder to Daughter. The trust has an independent trustee who has the right to give all or any portion of the income to Greg for the shorter of Greg's or Son's life. If Daughter transfers the remainder interest to her spouse, without any administrative intervention the transfer would be subject to IRC § 2702 since Greg "retains" an interest and Daughter transfers an interest in trust to a member of her family. However, under Reg. § 25.2702–1(c)(6) Greg's interest in the trust is disregarded and IRC § 2702 does not apply.

iii) Certain Transfers Made Pursuant to IRC § 2516

Under the Regulations, so long as the transferor's spouse holds all the remaining interests in the trust, IRC § 2702 will not apply to any transfers subject to IRC § 2516 made before a divorce is final. [Reg. § 25.2702–1(c)(7); *see supra* discussion of IRC § 2516, II. B. 4. a) (4) (a).] The Regulations effectively treat the soon to be ex-spouse as a former spouse, making him or her a non-family member.

> *Example:* One year before the divorce is final and pursuant to an agreement, Tom creates a trust with income to Lynette for life. The trust corpus reverts to Tom at her death. Assuming the agreement meets the other requirements of IRC § 2516, then even though this is a transfer to a member of Tom's family (a spouse) and Tom retains an interest in the transferred property, this transfer is outside the application of IRC § 2702. Effectively, Lynette is treated as an ex-spouse even though they are married at the time of transfer.

iv) Certain Transfers of Property in a Qualified Domestic Trust (QDOT) [Reg. § 25.2702–1(c)(8)]

The regulations provide IRC § 2702 does not apply when a non-citizen surviving spouse transfers an interest in a qualified domestic trust (QDOT) under IRC § 2056A. This means the deceased spouse remains the transferor of the property retained by the surviving spouse.

(3) Valuation

If no exceptions exist, IRC § 2702(a)(2) values a retained interest if there is a transfer of an interest in trust by gift to a member of the transferor's family and part of the interest in the trust is retained by the transferor. Valuation under IRC § 2702 depends on the type of interest being valued. "Qualified interests" are valued under the normal valuation rules for the gift tax under IRC § 7520. [IRC § 2702(a)(2)(B)] Non-qualified interests are valued at zero. [IRC § 2702(a)(2)(A)] The rationale behind such valuation is that qualified interests can be properly valued, and therefore normal valuation methods can be used.

(a) Qualified Interests Under IRC § 2702(b)

There are three types of "qualified interests": a qualified annuity interest, a qualified unitrust interest, and a qualified remainder interest.

i) Qualified Annuity Interests [IRC § 2702(b)(1)]

A qualified annuity interest arises in the context of a popular estate planning technique commonly known as a GRAT (**grantor-retained annuity trust**). A GRAT is an irrevocable trust where the grantor retains the right to receive not less than once per year either a stated dollar amount or a fixed percentage of the initial fair market value of the property transferred to the trust. The payments may increase by no more than 120% per year. If the trust's income exceeds the stated annuity amount, the excess may be distributed to the grantor; however, those additional amounts will not be taken into account in valuing the qualified interest. Additionally, the trust documents must prohibit prepayment of the annuity interest to the grantor. [Reg. § 25.2702–3(b), (d)(5)]

Example (1):   Alex transfers property to an irrevocable trust maintaining the right to receive income from the trust for ten years. After the ten-year term has expired, the trust will terminate and the trust corpus will be paid to Charles, Alex's son. If, however, Alex dies within the ten-year period the trust corpus is to be paid to Alex's estate. Since Alex transferred an interest in trust to a member of his family and retained an interest, IRC § 2702 applies. Both Alex's income interest and the contingent reversion are valued at zero because they are non-qualified interests. If, however, the trust allowed for a distribution of the greater of $10,000 or the trust income, the ten-year term interest would be a qualified annuity interest. In that situation, the income interest would receive its present value, but the contingent reversion would not. The amount of the gift to Charles would be the value of the trust corpus less the present value of the ten-year term interest. [Reg. § 25.2702–3(e)(ex. 1)]

Example (2): Urkle transfers property to an irrevocable trust, keeping the right to receive $10,000 for years 1 through 3, $12,000 for years 4 through 6, and $15,000 for years 7 through 10. After 10 years the trust will terminate, and the corpus will be distributed to Urkle's daughter, Karen. The basic elements of IRC § 2702 are met since Urkle transferred an interest in trust to a family member and also retained an interest therein. Since a qualified interest may only increase 120% from the previous year, Urkle has a qualified annuity interest for $10,000 in years 1 to 3, $12,000 in years 4 to 6, $14,600 in year 7, and $15,000 in years 8 to 10. [Reg. § 25.2702–3(e)(ex. 2)] The excess transfer amount in year 7 ($200) is not used in determining the value of the annuity.

The GRAT is an effective tool for achieving an "estate freeze" that will not trigger application of IRC § 7520's zero-value rule. Grantor usually sets the annuity amount below the amount of expected growth (the sum of the income from the trust assets plus the appreciation in value of those assets during the annuity period). That way, the grantor shifts more value to the remainder beneficiary than what the applicable valuation rule in IRC § 7520 assumes.

Example: Ernie transfers $100,000 in investment assets to an irrevocable trust, retaining the right to receive $5,000 annually from the trust for a term of ten years. Upon the end of the ten-year term, the trust will terminate and the remainder will be paid to Bert (Ernie's son) or Bert's estate. If Ernie dies during the ten-year term, payments will continue to be made to Ernie's estate. Ernie's retained right to the annual payment of $5,000 is a qualified income interest, so the value of the gift to Bert will be determined under IRC § 7520. Neither Ernie nor Bert pays additional tax of any kind when the trust terminates. Suppose the value of the gift to Bert is $70,000. If the trust assets grow in value by ten percent each year during Ernie's term interest, the annual growth will exceed the $5,000 annuity payable to Ernie each year. In fact, under these assumptions, the value of the remainder interest passing to Bert at the end of Ernie's term interest would be approximately $174,000. Thus, by reporting a $70,000 gift to Bert at the formation of the trust, Ernie is able to pass $174,000 of value to Bert upon the conclusion of the trust term.

ii) Qualified Unitrust Interests

A qualified unitrust interest arises when the grantor maintains a fixed percentage of the fair market value of the trust determined annually (instead of a fixed dollar amount or a fixed percentage of the initial value with the qualified annuity interest). [Reg. § 25.2702–3(c)(1)(i)]

iii) Qualified Remainder Interests

A qualified remainder interest is another interest that may be treated as a qualified interest. A qualified remainder interest is a non-contingent remainder interest where all of the term interests are either qualified annuity interests or qualified unitrust interests. Unlike either of the other qualified term interests, the governing instrument must prohibit the payment of income in excess of the annuity or unitrust amounts in order for the remainder to be a qualified remainder interest. [Reg. § 25.2702–3(f)(1)(i)–(iv)]

> *Example (1):* David creates an irrevocable trust with income to his child, Chris, for ten years, after which time the trust property will revert back to David or David's estate. Since David transferred an interest in trust to a member of his family and retained an interest, IRC § 2702 applies. Chris' ten-year income interest is neither a qualified annuity interest nor a qualified unitrust interest so David's reversion does not qualify as a qualified remainder interest. David will be treated as giving the entire trust corpus to Chris as a gift since his retained reversion will be valued at zero. [Reg. § 25.2702–3(f)(3)(ex. 1)]

> *Example (2):* Same facts as above, except that Chris is to receive $100 per year from the trust for ten years, regardless of the trust's income. Now Chris' interest is a qualified annuity interest and there is also a non-contingent remainder interest; therefore, David's reversion is a qualified remainder interest. While IRC § 2702 applies, the reversion is valued under the normal rules for the gift tax and will not be included in the taxable gift to Chris.

(4) Reduction in Taxable Gifts of Subsequent Transfer of a Retained Interest

Unless a qualified interest is retained by the transferor, IRC § 2702 assigns a zero value to the transferor's retained interest, thereby subjecting it to the gift tax even though it is retained by the transferor. If the retained interest is later transferred, it will be subject to a second round of taxation under the estate or gift tax. While relief from double gift taxation is not covered by the Code, the Regulations do allow for some relief. [Reg. § 25.2702–6(a)(1)]

The amount of taxable gifts is reduced by the lesser of: 1) the amount of increase in the taxable gifts due to the application of IRC § 2702 on the initial transfer, or 2) the increase in the amount of taxable gifts (or gross estate) due to the subsequent transfer of the interest. [Reg. § 25.2702–6(b)(1)]

Example: Xavier transfers property to an irrevocable trust, maintaining a ten-year income interest in the property. After ten years, the trust will terminate and the trust corpus will be distributed to Xavier's child, Dawn. The ten-year income interest has a value under IRC § 7520 of $40,000. Xavier is treated as making a taxable gift of the entire trust corpus to Dawn, and IRC § 2702 applies to value Xavier's retained interest at $0. If Xavier makes a gift of his ten-year income interest to a third party when it is valued at $31,000, he will be entitled to a reduction in his taxable gifts for the year in the amount of $21,000. $21,000 is the lesser of the amount of increase due to the application of IRC § 2702 on the initial transfer ($40,000) or the increase in the amount of taxable gift due to the subsequent transfer of the interest ($31,000 less $10,000 (the IRC § 2503(b) annual exclusion unadjusted for inflation) or $21,000). [Reg. § 25.2702–6(c)(ex. 1)]

(5)   Application of IRC § 2702 to Chapter 13 (Generation Skipping Tax)

IRC § 2702 does not apply to the generation-skipping tax of Chapter 13. [PS–92–90, 1991–1 C.B. 998, 1001–02]

3.   Treatment of Certain Lapsing Rights and Restrictions [IRC § 2704]

IRC § 2704 contains two sets of rules for measuring the value of transferred interests in a corporation or partnership. The first set of rules considers the effect of lapsing rights, and the second set of rules pertains to the effect of certain restrictions on liquidation of the entity.

Certain lapses in voting, liquidation, or similar rights in a corporation or partnership are treated as transfers of those rights by the holder. [IRC § 2704(a)(1)] If the lapse occurs while the holder of the right is alive, the transfer will be treated as a gift. If the lapse occurs upon the death of the holder of the right, the transfer is deemed to occur at death and included in the decedent's gross estate. [Reg. § 25.2704–1(a)(1)] The amount of the transfer (or the amount included in the gross estate, as the case may be) is the excess of the value of all interests in the entity held by the holder immediately before the lapse (determined as if the lapsed rights were non-lapsing) over the value of such interests immediately after the lapse. [IRC § 2704(a)(2)]

There are two elements to the application of IRC § 2704(a)(1). First, there must be a lapse of voting or liquidation right in a corporation or partnership. [IRC § 2704(a)(1)(A)] Second, the holder of the lapsed right and members of his or her family must control the entity both before and after the lapse. [IRC § 2704(a)(1)(B)] These elements work to ensure that the deemed transfer will only apply to those lapsed rights that were intended to drive down the transfer tax value of the holder's interest in the entity.

Example: George was a partner in a limited partnership. At his death, George held both a general partner interest and a limited partner interest. The general partner interest carried with it the right to liquidate the partnership. The limited partner interest had no such power to compel liquidation. Accordingly, the value of the limited partner interest was $59 million if it was held jointly with the general partner interest but only $33 million if it was held alone. A buy-sell agreement between George and his son, William Henry, required George's estate to sell the general partner interest to William Henry for $750,000. Absent IRC § 2704(a), the value of the limited partner interest included in George's estate was $33 million, for the right to liquidate the partnership lapsed at death due to the obligation to sell the general partner interest to William Henry. [*Estate of Harrison v. Commissioner*, 52 T.C.M. (CCH) 1306 (1987)] But IRC § 2704(a) applies, assuming George and members of his family (including William Henry) controlled the partnership before and after George's death. Accordingly, George is treated as having made a transfer of $26 million (the excess of the $59 million value of the limited partner interest assuming the liquidation right was non-lapsing over the $33 million value of the limited partner interest after the lapse) at death that is also included in his gross estate.

IRC § 2704(b) relates to restrictions imposed on a power to liquidate a corporation or partnership. If three requirements are met, then any "applicable restrictions" are to be disregarded when valuing a transferred interest in the entity. [IRC § 2704(b)(1)] These requirements are: (1) a transfer of an interest in a corporation or partnership (2) to or for the benefit of a member of the transferor's family (3) where the transferor and the members of the transferor's family control the entity immediately before the transfer. [IRC § 2704(b)(1)(A)–(B)] An **applicable restriction** is any limitation on the entity's ability to liquidate that either lapses to any extent after the transfer or can be removed after the transfer by the transferor or any member of the transferor's family. [IRC § 2704(b)(2)]

> *Example:* Wendy and Peter, a married couple, own general partner and limited partner interests in a limited partnership. Under their partnership agreement, Wendy and Peter have agreed that the partnership can be liquidated only with the written consent of all partners, though this restriction on liquidation may be removed by a unanimous vote of the partners. Wendy transfers her limited partner interest to her son, Michael. All of the requirements for IRC § 2704(b)(1) are met, for Wendy has transferred to her son an interest in the partnership controlled by Wendy and her husband. Consequently, the value of the limited partner interest transferred to Michael shall be valued without regard to the restriction that the partnership may be liquidated only with the consent of all partners, because this restriction can be removed upon the vote of Wendy, Peter, and Michael, all members of the same family.

Certain restrictions on liquidation are not disregarded even though the elements of IRC § 2704(b)(1) are met. Commercially reasonable restrictions on liquidation arising from a financing transaction with an unrelated party are not subject to IRC § 2704. [IRC § 2704(b)(3)(A)] In addition, restrictions on liquidation imposed by state or federal law do not trigger IRC § 2704(b). [IRC § 2704(b)(3)(B)] In effect, then, only those liquidation restrictions that are more stringent than those under applicable law or those found in commercially reasonable financing transactions will be disregarded. [Reg. § 25.2704–2(b)]

E. "Taxable gifts" [IRC § 2503(a)]

IRC § 2503(a) defines the term "**taxable gifts**" as the total amount of gifts made during the taxable year minus any gift tax deductions allowable. The amount of "taxable gifts" is one of the primary factors used to compute the gift tax under IRC § 2502(a) for the current year (the other being the amount of taxable gifts for all preceding years).

1. The Annual Exclusion [IRC § 2503(b)]

Unless excluded, the gift tax applies to all transfers of property by gift. [*See* IRC § 2501(a)(1)] "Gift" is defined by IRC § 2512(b) as the fair market value of property transferred less any consideration received. This definition includes such things as birthday, holiday, and graduation presents. However, since the commencement of the current gift tax in 1932, Congress has allowed a yearly per-donee exclusion to "obviate the necessity of keeping an account of and reporting numerous small gifts." [S. Rep. No. 665, 72d Cong., 1st Sess. (1932), *reprinted in* 1939–1 (Part 2) CB 496, 525]

Under IRC § 2503(b)(1) the first $10,000 of gifts (except for gifts of future interests) are excluded from "taxable gifts" under IRC § 2503(a). After 1998, the $10,000 exclusion amount is indexed for inflation using the 1997 Consumer Price Index as the base. However, the increase is only in $1,000 increments. [IRC § 2503(b)(2)] The first increase occurred in 2002 and as of 2011 the exclusion amount is $13,000.

The exclusion is mandatory and is as generous as it sounds. A donor may give up to $10,000 every year (before the adjustment for inflation) to any donee without incurring any gift tax liability, which is why it is called the **annual exclusion**. Presently, this means that if a donor had 20 grandchildren he or she could transfer up to $200,000 per year tax free ($10,000 to each grandchild). Additionally, if the donor is married and the couple chooses to use IRC § 2513 to split the gifts between the spouses, the amount transferred free of gift tax is doubled to $400,000. However, the exclusion does not carry-over to any other year, so any unused portion is lost. Moreover, the exclusion applies to transfers to unrelated donees as well.

Example: Gary gives several gifts to his niece during the year and makes no other gift transfers. He gives her a car (fair market value of $5,000) for her birthday, a necklace (fair market value of $4,000) for her graduation and cash of $4,000 for Christmas. The total gifts during the year amount to $13,000. However, after the IRC § 2503(b) exclusion is applied (before the adjustment for inflation), Gary's "taxable gifts" amount to only $3,000.

a) Application of IRC § 2503(b)

Before applying the IRC § 2503(b) exclusion, several issues need to be addressed, including the identification of the donee, whether the gift is of a present or future interest, and the application of the future interest rule to minors.

(1) Identification of the Donee

IRC § 2503(b) allows an exclusion for "gifts . . . made to any person by the donor." Under IRC § 7701(a)(1), "person" includes people, trusts, estates, partnerships and corporations. This means gifts to entities may qualify for the exclusion, but note that the courts have made it difficult to receive an exclusion for such transfers.

(a) Trusts

The Regulations provide that in a gift transfer of property through a trust, the donees are the beneficiaries of the trust and not the trustee or trust itself. [Reg. § 25.2503–2(a); *see also Helvering v. Hutchings*, 312 U.S. 393, 61 S.Ct. 653, 85 L.Ed. 909 (1941).] Accordingly, a gift of $20,000 to a trust with two beneficiaries is treated as a gift of $10,000 to each beneficiary.

(b) Partnerships

On gift transfers to partnerships, the donees are the individual partners. However, this does not automatically mean that the donor may take an exclusion amount for each partner. An exclusion amount may only be taken if the transfer is made to a general partnership (as opposed to a limited partnership) where the partners have unlimited access to their capital accounts. If the transfer is to a limited partnership, the transfer is treated as a future interest and no exclusion is allowed. [*Wooley v. United States*, 736 F.Supp. 1506 (S.D. Ind. 1990)] *See infra* the discussion of the rule prohibiting application of the annual exclusion to future interests, at II. E. 1. b) (1).

(c) Joint Interests in Property

Each joint tenant is a donee when a donor gifts property as a joint tenancy. This rule applies no matter whether the gift is made as tenants in common, joint tenants with rights of survivorship, or tenants by the entirety.

(d) Corporations

The individual shareholders are the donees on gift transfers to corporations. [Reg. § 25.2511–1(h)(1)] However, the donor may not take any IRC § 2503(b) annual exclusion for a transfer to a corporation because it is treated as the transfer of a future interest since the shareholders do not have present individual control over the gift property.

Example: Lavonna transfers a parcel of land to a corporation in exchange for a corporate note. Each year Lavonna discharges $10,000 of debt to the corporation with the intent to make a gift to the shareholders, each of which is her child or grandchild. Even though Lavonna makes a gift to each individual shareholder, she cannot take an IRC § 2503(b) annual exclusion since she did not transfer a present interest in property. [*See Stinson Estate v. United States*, 214 F.3d 846 (7th Cir. 2000)]

(e) Charities, Public or Political Organizations

Transfers to other organizations are generally treated as a gift to the entity as a whole since there are no easily identifiable beneficiaries, shareholders, or partners. [Reg. § 25.2511–1(h)(1); *see also* Reg. § 25.2502–1(d)(ex. 3)] These gifts also might not qualify for the annual exclusion under IRC § 2503(b) since they are gifts of future (as opposed to present) interests in property.

b) Present and Future Interests

(1) Future Interests

IRC § 2503(b) allows for an exclusion of gifts "other than gifts of future interests in property." The exclusion is denied for transfers of **future interests** due to the "difficulty, in many instances, of determining the number of eventual donees and the values of their respective gifts." [S. Rep. No. 665, 72nd Cong., 1st Sess. (1932), reprinted in 1939–1 (Part 2) CB 496, 526]

The Regulations define a future interest as any interest in property "limited to commence in use, possession, or enjoyment at some future date or time." [Reg. § 25.2503–3(a)] This means the exclusion is denied where the benefits of the gifted property cannot be immediately enjoyed. Examples of future interests are remainder interests in trust (vested or contingent), a trustee's unfettered discretion to distribute income from a trust (since the property may never be distributed, creating valuation difficulties), and other instances where circumstances prevent the income of the trust from being valued.

Example (1): Bob creates an irrevocable trust with income to Allen for Allen's life, remainder to Chris. Since Chris does not come into immediate possession of the property, his remainder interest is considered a future interest and does not qualify for the exclusion. Bob will receive an annual exclusion for the income interest transferred to Allen. The annual exclusion amount, before the adjustment for inflation, will be the lesser of the fair market value of Allen's life estate interest or $10,000.

Example (2):   Louise transfers one-twentieth of her mineral royalty interest in a parcel of real property to each of her ten children in trust on October 2, Year 1. The trust documents provide that the royalty payments will begin from mineral production starting after January 1, Year 2. Since the beneficiaries cannot immediately enjoy the benefits of the property transferred, the IRC § 2503(b) annual exclusion is denied. The fact that the trust could have been created or funded after the first of the year is inconsequential to the result. [*See Jardell v. Commissioner*, 24 T.C. 652 (1955)]

Example (3):   Elgin creates a trust whose terms provide that the income from the trust be distributed to his three children in whatever manner the independent trustee deems advisable, with no ascertainable standard provided for the distribution. Although all the income must be distributed, since the distributions are in total control of the trustee, the children's interest cannot be valued and no IRC § 2503(b) annual exclusions are allowed. [Reg. § 25.2503–3(c)(ex. 3); *see, e.g., Maryland Nat'l Bank v. United States*, 609 F.2d 1078 (4th Cir. 1979)]

Example (4):   Taxpayer creates an irrevocable trust for his three children. The trust documents provide that the income of the trust is to be paid annually in equal parts to each child until age thirty, after which a child may terminate his or her portion of the trust and receive a share of the corpus. To fund the trust, Taxpayer transferred stock from his closely held corporation that has never paid dividends. Since the stock is not publicly traded and no dividends have ever been paid, the income interest is unproductive and cannot be valued. As a result, no IRC § 2503(b) exclusion is permissible. [*See Stark v. United States*, 477 F.2d 131 (8th Cir. 1973)] An exclusion for "unproductive property" is disallowed only for gifts made in trust and not for direct gifts. Some scholars have challenged this rule by pointing to the lack of distinction between non-productive property and other assets which are allowed the exclusion but provide very little current income (e.g., growth stocks). [STEPHENS, ET AL., FEDERAL ESTATE AND GIFT TAXATION ¶ 9.04[3][b] (8th ed. 2002)]

(2) Present Interests

The Regulations define a **present interest** in property as the "unrestricted right to the immediate use, possession, or enjoyment of property or the income from property." [Reg. § 25.2503–3(b)] The focus is on the immediate enjoyment or benefits from the property, not on title or vesting. [*Fondren v. Commissioner*, 324 U.S. 18, 20, 65 S.Ct. 499, 501, 89 L.Ed. 668, 674 (1945)] When a present interest is transferred, the actuarial value of the interest can be excluded up to the maximum provided under IRC § 2503(b) ($13,000 in 2011).

The existence of a spendthrift clause or other condition that the property provide its primary benefits at a later point in time is not important, so long as the donee has access to the property at the time of transfer. For example, the Regulations provide that the transfer of a life insurance policy or promissory note, each of which would provide payments at some point in the future are transfers of present interests. This is because the property has immediate benefits, such as the possibility that it can be sold or used as security for a loan. [Reg. § 25.2503–3(a)]

Example (1): Larry transferred his life insurance policy to Mary when it had a fair market value of $50,000. Even though the benefits of the policy will not fully mature until Larry dies, it is treated as the transfer of a present interest in property. [Reg. § 25.2503–3(a)]

Example (2): Larry pays the premiums on a life insurance policy covering his life each year. Mary is in possession of all incidents of ownership in the policy. Larry's premium payments are treated as an indirect gift of a present interest in property to Mary and qualify for the exclusion. [Reg. § 25.2503–3(c)(ex. 6)]

Example (3): Payton creates an irrevocable trust with a five-year income interest going to Marvin and the remainder to Brandon. He funds the trust with $20,000 and the income interest is valued at $5,000, leaving the remainder to be valued at $15,000. The trust instrument has a spendthrift clause prohibiting Marvin from alienating, assigning or otherwise anticipating such income. Payton is still allowed an IRC § 2503(b) annual exclusion of $5,000 since the spendthrift provision does not make the income interest uncertain or postpone its immediate enjoyment. [Rev. Rul. 54–344, 1954–2 C.B. 319] After the application of the exclusion, Payton will have no taxable gifts to Marvin and a $15,000 taxable gift to Brandon.

Example (4): Payton transfers $10,000 to a qualified tuition plan (i.e., a "529 plan") for his brother Eli. The gift is a present interest and qualifies for the IRC § 2503(b) annual exclusion.

(a) Exceptions

i) Power to Invade Corpus for the Income Interest Holder [IRC § 2503(b)(1)(second sentence)]

One wrinkle in the present interest rule is for transfers in trust where the trustee has the power to give the corpus of the trust only to the income beneficiary. Since the trustee could terminate the income interest at any time, the interest is incapable of being valued absent some special rule. However, since in this instance the property may only go to the holder of the income interest, there is no harm in allowing the exclusion. The second sentence of IRC § 2503(b)(1) provides that the trustee's power in these situations is disregarded, allowing for the interest to be valued and the exclusion applied.

Example: Donor creates a trust which provides for payment of the net income of the trust to Frank for his life, with the remainder to Greg. A third-party trustee has the power to give the corpus of the trust to Frank at any time before Frank's death. Generally, the trustee's right to invade the corpus of the trust makes valuing the income interest impossible and no exclusion would be available. However, since the corpus may only be transferred to Frank, the holder of the income interest, the power is disregarded in valuing Frank's income interest. The power could not be disregarded if the trustee had the power to give the corpus to anyone else but Frank. [Reg. § 25.2503–3(c)(ex. 4)]

ii)   Lump Sum Payments to Qualified Tuition Plans

Gift transfers to qualified tuition programs are treated as present interests in property even though the property is used to pay future education expenses. [IRC § 529(c)(2)(A)(i)] The amounts can only be excluded under IRC § 2503(b) since they are not qualified transfers for IRC § 2503(e). [IRC § 529(c)(2)(A)(ii)]

IRC § 529(c)(2)(B) allows a donor to elect to prorate contributions in excess of the IRC § 2503(b) annual exclusion amount over a period of five years to a state sponsored qualified savings plan for higher education (more commonly called "529 plans"). In this way, before the adjustment for inflation, a lump sum gift of $50,000 can be excluded from the gift tax under IRC § 2503(b) over a five-year period. However, in this example, all other gifts made by the donor to that donee during the same five-year period are included in the taxpayer's taxable gifts, unless the exclusion amount increases. This election can be made for each donee's 529 plan to which the donor contributes.

Example: In Year 1, Dorothy Gale transfers $55,000 to the Kansas qualified tuition program for the benefit of her son. Dorothy elects to treat $50,000 (five years of present IRC § 2503(b) exclusions) ratably over a five-year period. Dorothy's total gifts in Year 1 are $15,000 ($10,000 from the

IRC § 529(c)(2)(B) election plus the $5,000 remainder not covered by the election). The IRC § 2503(b) exclusion, before the adjustment for inflation, excludes $10,000 and taxable gifts for Year 1 are $5,000. [IRC § 2503(a), (b)(1)] In Year 2 Dorothy will start with $10,000 of gifts to her son. Dorothy may still contribute amounts over $10,000 to qualified tuition programs for other individuals and use the IRC § 529(c)(2)(B) election to spread those contributions over a five-year period.

(b) *Crummey* Powers

If the beneficiaries of a trust do not have a present interest in the property transferred to the trust, an IRC § 2503(b) annual exclusion is not available to the donor. However, a general power of appointment given to the beneficiaries creates a present interest up to the amount the beneficiaries can appoint. In this way, gifts to trusts *can* qualify for the IRC § 2503(b) annual exclusion. Practitioners refer to the general power of appointment given to trust beneficiaries as "*Crummey* powers," after the Ninth Circuit case that upheld their validity, *Crummey v. Commissioner*, 397 F.2d 82 (9th Cir. 1968). The basic premise is that the possibility of possession (the right to withdraw) is equal to immediate possession and enjoyment of the property. *Crummey* powers are not limited to transfers in trusts, but they are used primarily in that capacity. *Crummey* powers are also used in partnerships where the gift transfer would not be treated as a present interest in property. [Priv. Ltr. Rul. 9710021 (Dec. 6, 1996)]

Example: Clifford transfers property into an irrevocable trust for his four minor children. The trust provides that the income of the trust is to accumulate until the children are 21, then any income from the trust is to be distributed from the ages of 21 to 35, and once they turn 35, the trustee has the discretion to distribute the income or accumulate it as he or she may see fit. The trust also allows each child the non-cumulative right to withdraw $10,000 each year. Under local law, a guardian is required to withdraw the money, but no guardian has been appointed for any of the children. Clifford transfers $40,000 to the trust in Year 1. Since the income is to be accumulated until the children are 21, without the power to withdraw funds, the children only have a future interest in the trust and no exclusions would be available. However, the right to withdraw funds is treated as a present right of possession for $10,000 and creates a present interest, even though there are no guardians for the children, and under local law they lack the capacity to file for the appointment of a guardian and could not demand the money without the help of their parents. Accordingly, Clifford can claim four annual exclusions and exclude the entire amount contributed to the trust from his taxable gifts for Year 1. [*Crummey v. Commissioner*, 397 F.2d 82 (9th Cir. 1968)]

The Tax Court has held that beneficiaries with only contingent remainder interests can possess valid *Crummey* powers. [*Estate of Cristofani v. Commissioner*, 97 T.C. 74 (1991)] By utilizing contingent beneficiaries, the number of IRC § 2503(b) annual exclusions increases without decreasing the amounts received by the vested primary beneficiaries. However, the Service maintains its position that it is improper to permit annual exclusions for transfers to trusts where the power holders have only contingent remainders or no interest in the trust at all. [*Estate of Cristofani v. Commissioner*, 97 T.C. 74 (1991), *action on dec.*, 1992–09 (Mar. 23, 1992)]

Example: Marie creates an irrevocable trust, with the income going to her two children, Frank and Lillian. At Marie's death, the trust will terminate and be equally divided between her surviving children. Marie's grandchildren take only if either Frank or Lillian dies before Marie. Upon the creation of the trust, Frank has two children and Lillian has three. All the beneficiaries of the trust (Frank, Lillian, and the five grandchildren) have the right to withdraw $10,000 from the trust up to fifteen days after any contributions to the trust are made. Frank and Lillian have vested interests, and the five grandchildren possess contingent remainders since they only take if their parents pre-decease Marie. Since the grandchildren possess the right to withdraw funds, Marie is allowed a total of seven IRC § 2503(b) annual exclusions when she contributes property to the trust, even though the grandchildren are contingent beneficiaries and might never receive any property from the trust. [*Estate of Cristofani v. Commissioner*, 97 T.C. 74 (1991) (the Service agreed not to appeal this case but said it will litigate this issue anywhere outside the Ninth Circuit).]

The Service has challenged the right to use the exclusion in those trusts where the power holder lacks knowledge or time to make a demand, or where there exists a prearranged understanding that the withdrawal rights will not be exercised. [Rev. Rul. 81–7, 1981–1 C.B. 474] In the above situations, the Service feels the withdrawal power is illusory and therefore does not create a present interest in property. However, to date the Service has not successfully litigated this point in court.

Example (1):   Gus created an irrevocable trust on December 29, Year 1, by contributing $5,000 to the trust. The trust instrument gave the right to income to Al for life, remainder to Ben. Under the terms of the trust Al has the non-cumulative right to withdraw $5,000 each calendar year, but that right was never communicated to him. Even though Al had the right to withdraw $5,000 Gus is not permitted to take any portion of the IRC § 2503(b) annual exclusion due to Al's lack of knowledge and because the two-day period (December 30 and 31) makes the demand right illusory and effectively deprives the donee of the power. [Rev. Rul. 81–7, 1981–1 C.B. 474]

Example (2):   Lieselotte transfers a commercial building worth $180,000 to an irrevocable trust. Lieselotte's two children receive the income interest, with the remainder going to whichever of her sixteen grandchildren they select. All eighteen persons with an interest in the trust are given *Crummey* powers to withdraw up to $10,000 following any transfer of property into the trust. After Lieselotte transfers the building the beneficiaries were notified of their withdrawal rights. However, none of the beneficiaries exercised their right. Since no evidence exists that the beneficiaries would be penalized for exercising their demand rights, or that the trustees purposefully withheld information from the beneficiaries, there is no implied agreement from the behavior of the beneficiaries. Thus, Lieselotte is entitled to eighteen IRC § 2503(b) annual exclusions. [*Estate of Kohlsaat v. Commissioner*, 73 T.C.M. (CCH) 2732 (1997)]

i)   Crossover Issues

The characterization of a *Crummey* power as a general power of appointment is an important planning issue to consider when using them in trusts. *Crummey* powers may have both estate and gift tax consequences to the holder of the power.

(1) Gift Tax Consequences

Under IRC § 2514(e), a "lapse" of a general power of appointment will be treated as a "release" to the extent the lapsed *Crummey* power exceeds the greater of $5,000 or 5% of the value of the assets from which the power could be satisfied. *See supra* discussion of IRC § 2514, at II. C. 1. If the withdrawal right pertains to the contribution only, the 5% will be computed from the contribution amount (not the trust corpus) since those are the proceeds from which the "lapsed powers could be satisfied." [IRC § 2514(e)(2)] If the withdrawal right is from the trust corpus, the corpus (including the new contribution) is used to compute the 5% amount.

The amount treated as "lapsed" is deemed a transfer to the beneficiaries of the trust. [IRC § 2514(b)] The consequence of the lapse is that a gift is made to the remaining beneficiaries of the trust, and those beneficiaries will probably not be allowed an exclusion since they do not have present interests in the trust. Furthermore, IRC § 2702 could apply if the other beneficiaries are family members of the power holder.

(2) Estate Tax Consequences

IRC § 2041 may also apply to the *Crummey* withdrawal power. This section definitely applies if the power holder dies while possessing the right to withdraw funds. [IRC § 2041(a)(2)] The amount of property over which the power holder had a power at death is included in his or her gross estate. Even if the power holder does not die, there could still be inclusion in the gross estate. If there is a lapse, the amount treated as lapsed (if the power holder receives an income interest in the trust) would constitute a release of a power and such property would be includable in the power holder's gross estate under IRC § 2036. The amount to be included would be the percentage of corpus that has lapsed, which would accumulate over time.

Example: Clara has a *Crummey* power to withdraw $5,000 from a trust. On Clara's death, IRC § 2041 will include $5,000 in her gross estate.

(3) Avoidance of Gift and Estate Tax Consequences

To avoid these results, *Crummey* powers can be limited to the greater of $5,000 or 5% of the trust corpus, even though the maximum annual exclusion amount under IRC § 2503(b) is $10,000 before the adjustment for inflation. Such a limitation prevents any amounts from lapsing and being included in the power holder's gross estate under IRC § 2041, or being a gift transfer under IRC § 2514.

Another way to avoid these results is to use a "**hanging**" *Crummey* **power**. A "hanging" *Crummey* power exists when the trust instrument states that the withdrawal power remains with the power holder for that amount in excess of the greater of $5,000 or 5% of the funds from which the exercise of the lapsed power could be satisfied. In this manner there will be no gift tax consequences upon the lapse of a *Crummey* power, though there will still be estate tax consequences if the power holder dies during the year since nothing has "lapsed."

c) Transfers to Minors

Parents or grandparents who want the IRC § 2503(b) exclusion but do not want to give the child or grandchild the money directly can use IRC § 2503(c) to create a present interest in property. IRC § 2503(c) applies when the property and income from the property (1) may be expended by, or for the benefit of, the donee before reaching age 21, and (2) the amount not distributed will either pass to the donee upon reaching 21 or, should the donee die before, be distributed to the donee's estate or by a general power of appointment of the donee. [IRC § 2503(c)]

IRC § 2503(c) provides yet another way to create a present interest in a transfer to trust for a minor, besides the use of a *Crummey* power. Because the donee of an IRC § 2503(c) trust does not hold a power to withdraw trust property, IRC § 2503(c) also avoids the problem of having the *Crummey* power lapse, triggering gift or estate tax consequences.

The decision of whether to distribute funds from the trust may be left to the complete discretion of the trustee, so long as there are no substantial restrictions on the exercise of the trustee's discretion. Thus, the donee is not required to have any authority over distribution of income; only the right to the income is important and not the likelihood of distribution from the trust.

The trust income may be distributed before the donee reaches age 21 and still satisfy IRC § 2503(c). [Rev. Rul. 73–287, 1973–2 C.B. 321] In addition, after the donee reaches the age of 21, the donee can possess the right to extend the terms of the trust. [Reg. § 25.2503–4(b)(2)]

A trust may also qualify under IRC § 2503(c) if only the accumulated income interest is distributed upon the donee reaching 21, and not the entire trust corpus. [*Commissioner v. Herr*, 303 F.2d 780 (3d Cir. 1962)] However, if this type of clause is present, only the income interest of the trust will qualify for the exclusion. [*Commissioner v. Thebaut*, 361 F.2d 428, 430–31 (5th Cir. 1966)]

Example (1):   Pop creates an irrevocable trust for the benefit of Pop's children. The trustee is authorized to spend trust funds only for the beneficiaries' education. Regardless of whether the other trust provisions satisfy IRC § 2503(c), the subsection does not apply since there are "substantial restrictions" on when the income may be distributed. [Reg. § 25.2503–4(b)] The trust may, however, still qualify for the IRC § 2503(b) annual exclusion to the extent the beneficiaries have present interests in the trust. [Reg. § 25.2503–4(c)]

Example (2):   Allene creates a trust for her minor grandchild, Ronald. The terms of the trust dictate that the trust income may be distributed as the trustee dictates until Ronald reaches the age of 21. At that point, any undistributed income is to be paid to Ronald. Thereafter, until Ronald reaches age 30, the trust will accumulate the income and then distribute the entire trust corpus, principal and income, to Ronald upon his reaching age 30. If Ronald dies before age 21, the accumulated trust income is to be paid to his estate. Even though only the accumulated income, and not the trust corpus, is distributed to Ronald at 21, this trust qualifies for IRC § 2503(c). The income from the trust is "property" for purposes of IRC § 2503(c), and the income may be separated from the corpus of the trust. Allene may only receive a IRC § 2503(b) annual exclusion (before the adjustment for inflation) for the fair market value of income interest of the trust up to $10,000. [*Commissioner v. Herr*, 303 F.2d 780 (3d Cir. 1962); Rev. Rul. 68–670, 1968–2 C.B. 413]

Example (3):   Same facts as above, except that the trustee is required to distribute the income from the trust to Ronald from the ages of 21 through 30. The income interest from 21 to 30 is a separate and distinct interest and cannot be combined with the income interest qualifying for IRC § 2503(c).

Therefore, it is a future interest and will not qualify for an IRC § 2503(b) annual exclusion. [*Estate of Levine v. Commissioner*, 526 F.2d 717 (2d Cir. 1975)]

d) Other Issues

(1) Application to the Generation–Skipping Tax (Chapter 13)

Gifts under the IRC § 2503(b) amount are given a zero inclusion ratio for the generation skipping transfer tax. [IRC § 2642(c)] *See infra* discussion of the zero inclusion ratio under IRC § 2642(c), at III. D. 2. b) (1) (a).

(2) Gift Tax Returns

No gift tax return is required to be filed if all gifts made are under the IRC § 2503(b) annual exclusion amount. [IRC § 6019(a)(1)] If a married couple consent to split gifts, however, a gift tax return is required by at least one spouse even if, after splitting gifts, neither spouse makes a gift in excess of the IRC § 2503(b) annual exclusion amount.

2. Deductions

a) Gift Tax Deduction for Charitable and Similar Gifts [IRC § 2522]

The charitable deduction is very similar under both the estate and gift tax. The primary difference is that inter vivos gifts made to charities may also be deducted for purposes of the donor's Federal income tax liability, while this is not allowed for testamentary gifts of the same nature.

IRC § 2522(a) provides for a charitable deduction for citizens and residents of the United States in an unlimited amount for gifts made to listed organizations. The types of charities included on the list are substantially similar to the types of organizations that are allowed deductions under both the estate [IRC § 2055(a)] and income tax [IRC § 170(a)]. The gift does not have to be made to a domestic entity in order to qualify for the gift tax deduction. [Reg. § 25.2522(a)–1(a)(flush)]

A deduction is also allowed for gifts by non-citizen, non-residents of the United States made to qualifying charities. The transfer, however, must be made only to domestic corporations or other organizations if used in the United States. [IRC § 2522(b)(3)–(4)]

The deduction is not allowed if the gift is subject to a condition unless "the possibility that the charitable transfer will not become effective is so remote as to be negligible." [Reg. § 25.2522(c)–3(b)(1)] This could create a situation where the transfer to a charity may be a complete gift, but is not deductible since the standard for when a gift is complete is less stringent then the standard for when a charitable gift is deductible.

Example: Charlie transfers land to City government for use as a public park. The gift is conditional so that if the land is ever used for a purpose other than a public park, the land will revert back to Charlie or his heirs. If the possibility that City will fail to use the land for a public park is not so remote as to be negligible, the gift is probably complete, but Charlie will not receive a gift tax deduction due to the condition placed on the gift. [*See* Reg. § 25.2522(c)–3(b)(2)(ex. 2)]

The charitable deduction is allowed in the year the gift is complete. *See supra* discussion at II. B. 3.

(1) Disallowance of Deductions [IRC § 2522(c)]

(a) Gifts to Disallowed Organizations or Trusts [IRC § 2522(c)(1)]

Gifts to certain organizations or trusts are disallowed a charitable deduction. For example, under certain circumstances, this includes gifts to an organization subject to tax under IRC § 507(c) (applying to formerly tax-exempt private foundations). [IRC § 508(d)(1)] In addition, gifts to private foundations or IRC § 4947 trusts are also disallowed a deduction under certain circumstances. [IRC § 508(d)(2)] Gifts to foreign organizations which engage in certain prohibited transactions or which are not taxable during the taxable year are also not allowed a charitable deduction. [IRC § 4948(c)(4)]

(b) Split Interest Gifts [IRC § 2522(c)(2)]

Gift transfers divided in time between charities and non-charities are either restricted in amount or disallowed under IRC § 2522(c)(2). Because these restrictions are similar to those present in the charitable estate tax deduction, they are covered in detail in I. B. 3. b).

Example: Neptune transfers property to an irrevocable trust, giving a life estate to Muriel with the remainder going to Atlantis University (A.U.). If the transfer does not meet the requirements of split interests gifts under IRC § 2522(c), the gift to A.U. will not qualify for a charitable deduction. Additionally, the transfer to A.U. does not qualify for the annual exclusion under IRC § 2503(b) since it is a transfer of a future interest.

(c) Fractional Gifts

Unless permitted by an exception, no deduction is allowed for contributions of fractional interests of tangible personal property. A charitable deduction is allowed if the taxpayer, or the taxpayer and the donee, hold all interests in the property. Also, a deduction may be allowed under situations provided for in the regulations (which to date have not been enacted) for proportional contributions made by co-owners of property. [IRC § 2522(e)(1)]

Example (1): Mr. Diesel owns several pieces of rare artwork. He transfers a one-third interest in one painting to a museum, which entitles it to possess the painting four months a year. While Mr. Diesel transferred a fractional interest in tangible personal property, he may take a deduction since he owned all the interests in the property before the transfer.

Example (2): The next year Mr. Diesel transfers another one-third interest in the painting to the museum. He may still take a deduction since the interests are held by the taxpayer (Mr. Diesel) and the donee (the museum).

Example (3): The transferred painting is owned equally by Mr. Diesel and Mr. Fairmont. Unless provided for in the regulations (which to date have not been enacted), Mr. Diesel cannot take a charitable deduction if he transfers less than 100% of his interest in the painting.

Even if a deduction is allowed it may be recaptured (plus interest and a 10% penalty) if the remaining interest is not transferred to the donee at the earlier of either: 1) 10 years from the date of the initial fractional contribution, or 2) the death of the donor. Even if the property is transferred within the required time period, a recapture will occur if the donee has not had "substantial physical possession" of the property and used the property in a way that is related to the organization's tax-exempt status. [IRC § 2522(e)(2)]

> *Example:* In the above examples, if the painting is used as an art exhibit sponsored by the museum and transferred within ten years, or if Mr. Diesel dies earlier, at his death, there should be no recapture of the deduction. If not, then all the deductions received by Mr. Diesel for the contribution of the painting plus interest and a ten percent penalty will be recaptured.

(2) Amount of Deduction

If a full interest in property is transferred to a qualifying charity, a deduction is allowed for the full fair market value of the property transferred. If a partial interest in property is transferred, and the requirements of IRC § 2522(c) are met, the partial interest is valued under IRC § 7520.

The deduction is reduced by any consideration received by the donor. [IRC § 2512(b)] Therefore, any amounts received by the donor from the charity serve to reduce the amount of the deduction allowed.

(3) Filing of Gift Tax Return

No gift tax return is required to be filed if the donor's only gifts consist of gifts made to charities that are fully deductible. [IRC § 6019(a)(3)]

b) Gifts to Spouses [IRC § 2523]

Originally enacted in 1948 to alleviate the disparity in estate and gift tax treatment in separate property and community property states, the marital deduction was made limitless in 1981 to reflect Congress' belief that a married couple should be treated as one economic unit. Now, transfers of fee interests in property during the marriage are fully deductible and not subject to the gift tax.

Under IRC § 2523(a), a deduction is allowed for the full value of gift transfers made to donor's spouse, unless the interest transferred is disqualified "terminable interest property" under IRC § 2523(b). In order to take the marital deduction, the donor and donee must be married at the time of transfer, since the section is inapplicable to transfers made either before marriage or after divorce.

The gift tax marital deduction under IRC § 2523 and the estate tax marital deduction under IRC § 2056 are very similar in language and scope. *See supra* discussion at I. B. 4., for extensive coverage of the estate tax marital deduction. Accordingly, this section only covers those areas where the gift tax marital deduction differs from the estate tax marital deduction.

(1) Terminable Interests [IRC § 2523(b)]

If all the interests in property are not transferred to the donee spouse, the transfer may not be deductible. When a portion of the transferred property passes to any person other than the donee spouse (including the donor) after the donee spouse's interest, or when the donor retains the power to appoint such an interest, no marital deduction is allowed unless an exception applies. The terminable interest rule in effect restricts the marital deduction only to those situations where the property will be subject to estate taxation at the donee spouse's death, or gift taxation if the property is transferred outside the marriage.

If the transferred property can be satisfied from a group of assets, the Code assumes the transferred assets do not qualify for the marital deduction. This is provided for in IRC § 2523(c), which is the gift tax counterpart to IRC § 2056(b)(2). If such an assumption is made, it serves to reduce the amount of marital deduction allowed.

Example: Harold creates a trust, with income to Harold for ten years. At the end of the ten-year period, the trustee is to transfer $100,000 to Harold's wife Maude, with any remainder going to their son. The trust has two assets. Asset 1 is corporate stock. Asset 2 is property that Harold previously transferred to Uncle Moe, retaining a twenty-year income interest in the property. Asset 2 is a terminable interest since Uncle Moe takes the property after the income interest terminates. [IRC § 2523(b)(1)] Therefore, the asset does not qualify for the marital deduction. [*Id.*] Assuming that the income interest in

Asset 2 is worth $30,000 at the end of ten years, the marital deduction is the present value of $70,000 due in ten years. The transfer to Maude at the end of the ten-year period is assumed to include the disqualified income interest regardless of the value of the corporate stock. [IRC § 2523(c); Reg. § 25.2523(c)–1(c)(ex.)]

(a) Donor Retains Interest or Third–Party Acquires Interest [IRC § 2523(b)(1)]

The terminable interest rule under IRC § 2523(b)(1) is substantially similar to its estate tax counterpart at IRC § 2056(b)(1). The primary coverage for this area is contained in the estate tax portion in I. B. 4. a) and only the differences are highlighted here. The most significant difference under the gift tax provision is that a donor's retained interest in the property can be a terminable interest. This is not present in the estate tax provision, since that provision covers transfers from a decedent rather than a donor. [IRC § 2523(b)(1)]

Another difference between the estate and gift tax marital deductions is found in the first sentence of the flush language (the penultimate sentence) of IRC § 2523(b). The rule provides that the exercise or release of a non-general power is treated as a transfer for the creation of a terminable interest. This means that a donor's spousal transfer of an interest originally created by someone outside the marriage may not qualify for the marital deduction.

Example: Raymond receives a ten-year income interest in trust, as well as the power to appoint the remainder to any of his children at his discretion. In default of any appointment, the remainder will go to Raymond's spouse. Raymond exercises the power and appoints the remainder to his son Seth. Raymond then transfers his income interest to his spouse. Since the power was a non-general power, IRC § 2514 does not apply to create a transfer. However, under the penultimate sentence of IRC § 2523(b), Raymond made a "transfer" to Seth creating a terminable interest. Since Raymond has transferred the remainder to a person other than his spouse and Seth may take the property after the ten-year period ends, it is a terminable interest and Raymond cannot claim a marital deduction for the gift of the income interest to his spouse.

The last difference between the gift tax's terminable interest rule and the estate tax's terminable interest rule is found in the last sentence of the flush language to IRC § 2523(b). This rule states that unless the donee has a life estate with a power of appointment that qualifies under IRC § 2523(e), an interest in property that can pass to either the donee spouse or some other person is treated as being transferable only to the other person. This means a transfer is treated as a terminable interest if it is not clear that the property interest can only pass to the donee spouse.

Example: Husband transfers property to an irrevocable trust giving his wife the right to the trust's income for ten years. After ten years, the corpus of the trust is to be distributed between the wife and the couple's three children in such a manner as the trustee determines. Even though some or all of the property may pass to the donor's spouse, after the application of the last sentence of IRC § 2523(b), for the purposes of determining if Husband transferred a terminable interest, the remainder interest will be treated as being completely transferred to a "person other than the donee spouse." [Reg. § 25.2523(b)–1(b)(3)(ex. 1)]

(b) Retained Powers of the Donor [IRC § 2523(b)(2)]

Under IRC § 2523(b)(2), a terminable interest is created if the donor retains a power to appoint the property after the complete termination of the donee spouse's interest. The donor does not actually have to own the property for this exception to apply, but if not, the donor must have a general power of appointment over the property, or no transfer will exist under IRC § 2514. For purposes of the application of IRC § 2523(b)(2), the fact that the power cannot be exercised until after the passage of time or the occurrence or non-occurrence of an event or contingency is disregarded.

Example (1):   A.J. gives Bart a general power of appointment (GPA) over some property owned by A.J. Bart exercises the GPA giving a life estate to his wife, Lisa, and retaining the power to appoint the remainder. Bart's power to transfer the property after Lisa's property interest terminates creates a terminable interest under IRC § 2523(b)(2). Bart receives no marital deduction for the transfer. [Reg. § 25.2523(b)–1(d)(3)(example)]

Example (2):   A.J. also gives Bart a life estate in the income interest of a trust, with the power to name the remainder beneficiary if Bart survives A.J. Bart gives the life estate interest to his spouse, but retains the right to appoint the remainder. The contingency is disregarded and Bart is treated as having the power to appoint the remainder. Bart receives no marital deduction for the transfer, since his spouse received a terminable interest under IRC § 2523(b)(2).

(c) Exceptions to the Terminable Interest Rule

There are several exceptions to the terminable interest rule. If an exception is found, a marital deduction from the taxable gifts may still be allowed even though the interest transferred to the donee spouse is a terminable interest. Most of the exceptions presented mirror the estate tax marital deductions and are covered more fully in that section. *See supra* the discussion of the estate tax marital deduction, I. B. 4. a) (2).

i)   Life Estate with Power of Appointment in Donee Spouse [IRC § 2523(e)]

This non-elective exception is permitted when the donee spouse has a life estate interest in the property and has the sole power to transfer the interest to whomever the donee spouse should choose. This provision is similar to IRC § 2056(b)(5) for the estate tax marital deduction.

ii)   Transfer of Qualified Terminable Interest Property (QTIP) [IRC § 2523(f)]

One of the most important and most utilized exceptions to the terminable interest rule is the exception for qualified terminable interest property (QTIP) found in IRC § 2523(f) and its estate tax counterpart at IRC § 2056(b)(7). For this exception to apply to the property 1) the donor spouse must transfer property, 2) the donee spouse must possess a qualifying income interest for life in the property, and 3) the donor must elect to have the exception apply. [IRC § 2523(f)(2)] The primary difference between the gift and estate tax QTIP exceptions is that the donor must elect to have the gift tax section apply, whereas the executor makes the election for estate tax purposes.

If the donee spouse transfers any portion of the qualified income interest, it will lead to the constructive transfer of all the remaining interests. *See supra* discussion at II. C. 3., for the application of IRC § 2519 to a transfer of a QTIP interest. If the donee spouse never transfers any portion of the interest at death, the entire interest will be included in the donee spouses' gross estate under IRC § 2044. *See supra* discussion at I. A. 3. e), for the application of IRC § 2044 where the spouse holds a QTIP interest at death.

If the other interests in the trust besides the donee spouse's interest qualify as a charitable remainder trust, a marital deduction is allowed even though a terminable interest is transferred. IRC § 2523(g) is the gift tax counterpart to IRC § 2056(b)(8). For the specific requirements of IRC § 2056(b)(8), *see supra* discussion at I. B. 4. a) (2) (c).

iii) Joint Interests Held Between Donor and Donee Spouse [IRC § 2523(d)]

If a donor spouse transfers a piece of property to the donee spouse as a joint tenant, the interest is a terminable interest under IRC § 2523(b)(1). The rationale is that if the donor spouse lives longer than the donee spouse, the donor takes the entire property. The survivorship right means 1) the donor has retained an interest in property and 2) by reason of that interest may enjoy the property after the completion of the donee spouse's interest. Therefore, without an exception, all transfers made in joint tenancy or tenancy by the entirety are not allowed a gift tax deduction.

IRC § 2523(d) avoids this result. It has no counterpart in the estate tax, as this situation cannot occur under the estate tax since the transferring spouse is deceased when the transfer is made. The exception disregards both the survivorship rights and the possibility of a severed interest for the purposes of applying the terminable interest rule. After the application of IRC § 2523(d) the donor spouse no longer retains any interest in the property, and the interest is not considered a terminable interest.

> *Example:*   With his separate property, Husband purchases $200,000 of stock and places it in joint tenancy with right of survivorship with his wife. The fact that Husband may take back all of the property after his wife's death is disregarded and, for the application of the terminable interest rule, no interest may return to Husband after his wife dies. Husband has given his wife a $100,000 gift that qualifies for both the IRC § 2503(b) annual exclusion and the marital deduction of IRC § 2523(a), resulting in zero taxable gifts.

(2) Spouse Not a U.S. Citizen [IRC § 2523(i)]

No marital deduction is allowed when the donor's spouse is not a citizen of the United States. While the deduction is disallowed, the IRC § 2503(b) annual exclusion is increased from a base of $10,000 to $100,000 for transfers to the non-citizen spouse, an amount that is adjusted for inflation. [IRC § 2523(i)] For 2011, the inflation adjusted amount is $136,000.

(3) Gift Tax Return [IRC § 6019(a)(2)]

A gift tax return is not required to be filed for any gift receiving a marital deduction, unless an election is made during the year to pass qualified terminable interest property under IRC § 2523(f). In that case, the election must be present on a gift tax return filed for the year. [Reg. § 25.2523(f)–1(b)(4)]

c) **Extent of Deductions [IRC § 2524]**

IRC § 2524 limits any gift tax deductions to the amount of gifts made after any exclusions. This prohibits the improper offset of deductions against gifts that do not qualify for either the charitable or marital deduction. After the application of IRC § 2524, the gift tax deductions can only create a zero net deduction.

Example: Adama gives a gift of $25,000 to Galactica University (G.U.) and a $22,000 gift to his son, Apollo. After using the $10,000 exclusion under IRC § 2503(b)(not adjusted for inflation), Adama will have a $15,000 gift to G.U. and a $12,000 gift to Apollo. IRC § 2524 limits the amount of the gift tax charitable deduction under IRC § 2522(a) to $15,000, the amount of the gift to G.U. after the application of IRC § 2503(b). Adama cannot claim a $25,000 gift tax charitable deduction in addition to the annual exclusion because that would effectively reduce the taxable gift to Apollo for which no gift tax deduction should be allowed. The amount of Adama's income tax charitable deduction is still $25,000. [IRC § 170(a)]

F. Computation of the Gift Tax [IRC § 2502]

The gift tax is computed on the amount of taxable gifts given during each calendar year. Taxable gifts are the base used for taxation, comparable to the "taxable estate" in the estate tax or "taxable income" in the income tax.

Since 1976, the gift tax and estate tax rates have been "unified," meaning a single rate schedule is used to compute both taxes. This rate schedule is located in IRC § 2001(c). The tax rate for the gift tax is computed based on progressive rates which increase based on the total amount of taxable gifts made during the donor's lifetime.

Computing the gift tax is a two-step process. First, a "tentative tax" is computed on all taxable gifts made by the donor after June 6, 1932, including those taxable gifts made during the current year. [IRC § 2502(a)(1)] Next, a "tentative tax" is computed using taxable gifts made after June 6, 1932, but does not include gifts made during the current year (called taxable gifts made during "preceding calendar periods"). [IRC § 2502(a)(2)] This amount is then subtracted from the first tentative tax (which includes the amount of gifts in the current year) to arrive at the gift tax liability for the current year. In this manner, only the current year's taxable gifts incur any tax liability and the taxable gifts made during prior years are used only to increase the marginal rate of taxation on the current year's taxable gifts. To arrive at the gift tax due, the donor's unified credit is applied against the computed gift tax liability. [IRC § 2505]

Example (1): Norm makes $3 million of taxable gifts during Year 1. Year 1 is the first year in which Norm has made any gifts over the annual exclusion amount [IRC § 2503(b)] to a single donee. To determine Norm's gift tax liability a tentative tax is first computed on the total amount of taxable gifts made by Norm after June 6, 1932. In this example the tentative tax is computed on $3 million using the tax rates found at IRC § 2001(c). Using the table the amount of tentative tax is $1,030,800, with a marginal rate of 35%. The second tentative tax is computed using only those taxable gifts made before the current year, here $0. Therefore Norm's gift tax liability is $1,030,800. However, to arrive at the amount of gift tax due, Norm must deduct his unified credit amount. [IRC § 2505]

Example (2): In Year 2, Norm makes another $3 million of taxable gifts. Now a tentative tax is first computed on $6 million, the sum of $3 million of taxable gifts made in the current year and the $3 million of taxable gifts made in Year 1. The tentative tax on $6 million under IRC § 2001(c) is $2,080,800. Next, a tentative tax is computed on all gifts made prior to Year 2 (the $3 million in gifts made in Year 1). As determined in the first example, the amount of gift tax on $1 million is $1,030,800. To find Norm's gift tax liability for Year 2 we take the excess of the first tentative tax ($2,080,800) less the second tentative tax ($1,030,800), leaving $1,050,000 in gift tax liability. As in the first example, Norm needs to utilize the unified credit (if any) to determine the amount of gift tax due. [IRC § 2505]

Note: the taxable gifts made in Year 1 were only used to place the taxable gifts made in Year 2 in the correct tax bracket on the progressive rate schedule of IRC § 2001(c).

1. "Taxable Gifts for Preceding Calendar Periods" [IRC § 2504]

To determine the current year's gift tax liability, "taxable gifts for preceding calendar periods" are used to calculate the rate of taxation. IRC § 2502(b) defines "preceding calendar periods" and the term includes all the years from June 6, 1932. [IRC § 2502(b)(flush)] "Periods" is used in the statute instead of "years," since between 1971 and March 3, 1982 the gift tax was computed quarterly. At all other times the gift tax was computed on a calendar year basis.

The amount of taxable gifts for preceding calendar periods is figured using the law as it existed at that time. This means that items that are not taxable under current law, but were taxable at an earlier time, are still included, and vice-versa. Also, if a transfer should have been included in the previous years' taxable gifts but was omitted on the gift tax return, that transfer must be included in computing the taxable gifts for preceding calendar periods. It does not matter if the statute of limitations has passed. It is important to note that the omitted amounts are not subject to the gift tax, but they merely increase the rate at which the current year's gifts are taxed.

Deductions and exemptions allowable in previous years, with one exception, are also utilized in determining the amount of taxable gifts for preceding calendar periods. [IRC § 2504(a)(2), (b)] The one exception is the application of former IRC § 2521, the specific exemption which was allowed in varying amounts between $30,000 and $50,000 before 1977, and was replaced with the unified credit of IRC § 2505. The now defunct IRC § 2521 exemption is used to reduce taxable gifts made before 1977 by $30,000, regardless of whether the taxpayer actually utilized the exemption. [IRC § 2504(a)(3)]

The valuation of different assets transferred in previous calendar years presents a problem. To alleviate the administrative burden and add some certainty, Congress enacted IRC § 2504(c). IRC § 2504(c) provides that after the statute of limitations has expired under IRC § 6501 (normally three years), the value of gifts made after August 5, 1997 cannot be changed for the purposes of computing the gift tax. IRC § 6501 provides that for the statute of limitations to expire so that no additional gift tax may be assessed or collected, and the value of the gift to be final, the item must be listed on the gift tax return in such a manner to give notice to the Secretary. [IRC § 6501(c)(9)] Therefore if no gift tax return is filed, or was filed but did not include the item, IRC § 2504(c) will not apply and the item may be revalued. Before the enactment of IRC § 2504(c), for a valuation to be final, the gift tax had to be assessed or paid on the transfer. Therefore, in cases where no tax was due because of the unified credit, valuation remained an open question.

2. Unified Credit Against Gift Tax [IRC § 2505]

After 1976, citizens and residents of the United States have a credit against any gift tax imposed. The amount of the gift tax credit is the applicable credit amount under IRC § 2010(c). [*See supra* discussion of IRC § 2010(c) at I. C. 2. a)] The applicable credit is the sum of the basic exclusion amount and the deceased spousal unused exclusion amount. The basic exclusion amount is the tentative tax under IRC § 2001(c) on $5 million, or $1,730,800. [IRC § 2505(a)(1)] The result of this credit is that until a donor's total amount of lifetime taxable gifts exceeds $5 million there is no tax liability. The amount of the credit is reduced by the amount of credit utilized in any preceding calendar period. [IRC § 2505(a)(2)] In order to compute the amount of credit used in preceding calendar periods the current rates under IRC § 2502(a)(2) are used. [IRC § 2505(a)(flush)] The amount of credit utilized under IRC § 2505 does not reduce the credit allowed under the estate tax under IRC § 2010.

Example: In the earlier example, Norm had a gift tax liability in Year 1 of $1,030,800. After application of the IRC § 2505(a) credit of the same amount Norm's gift tax due is zero. In Year 2, Norm would owe $350,000 in gift tax since the $6 million in gifts has fully exhausted his gift tax unified credit of $5 million.

The credit is mandatory and a donor may not elect when to utilize the credit. If a donor fails to utilize the credit it will still reduce the amount of available credit in later years.

Example: Gilbert transfers $1 million to his son Albert as a gift. Gilbert has not made any previous taxable gifts. Albert agrees to pay the gift tax due on the transfer, so Gilbert will not have to use his IRC § 2505 unified credit. Even if Gilbert files a gift tax return and does not utilize his IRC § 2505 credit, the statute provides that the available credit is reduced by the amount of "allowable" credits in preceding years, and Gilbert would have to reduce his available credit by $1 million. [Rev. Rul. 79–398, 1979–2 C.B. 338]

G. Procedural Rules

1. Who Must File

A gift tax return must be filed each calendar year an individual makes "any transfer by gift" unless the transfer falls into one of three categories. [IRC § 6019(intro.)] First, no return is required for transfers excluded under IRC § 2503(b) ["Exclusions from gifts" *see supra* II. E. 1. discussing the exclusion] or IRC § 2503(e) [exclusions from gifts for certain transfers for medical or educational expenses *see supra* II. B. 4. b) (2) discussing the exclusion]. [IRC § 6019(1)] Second, transfers deductible under the gift tax marital deduction [IRC § 2523] do not need to be reported. [IRC § 6019(2)] Third, no return is required for deductible charitable contributions under IRC § 2522, so long as the entire interest was deductible (only of present interests in property) or it was a qualified conservation contribution of an easement. [IRC § 6019(3)] Therefore, if all the individual's transfers for a given year do not fall into one of the three exceptions, a return is required regardless of whether gift tax is due or not. [Reg. § 25.6019–1(a), (f)] For example, a gift tax return is still required even if there is no gift tax liability due to the application of the unified credit under IRC § 2505. [Reg. § 25.6019–1(f)]

Non-gift transfers do not require a return. Non-gift transfers includes transfers of services, transfers in the ordinary course of business, transfers made for full and adequate consideration in money or money's worth, transfers made in satisfaction of support obligations, or transfers to political organizations, etc. [*See supra* II. B. 1. b) and II. B. 4. covering the exceptions to the gift tax and the general rule of when something is a "gift."]

A gift tax return is required from each individual making a qualifying transfer of property by gift. A husband and wife must each file their own gift tax return, since no provision allows for joint gift tax returns.

Death or incompetence does not terminate the obligation to file a return. If the donor dies before filing a gift tax return, the executor of the will or administrator of the estate is required to file the gift tax return. [Reg. § 25.6019–1(g)] If the donor becomes legally incompetent, the donor's guardian is required to file the return. [*Id.*]

2. Filing Date

A gift tax return may be filed as early as January 1, but no later than April 15, of the year following the transfer. [IRC § 6075(b)(1); 2009 IRS Instructions to Form 709, p. 3] An extension may be automatically granted for taxpayers who obtain an income tax extension under IRC § 6019. [IRC § 6075(b)(2)] Any extension is limited to six months, unless the taxpayer is abroad. [IRC § 6081(a)] If the taxpayer dies before filing, the gift tax return is due at the same time as the estate tax return, including any extensions. [IRC § 6075(b)(3)]

3. Payment of Gift Tax and Liens

Generally, payment of the gift tax by the donor occurs when the gift tax return is due "without regard to any extension of time for filing the return." [IRC § 6151(a)] An extension of time to pay the gift tax may be granted, but not for more than six months, unless the taxpayer is abroad. [IRC § 6161(a)(1)]

The donor assumes primary liability for any gift tax imposed. [IRC § 2502(c)] If spouses split any gifts during the year under IRC § 2513, the entire gift tax of each spouse is joint and several liability of the other, regardless of whether the gift tax due is from a split gift. [IRC § 2513(d); Reg. §§ 25.2502–2, 25.2513–4] If the donor dies before the payment of the gift tax, the executor or administrator must pay the debt from the donor's estate. [Reg. § 25.2502–2] If the donor does not pay the gift tax due on the gift, the donee is responsible for its payment up to the fair market value of the gift. [IRC § 6324(b)(second sentence)] The donee's liability does not depend on whether the donee's gift was under the IRC § 2503(b) exclusion amount or received a gift tax deduction (marital or charitable). [*Baur v. Commissioner*, 145 F.2d 338, 339 (3d Cir. 1944); *La Fortune v. Commissioner*, 263 F.2d 186, 194 (10th Cir. 1958)

If the gift tax is not paid, there is ten-year lien starting on the date the gifts were made on all property subject to the gift tax for such calendar year. [IRC § 6324(b)(first sentence)] The lien is terminated at the earlier of ten years, when the gift tax is paid, or when it "becomes unenforceable by reason of lapse of time." [*Id.*]

H. Carryover Basis Rules Applicable to Some Decedents Dying in 2010

At the election of the executor, decedents dying in 2010 may take advantage of the estate and generation-skipping transfer tax repeal in that year. If the election is made, then a new basis rule for property acquired from a decedent applies. The current basis rule for property acquired by a decedent is IRC § 1014. IRC § 1014 provides that the basis of property acquired from a decedent is its fair market value, or if some alternative estate tax valuation time or method is used, the value using such election. [IRC § 1014(a)]

For those estates making the election to not apply the estate tax, IRC § 1022 replaces IRC § 1014. IRC § 1022 applies to all property (1) acquired from a decedent, (2) dying after December 31, 2009. [IRC § 1022(a)] Property acquired in such a manner is treated for Subtitle A (Income taxes) as a gift transfer. This means that the property is not included in the transferee's gross income. [IRC § 102(a)] The basis of the acquired property is the lower of the decedent's transferred basis (similar to the rule for gift basis under § 1015 or transfers between spouses § 1041) or the fair market value at the time of the decedent's death. [IRC § 1022(a)(2)] This basis rule is augmented by allowable increases to the acquired property's basis of $1.3 million, with an additional $3 million increase for certain property acquired by a surviving spouse. [IRC § 1022(b), (c)]

IRC § 1022 also provides for non-recognition of gain incurred due to the transfer of property from the estate, where the liabilities of the property exceed its adjusted basis. [IRC § 1022(g)(1)] The rule does not apply to transfers to tax-exempt beneficiaries. [*Id.*]

1. Property Acquired from a Decedent [IRC § 1022(e)]

The adjusted basis rules of IRC § 1022 apply only to "property acquired from a decedent." [IRC § 1022(a)] IRC § 1022(e) broadly defines property acquired from a decedent, covering all property includable in the decedent's gross estate. Specifically, covered property includes both property acquired by bequest, devise or inheritance, and the property acquired by the decedent's estate from the decedent. [IRC § 1022(e)(1)] Also included is property received from a trust that the decedent could alter, amend, revoke, or terminate. [IRC § 1022(e)(2)] Finally, all property passed without consideration by reason of death from the decedent is also treated as property acquired from the decedent. [IRC § 1022(e)(3)]

2. Additional Basis Increase

IRC § 1014 allows for a fair market value basis to all property acquired from a decedent. A fair market value basis wipes out all the gain (and the losses) inherent in the property, a major consideration in many estate plans. To offset the loss of the fair market value basis rule, IRC § 1022 allows for a limited increase of the decedent's basis in property up to a maximum of the property's fair market value. As an overview, increases are allowed to all property "owned" by the decedent up to a total increase for all property of $1.3 million, with an additional $3 million in increases allowed for property acquired by a surviving spouse. [IRC § 1022(b), (d)] The executor determines the increases. [IRC § 1022(d)(3)(A)]

a) "Property to Which This Subsection Applies"

The executor may only increase the basis of "property to which this subsection [IRC § 1022(b) or (c)] applies." [IRC § 1022(b), (c)] IRC § 1022(d) provides when those subsections do, and do not, apply. The general rule is that the property must be "owned" by the decedent at the time of death [IRC § 1022(d)(1)(A)], but not be received by gift within three years of death (unless from a spouse). [IRC § 1022(d)(1)(C)] Additionally, the basis increase does not apply to certain types of stock. [IRC § 1022(d)(1)(D)]

(1) Property Owned by Decedent at Death

IRC § 1022 provides limited guidance for the determination of when items are, and are not, owned by the decedent at death. [IRC § 1022(d)(1)(B)] For example, the statute does not provide for an exact definition of when something is "owned," but it does provide for when certain items are to be included or excluded from the definition.

Property the decedent held as a joint tenant with rights of survivorship or in a tenancy in the entirety is treated as "owned" by the decedent. [IRC § 1022(d)(1)(B)(i)] There are three special rules for determining ownership of jointly held property. First, a decedent is treated as owning fifty percent of the property when jointly held with only a surviving spouse. [IRC § 1022(d)(1)(B)(i)(I)] Second, if the property was not jointly owned only with a surviving spouse, and the decedent furnishes consideration for the purchase of the property, the decedent is treated as owning a proportionate portion of the property. [IRC § 1022(d)(1)(B)(i)(II)] Finally, if the property was not jointly owned only with a surviving spouse and was not acquired by purchase (i.e., it was acquired by gift, bequest, devise, etc.) the decedent is treated as owning his or her fractional ownership portion. However, local law may overrule and determine the exact ownership interests. [IRC § 1022(d)(1)(B)(i)(III)]

A decedent is also considered as owning (1) property the decedent transferred to a qualified revocable trust, (2) all property over which the decedent holds a power of appointment, and (3) the entire amount of community property. [IRC § 1022(d)(1)(B)(ii)–(iv)] The community property rule mirrors IRC § 1014(b)(6) and allows for increases in the adjusted basis for small and medium size estates in the same manner as IRC § 1014.

One specific type of property not listed is property held by a surviving spouse in a QTIP trust or property receiving a marital deduction under IRC § 2056(b)(5). While the property may receive an increase after the first spouse's death, it will not get a second increase at the surviving spouse's death.

(2) Property Not Allowed a Basis Increase

Certain property is specifically excluded from receiving a basis increase. First, in a rule similar to, but much more broad than IRC § 1014(e), no basis increase is allowed for any property received as a gift (in whole or in part) or purchased for less than full consideration, by the decedent within three years of death. [IRC § 1022(d)(1)(C)(i)] This exception does not apply to property transferred by the decedent's surviving spouse, unless the surviving spouse received the property as a gift or for less than full consideration in the same time period. [IRC § 1022(d)(1)(C)(ii)]

Second, certain stock held by the decedent does not qualify for the basis increase. [IRC § 1022(d)(1)(D)] Stock in a foreign personal holding company, a current or former domestic international sales corporation ("DISC"), and stock in a foreign investment company or certain passive foreign investment company are all excluded from the basis increase provision. [IRC § 1022(d)(1)(D)(i–iv)]

b) Basic Basis Increase

Unless adjusted higher, the executor of the decedent's estate may increase the decedent's basis by an aggregate of $1.3 million. [IRC § 1022(b)(1), (2)(A,) (B)] However, the basis of the property cannot be increased beyond the property's fair market value at the time of the decedent's death. [IRC § 1022(d)(2)] The increases are made at the discretion of the executor on an asset-by-asset basis and must be indicated to the Service on a form to be proscribed under IRC § 6018. [IRC § 1022(d)(3)(A)] Once made, the basis of the property cannot be changed without the permission of the Secretary. [IRC § 1022(d)(3)(B)]

Three items may increase the basic $1.3 million aggregate amount. First, any unused capital loss carryover increases the limit under IRC § 1212(b). Second, any unused net operating loss carryovers under IRC § 172 that the decedent could have taken in the following year if alive, increase the amount. Finally, any built-in deductible losses under IRC § 165 increase the limit. [IRC § 1022(b)(2)(C)] Individuals can only deduct losses for trade or business property, property involved in transactions entered into for profit, and certain casualty losses. [IRC § 165(c)(1)–(3)]

For non-resident, non-citizens, the basis increase is limited to $60,000. [IRC § 1022(b)(3)(A)] Unlike the $1.3 million limit for United States citizens, the amount allowed for non-resident, non-citizens is fixed and cannot be increased by the adjustments described above. [IRC § 1022(b)(3)(B)]

c) Additional Basis Increase for Property Acquired by Surviving Spouse

The basis of "qualified spousal property" may be increased by an additional $3 million aggregate adjustment. [IRC § 1022(c)(1), (2)] Therefore, if the surviving spouse receives all decedent's property the basis could be increased, before any upward adjustments, by a total of $4.3 million. "Qualified spousal property" includes outright property transfers to a surviving spouse and all qualified terminable interest property ("QTIP"). [IRC § 1022(c)(3)] Outright transfers include all property acquired by the surviving spouse from the decedent, except terminable interest property. [IRC § 1022(c)(4)(A,) (B)] The terminable interest definition of IRC § 1022 exactly tracks the estate tax marital deduction definition and was designed to cover the same types of property. [IRC § 2056(b)(1)] The only exceptions allowed for IRC § 1022 are for the surviving spouse exception [IRC § 1022(d)(4)(C)] and for QTIP property [IRC § 1022(c)(3)(B)]. Therefore the other exceptions allowed for terminable interest property (i.e., life estates with power of appointment in a surviving spouse under IRC § 2056(b)(5)) are not allowed the additional increase. [*See supra* I. B. 4. a) (2) (a)–(d) covering the other exceptions to the terminable interest rule.]

The increase in basis is further limited to the fair market value of the property at the time of the decedent's death. [IRC § 1022(d)(2)]

d) Examples

Larry dies in 2010 with an estate worth a fair market value of $5 million. Larry's will bequeaths all his assets to his niece, Marta. Marta receives property with a basis equal to the lower of Larry's basis or the fair market value of the property. However, the estate's executor may increase the basis of those assets, up to each asset's respective fair market value, by an aggregate maximum amount of $1.3 million.

Same facts as above except that Larry's will transfers the property to his wife. Now the executor may increase the basis of the property by a total of $4.3 million up to the fair market value of the property at Larry's death ($1.3 million in basic increase plus $3.0 million for property passed outright to a surviving spouse).

I. Review Questions

1. Bill gives $1 million to the Green Party. Is that amount a gift?

2. Jason owes Laura $15,000. Without any business purpose, Laura forgives the debt. Has Laura made a gift to Jason?

3. By contract Jack owes Jill $10,000 which is due on April 15, Year 1. The payment date passes with no payment. Jill does not seek payment and lets the statute of limitations run out on the collection of the debt. Has Jill made a transfer of property to Jack?

4. Bill transfers to Steve several state bonds that are exempt from taxation under IRC § 103. Has Bill made a gift to Steve that can be subject to the gift tax?

5. Douglas creates a trust that pays income to Nancy for her life and the remainder to Bruce. Nancy and Bruce are unrelated to Douglas. Douglas

retains the right to change the remainder interest, but only with the consent of Nancy. Douglas does not maintain the power to change the income interest. Is there a completed transfer of any interest in property?

6. David's father promises to pay David $20,000 if he stops chewing tobacco. David quits and receives $20,000. Has a gift transfer been made?

7. Kitty pays for ice-skating lessons and rink time for her minor daughter at a cost of $20,000 per year. Has Kitty made a gift?

8. Kitty transfers $20,000 to Whatsamatta University Law School for her 35–year–old son's law school tuition. State law provides Kitty does not have any support obligations to her son. Has Kitty made a gift?

9. Wally has a general power of appointment over $20,000 per year from a trust created by Theodore. The trust provides income to Wally, and the remainder interest to Wally's son, Beaver. If Wally does not exercise the power it will lapse. What are the gift tax consequences, if any, if Wally fails to exercise the power in a year when the trust corpus is $300,000?

10. In the current year, Donor gives Mary an income interest in a trust for life, with the right to demand the corpus of the trust after 10 years. Donor's initial transfer to the trust is $20,000 and Mary's life estate interest, disregarding the right to demand the corpus, has a value of $17,280. What is the amount of taxable gifts from Donor to Mary from this transfer assuming the annual exclusion under IRC § 2503(b) is $10,000?

11. Using his separate property, Husband purchases a $100,000 annuity for his wife. The annuity provides annual payments to Wife for her life. If the total amounts of payments made before Wife's death are less than $100,000, additional payments are to be made to Son. Does the transfer of the annuity from Husband to Wife qualify for the marital deduction under IRC § 2523(a)?

12. Husband transfers an apartment building to Alan, an unrelated third-party, reserving a right to the rental income from the property for the next 10 years. The next year, Husband transfers his remaining income interest in the property to Wife for no consideration. What are the tax consequences of the transfer to Wife?

13. Generally, under which of the following circumstances (if any) is a gift tax return required to be filed? Assume the IRC § 2503(b) annual exclusion amount is $10,000.

A. A donor gives gifts to someone (other than a spouse) totaling more than $10,000.

B. A donor gives a gift of a future interest in property less than $10,000.

C. A donor gives a gift to an individual and splits the gift with donor's spouse.

D. All of the above.

14. Tom gifts a vase with a fair market value of $50,000 to his friend, Katie. Tom's adjusted basis in the vase is $10,000. What is the gross amount of the gift to Katie (without any reduction from IRC § 2503(b))?

A. $10,000

B. $29,000

C. $40,000

D. $50,000

15. True or false: All gifts over $10,000 to an unrelated individual 38 years younger than the donor are subject to both the gift and generation-skipping tax. Assume the IRC § 2503(b) annual exclusion amount is $10,000.

16. Bill transferred the following gifts to individuals during the current year. Which, if any, are "taxable gifts"?

1. $15,000 transferred to Bill's mother to offset medical expenses.

2. A $20,000 state bond exempt from Federal taxation under IRC § 103.

3. 500 shares of Macrohard stock transferred to Bill's sister, Tina. The stock had a basis of $3,000 and a fair market value of $20,000.

4. $17,000 paid to Whatsamatta University (a qualified educational organization) for his son's room and board.

A. All of the above

B. 2 and 3 only

C. 2, 3, 4, but not 1

D. 1, 2 and 3, but not 4

17. Jimmy transfers several assets in the current year.

- Transfer of his business to his son for $50,000. The fair market value of the business at the time of transfer was $125,000.

- Transfer of $20,000 to the Republican National Committee.

- Transfer of stock worth $20,000 to the University of Florida, where he got his LL.M. in taxation. The basis of the stock was $3,000.

- Payment directly to the school of $17,000 for the college tuition of his niece.

What is the total amount of taxable gift transfers, before any IRC § 2503(b) or unified credits, given by Jimmy?

A. $50,000

B. $75,000

C. $95,000

D. $132,000

E. None of the above

18. Dennis transfers a life insurance policy on his life valued at $100,000 to a trust. After Dennis dies, the insurance proceeds are to be held in trust with the income going to Steve, remainder to Trevor, Steve's son. Dennis transfers $10,000 to the trust each year to pay the premiums on the insurance policy. Steve has the non-cumulative yearly right to withdraw $10,000 from the corpus of the trust. What are the estate and gift tax results of the $10,000 yearly transfer? What are some ways to avoid any negative consequences? Assume the IRC § 2503(b) exclusion amount is $10,000.

CHAPTER III

Generation Skipping Transfer Tax

■ ANALYSIS

      (2) Tax Returns

          (a) Who Must File

          (b) Date and Type of Return to be Filed

   c) Taxable Distributions

      (1) Liability for Payment of GST Tax

      (2) Tax Returns

F.   **Review Questions**

A. Introduction

Chapter 13 of Subtitle B (covering estate and gift taxes) establishes the **generation-skipping transfer ("GST") tax**. The primary rationale behind the GST tax is not to generate revenue, but to ensure that transfer taxes are applied uniformly regardless of whether a transfer was made to the next succeeding generation or made in such a way to skip generations. [Staff of Joint Comm. on Taxation, 99th Cong., 2d Sess., General Explanation of the Tax Reform Act of 1986 at 1263 (Comm. Print 1987)]

For example, compare the results of transfers by two transferors to their heirs. The first transferor, D, leaves all of his property at his death to his child, E. As a result of the transfer, D's gross estate is subject to an estate tax at D's death. E then leaves all of his property at his death to his child F, where it is subject to another estate tax, as is F's gross estate on the transfer to his child (D's great-grandchild).

The second transferor, T, creates a trust with the income to his child, C, for life, then to his grandchild, GC, for life, then to GC's issue per stirpes (the great-grandchildren of T). Except for the rule against perpetuities (which has been repealed in several states) and the lack of funds to create a trust fund large enough to withstand consumption from multiple generations of beneficiaries without totally eroding the trust corpus, there is no limit as to how long this type of arrangement could continue. T is taxed under the estate tax, if the trust is created at T's death, or the gift tax, if the trust is established inter vivos. However, C does not have any estate tax liability at his death since C does not have an "interest" in property [IRC § 2033], and never owned the property. Therefore, the re-inclusion provisions of the estate tax [IRC §§ 2035–2038] do not apply. At GC's death, a similar situation occurs and no estate tax is imposed. Therefore, unlike D's family, which was subject to three transfer taxes (at D's, E's and F's death), T's property passed through three generations with the imposition of only one transfer tax.

Without the GST tax, the inequity between the classes is exacerbated, since generally only the wealthy can afford to have large amounts of property committed to an irrevocable trust and afford to tap the knowledge and expertise of estate planners to have the trusts created. Therefore, to treat both transferors in a similar fashion, the GST tax of Chapter 13 was created. Applying the GST tax to T's trust will correct the absence of taxation under both the estate and gift taxes and impose a tax on the termination of both C and GC's interest.

The GST tax, in addition to whatever estate and gift tax liability exists on the transfer, is imposed on every "generation-skipping transfer." [IRC § 2601]

Generation-skipping transfer is defined in IRC § 2611 as any "direct skip," "taxable termination," or "taxable distribution." These terms are individually defined in IRC § 2612. Once a generation-skipping transfer is found, the tax rate (the computation of which is fairly complicated) is applied against the "taxable amount" as determined under IRC §§ 2621 to 2623. One important note: for the most part Chapter 13 only applies to transfers completed and trusts created after Chapter 13's effective date of October 22, 1986. Therefore, any irrevocable trusts created before that date are not subject to the generation-skipping tax, even though they may skip multiple generations. However, any additional funds added to those trusts after the effective date will be subject to Chapter 13. [*See infra* discussion on effective dates, III. C. 2. (d) (1)]

The key to understanding and utilizing the GST tax is to grasp its terminology. Some terms used in Chapter 13 (i.e., "skip person," "direct skip," "inclusion ratio") are not used in either the estate or gift taxes, and others have their own special meaning for Chapter 13 (i.e., "interest" and "transferor"), which makes the study of Chapter 13 difficult. However, once the terminology is understood and mastered, determining when a generation-skipping transfer is present and computing the tax is relatively straightforward.

This portion of the outline is organized around determining when and how to apply the GST tax. First, the various terms are defined. The next section applies those terms to determine when and what type of generation-skipping transfer has occurred. Afterward, the computation of the GST tax will be covered. Finally, in the last section some collateral and procedural issues will be discussed.

For simplicity and clarity, individuals are given standard names in this section. Generally, "T" will refer to the transferor of the property, "TS" is the transferor's spouse, "C" is the transferor's child, "GC" is transferor's grandchild, "GGC" is the great-grandchild of the transferor, "TP" is transferor's parent, and "TGP" is transferor's grandparent. These designations are repeated in the following examples for clarity. Creating diagrams of the family relationships, as well as the transactions, is very helpful to determine whether the GST tax applies to any given situation.

B. Terminology

1. Introduction

Much of the GST tax's terminology is unique to Chapter 13. Many of the terms apply only to the application of the GST tax (e.g., "skip person"), or are used differently from the other transfer taxes (e.g., "interest"). The terms must be defined before analyzing a transaction to determine possible GST tax consequences.

As an overview, Chapter 13 imposes a tax on all "generation-skipping transfers." [IRC § 2601] Three types of generation-skipping transfers exist: a direct skip, a taxable termination, and a taxable distribution. [IRC § 2611(a)] Very generally, the three types of generation-skipping transfers require a "skip person" to receive an "interest in property" under Chapter 13. The interest may be transferred directly or through a trust. If no one has a Chapter 13 interest in the trust (e.g., the trust is not distributing income), the trust can be still be a skip person if no non-skip person may ever take the property. [IRC § 2612(a)–(c)] A skip person can either be a natural person or a trust. [IRC § 2613(a)] For an individual to qualify as a skip person, the transferee or beneficiary of the trust must be two or more "generational assignments" below the "transferor." [IRC § 2613(a)(1)] For a trust to be a skip person all persons holding "interests" must be skip persons, or if no one holds an "interest" in the trust, only skip persons may hold an interest in the trust in the future. [IRC § 2613(a)(2)]

Therefore, figuring out who (in the case of an individual) or what (in the case of a trust) is a skip person is crucial for determining if a "generation-skipping" transfer exists. To establish who is a skip person (or, conversely, a "non-skip person") one must establish the identity of the "transferor" of the property [IRC § 2652(a)]. For transfers in trust, one must determine who has an "interest in property" [IRC § 2652(c)], which requires a finding of a "trust" [IRC § 2652(b)], and the "generational assignment" of individuals [IRC § 2651(a)].

2. Transferor

a) General Rule

The first order of business for any possible generation-skipping transfer is identifying the "transferor." Determining the transferor is important in order to determine generational assignments [IRC § 2651], which are used to determine who is either a skip or non-skip person. [IRC § 2613]

With one exception, a transferor is present any time property is subject to either the estate or gift tax. [IRC § 2652(a)(1)] In the case of the estate tax, the transferor is the decedent. [IRC § 2652(a)(1)(A)] For property "subject to" the gift tax, the transferor is the donor. [IRC § 2652(a)(1)(B)] It is important to note that an actual transfer under local law does not need to be present; the definition treats a transfer as being made for all property in which an individual is deemed the transferor because the property was either included in their gross estate or they were treated as having transferred property by gift. The exception to the general rule is for the reverse QTIP election, covered *infra* at III. B. 2. c). [IRC § 2652(a)(3)]

Example (1):   T transfers $100,000 to GC, his grandchild. The transfer is subject to the gift tax under IRC § 2501(a). Since the transfer is subject to the gift tax and T is the donor, T will be treated as the transferor of the property for Chapter 13. [IRC § 2652(a)(1)(B); Reg. § 26.2652–1(a)(5)(ex. 1)]

Example (2):   T transfers property to an irrevocable trust, with income to TS, T's spouse, and remainder to GC, T's grandchild. T elects to treat the property as qualified terminable interest property ("QTIP") under IRC § 2523(f), but does not make the reverse QTIP election under IRC § 2652(a)(3). When TS dies, the trust corpus is included in TS's gross estate under IRC § 2044. Since the trust corpus is subject to the estate tax, and TS is the decedent, TS is treated as the new transferor of the property for Chapter 13. It does not matter that TS never made an actual transfer of the property. [IRC § 2652(a)(1)(A); Reg. § 26.2652–1(a)(5)(ex. 3)]

Example (3):   T transfers property to an irrevocable trust that pays the income to C, T's child. T also gives C a testamentary general power of appointment over the trust corpus, but if C does not transfer the property by will, the property passes by default to GC. Since the transferred property is subject to the gift tax on transfer, T is the initial "transferor" for Chapter 13. [IRC § 2652(a)(1)(B)] However, if C dies in possession of the general power of appointment, regardless of whether it is exercised, the trust corpus is included in C's gross estate. [IRC § 2041(a)(2)] Since the trust corpus is subject to the estate tax, and C is the decedent, C is treated as the new transferor of the property for Chapter 13 purposes. It does not matter that C never made an actual transfer of the property. [IRC § 2652(a)(1)(A)]

Example (4):   Same facts as Example (3), except that the T gives C a testamentary non-general power of appointment over the property. Now the trust corpus is not included in C's gross estate at death, and T continues as the transferor of the trust corpus.

The property needs only to be "subject to" the estate or gift taxation, not create an actual tax liability. Exemptions, exclusions, deductions and credits are not taken into account to determine if a transfer is "subject to" the other transfer taxes. [Reg. § 26.2652–1(a)(2)]

Example (1): T makes a $20,000 taxable gift to GC, T's grandchild. Assume that until this transfer T has not used any of T's unified credit, and T therefore does not owe any gift tax. [IRC § 2505(a)] Even though the gift incurs no gift tax liability, it is still treated as a transfer of property by gift and "subject to" the gift tax. Therefore, under Chapter 13 T is the transferor of $20,000 to GC. [Reg. § 26.2652–1(a)(2)]

Example (2): T pays GC's college tuition of $20,000 and makes the payment directly to GC's college. Because the payment was made for tuition directly to an educational organization, it is not treated as a "transfer of property by gift." [IRC § 2503(e)(1)] Since the payment is not a "transfer of property by gift" it is not "subject to" the gift tax [IRC § 2501(a)(1)] and T is not treated as a "transferor" of the $20,000 under Chapter 13. [IRC § 2652(a)(1)]

Example (3): T places property into a revocable trust for the benefit of GC. Since the trust is revocable, T has not given up dominion and control over the property, and the transfer is not "subject to" the gift tax at the time of transfer. [Reg. § 25.2511–2(b)] Because the transfer is not "subject to" the gift tax, T is not a "transferor" of the property under the GST tax.

b) Treatment of Split Gifts Under IRC § 2513 [IRC § 2652(a)(2)]

To determine the amount of property transferred by gift, spouses may elect to treat any transfers of property made during the year as made one-half by each spouse. [IRC § 2513(a)(1)] As discussed in more detail in the gift tax section of this outline, the gift splitting provision allows for the utilization of each spouse's annual exclusion, unified credit, and lower tax brackets. [*See supra* II. C. 4.; IRC §§ 2001(c), 2502(a), 2503(b), 2505(a)]

When a married couple elects to treat a transfer of property as a split gift, they can also treat it as a split gift for the purposes of Chapter 13. [IRC § 2652(a)(2), Reg. § 26.2652–1(a)(4)] This allows for the utilization of the GST exemption [discussed *infra* III. D. 2. b) (2) (a)] of both spouses, even though one spouse transfers the property.

> *Example:* T transfers $100,000 to GC, T's grandchild. The transfer is subject to the gift tax under IRC § 2501(a). T's spouse, TS, consents to treat the gift as split between the two of them. [IRC § 2513(a)(1)] For Chapter 13 both T and TS are treated as the "transferor" of $50,000 each to GC. [IRC § 2652(a)(1)(B), (a)(2); Reg. § 26.2652–1(a)(5)(ex. 2)]

c) Reverse QTIP Election [IRC § 2652(a)(3)]

Under the general definition, the "transferor" for purposes of the GST tax is the decedent or donor when the property is subject to the estate or gift tax. The exception to this general rule is the **reverse QTIP election**. [IRC § 2652(a)(3)]

In brief, to receive an estate tax or gift tax marital deduction for terminable interest property, a decedent or donor spouse may elect to treat the property as "qualified terminable interest property" ("QTIP"). [IRC §§ 2056(b)(7), 2523(f)(1)] However, the "cost" of making the election is deferred taxation of the property, either by inclusion of the trust corpus into the receiving spouse's gross estate [IRC § 2044(a)] or treatment as a transfer by gift of the remainder interest if the donee spouse makes an inter vivos transfer of any portion of the qualifying income interest [IRC § 2519(a)]. Without any exception to the general rule, there would always be a new transferor created for any qualified terminable interest property since the property is later "subject to" either the estate or gift tax. This would result in the loss of any GST exemption amount granted to the trust by the transferring spouse. [*See infra* the discussion of the GST exemption, III. D. 2. b) (2) (a); IRC § 2631(a)]

The election under IRC § 2652(a)(3) solves this dilemma by treating the property for purposes of Chapter 13 "as if the election to be treated as qualified terminable interest property had not been made." [IRC § 2652(a)(3)(flush)] This way the transferor of the trust does not change even though it is later subject to either the estate or gift tax. [Reg. § 26.2652–1(a)(3)]

The election may be made on a trust-by-trust basis, but all the qualified terminable interest property in any given trust is subject to the election.

[IRC § 2652(a)(3)(flush); Reg. § 26.2652–2(a)] The election may be made by the estate of the deceased spouse (in the case of the estate tax marital deduction) or by the donor spouse (in the case of the gift tax marital deduction) and is made at the same time and on the same return as the election to treat the trust as qualified terminable interest property. [IRC § 2652(a)(3)(flush); Reg. § 26.2652–2(b)] Once the election is made it is irrevocable. [Reg. § 26.2652–2(a)]

Example: T transfers property to an irrevocable trust that pays income to TS, T's spouse, at least annually for TS's life. Upon TS's death, the remainder passes to GC, T's grandchild. T elects to treat the property as qualified terminable interest property under IRC § 2523(f) and makes a reverse QTIP election under IRC § 2652(a)(3). When TS dies, the trust corpus is included in TS's gross estate under IRC § 2044. Without the reverse QTIP election, TS would be treated as the new "transferor" of the property for Chapter 13, since the trust is subject to the estate tax and TS is the decedent. However, because T made the reverse QTIP election, T will continue to be the Chapter 13 transferor. [Reg. § 26.2652–1(a)(5)(ex. 6)] On TS's death, a taxable termination generation-skipping transfer will be made from T to GC. [Reg. § 26.2652–2(d)(ex. 1)]

3. "Interest"

a) General Rule

For a generation-skipping transfer to be either a direct skip or a taxable termination, someone must have an "interest" in the property transferred. [IRC § 2612(a)(1)(A), (c)(1)] If property is transferred directly to an individual there is no need of statutory help since the individual receiving the property clearly has an interest therein. However, statutory assistance is required to establish an "interest in property" for transfers made to a trust. [IRC § 2652(c)(1)] Moreover, if an interest in property is properly disclaimed under IRC § 2518 it is treated as if the interest never existed. [IRC § 2654(c); Reg. § 26.2612–1(e)(3)]

There are three different types of Chapter 13 interests in property held in trust. The first type includes individuals, trusts, corporations, and the like, who have a present right to receive income or corpus from the trust. [IRC § 2652(c)(1)(A)] The second includes those individuals or entities other than charities, which are permissible current recipients of the trust's income or corpus. [IRC § 2652(c)(1)(B)] The third type includes charities treated as having an interest in trust even though they do not have any present right to trust income, so long as the trust is either a charitable remainder annuity trust (CRAT), charitable remainder unitrust (CRUT) or pooled income fund. [IRC § 2652(c)(1)(C)]

If trust income can be used to satisfy an individual's support obligations, then that individual is treated as having a Chapter 13 interest in the trust. However, if the trust income may only be distributed for an individual's support at the discretion of an independent trustee, the individual does not have a Chapter 13 interest in the trust because of the uncertainty as to whether a distribution will be made. [Reg. § 26.2612–1(e)(2)(i)]

Example (1):   T creates two irrevocable trusts. In the first trust, T gives GC, T's grandchild, an income interest for life. In the second trust, T gives GC a general power of appointment over the corpus of the trust. Because GC has "a right (other than a future right) to receive income or corpus from the trust," GC has an interest in property in both trusts. [IRC § 2652(c)(1)(A)] If GC's power in the second trust was a non-general power of appointment, GC would not have a Chapter 13 interest in property since GC would have no right to the income from that trust.

Example (2):   T creates an irrevocable trust, naming P the trustee. The trust grants P the power to give C, T's child, any portion of the income from the trust during C's life. After C dies, the corpus of the trust goes to GC. For purposes of Chapter 13, C has an interest in the property of the trust since C is a "permissible current recipient of income" from the trust. [IRC § 2652(c)(1)(B)] The trustee, P, does not have a Chapter 13 interest since P does not have any right to income from the trust. GC has no Chapter 13 interest since GC only possesses a future right to the corpus of the trust. [IRC § 2652(c)(1)(A)(parenthetical); Reg. § 26.2612–1(e)(1)(i)]

Example (3):   T creates an irrevocable trust in which a fixed amount will be paid to GC for life, with the remainder interest pledged to a charity. GC enjoys an interest because of

GC's present right to receive trust income. [IRC § 2652(c)(1)(A)] Even though the charity does not receive any income from the trust, it is deemed to have a Chapter 13 interest in property. [IRC § 2652(c)(1)(C)] As will be discussed in a later section, the trust is not a skip person since the charity is considered to be at the same generational level as T. [IRC §§ 2613(b), 2651(f)(3)]

Example (4): T creates an irrevocable trust, with the income used to support GC, a minor, until GC reaches age 18. C, GC's parent, will receive the remainder when GC reaches age 18. Since the income of the trust will be used to satisfy C's parental support obligations, C is treated as having a Chapter 13 interest in the trust. [Reg. § 26.2612–1(e)(2)(i)]

b) Disregarded Interests [IRC § 2652(c)(2), (3)]

Interests, in two situations, may be disregarded in determining the presence of a generation-skipping transfer. First, an interest is disregarded if it is created primarily to postpone or avoid the generation-skipping tax. [IRC § 2652(c)(2)] Second, disbursements of trust assets used to satisfy support obligations in a discretionary manner, or pursuant to laws equivalent to the Uniform Gifts to Minors Act, are not treated as giving the individuals whose support obligations are satisfied a Chapter 13 interest in property held in trust. [IRC § 2652(c)(3)]

Example (1): T creates an irrevocable trust where the income is divided between GC, T's grandchild, and a charity. The trust terminates upon the death of GC, with the remainder payable to GGC, T's great-grandchild. The charity receives a de minimis amount of income, while GC accepts the balance. Unless the charity's income interest is disregarded, the trust will not be treated as skip person since the charity is treated at the same generational level as T. [IRC § 2651(f)(3)] However, the charity's interest must be disregarded if the interest was only created to avoid the generation-skipping tax due on the creation of the trust. [IRC § 2652(c)(2)]

Example (2): T creates an irrevocable trust where the income is to be used to satisfy C's (T's child) state law support obligation of GC, T's grandchild, for so long as GC is a minor.

C is treated as having an interest in the trust since the income is used to fulfill C's support obligation. [IRC § 2652(c)(1)(B); Reg. § 26.2612–1(e)(2)(i)] If the trustee possessed sole discretion over distribution of the funds for GC's support C would not have an interest in the trust. [IRC § 2652(c)(3)(A); Reg. § 26.2612–1(f)(ex. 13)]

c) Disclaimed Interests [IRC § 2654(c)]

Chapter 13 incorporates the gift tax rules for disclaimers. [IRC § 2654(c)] Therefore, if a qualified disclaimer is made pursuant to IRC § 2518, the interest is treated as if it never existed. [Reg. § 26.2612–1(e)(3)] Any additional analysis must consider the recipient of the interests after the disclaimer is made.

4. Generational Assignments [IRC § 2651]

In most cases, a generation-skipping transfer occurs after a transfer of property to a "skip person." [IRC § 2612] The classification of an individual or trust as a skip person or a non-skip person depends on their generational assignment. [IRC § 2613] Generational assignments are determined by comparing the individual receiving the interest with the Chapter 13 "transferor" (defined *supra* III. B. 2.). [IRC § 2652(a)] Generational assignments are provided in IRC § 2651. This section provides rules establishing generational assignments for lineal descendants of the transferor's grandparent [IRC § 2651(b)] and those who are not lineal descendants of the transferor's grandparent [IRC § 2651(d)], as well as special rules for determining generational assignments of lineal descendants with deceased parents, individuals with more than one generational assignment, and entities. [IRC § 2651(e), (f)]

a) Lineal Descendants of the Transferor's Grandparent [IRC § 2651(b)]

(1) General Rule

If an individual is a lineal descendant of the transferor's grandparent, his or her generational assignment is calculated by comparing the number of generations between the grandparent and such individual to the number one (the generations between the transferor's grandparent and the transferor). Two aspects of this rule should be highlighted. First, only those individuals in generations below the transferor receive generational assignments. Therefore, the generation-skipping tax only applies to transfers to younger generations.

Second, including the descendants of the transferor's grandparent instead of just the transferor casts a very wide net that includes many remote relatives (i.e., third and fourth cousins), the likely beneficiaries of the transferor.

Example: T gifts property to GC, T's grandchild. Since T's transfer is subject to the gift tax and T is the donor, T is the transferor for Chapter 13. [IRC § 2652(a)(1)(B)] T's generational assignment is "1" since there is only one generation between T's grandparent (TGP) and T, namely TP (T's parent) [TGP→TP→T]. GC has a generational assignment of "3" since there are three generations between GP and GC: TP, T, and C (T's child) [TGP→TP→T→C→GC]. [IRC § 2651(b)(1)]

(2) Spouses

The transferor's spouse is assigned to the same generation as the transferor. [IRC § 2651(c)(1)] This rule applies to an individual married "at any time" to the transferor, so death and divorce do not alter the generational assignment. The spouses and former spouses of descendants of the transferor's grandparent are also assigned to the same generational level as their spouse or former spouse. [IRC § 2651(c)(2)]

Example (1): T gifts property to SGC, the ex-spouse of T's grandchild, GC. Since SGC and GC were married at one time, SGC receives the same generational assignment ("3") as GC. [IRC § 2651(c)(2)]

Example (2): T gifts property to SOGC, the "significant other" of T's grandchild, GC. Since SOGC and GC are not married, the rules of IRC § 2651(d) (discussed *infra* at III. B. 4. b) covering non-lineal descendants) must be used, unless SOGC is a descendent of T's grandparents.

The same rules applicable to the transferor apply to determine the generational assignment of the lineal descendents of the transferor's spouse. [IRC § 2651(b)(2)] A comparison of the number of generations between the grandparent of the transferor's spouse and the lineal descendant of the transferor's spouse to the number "1" (the number of generations between the spouse and the spouse's grandparent) determines the individual's generational assignment.

(3) Adoption and Step–Children

Lineal descendants related by adoption or with only one parent in common ("half-blood") are treated as whole-blood descendants. [IRC § 2651(b)(3)]

Example (1): T has three brothers, Alfred, Bob, and Charlie. Alfred is the child of T's mother and father. T's parents adopted Bob. Charlie is the child of T's father and T's father's second wife. Even though Bob is adopted and Charlie is a half-blood relation of T, both are treated as whole-blood relatives. [IRC § 2651(b)(3)]

Example (2): T's child, C, adopted GC from Russia. GC will have the same generational assignment as if born to C.

b) Non–Lineal Descendants of the Transferor's Grandparent [IRC § 2651(d)]

Individuals who are not lineal descendants of the transferor's grandparent are given generational assignments based on set age ranges. Individuals older than the transferor or not more than 12.5 years younger are deemed to be in the same generational level as the transferor. [IRC § 2651(d)(1)] Individuals more than 12.5 years younger, but not more than 37.5 years younger than the transferor, are assigned one generational level below the transferor. This equals the same generational level as the transferor's child. [IRC § 2651(d)(2)] Individuals more than 37.5 years younger, but not more than 62.5 years younger than the transferor, are classified two generational levels below the transferor. This is the same generational level as the transferor's grandchild. The generational assignments increase every 25 years thereafter. [IRC § 2651(d)(3)]

Example: Paul and Anna are both unrelated to T. Paul was born 50 years after T, and Anna was born 63 years after T. Paul is deemed to be two generations below T, while Anna's assignment is three generations below T. [IRC § 2651(d)(3)]

c) Special Rules

(1) Predeceased Parent Rule [IRC § 2651(e)]

The **predeceased parent rule** is easier to understand after considering the rationale behind the rule. As an example, assume T's only heir is GC, T's grandchild, due to the fact that C, T's child and GC's parent, died before T distributes any of T's wealth. Without the predeceased parent rule, GC's generational assignment would be determined by comparing GC with T's grandparent (TGP→TP→ T→C→GC). Therefore, there would be three generations between TGP and GC, providing GC with a generational assignment of "3." Consequently, any direct transfer to GC would be a generation-skipping transfer. Applying Chapter 13 to this transfer does not fit with its rationale, since the estate or gift tax did not skip a generation because C is deceased.

Under the predeceased parent rule of IRC § 2651(e), an individual is moved up to the generational level of his or her predeceased parent (or higher if the individual's grandparents are also deceased) if (1) the individual is the descendant of the transferor's parent, (2) the parent died before the transfer was subject to the estate or gift tax, and (3) the individual is a lineal descendant of the transferor (i.e., child, grandchild, etc.), unless the transferor has no living descendants. [IRC § 2651(e)(1)] The rule also applies to the descendants of T's spouse or former spouse. If the transferor has no living lineal descendants at the time of transfer, the predeceased parent rule may apply to all lineal descendants of T's parent. [IRC § 2651(e)(2); Reg. § 26.2651–1(b)]

This rule does not apply to all who would have their generational assignments completed under the lineal descendant rule of IRC § 2651(b), since, unless the transferor has no living descendents, the predeceased parent rule only applies to descendants of the transferor's parents, and not descendants of the transferor's grandparents. The general rule of IRC § 2651(b) includes all the descendants of the transferor's grandparents. Therefore, the descendants of the transferor's aunts and uncles do not qualify for the predeceased parent rule.

The regulations provide an exception to the strict survivorship requirement. In determining if a transferee's parents died before a covered transfer, individuals who die within 90 days of a transfer subject to the estate or gift tax are treated as if they predeceased the transferor. [Reg. § 26.2651–1(a)(2)(iii)] This determination is not dependant on local survivorship law.

Transfers made to trusts created before the predeceased parent rule changed the generational assignment of any individual are bifurcated and treated as a transfer to two separate trusts. One created before, and the other after, the application of the predeceased parent rule. [*See* Reg. § 26.2651–1(a)(4)]

Once an individual generational assignment is changed under IRC § 2651(e), a corresponding adjustment is also made to the generational assignment of the individual's spouse (or former spouse), descendants, and their spouses (or former spouses). [Reg. § 26.2651–1(a)(2)(i)] In other words, the changes are made to everyone related to the effected individual.

Example (1): T transfers property to GC, T's grandchild. C, GC's parent and T's child, is dead at the time the transfer is made. In order to determine GC's generational assignment, GC moves up to C's generational level. [IRC § 2651(e)(1); Reg. § 26.2651–1(c)(ex. 1)] Because of GC being moved up one level, GC does not qualify as a skip person and any transfer from T to GC will not be a generation-skipping transfer.

Example (2): T transfers property to GC, T's grandchild. C, T's child, is living, but GC's other parent, CS (T's daughter-in-law), is dead at the time of transfer. Since CS is not a lineal descendant of T's parent (or T's spouse or former spouse), the predeceased parent rule does not apply and GC's generational level does not change. [IRC § 2651(e)(1)]

Example (3): T transfers property to his sister's grandchild (S's GC) after his sister's child is dead. T has a living lineal descendant at the time the transfer is made. Even though S's GC is a lineal descendant of T's parent, and his sister's child is dead at the time of transfer, the predeceased parent rule does not apply because S's GC is not a lineal descendant of T at a time when T has a living lineal descendant. [IRC § 2651(e)(2)]

Example (4): Same facts as Example (3), except that T has no lineal descendants. Now the deceased parent rule applies and S's GC moves up one generational level. [*Cf.* IRC § 2651(e)(2); Reg. § 26.2651–1(c)(ex. 5)]

Example (5):   T dies survived by T's spouse (TS), T's child (C) and T's grandchild (GC). T's will creates a trust with a life estate to TS, remainder to C. The trust qualifies as a QTIP trust. T's will provides that if C dies before TS, GC receives the remainder interest. T's executor makes the reverse-QTIP election under IRC § 2652(a)(3). [*See supra* III. B. 2. c) for the effect of a reverse-QTIP election.] Even if C dies before TS, the predeceased parent rule will not apply since at the time the property was first subject to the estate tax (T's death), C was not dead. [Reg. § 26.2651–1(a)(3), (c)(ex. 4)]

Example (6):   Same facts as Example (5) except that T's executor fails to make the reverse-QTIP election under IRC § 2652(a)(3). C dies before TS. When TS dies the predeceased parent rule will apply since TS is the "transferor" of the trust corpus for Chapter 13 purposes. [IRC § 2652(a)(1)(A)] Since GC's interest is established at TS's death, and C is dead at that time, the predeceased parent rule applies and GC is one generational level below TS. [Reg. § 26.2651–1(c)(ex. 3)]

(2)   Individuals Assigned to More than One Generation [IRC § 2651(f)(1)]

Unless provided otherwise in the regulations, any individual assigned to more than one generation after applying the rules is assigned to the youngest possible generation level. [IRC § 2651(f)(1); Reg. § 26.2651–2(a)] This rule avoids a generational assignment by marriage or adoption as a method to avoid the GST tax.

After July 18, 2005, an exception for "adopted individuals" exists in the regulations to the ordering rule of IRC § 2651(f)(1). [Reg. § 26.2651–2(b)] An "adopted individual" is one who is: 1) legally adopted, 2) a descendant of the adoptive parent's parent or their spouse or former spouse (e.g., grandchild, niece, nephew), 3) under 18 at the time of adoption, and 4) not adopted for the primary purpose of avoiding the GST tax. [*Id.*] In looking at the reason for the adoption, all facts and circumstances are considered. The primary consideration is if a "bona fide parent/child relationship" exists between the adoptive parent and child. This is present if the adoptive parents assume "significant" responsibilities for raising the adoptive child. Other facts considered include the age of the adopted individual (the younger the child the less likely the adoption is for avoidance purposes), and the relationship between the adopted individual and his or her parents (for example, the parents' absence or incapacity). [Reg. § 26.2651–2(b)(4)(i, ii)]

Example (1):   T adopts the grandchild of T's significant other (SOGC) at a time when all of T's lineal descendants are living. Under the adoption rule, SOGC is treated as T's child. [IRC § 2651(b)(3)(A)] The special rule of IRC § 2651(f)(1) does not apply because there is only one generational level assigned to SOGC. The rules for non-lineal descendants under IRC § 2651(d) only apply if the rules for lineal descendants do not apply, but they do apply after T makes the adoption. [IRC § 2651(d) ("an individual who is not assigned to a generation by reason of the foregoing provisions . . . ")]

Example (2):   T adopts T's 20-year-old great-great-great-grandchild (GGGGC) when all of T's lineal descendants are living. Under the rules for generational assignments, GGGGC is assigned to two generational levels: a generational level of six under IRC § 2651(b)(1), and a generational level of two after applying the adoption rule treating GGGGC as T's child. [IRC § 2651(b)(3)(A)] Since the younger of the two assignments is six, GGGGC's generational level is six. [IRC § 2651(f)(1); Reg. § 26.2651–2(d)(example)]

Example (3):   Same facts as Example (2) except that GGGGC is not 18 years old when adopted and the adoption did not have as its primary purpose the avoidance of the GST tax. Since GGGGC is an "adopted individual," the general rule under IRC § 2651(f)(1) is disregarded and GGGGC is one generational level below T. [Reg. § 26.2651–2(b)]

(3) Generational Assignments of Entities

Except for transfers to charitable or governmental entities, transfers to entities are treated as transfers to the individuals holding the entities' beneficial interests and the above rules are then applied to find each individual's generational assignment. [IRC § 2651(f)(2)] If the entity is a charitable organization, charitable trust, or governmental entity, however, the entity is not pierced and is assigned the same generational level as the transferor. [IRC § 2651(f)(3); *see also infra* at III. B. 6. c) (expanding on this topic)]

d) Multiple Skips [IRC § 2653(a)]

The generational assignment of the transferor changes if there is (1) a generation-skipping transfer of property, and (2) immediately after such transfer the property is held in trust. [IRC § 2653(a)] If both conditions are met, the transferor is deemed to be only one generational level above the person with the highest generational level possessing a Chapter 13 interest in the trust immediately after transfer. This rule prevents the GST tax from being applied twice to any given transfer of property.

Example: T creates an irrevocable trust that pays income to GC, T's grandchild, for GC's life, followed by the remainder to GGC, T's great-grandchild. Assume GC's parents are alive so the predeceased parent rule does not apply. Both GC and GGC are skip persons since each are two or more generational assignments below T. Upon creation, the transfer is a generation-skipping transfer (direct skip). Without any special rules, any distributions of income would again be subject to the GST tax as generation-skipping transfers (taxable distributions). This result is avoided since T's generational assignment is moved to one higher than GC, the holder of the Chapter 13 interest in trust. This shift occurs immediately after the direct skip upon formation of the trust. Therefore, when the property is distributed from the trust, GC is no longer a skip person, being only one generation removed from the "new" transferor. [IRC § 2653(a); Reg. § 26.2653–1(b)(ex. 1)]

If a trust described by IRC § 2653(a) makes a distribution to another trust (called a "pour-over trust"), the inclusion ratio in the receiving must be recomputed in a special manner. [IRC § 2653(b)(2)] This is covered *infra* at III. D. 2. b) (3) (e) discussing IRC § 2653(b)(2).

5. "Trust" and "Trustee"

a) "Trust" [IRC § 2652(b)(1), (3)]

(1) General Rule

In order for a generation-skipping transfer to be either a taxable termination or taxable distribution (two of the three types of generation-skipping transfers) the property must be held in trust. "Trust" is not specifically defined in the Code, even though the finding of a trust is critical for certain generation-skipping transfers. The Regulations define a trust as "an arrangement created either by a will or by an inter vivos declaration whereby trustees take title to property for the purpose of protecting or conserving it for the beneficiaries." [Reg. § 301.7701–4(a)]

The term "trust" also includes arrangements, while not formally trusts, which have the same effect and are treated as trusts for Chapter 13. [IRC § 2652(b)(1)] These include property interests with life estates and remainders, insurance and annuity contracts, and arrangements where a contingency controls the determination of the transferee, unless the contingency will be satisfied within six months. [IRC § 2652(b)(3); Reg. § 26.2652–1(b)(1)] However, the Code expressly excludes estates from treatment as nonexplicit trusts. [IRC § 2652(b)(1)(parenthetical)]

Example: T makes a bequest of property in his will to C, T's child, which is contingent upon C surviving T by seven months. If C dies within that period, the property passes to GC, T's grandchild. Since the contingency cannot be satisfied within six months of the transfer, the bequest is treated as a transfer in trust. [Reg. § 26.2652–1(b)(2)(ex. 3)] If GC takes property from the bequest (the trust equivalent), it will be treated as a generation-skipping transfer (a "taxable distribution").

(2) Multiple Trusts [IRC § 2654(b)]

In three instances a single trust can be treated as separate trusts for the purposes of Chapter 13, although actual severance does not occur. The first is where there is more than one transferor. Each transferor is treated as having a separate trust for Chapter 13 purposes, but only one return is filed and the trust is not treated as separate for purposes of any other chapter of the Code. [IRC § 2654(b)(1); Reg. § 26.2654–1(a)(2)(i)] The second instance is where beneficiaries have separate and independent portions for the entire term of the trust. Again, the trust is separated for Chapter 13 purposes only, and only one return is filed for the trust. [IRC § 2654(b)(2); Reg. § 26.2654–1(a)(1)(i)]. The regulations provide for a third instance outside the scope of this general outline. [Reg. § 26.2654–1(a)(2)(ii)]

> *Example (1):*   T transfers property in trust, with the income split equally for twenty years between C, T's child, and GC, T's grandchild. After twenty years the corpus of the trust will be divided equally between the two, or their estates if one or the other is not living at the time the corpus is distributed. Since the portions are separate and independent at all times, each is treated as a separate trust for Chapter 13. [IRC § 2654(b)(2); Reg. § 26.2654–1(a)(5)(ex. 1)]

> *Example (2):*   Same facts as Example (1), except that in the last year of the twenty year term the trustee may allocate the income in any manner. Since the shares are not separate and independent for the trust's entirety, the trust is treated as a single trust from its conception. [Reg. § 26.2654–1(a)(5)(ex. 2)]

> *Example (3):*   T and T's brother, BT, simultaneously transfer $1 million each to an irrevocable trust. For purposes of Chapter 13, both T and BT are treated as transferors of one-half of the trust. They may allocate their GST exemptions to their shares of the trust. [IRC § 2654(b)(1); Reg. § 26.2654–1(a)(5)(ex. 5)]

b)   "Trustee" [IRC § 2652(b)(2)]

The trustee of a true trust is the person so designated by local law. [Reg. § 26.2652–1(c)] In a nonexplicit trust, the trustee of the trust is the person in "actual or constructive possession" of the property held in the deemed trust. [IRC § 2652(b)(2); Reg. § 26.2652–1(c)] The determination of the trustee is important since certain types of generation-skipping transfers require the trustee to file the return and the trustee is liable for payment of any GST tax due. [IRC §§ 2603(a), 2662(a)]

6. **Skip Person and Non–Skip Person [IRC § 2613]**

    All generation-skipping transfers require a transfer or distribution, either directly or indirectly, to a "skip person." [IRC § 2612(a)–(c)] A **skip person** is a Chapter 13 term used to designate when a generation is skipped. There are two different definitions of a skip person. Skip persons can either be "natural persons" (individuals), or trusts. [IRC § 2613(a)(1)–(2)] Any individual or trust that is not a skip person is classified as a "non-skip person." [IRC § 2613(b)]

    a) **Individuals (a.k.a. "Natural Persons") [IRC § 2613(a)(1)]**

        In order to determine whether an individual is a skip person, there must be a comparison of the generational assignment of the transferor with the individual in question. Skip persons have a generational assignment (*see supra* III. B. 4.) two or more generations below that of the transferor. Therefore, a skip person is an individual with a generational assignment of three or more since the transferor's generational assignment is always "1." [IRC § 2613(a)(1); Reg. § 26.2612–1(d)(1)]

        Example: T gifts $20,000 to GC, T's grandchild, at a time when GC's parents are living. Because T is the donor in a transfer subject to the gift tax, T is the transferor. [IRC § 2652(a)(1)(B)] As the transferor, T has a generational assignment of "1" (TGP→TP→T). GC has a generational assignment of "3" since the generations between T's grandparent and GC are T's parent, T and T's child (TGP→TP→T→C→GC). [IRC § 2651(b)(1)] Since GC has a generational assignment two below T, GC is a "skip person." [IRC § 2613(a)(1)] This transfer is a generation-skipping transfer (a "direct skip"). [IRC § 2612(c)]

    b) **Trusts [IRC § 2613(a)(2)]**

        A trust can be a skip person in two ways. First, a trust is a skip person when all of the current Chapter 13 interests in the trust are held by skip persons. [IRC § 2613(a)(2)(A)] Second, if no one has a current Chapter 13 interest in the trust, a trust is deemed a skip person if no distributions, including upon termination of the trust, can ever be made to a non-skip person. [IRC § 2613(a)(2)(B)]

        (1) **All Chapter 13 Interests in Trust Held by Skip Persons [IRC § 2613(a)(2)(A)]**

            If all the Chapter 13 interests in a trust are held by skip persons, the trust itself is classified as a skip person. As discussed in more depth *supra* at III. B. 3., an "interest" for Chapter 13 purposes does not include all beneficial interests in trusts. Only a present or permissible right to the income of the trust, or certain charitable interests, are treated as "interests" for purposes of Chapter 13 and defining who is, and who is not, a skip person. [IRC § 2652(c)]

If a corporation, partnership, estate, or other entity possesses a Chapter 13 interest in the trust, the entity is pierced to determine if a skip person owns the interest. [IRC § 2651(f)(2)] These rules are covered *infra* in III. B. 6. c).

Example (1):   T transfers property to an irrevocable trust that pays income to C, T's child, for life, with the remainder to GC, T's grandchild. Because T is the donor in a transfer subject to the gift tax, T is the transferor. [IRC § 2652(a)(1)(B)] Since C has the sole right to income, C possesses the only Chapter 13 interest in the trust [IRC § 2652(c)(1)(A)]. C is only one generational level below T, so C is not a skip person. [IRC § 2613(a)] Therefore, the trust is not a skip person under IRC § 2613(a)(2)(A) because all interests in the trust are not held by skip persons. [IRC § 2613(b)] *Caveat:* While no generation-skipping transfer exists on the formation of the trust, a generation-skipping transfer will exist when C dies (a taxable termination). [Reg. § 26.2612–1(f)(ex. 4)]

Example (2):   T creates another irrevocable trust, this time giving GC the right to income for life, followed by distribution of the remainder to C. Since GC has the sole right to income, GC possesses the sole Chapter 13 interest in trust. [IRC § 2652(c)(1)(A)] GC has a generational assignment of "3" and is a skip person. [IRC §§ 2651(b)(1); 2613(a)(1)] Since GC possesses the only Chapter 13 interest in the trust, and GC is a skip person, the trust is treated as a skip person. [IRC § 2613(a)(2)(A)] C's classification as a non-skip person is irrelevant, because C does not have a Chapter 13 interest in the trust.

Example (3):   T creates a third irrevocable trust that pays income to GC for life and gives GGC (T's great-grandchild) the remainder. Additionally, the trustee has the power to give a portion of the income to C. Since both C and GC have a right to income from the trust, both have Chapter 13 interests. [IRC § 2652(c)(1)(A)–(B)] C, however, is not a skip person, therefore the trust is designated as a non-skip person (not all Chapter 13 interests in the trust are held by skip persons). [IRC § 2613(a)(2)(A), (b)] *Caveat:* while there is no generation-skipping transfer on the formation of the trust, there will be a generation-skipping transfer on the distribution of income to GC (a taxable distribution). [Reg. § 26.2612–1(f)(ex. 11)]

Example (4):   After living a good, long life, T dies, survived by C (GC's parent). T held an insurance policy, which provides that the proceeds are to be held by the insurer and GC is to receive monthly payments of $750 for life. At GC's death, any remaining death benefit is to be paid to GGC or GGC's estate. While not a formal trust, this arrangement will be treated as a trust equivalent, with the insurance company as trustee. [IRC § 2652(b)] Since GC holds the only Chapter 13 interest and GC is a skip person, the "trust" is deemed a skip person. [Reg. § 26.2662–1(c)(2)(vi)(ex. 3)]

(2)   No Chapter 13 Interests in Trust [IRC § 2613(a)(2)(B)]

If no person holds a Chapter 13 interest in trust (e.g., when all trust income is to be accumulated) the trust may still be a skip person if no future distributions from the trust will be made to non-skip persons. [IRC § 2613(a)(2)(B)] Any distribution that has less than a five percent probability of occurring (determined by applying actuarial standards) is not considered in determining who has a Chapter 13 interest in the trust. [Reg. § 26.2612–1(d)(2)(ii)]

Example: T creates an irrevocable trust with income to be accumulated for twenty years, after which time the current (but not the accumulated) income will be distributed to GC, T's grandchild, for life. At GC's death, the remainder is to be paid to GGC, T's great-grandchild. For the first twenty years when the income is accumulated, no person has a Chapter 13 interest. However, both GC and GGC are classified as skip persons since both have a generational assignment two or more below T. [IRC § 2613(a)(1)] Since the trust cannot make any distributions to a non-skip person, even on termination of the trust, the trust is treated as a skip person. [IRC § 2613(a)(2)(B)]

c) Treatment of Entities

Entities are not themselves treated as skip persons or non-skip persons. [IRC § 2651(f)(2)] When a transfer to an entity is involved, the generational levels of the individual beneficial interest holders control in determining whether the transfer is made to skip persons. However, charitable organizations, charitable trusts, and governmental entities are considered non-skip persons since they have the same generational assignment as the transferor. [IRC § 2651(f)(3)]

Example (1): T gifts property to Corporation X. Corporation X has two equal shareholders, C, T's child, and GC, T's grandchild. As shareholders, C and GC hold the beneficial interest in the corporation. Both C and GC's generational assignments are considered in the determination of whether a generation-skipping transfer has occurred. [IRC § 2651(f)(2)] Since C is only one generational level below T, C is a non-skip person. [IRC § 2613(b)] GC is a skip person since GC is two generational levels below T. [IRC § 2613(a)(1)] Therefore, one-half of T's transfer to X Corporation will be treated as a generation-skipping transfer (a "direct skip"). [IRC § 2612(c)]

Example (2): T dies and provides in his will for his estate to make payments to GC for ten years. Estates cannot be treated as trusts, so the generational assignment of the beneficial interest holder, GC, must be considered to determine whether a transfer to a skip person has been completed. [IRC § 2651(b)(1)] GC is a skip person and the payments to GC will be generation-skipping transfers ("taxable distribution"). [IRC § 2612(b)]

Example (3): T transfers property to an irrevocable trust with the income split between GC and his church (an IRC § 501(c) organization). Neither payment was made primarily to postpone or avoid the GST tax therefore neither is disregarded. [IRC § 2652(c)(2)] Because charities with valid Chapter 13 interests are not pierced, they are treated as non-skip persons. [IRC §§ 2651(f)(3); 2613(b)] The trust is a non-skip person since not all Chapter 13 interests in the trust are held by skip persons. [IRC § 2613(a)(2)(A)]

C. Generation–Skipping Transfers

Once the above terminology is understood and applied to any given transfer, the next step is to determine if the result is a "generation-skipping" transfer. Chapter 13 will not apply if there are no skip persons involved in the transaction. However, if a skip person is involved, one must determine whether a generation-skipping transfer is present, regardless of whether the skip person has a Chapter 13 interest in property.

Unless excluded, a "generation-skipping transfer" includes any "direct skip," "taxable termination," or "taxable distribution." [IRC § 2611(a)] Direct skip, taxable termination, and taxable distribution are all defined terms in the Code and are separately explained below. [IRC § 2612(a)–(c)] Any given transfer or event may meet the basic elements of more than one type of generation-skipping transfer, but ordering rules qualify each transfer so that only one generation-skipping transfer results. In general, direct skips apply over taxable terminations and taxable distributions, taxable terminations apply over taxable distributions, and taxable distributions are present only when no other generation-skipping transfer is present. The determination of the specific type of transfer is important since such things as the taxable base (called the "taxable amount"), liability for payment of the tax, and the person required to file a return varies for each type of generation-skipping transfer. [IRC §§ 2603, 2621–23]

1. Defining Generation–Skipping Transfers

a) Direct Skips

A **direct skip**, as defined in IRC § 2612(c)(1), is a transfer of a Chapter 13 interest to a skip person that is subject to the estate or gift tax. A direct skip covers both transfers of an interest in property directly to a skip person either by will (e.g., "I leave Blackacre to my grandson") or by gift (e.g., T transfers Blackacre to T's granddaughter inter vivos). A direct skip can occur on direct transfers of property (like the two previous examples) or on transfers to irrevocable trusts. However, transfers to trusts are direct skips only if the trust itself is a skip person. [IRC § 2612(c)(2); Reg. § 26.2612–1(a)] Regardless of the number of generations skipped on the transfer only one direct skip results from the transfer. [Reg. § 26.2612–1(a)]

Example (1):   T's will transfers Blackacre to GGGC, T's great-great-grandchild. Blackacre is subject to the estate tax since it is included in T's gross estate under IRC § 2033. GGGC is a skip person, being three generation assignments below T. This transfer is a direct skip since it is a transfer of a Chapter 13 interest in property to a skip person that is subject to the estate tax. [IRC § 2612(c)(1)] Even though the transfer skips three generations, only one direct skip generation-skipping transfer is present. [Reg. § 26.2612–1(f)(ex. 2)]

Example (2):   T creates an irrevocable trust that pays income to GC, T's grandchild, for life. At GC's death, the remainder will be paid to C, T's child and GC's parent. The trust is a skip person since GC is a skip person and possesses the sole Chapter 13 interest in the trust. [IRC §§ 2652(c)(1)(A), 2613(a)(2)(A)] Both the transfer creating the trust and any additional transfers to the trust will be treated as direct skips. [IRC § 2612(c)(1)]

Example (3):   T creates another irrevocable trust where C has the income interest for life and GC possesses the remainder interest. The trust also allows GC and T's three other grandchildren to withdraw up to $10,000 from the trust for 60 days after any transfers to the trust. T makes a transfer of $50,000 to the trust. Since a non-skip person, C, has a Chapter 13 interest in the trust, the trust is not a skip person. Therefore the transfer is not a direct skip. [Reg. §§ 26.2612–1(a), 26.2612–1(f)(ex. 3)] For the Chapter 13 treatment upon C's death, or for any distributions from the trust to the grandchildren, *see infra* the discussion of taxable terminations and taxable distributions at III. C. 1. b) and c).

Example (4):   T creates an irrevocable trust which will accumulate income for ten years. After that time, the current (but not the accumulated) income will be paid to T's grandchildren until the last of them dies, at which point the corpus is to be distributed to T's great-grandchildren then living. The transfer is subject to the gift tax. [IRC § 2501(a)(1)] Upon creation of the trust, no one has a Chapter 13 interest since the income is to be accumulated. [IRC § 2652(c)] However, the trust is still a skip person since there can be no distributions made to a non-skip person. [IRC § 2613(a)(2)(B)] Since T has made a transfer of an interest in property to a skip person subject to the gift tax, it constitutes a direct skip. [IRC § 2612(c)]

(1) Elements of a Direct Skip

(a) Interest Transferred to a Skip Person

i) General Rule

For a direct skip an "interest" must be transferred to a skip person. The interest in direct transfers (e.g., T transfers Blackacre to grandchild) is easy to identify without statutory assistance. However, the identification of a Chapter 13 interest in trust or a trust equivalent requires statutory help (*see supra* III. B. 3.). A Chapter 13 interest in a trust or trust equivalent is not the same as any beneficial interest, and unless a charity is involved, a Chapter 13 interest requires a current or permissible right to income. [IRC § 2652(c)(1)]

Example: T possesses the beneficial right to a remainder interest in a trust created by TP, T's parent. T transfers the remainder interest to GC, T's grandchild. The transfer is subject to the gift tax, but is not a direct skip. Even though the property is transferred to a skip person a Chapter 13 interest was not passed since T did not have a right to income from the trust. [IRC §§ 2652(c)(1), 2612(c)(1)]

ii) Anti–Look–Through Rule for Transfers to Trusts [IRC § 2612(c)(2)]

The general rule for entities is that they are first pierced to determine the generation assignment of those with a beneficial interest in the entity. [IRC § 2651(f)(2)] However, if the transfer is to a trust and subject to the gift or estate tax, the look-through rule does not apply. [IRC § 2612(c)(2)] In order for any transfer to a trust to be a direct skip, the trust itself must be deemed a skip person under IRC § 2613(a)(2). A similar rule also applies to taxable distributions (*see infra* the discussion of taxable distributions, III. C. 1. c)).

Example: T creates an irrevocable trust that may, at the discretion of an independent trustee, pay income. Any such distributed income is to be split between C, T's child, and GC, T's grandchild. Upon the death of C, the trust will terminate and the remainder will be paid to GC. The transfer is subject to the gift tax. [IRC § 2501(a)(1)] Since both C and GC have a permissible right to the trust income, both have a Chapter 13 interest in the trust. [IRC § 2652(c)(1)] C is not a skip person; therefore, the trust is not a skip person. [IRC § 2613(a)(2)] Even though IRC § 2651(f)(2) says to look-through an entity to see who has a Chapter 13 interest, the anti-look-through rule applies and prevents an examination of the trust interests. [IRC § 2612(c)(2)] *Caveat:* Any distributions to GC from the trust will be a generation-skipping transfer (a "taxable distribution") and when C dies another generation-skipping transfer is present (a "taxable termination").

(b) Subject to Estate or Gift Tax

In order to have a direct skip the transfer must be "subject to" either the estate or the gift tax. This does not necessarily mean that a tax liability must be imposed or that any tax becomes due. Technically, it is enough that the transferred property be included in the decedent's gross estate or be treated as a transfer of property by gift.

The "subject to" requirement is one of the primary differences between direct skips and taxable termination generation-skipping transfers (the other difference being that a taxable termination requires a transfer to a trust whereas direct skips do not). A direct skip requires the possible imposition of the gift or estate tax, and such a feat is impossible under the Regulations for a taxable termination. [IRC § 2612(c); Reg. § 26.2612–1(b)(1)(i)] Since the GST tax is a separate tax it will be imposed on top of any estate or gift tax present. [IRC § 2601]

For inter vivos gifts, if the transfer is excluded, or not treated as a "taxable gift," it does not satisfy the direct skip requirement of being "subject to" a gift tax. Therefore, transfers made for tuition or medical care that are not treated as taxable gifts under IRC § 2503(e) are not direct skips.

Gift transfers under the IRC § 2503(b) exclusion dollar amount (in 2011 $13,000) are "subject to" gift taxation since they are still "property transferred by gift" and only excluded from the "total amount of gifts" for the gift tax calculation. However, the Service does not require returns for direct (i.e., not through a trust) gift transfers to any donees that total less than the exclusion amount. [2009 IRS Instructions to Form 709, at 1] Additionally, even if the amounts subject to the IRC § 2503(b) exclusion were treated as taxable gifts, they would receive a tax rate of 0%. [IRC § 2642(c)(1)] This allows grandparents to give gifts to their grandchildren without the result of a direct skip. Payments made to political organizations excluded from the gift tax also are not treated as direct skips. [IRC § 2501(a)(4)]

Example (1): T creates an irrevocable trust, reserving the right to the income for life. At T's death, GC, T's grandchild, will receive the remainder. While the trust is subject to the gift tax upon creation, no generation-skipping transfer is present since GC does not have a Chapter 13 interest in the trust and the trust is not a skip person. [IRC §§ 2652(c); 2613(b)] At T's death, the corpus of the trust is included in T's gross estate under IRC § 2036. Assuming that GC's parent survives T (so the predeceased parent rule does not apply) the trust's termination results in a direct skip. The transfer was subject to the estate tax and GC, a skip person, receives an interest in property. [IRC § 2612(c)(1)] Although the transfer could also qualify as a taxable termination, the Regulations preserve the transfer's status as a direct skip. [Reg. § 26.2612–1(b)(1)(i)]

Example (2): T creates an irrevocable trust where the income, at T's discretion, will be paid either to GC, T's grandchild, or GGC, T's great-grandchild. Upon GC's death, the remainder will be paid to GGC. T also has the power to revoke the trust. Since T has maintained dominion and control over the trust, it is not "subject to" the gift tax and no direct transfer exists on the creation of the trust. [Reg. § 25.2511–2(b)] Therefore, a direct skip is not present. However, any distributions of income will be a generation-skipping transfer (a "taxable distribution"). [IRC § 2612(b)]

(2) Generational Assignment After Direct Skip in Trust [IRC § 2653(a)]
As discussed *supra* at III. B. 4. d), the generational assignments of individuals with a Chapter 13 interest in trust change to one below the transferor if (1) a generation-skipping transfer of property exists, and (2) immediately after such transfer the property is held in trust. [IRC § 2653(a)] This applies to all direct skip transfers in trust in order to modify the generation assignment of the oldest generation of the trust's Chapter 13 interest holders to one below that of the transferor. *Caveat:* Distributions and terminations from the trust may still be generation-skipping transfers depending on who has a Chapter 13 interest in the trust or the remainder interest.

Example: T transfers property to an irrevocable trust for the benefit of T's grandchild, GC, great-grandchild, GGC, and great-great-grandchild GGGC. The trust's income may be distributed among GC, GGC, and GGGC at the trustee's discretion. After GC and GGC die, the property will be distributed to GGGC or GGGC's heirs. Assume T's child, C, is alive (this avoids application of the predeceased parent rule). [IRC § 2651(e)] Based on their right to income, all three of T's descendants have a Chapter 13 interest in the trust. [IRC § 2652(c)(1)(B)] Therefore, the transfer to the trust is a direct skip. [IRC § 2612(c)] After the transfer, the "transferor" for the trust is deemed to be one generational assignment above GC, the person with the highest generational assignment holding a Chapter 13 interest. [IRC § 2653(a)] Therefore, after the transfer, GC is not a skip person, but GGC and GGGC, two or more generational assignments below the deemed transferor, are considered skip persons. [IRC § 2613(a)(1)] On all distributions of property to GGC or GGGC, and upon the termination of the trust, there will be additional generation-skipping transfers present (respectively, a "taxable distribution" and "taxable termination"). [IRC § 2612(a)–(b)] After any taxable distribution the generational assignments will not change because any additional transfers will not be from "such property" distributed to GGC or GGGC. [IRC § 2653(a)(flush); Reg. § 26.2653–1(b)(ex. 1)]

(3) Exceptions and Exclusions

(a) General Exclusions to Generation–Skipping Transfers [IRC § 2611(b)]

There are two general exclusions to all generation-skipping transfers provided in IRC § 2611(b). The exclusions apply to all three types of generation-skipping transfers and are covered *infra* at III. C. 2.

(b) Deceased Parents at Time of Transfer

Before 1998, the predeceased parent rule of IRC § 2651(e) only applied to direct skips. Since 1998 the rule applies to all generation-skipping transfers. *See supra* the complete discussion of the predeceased parent rule at III. B. 4. c) (1).

(c) The "Gallo" Amendment

As an example of special interest legislation, transfers of up to $2 million made before January 1, 1990 to the transferor's grandchildren are not considered direct skips. [Tax Reform Act of 1986, Pub. L. No. 99–514, § 1433(b)(3), 100 Stat. 2085, 2731 (1986)] This was reportedly included in the Code due to the lobbying of winemakers Ernest and Julio Gallo who are reported to have transferred $80 million without the GST tax under this exception.

b) Taxable Terminations [IRC § 2612(a)]

Taxable terminations cover certain trusts that precipitated the Congressional desire to tax generation-skipping transfers. The following example was given at the beginning of the section covering the GST tax: "T, creates a trust with the income to his child, C, for life, then to his grandchild, GC, for life, then to GC's issue per stirpes (the great-grandchildren of T)." [*See supra* III. A.] No estate tax or gift tax would be paid upon the death of the grantor's child or grandchild. Under the GST tax regime, however, such a trust is potentially subject to the GST tax twice (when the child and grandchild die) because upon each death a taxable termination occurs. [IRC § 2612(a)(1)]

A taxable termination is present when there is (1) a termination, (2) of an "interest in property," (3) held in trust, (4) unless, immediately after the termination, a non-skip person has a Chapter 13 interest in the trust or no future distributions (including those on termination of the trust) may be made to a skip person. [IRC § 2612(a)(1)] A fifth element from the Regulations requires that no federal estate or gift tax can exist on the termination of the trust. [Reg. § 26.2612–1(b)(1)(i)] This additional regulatory rule provides that when the statutory elements of both a direct skip and a taxable termination apply, the transfer will be treated as a direct skip rather than a taxable termination.

If a trust's termination simultaneously satisfies the elements of both a taxable termination and taxable distribution (discussed *infra* at III. C. 1. c)), the Code specifically states that a taxable termination takes precedence. [IRC § 2612(b)(parenthetical)]

Example: T creates an irrevocable trust that pays income to C, T's child, for life. After C's death, the corpus is to be distributed to GC, T's grandchild. The creation of the trust, while subject to the gift tax, is not subject to the GST tax. No direct skip generation-skipping transfer occurs since C, a non-skip person, holds the Chapter 13 interest in the trust and the trust is classified as a non-skip person. [IRC § 2612(c)(1)] However, a taxable termination occurs at C's death because C's interest in the trust ends and, immediately after such termination, GC, a skip person, takes the distribution of the corpus. [IRC § 2612(a)(1)] This transfer is not considered a direct skip since no estate tax is present on C's death. [Reg. § 26.2612–1(f)(ex. 4)]

(1) Elements of a Taxable Termination

(a) "Termination"

"Death, lapse of time, release of power, or otherwise" satisfies the termination requirement. [IRC § 2612(a)(1)(intro.)(parenthetical)] Any termination of a Chapter 13 interest in the trust satisfies this requirement, even the termination of the possibility of income from the trust. This is why it is important to determine who has a Chapter 13 interest in the trust and track what happens to those interests over time.

Example: T creates an irrevocable trust that pays income equally to C, T's child, and GC, T's grandchild for ten years. After ten years, GC will receive all of the income for life. At GC's death, the remainder will go to GGC, T's great-grandchild. Upon creation of the trust, no direct skip occurs since C, a non-skip person, holds an interest in the trust and the trust is not considered a skip person. [IRC § 2613(b)] After the expiration of the ten-year period, Chapter 12 does not apply since there is no transfer of property by gift. However, a taxable termination occurs since upon the termination of C's interest in the trust a skip person (GC) obtains a Chapter 13 interest in the trust. [Reg. § 26.2612–1(f)(ex. 6)]

i) Simultaneous Terminations

More than one Chapter 13 interest can simultaneously terminate in a trust. When this happens the potential exists for simultaneous multiple generation-skipping transfers. However, under the Regulations the termination of more than one interest in a single trust results in only one taxable termination generation-skipping transfer. [Reg. § 26.2612–1(b)(3)]

Example: T creates an irrevocable trust where the income will be distributed equally between C

(T's child), GC (T's grandchild), and GGC (T's great-grandchild). At C's death the corpus of the trust will go to GGC. The creation of the trust is subject to the gift tax, but is not a direct skip since C, a non-skip person, has a Chapter 13 interest in the trust. [IRC § 2612(c)(1)] On C's death, both C's and GC's Chapter 13 interests terminate. Even though more than one interest is simultaneously terminated at C's death, only one taxable termination occurs. [Reg. § 26.2612–1(f)(ex. 8)]

ii) Partial Terminations [IRC § 2612(a)(2)]

A taxable termination can exist even though one or more of the elements of IRC § 2612(a)(1) are missing. If (1) a Chapter 13 interest held in trust by a lineal descendant of the transferor, (2) is terminated by death, and (3) trust assets are distributed out of the trust to a skip person, a taxable termination is present for that portion of the property so distributed. [IRC § 2612(a)(2)] The partial termination rule does not apply when the Chapter 13 interests are transferred after death to both skip and non-skip persons but all the property is held in the trust and not distributed.

Example (1): T creates an irrevocable trust that pays income in equal shares to C1 and C2, T's children. After one child dies, one-half of the trust corpus is to be distributed in equal shares to T's grandchildren then living. On the death of the second child, the remaining trust corpus is to be distributed in equal shares among T's grandchildren then living. Under IRC § 2612(a)(1), no taxable termination occurs when C1 dies since a non-skip person, C2, retains a Chapter 13 interest in the trust. [IRC § 2612(a)(1)(B)] However, since a lineal descendant of the transferor (C1) caused the termination and one-half of the trust assets were distributed to skip persons (T's grandchildren), a partial taxable termination is present. [IRC § 2612(a)(2)] There is, consequently, a generation-skipping transfer of one-half of the trust property. [Reg. § 26.2612–1(f)(ex. 9)]

Example (2): T creates an irrevocable trust that pays income to X, T's friend, for X's life. After X's death the corpus is to be distributed equally between C, T's child and GC, T's grandchild. At X's death no taxable termination transpires since some of the property passes to C, a non-skip person. Also, there is no partial termination since X is not a lineal descendant of T. [IRC § 2612(a)(2)] However there is a taxable distribution for the portion of the trust distributed to GC. [IRC § 2612(b)]

(b) **Interests in Property Held in Trust**

IRC § 2652(c)(1) defines "interests in property held in trust" for Chapter 13 purposes. [*See supra* III. B. 3., explaining the term in detail] When determining possession of a Chapter 13 interest, apply the look-through rules of IRC § 2651(f)(2). [*See supra* III. B. 6. c)] Interests created merely to postpone or avoid the tax, as well as those interests which are de minimis, are disregarded. [IRC § 2652(c)(2)]

(c) **Trusts**

As explained in more detail *supra* III. B. 5. a), "trusts" for Chapter 13 purposes include formal as well as nonexplicit trusts. [IRC § 2652(b)(1), (3); Reg. § 26.2652–1(b)]

Example: T irrevocably transfers T's house to T's child, C, for life giving the remainder to GC, T's grandchild. The transfer is subject to the gift tax, but is not classified as a direct skip generation-skipping transfer since C is a non-skip person and therefore, the trust is a non-skip person. [IRC § 2613(b)] The transfer is treated as a transfer in trust since it involves a life estate. [IRC § 2652(b)(3); Reg. § 26.2652–1(b)(1)] When C dies, there is a termination of a Chapter 13 interest in trust, and a skip person takes the property. Therefore, upon C's death a taxable termination generation-skipping transfer occurs. [IRC § 2612(a)(1)]

(d) Not Subject to Estate or Gift Tax

The Regulations provide that a taxable termination cannot occur if the transfer is subject to estate tax or gift tax. [Reg. § 26.2612–1(b)(1)(i)] The sole reason for this requirement is to ensure that where a transfer is both a direct skip and taxable termination, the direct skip takes precedence.

The one exception to this rule is the reverse QTIP election pursuant to IRC § 2652(a)(3). Even though the termination of a QTIP interest in property would be subject to either the estate tax [IRC § 2044(a)] or treated as a transfer of property by gift [IRC § 2519], the reverse QTIP election treats the property as if the QTIP election were not made (in other words, constructively "reversing" the election). If the election was not made, neither the estate tax nor the gift tax would apply and a taxable termination would occur.

Example (1): T creates an irrevocable trust reserving the right to income from the trust for life, with the remainder payable to GC, T's grandchild. At T's death, the trust corpus is included in T's gross estate. [IRC § 2036] Even though this is a termination of a Chapter 13 interest in trust in which a skip person takes after the termination, it is not a taxable termination since the trust is subject to the estate tax. [Reg. § 26.2612–1(b)(1)(i)] Instead of a taxable termination this is classified as a direct skip generation-skipping transfer. [IRC § 2612(c)(1)] For the timing of when the transfer occurs, see the material on the estate tax inclusion period *infra* III. D. 2. b) (3) (b).

Example (2): For an example illustrating a taxable termination in the context of the reverse QTIP election, *see supra* III. B. 2. c).

(e) "Unless" Rules

Not all terminations of interests in property not subject to estate or gift tax are taxable terminations. In two instances, such a termination does not result in a taxable termination: (1) when, immediately after the termination, a non-skip person has a Chapter 13 interest in the trust; or (2) if no one has a Chapter 13 interest in the trust, and after the termination, no distributions can be ever made to skip persons.

i) Post–Termination Interests Held by Non–Skip Persons [IRC § 2612(a)(1)(A)]

If after the termination of a Chapter 13 interest a non-skip person holds a Chapter 13 interest in the trust's property, no taxable termination occurs.

Example: T creates an irrevocable trust in which C1, C2 (two of T's children) and GC (T's grandchild) are all permissible recipients of the trust's income. Upon C1's death, even though a Chapter 13 interest is terminated in the trust, no taxable termination takes place because a non-skip person (C2) retains an interest in the trust property. Furthermore, the partial termination rule does not apply because the property was kept in trust and not distributed to a skip and non-skip person. [IRC § 2612(a)(2)]

ii) No Possibility of Future Distributions to Skip Persons [IRC § 2612(a)(1)(B)]

If no person holds a Chapter 13 interest in the trust, the termination is not a taxable termination if at no future time can a skip person receive property from the trust. That means a taxable termination will occur if even one skip person may receive a distribution, unless the possibility of them receiving property is "so remote as to be negligible." The Regulations deem an interest remotely negligible if the probability of distribution is less than 5% by actuarial standards. [Reg. § 26.2612–1(b)(1)(iii)]

Example (1): T creates an irrevocable trust for the benefit of C, T's child, for life. After C's death the trust is to accumulate income for ten years, then distribute the corpus and accumulated income to TS, T's spouse. On C's death, there is a termination of a Chapter 13 interest in property. Since the income is to be accumulated for ten years after the termination of the trust, IRC § 2612(a)(1)(A) does not apply. However, C's death does not create a taxable termination since only a non-skip person (TS) can receive a distribution from the trust. [IRC § 2612(a)(1)(B)]

Example (2): T creates a trust that pays the income to C, T's child, for life. After C dies, the income is to accumulate until D, T's daughter, reaches the age of 21, after which time the income will be paid to D for life. After D dies, the corpus is to be distributed to GC. The trust is subject to the gift tax on its creation, but no direct skip generation-skipping transfer occurs since the Chapter 13 interest is held by a non-skip person (C) and the trust is not a skip person. [IRC § 2612(c)(1)] If C should die before D's twenty-first birthday, a taxable termination generation-skipping transfer would occur since C's Chapter 13 interest in the trust terminates. Additionally, since the income of the trust must be accumulated, there is no Chapter 13 interest holder even though D (a non-skip person) will take the income after her 21st birthday. As a result, the exception under IRC § 2612(a)(1)(A) does not apply. Also the IRC § 2612(a)(1)(B) "unless" clause is not met since a skip person (GC) may receive a distribution from the trust after the termination.

Example (3): T creates an irrevocable trust for the benefit of T's child, C1, for life, remainder to C2, T's second child. The trust instrument provides that if T has any great-great-great-great grandchildren living at the time of C1's death, such persons will take the property instead of C2. If the actuarial probability of T having a conforming grandchild is less than 5%, it is disregarded and no taxable termination will be present. If the probability is 5% or greater, a taxable termination is present since a skip person can take a distribution from the trust. [IRC § 2612(a)(1)]

(2) Exclusion and Exceptions

(a) General Exclusions to Generation–Skipping Transfers [IRC § 2611(b)]

IRC § 2611(b) provides two general exclusions to all the generation-skipping transfers. Since these exceptions apply to all three types of generation-skipping transfers, they are covered *infra* at III. C. 2.

(b) Trusts Created Before September 25, 1985

See infra the discussion of the effective date of the GST tax, III. C. 2. d).

c) **Taxable Distributions [IRC § 2612(b)]**

Taxable distributions are the backstop provision for generation-skipping transfers. This catchall status reflects the fact that all others types of generation-skipping transfers take precedence over taxable distributions. By definition, a taxable distribution only occurs when a direct skip or taxable termination is not present. [IRC § 2612(b)(parenthetical)] The additional requirements of a taxable distribution are simple—there must be a distribution from a trust (which includes non-explicit trusts) to a skip person. [IRC § 2612(b); Reg. § 26.2612–1(c)(1)]

Example (1): T creates an irrevocable trust that pays income to C, T's child, for life. When GC, T's grandchild, reaches age twenty, one-half of the corpus is to be distributed to GC. The remainder of the corpus is to be distributed to GC on C's death. GC reaches age twenty with C still alive and receives one-half of the corpus. The distribution is not a direct skip since the transfer is not subject to the estate or gift tax. [IRC § 2612(c)(1)] No taxable termination is present since there is not a termination of a Chapter 13 interest (C retains the right to income from the trust). [IRC § 2612(a)(1)] However, there is a taxable distribution since there is a distribution from a trust to a skip person (GC). [IRC § 2612(b); Reg. § 26.2612–1(f)(ex. 10)]

Example (2):   Same facts as Example (1), except that GC also has the right to withdraw $10,000 from the trust each year. Assume GC exercises her right and withdraws $10,000 from the trust. A direct skip is not present since there is no estate or gift tax due on the distribution. [IRC § 2612(c)(1)] Assuming that the trust contains more than $10,000, no Chapter 13 interest in the trust is terminated, so a taxable termination is not present. [IRC § 2612(a)(1)] A taxable distribution does occur, however, since there was a distribution from a trust to a skip person (GC). [IRC § 2612(b); Reg. § 26.2612–1(f)(ex. 11)]

Example (3):   Same facts as Example (2), except that the withdrawal power is held by GGC, T's great-grandchild. Even though the distributions skip more than one generation only a single taxable distribution generation-skipping transfer occurs.

(1) Elements of a Taxable Distribution

Any distribution from a trust qualifies as a taxable distribution, no matter whether it is required or discretionary (i.e., under a power of appointment), and no matter whether it is paid from the income (current or accumulated) or corpus of the trust. [IRC § 2612(b)]

A skip person can include both individuals and trusts. [IRC § 2613(a)] However, only distributions to trusts deemed skip persons under IRC § 2613(a)(2) are treated as taxable distributions, and therefore the look-through rules of IRC § 2651(f)(2) do not apply. [Reg. § 26.2612–1(c)(2)] The look-through rules have continued application to see if skip persons are receiving distributions to entities, such as to corporations or partnerships.

Example (1):   T's will provides that T's estate shall make payments to GC for ten years. The distribution is not to another trust so the look-thru rules may be applied. [Reg. § 26.2612–1(c)(2)] Estates cannot be treated as trusts [IRC § 2652(b)(1)(parenthetical)], so the generational assignment of the beneficial interest holder, GC, must be considered to determine if a transfer to a skip person has been completed. [IRC § 2651(b)(1)] GC is a skip person so the distributions from the trust to GC are taxable distributions. [IRC § 2612(b)]

Example (2):   T creates an irrevocable trust where the trustee has the power to distribute the income among T's lineal descendents. The trustee distributes some trust income to a separate trust in which both C, T's child, and GC, T's grandchild, are permissible income recipients. Since both C (a non-skip person) and GC (a skip person) have Chapter 13 interests, the recipient trust is classified as a non-skip person. [IRC § 2613(b)] If the look-through rules of IRC § 2651(f)(2) are applied, a taxable distribution would be present. However, under the Regulations, on a trust-to-trust transfer, the look-through rules do not apply and the distribution is not considered a taxable distribution. [Reg. § 26.2612–1(c)(2)]

(2) Trust's Payment of GST Tax on a Taxable Distribution

The transferee is liable for any GST tax due on the taxable distribution. [IRC § 2601] Therefore, if the trust pays the tax, the transferee's liability has been discharged by a third party and should be treated as additional income from the trust. [*Old Colony Trust Co. v. Commissioner*, 279 U.S. 716, 49 S.Ct. 499, 73 L.Ed. 918 (1929)] If the trust pays the tax on a taxable distribution generation-skipping transfer, the payment is treated as a second taxable distribution. [IRC § 2621(b)] The distribution includes any GST tax as well as any associated penalties and interest paid. [Reg. § 26.2612–1(c)(1)] This second taxable distribution is treated as being have made on the last day of the calendar year the root taxable distribution was made. [Reg. § 26.2612–1(c)(1)]

(3) Exclusion and Exceptions

(a) General Exclusions to Generation–Skipping Transfers [IRC § 2611(b)]

IRC § 2611(b) provides two general exclusions to all the generation-skipping transfers. Since these exceptions apply to all three types of generation-skipping transfers they are covered *infra* at III. C. 2.

(b) Multiple Skip Rule [IRC § 2653(a)]

If there is a generation-skipping transfer of property and the property is immediately held in trust after the transfer, the generational assignment of the transferor changes. The change in the transferor's generational assignment can affect whether subsequent transfers from the trust are taxable distributions. *See supra* the detailed discussion of the multiple skip rule of IRC § 2653(a) at III. B. 4. d).

(c) Trusts Created on or Before September 25, 1985

See infra the discussion of the effective date of the GST tax, III. C. 2. d).

2. Excluded Transfers

The GST tax will not necessarily apply, even if a generation-skipping transfer is present under IRC § 2611(a). Several exclusions or exceptions must be considered. These include certain transfers to pay for medical or educational expenses and transfers of property already subjected to the GST tax. Three other exceptions are transfers which skip multiple generations (multiple skips), certain irrevocable trusts created on or before September 25, 1986 and certain transfers during the year 2010.

a) Indirect Payments of Medical or Educational Expenses [IRC § 2611(b)(1)]

Transfers which would not be treated as taxable gifts under IRC § 2503(e) if made by the transferor directly are not generation-skipping transfers. [IRC § 2611(b)(1)] IRC § 2503(e) excludes all direct payments of tuition to an educational organization and all direct payments for medical care to the medical provider from being transfers of property by gift.

It is important to note that this provision only excludes the payment of such expenses by a trust; the exclusion does not require direct payments by the transferor. The rationale is that a payment made directly would not be "subject to" the gift tax and therefore, no Chapter 13 transferor exists and there could be no determination of a skip person. [IRC § 2652(a)(1)(B)] Therefore, the exclusion applies only to testamentary transfers and transfers from a trust not already subjected to the GST tax.

Example (1): T creates an irrevocable trust that pays income to C, T's child, for life. At C's death, the remainder will be paid to GC, T's grandchild. The trust also allows for the trust's income and corpus to be used to pay for GC's college tuition or medical care. Later, the trust makes a direct payment to GC's college to cover GC's tuition. If T made the payment, it would have been covered by IRC § 2503(e). Therefore, even though the transfer qualifies as a generation-skipping transfer (a "taxable distribution") it is excluded because it would be excluded from gift taxation if paid by T under IRC § 2503(e). [IRC § 2611(b)(1)]

Example (2): T creates an irrevocable trust to pay for GC's college tuition. Even though the trust will be used to pay for tuition, T's transfer was not made directly to the educational organization and is, therefore, not covered by IRC § 2503(e). The transfer is considered a generation-skipping transfer (a "direct skip"). [IRC § 2612(c)(1)] For what happens to the trust after its creation *see supra* the discussion of IRC § 2653(a), the multiple skip rule, at III. B. 4. d).

Example (3): T makes a payment directly to the hospital for GC's medical costs. Here the payment is not treated as a transfer of property by gift since it is excluded by IRC § 2503(e). Since the gift is not subject to the gift tax, it will not be subject to any Chapter 13 consequences and it is unnecessary to utilize the exclusion under IRC § 2611(b)(1) to shield the transfer from GST tax consequences.

b) Property Previously Subject to the GST Tax [IRC § 2611(b)(2)]

The general policy underlying Chapter 13 is to ensure the uniform application of the transfer taxes, even in situations where generations are skipped. For property already subjected to the GST tax, however, there is no reason to subject the property to another round of GST taxation.

A transfer is not treated as a generation-skipping transfer to the extent (1) it involves property previously subject to a GST tax, (2) the previous transferee had the same or lower generational assignment as the current transferee, and (3) the effect of the transfer is not avoidance of the GST tax. [IRC § 2611(b)(2)] Commentators differ on whether the exclusion is limited to the value of the property at the time it was subjected to the previous GST tax. Some commentators advocate a limit to the exclusion equal to the fair market value previously taxed, while others say that the exclusion applies to "the property transferred" and therefore, is not limited to its former value. Commentators also differ on whether the exclusion applies to the proceeds from the sale of property previously subjected to the GST tax, but then sold, and other property purchased. Some believe the property subjected to the previous GST tax can be sold and the proceeds used to purchase another piece of property and still have the exclusion apply. Others state that tracing difficulties prohibit the application of the rule in this fashion.

If the property is held in trust, before the application of the exclusion, one should look at IRC § 2653(a) to see if the generation assignments of the trust beneficiaries change. *See supra* the detailed discussion of the multiple skip rule of IRC § 2653(a) at III. B. 4. d).

Example: T gives Blackacre to GGC, T's great-grandchild, when it is worth $200,000. This transfer is a direct skip and subject to the GST tax. [IRC §§ 2612(c), 2601] Later, GGC transfers the property to TS, GGC's grandmother and T's spouse. When the property is worth $300,000, TS transfers the property to GC, GGC's parent. Without an exclusion, the transfer of property from TS to GC would be a direct skip and subject to another round of Chapter 13 taxation. However, since the property was formerly subjected to taxation under Chapter 13 and GC has the same or lower generation assignment compared to GGC, (assuming the transfer was not completed to avoid taxation) this transfer is not treated as a generation-skipping transfer. [IRC § 2611(b)(2)] Commentators differ as to whether the $100,000 appreciation in value between the two direct skip transfers should be subject to Chapter 13 taxation.

c) Multiple Skips

While not technically considered an exclusion, skips over multiple generations are not subject to more than one GST tax. [Reg. § 26.2612–1(a)]

Example: T transfers property to GGGC at a time when all of T's descendents were living. The transfer skips multiple generations (C, GC, GGC), but is only treated as one generation-skipping transfer (a "direct skip"). [Reg. § 26.2612–1(a)]

d) Trusts Created Before the GST Effective Date

The effective date for the GST tax is October 23, 1986. Therefore, trusts created on or after this date are subjected to the GST tax on generation-skipping transfers. [Reg. § 26.2601–1(a)(1)] The effective date is expanded to cover trusts created after September 25, 1985, that are subject to the gift tax upon creation. [Reg. § 26.2601–1(a)(2)] This makes the effective date for inter vivos trusts September 26, 1985, corresponding to the date Congress started its consideration of the tax changes passed in 1986. All trusts created prior to this date can have no GST tax liability, even if they have generation-skipping transfers, unless an exception is present.

Example: On February 1, 1986 T creates an irrevocable trust potentially triggering later generation-skipping transfer tax consequences for any distributions from the trust or on the trust's termination. The trust faced gift tax consequences upon creation. Since the trust was created after September 25, 1985, the trust is deemed to be created on October 23, 1986, and is therefore not excluded from future GST tax consequences. [Reg. § 26.2601–1(a)(2)]

(1) Irrevocable Trusts Created Before September 26, 1985

(a) General Rule

The GST tax does not apply to any taxable distributions from, or taxable terminations of, irrevocable trusts created before September 26, 1985. [Reg. § 26.2601–1(b)(1)(i)] Interestingly, any trust in existence on September 25, 1985, is treated as an "irrevocable trust" for purposes of this rule. [Reg. § 26.2601–1(b)(1)(ii)(A)] Trusts with qualified terminable interest property (QTIP) created before September 25, 1985, are treated as if a reverse QTIP election was made, regardless of whether an election actually occurred. [Reg. § 26.2601–1(b)(1)(iii)(A)] This results in the trust's transferor remaining the same, and the trust remains exempt from the GST tax. [*See, e.g.,* Reg. § 26.2601–1(b)(1)(iii)(B)(ex. 2)]

> *Example:* In 1983, T created an irrevocable trust that paid income to C, T's child for C's life, and the remainder to GC, T's grandchild. C's death in 2009 results in a taxable termination generation-skipping transfer from the trust. [IRC § 2612(a)(1)] However, since the creation of the trust occurred before September 25, 1985, the GST tax does not apply. [Reg. § 26.2601–1(b)(1)(i)]

(b) **Trust or Trust Assets Not Treated as an Irrevocable Trust**

Not all trusts created before September 26,1985, are exempted from GST tax liability. If the trust's property is includable in the transferor's gross estate under IRC §§ 2038 or 2042 and the settlor of the trust dies after September 25, 1985, then Chapter 13 applies. [Reg. § 26.2601–1(b)(1)(ii)(B)–(C)] Additionally, any property transferred to the trust after September 25, 1985, is not excluded. [Reg. § 26.2601–1(b)(1)(i)]

(i) **Trusts Included in Settlor's Gross Estate Under IRC § 2038**

Trusts created before September 26, 1985, with trust assets that would be includible in the settlor's gross estate under IRC § 2038 if the settler died on September 25, 1985, are not considered "irrevocable trusts." [Reg. § 26.2601–1(b)(1)(ii)(B)] Generally, IRC § 2038 includes in a settlor's gross estate transfers to trusts where the settlor has the power to "alter, amend, revoke or terminate" the trust. [IRC § 2038; *see supra* I. A. 2. c) covering IRC § 2038]

> *Example (1):* T created a trust in 1984 that paid the income to GC, T's grandchild, for GC's life, followed by the remainder to GGC, T's great-grandchild. On September 25, 1985, T held a testamentary power to add beneficiaries to the trust. If T died on that date,

the power to add beneficiaries forces inclusion of the trust's assets into T's gross estate under IRC § 2038. If T died on September 25, 1985, the trust assets would have been included under IRC § 2038. Therefore, the trust is not an irrevocable trust for purposes of the effective date and potentially faces GST tax liability. [Reg. § 26.2601–1(b)(1)(ii)(D)(ex. 1)]

Example (2):   T created a trust in 1984 and retained the power to give a remainder interest in the trust to any after-born grandchildren. On September 25, 1985, all of T's grandchildren possessed a remainder interest in the trust. Even though T owned the right to add remainder persons, the contingency for the power to exist was not satisfied on September 25, 1985, since at that time there were no after-born grandchildren who were not in the class of the remainderpersons. Since no power existed at that time, IRC § 2038 would not include the trust in T's gross estate (if T died on September 25, 1985). Therefore, the trust is an irrevocable trust for purposes of the effective date and is not subject to the GST tax, regardless of whether T has after-born grandchildren (post-September 1985). [Reg. § 26.2601–1(b)(1)(ii)(D)(ex. 3)]

(ii) Trusts Included in Settlor's Gross Estate Under IRC § 2042

Insurance policies are treated as trusts for Chapter 13 purposes. [IRC § 2652(b)(1), (3); *see supra* the discussion of trusts and trust-like instruments, III. B. 5. a)] An insurance policy created before September 25, 1985, that is includible in the individual's gross estate under IRC § 2042 (if the individual died on September 25, 1985) is not treated as an irrevocable trust and is possibly subject to the GST tax to the extent that the insured possessed any incident of ownership on September 25, 1985. [Reg. § 26.2601–1(b)(1)(ii)(C)]

Example: T purchased a life insurance policy in 1983 designating GC, T's grandchild, as the beneficiary of the policy. On September 25, 1985, T held the right to obtain a loan from the insurance carrier against the surrender value of the policy. The insurance policy is considered a "trust" for purposes of Chapter 13. [IRC § 2652(b)(1), (3); Reg. § 26.2652–1(b)(1)] T owned an incident of ownership over the policy on September 25, 1985, causing the policy's inclusion in T's gross estate, if T had died on or before that date. Therefore, the policy is not considered an irrevocable trust for purposes of the effective date and potentially faces GST tax liability. [Reg. § 26.2601–1(b)(1)(ii)(D)(ex. 4)]

(iii) Transfers to Irrevocable Trusts after September 25, 1985

Property transferred after September 25, 1985, to an irrevocable trust created prior to September 25, 1985, is subject to the GST tax. [Reg. § 26.2601–1(b)(1)(i)] A pro-rata portion of each generation-skipping transfer becomes taxable. The taxable portion is determined by calculating the allocation fraction, the numerator equal to the amount of the additional transfer and the denominator equal to the fair market value of the trust immediately following the addition. [Reg. § 26.2601–1(b)(1)(iv)(C)(1)] If multiple additions occur over time, the numerator of the allocation fraction equals the non-exempt portion of the trust plus the value of the additional property. The denominator remains the value of the trust immediately after any subsequent additional transfer. [Reg. § 26.2601–1(b)(1)(iv)(C)(1), (C)(2)(ex. 3)] GST exemption can be allocated to the trust and will be applied only to the non-exempt portion. [Reg. § 26.2601–1(b)(1)(iv)(A); *see infra* III. D. 2. b) (2) (a) for discussion of the GST exemption]

Example: T created a trust in 1985 with $100,000 in property. In 1987, when the trust was worth

$150,000, T added an additional $50,000 to the trust. The taxable portion of any future generation-skipping transfers is determined using an applicable fraction of 1/4. The numerator is $50,000 (the value of the additional property) and the denominator equals $200,000 (the total value of the trust immediately after the addition: $150,000 plus the $50,000 additional transfer). [Reg. § 26.2601–1(b)(1)(iv)(C)(2)(ex. 1)]

A deemed transfer potentially occurs for property subject to a general power of appointment. Property is deemed an additional transfer to the trust if (1) the property is subject to a power of appointment, (2) the exercise, release, or lapse of the power occurs after September 25, 1985, and is treated as a taxable transfer under the estate or gift tax, and (3) the property remains in the trust after the exercise, release or lapse. [Reg. § 26.2601–1(b)(1)(v)(A)]

If a power is non-general, the exercise, release or lapse of the power will not be a deemed transfer if (1) the power is from an excluded trust, and (2) it does not violate the Uniform Statutory Rule Against Perpetuities. [Reg. § 26.2601–1(b)(1)(v)(B)]

(2) Continuous Mental Incompetence of Transferor from October 22, 1986

Certain transfers are not subject to the GST tax if the settlor of the trust suffered under a mental disability at all times from October 22, 1986, until the settlor's death. [Reg. § 26.2601–1(b)(3)(i)] Excludable transfers are (1) direct skips caused by the settlor's death (e.g., T gives Blackacre to GC), and (2) testamentary transfers from trusts included in the individual's gross estate (e.g., where the individual had the right to income from the trust). [*Id.*] A qualified physician can certify to the mental incompetence; however, court adjudication is not required. [Reg. § 26.2601–1(b)(3)(ii)–(iii)] If additional property is added to the trust after October 22, 1986, to the trust by or on behalf of the disabled individual during his or her life, such transfers are covered by the GST tax. [Reg. § 26.2601–1(b)(3)(i)(A)]

(3) Revocable Trusts and Wills of Decedents Dying Before 1987

Chapter 13 excludes generation-skipping transfers from revocable trusts or wills created before October 22, 1986, if: (1) the trust was not amended (except for certain changes listed below) after October 22, 1986, (2) the trust received no additions after such date, and (3) the decedent died before January 1, 1987. [Reg. § 26.2601–1(b)(2)(i)] The only changes permitted are administrative or clarifying changes, or those changes ensuring an existing bequest or transfer qualifies for a marital or charitable deduction, but neither change can increase the amount transferred more than an "incidental" amount. [Reg. § 26.2601–1(b)(2)(iv)]

(4) "Gallo" Amendment

Before 1990, direct skips to the transferor's grandchildren up to $2 million were excluded transfers. [*See supra* the discussion of the Gallo amendment, III. C. 1. a) (3) (c).]

e) Generation–Skipping Transfers Occurring During 2010

One "exception" to the GST tax applies to generation-skipping transfers made in the year 2010. The Economic Growth and Tax Relief Reconciliation Act of 2001 (EGTRRA) repealed the GST tax after December 31, 2009. While the repeal was itself repealed in 2010, Congress allowed executors of decedents dying in 2010 to elect to have the estate and GST tax not apply. Additionally, the Act also provides for an applicable rate of 0% for all transfers made in 2010, which effectively precludes any GST tax from being collected on such transfers. [Tax Relief, Unemployment Insurance Reauthorization, and Job Creation Act of 2010, Pub. L. No. 111–312, §§ 301(c), 302(c) (2010)]

D. Computation of the Generation Skipping Transfer Tax

The Chapter 13 GST tax is computed by multiplying the "taxable amount" by the "applicable rate." [IRC § 2602] The tax base for the generation-skipping tax is the taxable amount, which is analogous to the "taxable income" of the income tax, the "taxable estate" of the estate tax, and "taxable gifts" of the gift tax. [IRC §§ 1, 2001(b), 2502(a)] Generally, the taxable amount equals the value of the property involved in the generation-skipping transfer, but the taxable amount can vary by the type of generation-skipping transfer (i.e., a direct skip, taxable termination, or taxable distribution) involved. [IRC §§ 2621–2623] The applicable rate is determined by multiplying the maximum federal estate tax rate by the "inclusion ratio." [IRC § 2641] While Congress intended to simplify computation of the GST by utilizing an applicable rate in lieu of a rate table, the computation remains complex. The maximum federal rate equals the maximum federal estate tax rate applicable at the time of the generation-skipping transfer. [IRC § 2641(b)] The computation of the inclusion ratio is much more complex and is discussed *infra* at III. D. 2. b). After applying the applicable rate to the taxable amount, the the final GST tax due is reached after subtracting any credit allowed for state taxes paid on generation-skipping transfers. [IRC § 2604; *see infra* III. D. 3.] This credit does not apply, however, to generation-skipping transfers occurring after 2004. [IRC § 2604(c)]

1. Taxable Amount

The tax base for Chapter 13 is the "taxable amount." [IRC § 2602] To determine the taxable amount, one must first identify the type of generation-skipping transfer that occurred. The appropriate taxable amount is then ascertained by applying the appropriate statute. [IRC §§ 2621–2623] After determining what to include, the time and method of valuation must be determined (generally, the fair market value at the time of the generation-skipping transfer). [IRC § 2624(a)] Finally, the taxable amount is reduced by any consideration given by the transferee. [IRC § 2624(d)]

a) Direct Skip [IRC § 2623]

(1) Taxable Amount

The taxable amount for a direct skip generation-skipping transfer is the value of the property received by the transferee less any consideration paid by the transferee. [IRC §§ 2623, 2624(d)] No deductions are allowed in the computation of the taxable amount on direct skips (while deductions are allowed for taxable terminations and taxable distributions).

Important to remember, although not directly related to the computation of the GST tax, is that the payment of the Chapter 13 tax on inter vivos direct skips by the transferor/donor is treated as a taxable gift. [IRC § 2515] This can lead to a combined tax payment (for the gift and GST tax) of more than the original gift transfer. The rule and an example are explained further *supra* at II. C. 5.

(2) Method and Time of Valuation

The time and method of valuation for the taxable amount of a direct skip is controlled by the type of transfer. Three types of direct skip transfers exist: a direct skip by gift (either direct or through a trust, but not within the estate tax inclusion period), a testamentary direct skip, and a direct skip within the estate tax inclusion period.

Any consideration provided by the transferee reduces the taxable amount for all three types of generation-skipping transfers. [IRC

§ 2624(d)] Consideration can be in any form and includes anything from the transfer of money to the assumption of liability on the property (e.g., a recourse loan). Non-recourse loans also reduce the taxable amount, but do so by reducing the value of the property transferred and not by a reduction as consideration paid. [*See, e.g.,* Reg. § 20.2053–7]

(a) Inter Vivos Gift

The value of a direct skip made by gift directly or through a trust is the fair market value of the property determined at the time of the transfer. [IRC § 2624(a)] This is the only method of valuation available. [Reg. § 20.2031–1(b); *C.f.* IRC § 2032A (where under certain circumstances the taxpayer may elect to use an alternative valuation method)]

> *Example:* On January 1, T creates an irrevocable trust that pays the income to GC, T's grandchild, for life. At GC's death, the remainder will be paid to GGC, T's great-grandchild. At the time of the transfer, the property has a value of $1 million. By the time T files Form 709 (required for gift and generation-skipping tax), the property increases in value to $2 million. The taxable amount is still $1 million, since that was the value of the property at the time of the transfer. [IRC § 2624(a)]

(b) Testamentary Transfer

Property included in the transferor's gross estate subject to a testamentary direct skip is valued at the same time and in the same manner as under the estate tax. If the transferor's estate elects to use the alternate valuation date [IRC § 2032] or special use valuation [IRC § 2032A] instead of the fair market value at death, those methods are likewise utilized to determine the taxable amount for Chapter 13. [IRC § 2624(b)]

(c) Estate Tax Inclusion Period

If a transfer is a direct skip but the property would be includible in the transferor's gross estate after the transfer, it is subject to the estate tax inclusion period ("ETIP"). [IRC § 2642(f)] Since the transfer is in part a gift and part a testamentary transfer, the direct skip is treated as occurring at the termination of the ETIP. [IRC § 2642(f)(1)(flush)] For a full discussion of the ETIP *see infra* at III. D. 2. b) (3) (b).

b) Taxable Termination [IRC § 2622]

(1) Taxable Amount

The taxable amount for taxable termination generation-skipping transfers includes all property involved in the taxable termination. Since the tax liability in a taxable termination is borne by the trust [IRC § 2603(a)(2)] this means the taxable amount includes amounts that will be used to pay the GST tax. In other words, the computation is tax inclusive. The taxable amount is reduced by any amounts "similar to the deduction allowed by [IRC § 2053]" (e.g., administration expenses, claims, unpaid mortgages, etc.) and any consideration paid by the transferee. [IRC §§ 2622(b), 2624(d)] However, any IRC § 2053–like expenses used to reduce the taxable amount may not also be used to reduce taxable income for income tax purposes. [IRC § 642(g)]

(2) Method and Time of Valuation

The method of valuation for a taxable termination is the fair market value of the property, no exceptions. [IRC § 2624(a)] However, the time of valuation can vary. Generally, the valuation date is the termination of the trust. [*Id.*] The one exception to the general rule is for taxable terminations that take place due to the death of an individual. In such a case, the trustee may elect to use the alternate valuation date under IRC § 2032 to postpone the valuation date until six months after the decedent's death. [IRC § 2624(c)] The property is not required to be in the decedent's gross estate to utilize this rule, but if the property is included in the decedent's gross estate, the estate must make a similar election to use IRC § 2032 to value the property.

c) Taxable Distribution [IRC § 2621]

(1) Taxable Amount

The taxable amount for a taxable distribution is the value of the property received by the transferee reduced by any expenses incurred "by the transferee in connection with the determination, collection, or refund" of any GST tax imposed on the distribution. [IRC § 2621(a)] The deductible expenses are similar to those allowed for the income tax under IRC § 212(3), but they only need be "incurred" (not paid) by the time the return is filed. For examples of deductible expenses *see* Reg. § 1.212–1(a)(1). Any expenses used to reduce the taxable amount may not be used to reduce income taxes. [IRC § 642(g)] The taxable amount can also be reduced by any consideration paid by the transferee (similar to a direct skip or taxable termination). [IRC § 2624(d)]

Chapter 13 imposes tax liability on the transferee for taxable distributions. [IRC § 2603(a)(1)] If the trust pays the tax for the transferee, the amount paid is treated as an additional taxable distribution and included in the taxable amount. [IRC § 2621(b); Reg. § 26.2612–1(c); *see also* the discussion of IRC § 2621(b) *supra* at III. C. 1. c) (2).]

(2) Method and Time of Valuation

The only allowable valuation method for a taxable distribution is the property's fair market value at the time of distribution. [IRC § 2624(a)] No other time periods are available, and no elections are available to change this result.

d) Tax Inclusive v. Tax Exclusive

The terms "tax inclusive" and "tax exclusive" describe, respectively, the estate and gift tax, and both are present in Chapter 13. To be tax inclusive means the tax base includes amounts used to pay the tax. The estate tax is considered tax inclusive since the gross estate (the base for the estate tax) is used to compute the tax and is the source from which the estate tax, if any, is paid. The gift tax is tax exclusive since taxable gifts (the base for the gift tax) include only those amounts received by the donee; the gift tax is paid from the donor's other funds. Since no tax is paid on the funds used to pay the tax, it is cheaper tax-wise to give a gift rather than a testamentary transfer.

The difference in the amount of funds required to pass on any given sum can best be illustrated by example. Suppose T wants to transfer $1 million to X, but does not care if the transfer occurs during T's lifetime or at T's death. For simplicity, assume that the estate and gift tax have a flat rate of 35% and there are no estate or gift tax exclusions or credits. To transfer $1 million at death, $1,538,462 is required in T's gross estate since 35% of $1,538,462 is (rounded) $538,462. The $538,462 in tax liability reduces the available funds to make the $1 million transfer. In contrast, to pass $1 million by inter vivos gift, "only" $1.35 million is needed. The $1 million gift is used as the tax base (as compared to $1,538,462 for the estate tax) and only $350,000 is due in gift tax (35% of

$1 million). The difference in the amount required between the estate and gift taxes ($188,462) represents the tax (35%) on the amount used to pay the tax ($538,462).

Chapter 13 contains both tax inclusive and tax exclusive transfers. Taxable terminations and taxable distributions are tax inclusive transfers. The tax liability for each is paid from the amount used to compute the tax. [IRC §§ 2603(a)(1), (2), 2621, 2622] Testamentary direct skips are tax exclusive transfers; no amount of tax is due from the property transferred. [IRC §§ 2603(a)(3), 2623] Since the GST tax imposed as a result of a direct skip is treated as a taxable gift, it increases the overall amount of gift tax, but not as high as a tax inclusive transfer. [IRC § 2515]

Example (1):   Assume for the following examples that the rate of tax for Chapter 13 is 35% and no GST exemption amount is utilized.

   If a taxable termination occurs in a trust containing $1 million in property, the "taxable amount" is $1 million. [IRC § 2622] The GST tax, paid by the trustee, is $350,000. [IRC § 2603(a)(2)] Therefore, $650,000 passes after payment of the GST tax. (Note: A taxable termination is tax inclusive since tax was computed on the $350,000 used to pay the GST tax).

Example (2):   Assume a trust distributes $1 million to a skip person generating a taxable distribution generation-skipping transfer. [IRC § 2612(b)] The taxable amount is $1 million (the amount received by the transferee). [IRC § 2621(a)] The GST tax due is $350,000 and is to be paid by the transferee. [IRC § 2603(a)(1)] Since the tax is computed on the amount used to pay the tax, the transfer is tax inclusive.

Example (3):   T's will bequeaths $650,000 to a skip person, creating a direct skip. [IRC § 2612(c)] The taxable amount is $650,000. [IRC § 2623] GST tax on $650,000 is $227,500 (35% of $650,000) and is paid by the estate. [IRC § 2603(a)(3)] Therefore, the tax and property transferred totals $877,500, or $122,500 less than the prior Examples because a testamentary direct skip is a tax exclusive transaction.

Example (4): T transfers $650,000 to a skip person inter vivos, creating a direct skip generation skipping transfer. [IRC § 2612(c)] The taxable amount is $650,000. [IRC § 2623] GST tax on $650,000 is $227,500 (35% of $650,000) and is to be paid by the transferor. [IRC § 2603(a)(3)] However, the GST tax due is treated as another taxable gift and will increase T's gift tax (but not GST tax) liability. [IRC § 2515] Since a tax will be imposed on the amount used to pay the tax, this is not a purely tax exclusive situation.

2. Applicable Rate

To compute the GST tax, the "taxable amount" is multiplied by the "applicable rate." [IRC § 2602] The applicable rate is the product of the "maximum Federal estate tax rate" multiplied by the "inclusion ratio." [IRC § 2641(a)] The inclusion ratio is computed by subtracting from the number 1 the "applicable fraction" (1 – applicable fraction). [IRC § 2642(a)(1)] To determine the applicable fraction, divide the GST exemption amount allocated to the transfer or trust by the value of the property. [IRC § 2642(a)(2)] The GST exemption "simplifies" the Chapter 13 tax rate by utilizing the inclusion ratio instead of a straight reduction of the transfer amount. Although hard to believe, simplification occurs since the GST exemption applied to a trust remains constant unless some event (like the transfer of additional assets or the allocation of additional GST exemption) creates a need to modify it. [*See* Staff of Joint Comm. on Tax'n, 99th Cong. 2d Sess., General Explanations of the tax Reform Act of 1986 at 1263] This can be very advantageous to a transferor if the trust carries an applicable rate of zero since no GST tax liability exists regardless of the growth of the trust corpus. For 2010 all GST have an applicable rate of zero. [Tax Relief, Unemployment Insurance Reauthorization, and Job Creation Act of 2010, Pub. L. No. 111–312, § 302(c), 124 Stat. 3296, 3300 (2010)]

Example (1): For the following examples assume all transfers occurred in 2011 and that all of T's descendants are living at the time of the transfer.

T transfers $5 million to an irrevocable trust. The trust pays income to GC, T's grandchild, for life, and the remainder to GGC, T's great-grandchild. The trust qualifies as a skip person because GC is a skip person and possesses the trust's only Chapter 13 interest. [IRC §§ 2652(c)(1)(A), 2651(b)(1), 2613(a)] T's transfer is a direct skip generation skipping transfer and is subject to gift tax liability. [IRC § 2612(c)(1)] The taxable amount is $5 million (the value of the property at the time of the transfer). [IRC §§ 2623, 2624(a)] If the entire amount of T's GST exemption is transferred to the trust ($5 million in 2011), the applicable rate will be zero. [IRC §§ 2010(c); 2631(c), 2641(a), 2642(a)] This results in T not paying any Chapter 13 tax on the transfer of the property to the trust. Moreover, when GC dies, no GST tax will be due upon the taxable termination of the trust, since the applicable rate remains zero, even if the corpus of the trust appreciates by the time of GC's death. [IRC §§ 2612(a), 2653(b)(1)]

Example (2): T transfers $5 million to an irrevocable trust, giving the income interest to TS, T's spouse, for TS's life, and the remainder interest to GC. T elects to treat TS's interest as qualified terminable interest property to claim the gift tax marital deduction, but does not make the reverse QTIP election. [IRC §§ 2523(a), (f), 2652(a)(3)] T is subject to gift tax for the gift of GC's remainder interest upon formation of the trust, but since the only Chapter 13 interest in trust is held by a non-skip person (TS), no generation-skipping transfer occurs upon formation. [IRC §§ 2611(a), 2651(c)(1), 2652(c)(1)] When TS dies, the trust corpus is included in TS's gross estate under IRC § 2044(a) and, for Chapter 13 purposes, TS becomes the new transferor. [IRC § 2652(a)(1)(A)] The death of TS creates a direct skip since the transfer was to a skip person (GC) and subject to the estate tax. [IRC § 2612(c)] If T was permitted to allocate any GST exemption upon creation of the trust, it would be lost since no generation-skipping transfer took place while T was the transferor of the trust. [IRC § 2631(a); Reg. § 26.2652–2(d)(ex. 3)]

Example (3): Same facts as Example (2), except that T makes the reverse QTIP election. [IRC § 2652(a)(3)] The reverse QTIP election results in the property being "treated as [if the election] had not been made." [IRC § 2652(a)(3)(flush)] The consequence (for Chapter 13 purposes only) is that no gift tax (on the transfer of the QTIP interest) or estate tax (if TS retains the QTIP interest until death) occur. [IRC §§ 2044, 2519] The applicable rate would be zero, assuming the transfer of T's entire GST exemption to the trust. [IRC §§ 2631(c), 2641(a),

2642(a)] Moreover, T remains the transferor at TS's death (since no estate or gift tax consequences occur for Chapter 13 purposes due to the reverse QTIP election) and the applicable rate of the trust is zero. [IRC § 2641(a)] No Chapter 13 tax is due regardless of how much the trust corpus appreciates and regardless of whether the death of TS results in a taxable termination generation-skipping transfer. A taxable termination occurs instead of a direct skip because no estate tax for Chapter 13 purposes exists on TS's death. [IRC § 2612(a); Reg. § 26.2612–1(b)(1)(i)] This is due to the reverse QTIP election, which treats the QTIP election as having not been made so that IRC § 2044 does not apply for the purposes of Chapter 13. [Reg. § 26.2652–2(d)(ex. 1)]

a) Maximum Estate Tax Rate [IRC § 2641(b)]

The applicable rate is determined by multiplying the maximum Federal estate tax rate by the inclusion ratio. [IRC § 2641(a); Reg. § 26.2641–1] The maximum Federal estate tax rate is easy to determine: it is the highest marginal rate provided for by IRC § 2001(c) at the time the generation-skipping transfer occurs. Currently this is 35%, but from 2003 to 2009 the maximum rate fluctuated and the current 35% rate is scheduled to return to a maximum of 55% in 2013. Because of this fluctuation, if the inclusion ratio is not zero (resulting in a zero tax rate) for a trust, then the rate is computed at the time the generation-skipping transfer occurs and not at the moment property is transferred to a trust. [IRC § 2641(b)]

b) Inclusion Ratio

(1) General Rule

Chapter 13's tax rate is expressed in a single figure, the applicable rate. The applicable rate is computed by multiplying the maximum Federal estate tax rate by the **inclusion ratio**. The maximum Federal tax rate is discussed above and is easy to determine; all that is required to know is the year in which the generation-skipping transfer took place and the estate tax rate tables for the highest marginal rate for that year. The inclusion ratio is more difficult to determine because it incorporates the GST exemption into the computation of the Chapter 13 tax. In general, the inclusion ratio is computed by subtracting the applicable fraction from the number 1. [IRC § 2642(a)(1)] The applicable fraction is computed by taking the amount of GST exemption allocated (if any) to the transaction or trust, divided by the value of the property received (for direct skips or taxable distributions) or the value of the trust (for taxable terminations), less any federal or state tax paid and charitable deductions allowed on the property. [IRC § 2642(a)(2)]

Inclusion ratio = 1 – [applicable fraction]

Applicable fraction = (GST exemption) ÷ [value – (federal and state death taxes + charitable deductions)]

The inclusion ratio adjusts the applicable rate between the maximum Federal estate tax rate (35% in 2011) and zero. If the transferor of property assigns an amount of GST exemption equal to the value of the property transferred (less certain taxes and charitable deductions), the applicable fraction is 1 and the inclusion ratio equals zero (1 – 1), providing for a zero applicable rate and no Chapter 13 taxation. If no GST exemption is allocated, the applicable fraction is zero, the inclusion ratio is 1 (1 – 0), resulting in an applicable rate equal to the maximum Federal estate tax rate at the time of the generation-skipping transfer. If the GST exemption allocated to the transaction is somewhere in between zero and the value of the property, the applicable fraction (and, thus, the inclusion ratio) will be between zero and one. This creates an applicable rate somewhere between the maximum estate tax rate and zero.

Unless one of several events occurs, the inclusion ratio remains with the trust and assists in the computation of the applicable rate for any future taxable distributions or taxable terminations [IRC § 2653(b)(1)], regardless of whether the trust's value increases or decreases over time. The inclusion ratio can change if the transferor changes (because the trust is subject to the gift or estate tax) [IRC § 2652(a)(1)] if property is added to the trust or additional GST exemption is allocated to the trust [IRC § 2642(d)(1), (4)], if the trust is severed [IRC § 2642(a)(3)] or consolidated with another trust [Reg. § 26.2642-4(a)(2)], and if a trust undergoes a taxable termination. [IRC § 2653(b)(1)] These and other provisions dealing with the recomputation of the inclusion ratio are discussed *supra* in III. D. 2. b) (3) [Exceptions to the General Rules for Computation of the Applicable Fraction and Inclusion Ratio].

The issues analyzed here are the amount of GST exemption, the valuation of the property or trust (how and when), and any exceptions to either the general rule of the inclusion ratio or the valuation rules. Like most things in the Code, if completed in a step-by-step manner the material is more easily understood rather than trying to achieve a global understanding in the first read.

Example (1):   T creates an irrevocable trust that will accumulate income for ten years, after which the accumulated income is to be distributed to C, T's child, and the trust's corpus paid to GC, T's grandchild. T transfers $100,000 to the trust, and also allocates $100,000 of T's GST exemption to the trust on a timely filed gift tax return. The applicable fraction is 1 ($100,000 of GST exemption divided by the $100,000 value of the trust). [IRC § 2642(a)(2)] Since the applicable fraction is 1, the inclusion ratio is zero (1 – 1). [IRC § 2642(a)(1)] An inclusion ratio of zero means that the applicable rate is also zero, since applicable rate is calculated by taking the maximum Federal estate tax rate and multiplying it by a zero inclusion ratio, giving a product of zero. [IRC § 2641(a)] After ten years when the taxable termination takes place no GST tax will be due.

Example (2):   Same facts Example (1), except that T allocates no GST exemption to the trust. Now the applicable fraction equals zero ($0 GST exemption divided by the $100,000 value of the trust) and the inclusion ratio totals 1 (1 – 0). [IRC § 2642(a)] The applicable rate is the maximum federal estate tax rate when C's interest in the trust terminates after ten years.

Example (3):   Same facts as Example (1), except that T allocates $40,000 of GST exemption to the trust on a timely filed gift tax return. [IRC § 2632(a)] The applicable fraction is 0.4 ($40,000 GST exemption divided by the $100,000 value of the trust). [IRC § 2642(a)(2)] The inclusion ratio is 0.6 (1 minus the applicable fraction of 0.4). [IRC § 2642(a)(1)] Assuming the maximum federal estate tax rate upon termination of the trust is 35%, the applicable rate is 14%, which equals the product of the maximum Federal estate tax rate (35%) and the inclusion ratio (40%). [IRC § 2641(a)] [Reg. § 26.2642–1(d)(ex. 1)]

(a) Exceptions to General Rule for Inclusion Ratio: Zero Inclusion Ratio for Direct Skips of Transfers Excluded from Gift Tax Under IRC § 2503(b)

The one exception to the general rule for computing the inclusion ratio concerns certain direct skips resulting from nontaxable gift transfers. [IRC § 2642(c)] Chapter 13 provides two types of "nontaxable gifts." [IRC § 2642(c)(3)] The first is for amounts equal to or less than the gift tax annual exclusion amount under IRC § 2503(b) ($13,000 in 2011). [IRC § 2642(c)(3)(A)] The second is for direct payment of educational or medical expenses to providers under IRC § 2503(e). [IRC § 2642(c)(3)(B); for a complete discussion of IRC § 2503(e) *see supra* II. B. 4. b) (2).] However, the zero inclusion ratio for IRC § 2503(e) payments is unnecessary since those amounts are never considered a direct skip because they are not "subject to" the gift tax (one of the requirements of a direct skip). [IRC § 2612(c)(1)]

Where a nontaxable gift transfer results in a direct skip, the transfer, in whole or in part, receives a zero inclusion ratio, even if no GST exemption has been allocated. The automatic zero inclusion ratio only applies to direct skips and does not apply to a generation-skipping transfer by taxable termination or taxable distribution.

i) Transfers Not In Trust

Any direct skip resulting from a nontaxable gift transfer not in trust is automatically given a zero inclusion ratio. [IRC § 2642(c)(1); Reg. § 26.2642–1(c)(3)] If the total amount transferred as a direct skip is less than the IRC § 2503(b) exclusion amount, it does not have to be reported to the Service. [2009 Instruction for Form 709, p. 1, 3] Note that direct skips in trust must always be reported to the IRS. If the amount of the inter vivos transfer is greater than the IRC § 2503(b) exclusion amount, the application of the zero inclusion ratio rule requires treating the transaction as two separate transfers: one with a zero inclusion ratio, the other with an inclusion ratio computed in the normal manner.

Example: In 2011, T gifts $33,000 to GC, T's grandchild, at a time when T's daughter (GC's mother) is living. The transfer constitutes a direct skip since the transfer was to a skip person and subject to the gift tax. [IRC § 2612(c)(1)] The transfer is split into two separate transfers for GST purposes. The first transfer in the amount of $13,000 (the IRC § 2503(b) limit in 2011), is given an inclusion ratio of zero. [IRC § 2642(c)(1)] The second transfer, in the amount of $20,000, has an inclusion ratio determined under the normal rules.

ii) Transfers in Trust

Direct skip transfers made by a trust have additional requirements to qualify for the automatic zero inclusion ratio. These additional requirements prevent the automatic zero inclusion ratio from shielding subsequent generation-skipping transfers from the trust. Absent these requirements, remote beneficiaries with *Crummey* powers could permanently shield transfers to trusts from the GST tax. [S. Rep. No. 445, 110th Cong., 2d Sess. 367, 376 (1988)]

The first additional requirement is that trust income may only be distributed for the benefit of the beneficiary during the beneficiary's life. [IRC § 2642(c)(2)(A); Reg. § 26.2642–1(c)(3)(i)] Trust income may be used for another person's support only if it is disregarded as an interest under IRC § 2652(c)(3). [*See* III. B. 3. b) discussing when an interest is disregarded.] The second requirement is that the trust corpus must be included in the beneficiary's gross estate if the individual dies before the termination of the trust. [IRC § 2642(c)(2)(B); Reg. § 26.2642–1(c)(3)(ii)] In effect, then, the automatic zero inclusion ratio for transfers in trust applies where the beneficiary is treated as owning the property and the trust assets are not held for the benefit of (and will not be distributed to) others.

These rules only apply to transfers made on or after April 1, 1988. [P.L. 101–508, § 11703(c) (1990)] The rules before that time were similar, but are outside the scope of this work.

Example (1):   T creates an irrevocable trust that pays income to GC, T's grandchild, for life. At GC's death, the remainder is to be divided among T's three great-grandchildren. The trust gives each of T's great-grandchildren a right to withdraw up to $120,000 from the corpus of the trust for 30 days following any transfers to the trust (a.k.a. a *Crummey* power). T transfers $40,000 to the trust. The transfer is not included in T's taxable gifts for the year due to the IRC § 2503(b) exclusion (not adjusted for inflation), one for GC and three for the great-grandchildren. However, this is a direct skip generation-skipping transfer (the interest in property goes to GC who is a skip person and is "subject to" the gift tax). [*See* III. C. 1. a) (1) (b), discussing the "subject to" element for direct skips] Since the corpus of the trust is not limited to GC, and it is not included in GC's gross estate at GC's death, the transfer does not receive an automatic zero inclusion ratio even though it is a nontaxable direct skip. [IRC § 2642(c)(2), (3)]

Example (2):   T creates an irrevocable trust that pays income to GC, T's grandchild, for life. T also gives GC a testamentary general power of appointment (GPA) over the trust corpus. If GC does not exercise the power, T's great-grandchildren receive the trust corpus in equal shares at GC's death. T transfers $10,000 to the trust and assumes the entire amount is excluded from gift tax under IRC § 2053(b). Since GC is the only person that can take income or corpus during GC's life, and the property will be included in GC's gross estate under IRC § 2041 due to GC's GPA, the $10,000 receives a zero inclusion ratio. [IRC § 2642(c)(1)–(2); Reg. § 26.2642–1(d)(ex. 2)]

Example (3): Same facts as Example (2), except that T transfers $21,000 to the trust. For Chapter 13 purposes the transfer is bifurcated. The $10,000 excluded under IRC § 2503(b) (not adjusted for inflation) receives a zero inclusion ratio. [IRC § 2642(c)(1–2)] The inclusion ratio for the $11,000 excess is computed under the general rules of IRC § 2642. [Reg. § 26.2642–1(d)(ex. 3)]

(2) Applicable Fraction

The **applicable fraction** incorporates the GST exemption amount into the computation of the GST tax. Unless a special rule applies (*see infra* III. D. 2. b) (3)), the applicable fraction is computed by dividing the GST exemption allocated to the transfer (in the case of a direct skip) or trust (in the case of all other generation-skipping transfers) by the value of the property. The value of the property is reduced by certain federal estate or state death taxes and any charitable deductions allowed under IRC sections 2055 or 2522 attributable to the property. [IRC § 2642(a)(2)(B)] This fraction is then put into decimal form and rounded to the nearest one-thousandth (.001). The applicable fraction is then subtracted from 1 to compute the inclusion ratio. [Reg. § 26.2642–1(a)]

Certain types of transactions or transfers receive a special applicable fraction. These are covered *infra* in III. D. 2. b) (3) "Exceptions to the General Rules for Computation of the Applicable Fraction and Inclusion Ratio."

(a) The Numerator of the Applicable Fraction

The numerator of the applicable fraction is generally the amount of GST exemption allocated to the trust or the transferred property (for direct skips not in trust). [Reg. § 26.2642–1(b)(1)] However, in three instances the GST exemption is not necessarily the amount allocated. These instances are generation-skipping transfers within the estate tax inclusion period (ETIP) [Reg. § 26.2642–1(b)(2)], transfers to charitable lead annuity trusts [IRC § 2642(e)], and where there are additional transfers to a trust of property or GST exemption [IRC § 2642(d)]. These exceptions to the general rule of GST exemption allocation are covered in *infra* III. D. 2. b) (3).

Allocation of GST exemption to a transfer or a trust shields the property from GST tax by increasing the applicable fraction (since there is a number greater than zero divided by the value of the property) thereby lowering the inclusion ratio (computed by 1 – (applicable fraction)). If the GST exemption is assigned to a trust, it shelters all or part of the trust property from future GST tax. This is why Congress used the tax rate as opposed to the tax base to apply the exemption amount. The exemption protects trust assets from the GST tax regardless of the amount of appreciation (or depreciation) in value of the property in trust.

Example: T creates an irrevocable trust that pays income to GC, T's grandchild, for life, then to GGC, T's great-grandchild, for life. At GC's death, the remainder will be paid to GGGC, T's great-great-grandchild. T transfers $100,000 to the trust upon its creation and also allocates $100,000 of GST exemption to the transfer on a timely filed gift tax return. The applicable fraction is 1 (the $100,000 GST exemption divided by the $100,000 value of the property). [IRC § 2642(a)(2)] The inclusion ratio is zero (1 less the applicable fraction of 1). [IRC § 2642(a)(1)] The applicable rate is also zero (the product of the highest federal estate tax rate and zero applicable rate is zero). [IRC § 2641] Regardless of the value of the trust when property is distributed (creating taxable distributions) or when GC or GGC die (both events are taxable terminations) the trust will incur no Chapter 13 tax liability.

The analysis for determining the basic GST exemption can be broken down into three primary areas: identifying who can transfer GST exemption, ascertaining how much each permissible transferor can allocate, and the rules for making an allocation of GST exemption. All three areas are covered in turn below.

i) Who is Allowed to Allocate the GST Exemption [IRC § 2631(a)]

(1) General Rule

Every individual has a GST exemption amount that may be allocated to any property for which they are the Chapter 13 transferor. [IRC § 2631(a)] The allocation of the GST exemption can be applied to inter vivos transfers by the donor or to testamentary transfers by the individual's executor. For transfers to a trust with more than one transferor, the trust is split into separate portions and the GST exemption for any one transferor will only serve to reduce the tax on his or her specific portion of the trust. [IRC § 2654(b)(1)]

Recall that the determination of the "transferor" occurs each time the property is subject to either the estate or gift tax. [IRC § 2652(a)(1)] Therefore, if trust property is subject to either the estate or gift tax after the initial transfer creating the trust, the transferor can change, as can the amount of GST exemption required to be allocated.

Example: T creates an irrevocable trust that pays income to C, T's child, for life. C is also given a general power of appointment (GPA) over the trust property, but, if C does not exercise the GPA, the remainder interest goes to GC, T's grandchild. On the initial transfer to the trust, no generation-skipping transfer occurs since C, a non-skip person, has the Chapter 13 interest in the trust. [IRC §§ 2652(c)(1), 2613(b), 2612] In this situation, any GST exemption T assigns to the trust will be wasted since C, and not T, will be the Chapter 13 transferor at C's death. C's GPA causes the trust corpus to be included in C's gross estate and changes the trust's Chapter 13 transferor to C. [IRC §§ 2041(a)(2), 2652(a)(1)(A)] In situations where the possibility of a generation skipping transfer from the trust does not exist the Regulations provide that any GST exemption allocated by T is void. [Reg. § 26.2632–1(b)(4)(i)]

(2) Marital Planning and the GST Exemption

Married couples have the advantage of utilizing two GST exemption amounts, one for the husband and another for the wife. The GST exemption does not transfer, so spouses may only use their GST exemption for those amounts for which they are deemed the transferor. Two techniques help married couples maximize their respective GST exemptions.

The first technique, authorized by IRC § 2652(a)(2), incorporates the gift-splitting provision of the gift tax under IRC § 2513 into Chapter 13. [IRC § 2652(a)(2); *see supra* III. B. 2. b) discussing gift splitting in Chapter 13] By splitting the gift between husband and wife, both spouses may utilize their respective GST exemptions to reduce GST tax consequences.

Example: T gives $2 million in property to GC, T's grandchild. TS, T's wife, consents to split the gift between them. [IRC §§ 2652(a)(2); 2513] The GST exemptions of both T and TS may be used to determine the applicable fraction and inclusion ratio.

The second technique is the reverse QTIP election. [IRC § 2652(a)(3)] Generally, if terminable interest property is transferred to a spouse it will not qualify for the marital deduction for either estate or gift tax purposes. [IRC §§ 2056(b)(1), 2523(b)] The terminable interest rule does not apply, however, when the donor or executor elects to treat the property as "qualified terminable interest property" (QTIP). [IRC §§ 2056(b)(7), 2523(f)] The cost of the election, however, is the later inclusion into the spouse's gross estate if the surviving spouse dies with the interest (or a deemed gift transfer of the remainder interest if the qualified terminable interest property is transferred inter vivos). [IRC §§ 2044(a), 2519(a)] This causes the trust property to be "subject to" the estate or gift tax and creates a new Chapter 13 transferor. Yet if the reverse QTIP election is made, the QTIP election made for estate or gift tax purposes is treated as having not been made for Chapter 13 purposes, thereby allowing the original spouse to remain the transferor, and thus protecting any GST exemption allocated to the trust. [IRC §§ 2652(a)(3), 2631(a)]

Example: In 2011, T transferred $1 million in property to an irrevocable trust that paid income to TS, T's spouse, for life. At TS's death, the remainder would pass to GC, T's grandchild. T elected to treat the property as qualified terminable interest property under IRC § 2523(f) and made a reverse QTIP election under IRC § 2652(a)(3). T transferred all of T's GST exemption amount ($5 million in 2011) to the trust, thereby giving an applicable fraction of "1" and inclusion ratio of "0." [IRC § 2642(a)] When TS dies, the trust corpus is included in TS's gross estate under IRC § 2044. Without the reverse QTIP election, TS would be treated as the new "transferor" of the property for Chapter 13 and the GST exemption would be lost, since the trust is being subject to the estate tax and TS is the decedent. However, because T made the reverse QTIP election, T will continue to be the Chapter 13 transferor. [Reg. § 26.2652–1(a)(5)(ex. 6)] On TS's death, therefore, a taxable termination from T to GC will occur with no GST tax due. [Reg. § 26.2652–2(d)(ex. 1)]

Since 2004, the estate tax applicable exemption amount and the GST exemption are unified. As a result, one can expect the reverse QTIP election to become less popular. Before 2004, the GST exemption amount was greater than the estate tax applicable exemption amount. Therefore, to fully utilize both amounts on the death of the first spouse two trusts were used (also known as "A/B trusts" or "**credit shelter trusts**"). One trust was funded to the amount allowed under the estate tax applicable exemption amount and assigned the same amount of GST exemption. The other trust, a QTIP trust, was allocated the remaining amount of GST exemption. The reverse QTIP election was made to retain the original transferor of the trust in case the surviving spouse transferred the QTIP interest or died with it. Since the amounts are now unified, the entire GST exemption can be allocated to the same trust as the one utilizing the entire estate tax credit. Since the GST exemption is fully allocated, none will remain to shelter amounts in the trust created to take advantage of the marital deduction.

ii) GST Exemption Amount [IRC § 2631(c)]

Over the years the amount of GST exemption has increased. Before 1998, the amount of GST exemption was $1 million. From 1998 until the end of 2003, the GST exemption was indexed for inflation and the amount increased over the years:

Year	Amount
1999	$1,010,000
2000	$1,030,000
2001	$1,060,000
2002	$1,100,000
2003	$1,120,000

Since 2004, the GST exemption amount equals the estate tax applicable exemption amount provided by IRC § 2010(c). [IRC § 2631(c)] Before 2004, the GST exemption amount was always greater than the applicable exemption amount and multiple trusts were used to fully utilize both credits. Starting in 2011 the GST exemption amount is equal to the "basic exclusion amount" under IRC § 2010(c) ($5 million in 2011) and does not include any of the deceased spousal unused exclusion amount. [For an explanation of the deceased spousal unused exclusion amount *see* I. C. 2. a) *supra*] However, the $5 million credit amount is set to expire after 2012, and without Congressional action would return to $1 million. [P.L. 107–16, § 901(a) (2001) as modified by P.L. 111–312, § 101(a)(1) (2010).]

iii) Allocation of GST Exemption

Since the GST exemption lowers the tax rate for generation-skipping transfers, and is not unlimited, prudent use of the GST exemption is important. Due to the GST tax's complexity, several rules assist taxpayers in allocating their GST exemption. This creates a system where the GST exemption may either be automatically allocated [IRC § 2632(b)], allocated by the transferor [IRC § 2631(a)], or, in certain circumstances, allocated as if timely allocated even though the transfer originally did not have any GST exemption allocated to it [IRC § 2632(d)].

The GST exemption amount may be allocated up until the date for filing the individual's federal estate tax return (also taking into account any granted extensions to file). This time period applies even if the filing of an estate tax return is not required. [IRC § 2632(a)(1)] For any inter vivos transfers, any election to allocate must be made subsequent to the transfer of property and may not be made prospectively. [Reg. § 26.2632–1(a)]

Transfers of the GST exemption to trusts must be made to the trust itself and not specific trust assets. [Reg. § 26.2632–1(a)] Additionally, the GST exemption for the trust may be allocated by a formula located in a will or trust document. [Reg. § 26.2632–1(b)(4)(i)]

(1) Inter Vivos Transfers

(a) Direct Skips

The GST exemption amount may be allocated either by default or specific election. The specific election may be made at any time before the federal estate tax return is due, but in most cases will not have the same effect as a timely election. [IRC § 2632(a)(1)] Generally, property is valued as of the time of the late election and not at the time of transfer. [IRC § 2642(b)(3); *see infra* III. D. 2. b) (2) (b) (discussing the valuation of property for the applicable fraction)] However, once made, the election is irrevocable.

i)   Deemed Allocations for Inter Vivos Direct Skips [IRC § 2632(b)]

Any remaining GST exemption (called the "unused portion" in the Code) automatically creates a zero inclusion ratio on all inter vivos direct skips. [IRC § 2632(b)(1); Reg. § 26.2632–1(b)(1)(i)] The amount automatically allocated equals the fair market value of the property at the time of transfer. To forgo the automatic allocation of GST exemption, a transferor must either affirmatively elect to do so on a timely filed gift tax return or pay the GST tax due with respect to the transfer. [IRC § 2632(b)(3); Reg. § 26.2632–1(b)(1)(i)]

The unused portion of the GST exemption is the GST exemption not previously allocated by the transferor or automatically allocated to a direct or indirect generation-skipping transfer. [IRC § 2632(b)(2)] If the amount of the inter vivos direct skip exceeds the value of the unused GST exemption, all of the GST exemption will be allocated to that transfer. [IRC § 2632(b)(1)]

Example: T transfers $100,000 to a trust, resulting in a direct skip generation-skipping transfer. T timely files a gift tax return (Form 709) on which both T and T's spouse elect to treat the gift as split under IRC § 2513, but do not elect out of the automatic allocation of GST exemption.

The transfer is treated as $50,000 each from T and TS, with both being treated as the transferor of the property to the trust. [IRC 2652(a)(2)] Both spouses will have automatically allocated $50,000 of their respective GST exemption amount. The automatic allocation creates an inclusion ratio and applicable rate of zero. [IRC § 2632(b)(1); Reg. § 26.2632–1(b)(4)(iii)(ex. 5)]

ii)   Transferor's Election to Allocate GST Exemption

A transferor must affirmatively elect out of the automatic allocation of GST exemption to inter vivos direct skips. [IRC § 2632(b)(3)] The election may be made in two ways. First, the election may be made on a gift tax return that clearly describes the transaction and states that the transferor elects out of the deemed allocation. [2009 IRS Instructions for Form 709, p. 11] Second, a payment of the GST tax due will prevent the automatic allocation. If a return is filed and payment is made on the transfer it is treated as an election to allocate zero GST exemption. [Reg. § 26.2632–1(b)(1)(i)]

The Regulations provide some relief so that a transferor's erroneous allocation of a GST exemption is not wasted. Except in the case of charitable lead trusts [IRC § 2642(e), discussed *infra* in III. D. 2. b) (3) (a)], a transferor may elect to transfer GST exemption only to the extent of the fair market value of the property, and any amounts of exemption utilized in excess of that amount are void. The allocation is also void if it is made to a trust where there is no possibility of a generation-skipping transfer at the time of the transfer. [Reg. § 26.2632–1(b)(1)(i)]

In order to get a zero inclusion ratio, the applicable fraction must be 1. The applicable fraction is 1 only if the GST exemption equals the value of the property transferred. [IRC § 2642(a)] Since property values fluctuate, the proper time for valuation is important to allocate a sufficient GST exemption. As described in more detail *infra* at III. D. 2. b) (2) (b) (i) (describing the denominator of the applicable fraction), the property value is determined at the time of transfer when the GST exemption is allocated on a timely filed return.

Any modification (increase or decrease) of the GST exemption may be made until the due date of the gift tax return, taking into consideration any granted extensions for filing. With one exception, the allocation becomes irrevocable after the time for filing. [IRC § 2632(b); Reg. § 26.2632–1(b)(1)(ii)]

The exception to the above is IRC § 2642(g). In 2001, Congress attempted to help taxpayers avoid the GST tax by allowing that, if an allocation is not sufficient to create a zero inclusion ratio, any unused GST exemption is deemed allocated if the transferor "demonstrates an intent to have the lowest possible inclusion ratio." [IRC § 2642(g)(2)] Examination of the trust instrument, transfer documents, or other factors the Service deems relevant can be used to determine the transferor's intent. [IRC § 2642(g)(2)(last sentence)]

Also, in 2001 Congress provided that the Service could proscribe regulations allowing for circumstances to grant extensions of time to make the election to allocate GST exemption for direct skips. [IRC § 2642(g)(1)(A)(ii)] The proposed regulations allow for relief when facts indicate the taxpayer "acted reasonably and in good faith, and that the grant of relief will not prejudice the interests of the Government." [Prop. Reg. § 26.2642–7]

Example (1): On December 1, Year 1, T transfers $30,000 to an irrevocable trust. The transfer is a direct skip generation-skipping transfer. On February 1, Year 2, T files a gift tax return and allocates $20,000 of GST exemption to the transfer. On April 1, Year 2, before the April 15 due date for the gift tax return for Year 1, T files an amended return clearly allocating $30,000 of GST exemption to the December 1, Year 1, transfer. The April 1 allocation supersedes the February 1 allocation and applies to the December 1 transfer. [Reg. § 26.2632–1(b)(1)(ii), –1(b)(4)(iii)(ex. 1)]

Example (2): Same facts as Example (1), except T files the amended return after April 15, Year 2. The February 1 allocation of $20,000 is irrevocable and may not be changed by an untimely modification. [Reg. § 26.2632–1(b)(1)(ii), –1(b)(4)(iii)(ex. 2)]

Example (3): T made $1.5 million of inter vivos generation-skipping transfers through Year 5 and allocated all of T's GST exemption ($1.5 million through Year 5) to those transfers. In Year 6, the GST exemption amount increased to $2.0 million. [IRC § 2631(c)] T could allocate the unused portion of T's GST exemption ($500,000) to future generation-skipping transfers, but T may not allocate that amount to any former transfers, unless those transfers were in trust. [2009 IRS Instructions to Form 709, p. 11] Any allocation of the amount to a trust will be under IRC § 2642(d)(4) discussed *infra* at III. D. 2. b) (3) (d).

iii) Estate Tax Inclusion Period

If a transfer is a direct skip but the property would be includible in the transferor's gross estate after the transfer, it is subject to the estate tax inclusion period ("ETIP"). [IRC § 2642(f)] Any GST exemption allocation is irrevocable, but not effective until the termination of the ETIP. [IRC § 2642(f)(1)(flush); Reg. § 26.2632–1(c)(1)(ii)] For a full discussion of the ETIP *see infra* III. D. 2. b) (3) (b).

(b) Transfers, Not Direct Skips, to a Trust

GST exemption may be allocated to a trust created after 2001 in three different ways. First, certain trusts receive an automatic allocation if the transferor does not elect out. [IRC § 2632(c)] Second, the transferor may make a specific GST exemption allocation to the trust. [IRC § 2631(a)] Third, under certain specific circumstances a transferor may retroactively make an allocation of GST exemption to trusts. [IRC § 2632(d)]

i) Automatic Allocation of GST Exemption to Trusts [IRC § 2632(c)]

While there has always been a deemed allocation of GST exemption for direct skips, before 2001 no corresponding automatic allocation existed for other transfers to a trust. After 2001, transfers to certain trusts are allowed a deemed allocation of GST exemption. Congress added this provision to provide relief for missed allocations due to inadvertent omissions or defective elections. [H. Rep. No. 107–37, 35].

The automatic allocation is allowed for all "indirect skips." [IRC § 2632(c)(1)] An indirect skip occurs when there is a (1) transfer of property "subject to" gift taxation, (2) not a direct skip, (3) made to a "GST trust." [IRC § 2632(c)(3)(A)] To be "subject to" gift taxation does not require actual gift tax liability, therefore transfers shielded from the gift tax by exclusions or deductions are eligible for the deemed allocation. The determination of what is a "GST trust" is discussed directly below in the next section.

If the deemed allocation applies, any unused GST exemption is allocated to the trust to the extent required for a zero inclusion ratio. If the value of property transferred to the trust exceeds the unused GST exemption, then the entire unused portion is allocated to make the inclusion ratio as small as possible. [IRC § 2631(c)(1)] In order to avoid the deemed allocation, an affirmative election out is required. [IRC § 2632(c)(5)]

(1) GST Trusts [IRC § 2632(c)(3)(B)]

A "GST trust" is any trust subject to a possible future taxable termination or taxable distribution not specifically exempt from such consideration. [IRC § 2632(c)(3)(B) (intro language)] There are six different types of trusts not treated as GST trusts. These trusts can be sorted into two categories: 1) trusts with significant distributions to non-skip persons, and 2) trusts which will be included in non-skip person's gross estates. [IRC § 2632(c)(3)(B)(i)–(vi); RICHARD STEPHENS ET. AL., FEDERAL ESTATE & GIFT TAXATION ¶ 15.03[4][b][iii] (8th ed. 2002)] These six trusts do not receive the deemed allocation since the principal amount of these trusts is likely to be distributed to (or included, in the gross estates of) non-skip persons, which would mean the GST exemption would either not be fully utilized or lost.

Two special rules apply to determine the treatment of a GST trust. First, any right to withdraw property from the trust that is limited to the annual exclusion amount or less (as of 2011, $13,000) is disregarded, meaning that *Crummey* powers do not affect the determination. Second, in valuing the property, all powers of appointment (special or general) held by non-skip persons are treated as if they will not be exercised. [IRC § 2632(c)(3)(B)(flush)]

(a) Trusts With Significant Distributions to Non–Skip Persons

If the trust instrument allows for more than 25% of the trust corpus to be withdrawn by a non-skip person before such person reaches the age of 46, the trust is not a GST trust. [IRC § 2632(c)(3)(B)(i)] Also excluded are trusts where more than 25% of the corpus must be distributed or withdrawn by a non-skip person who receives the interest only if he or she must survive a person that is ten years older than that individual. [IRC § 2632(c)(3)(B)(ii)]

Moreover, trusts that either contain certain charitable interests or were allowed a deduction for certain charitable interests are also excluded. [IRC § 2632(c)(3)(B)(v)] Therefore, charitable lead annuity trusts [IRC § 2642(e)(3)(A)], as well as charitable remainder annuity or unitrusts [IRC § 664(d)] are not treated as GST trusts since charitable trusts are non-skip persons. [IRC § 2651(f)(3); 2613(b)] Finally, charitable lead trusts are not GST trusts if a non-skip person takes the corpus of the trust after the completion of the charitable lead interest. [IRC § 2632(c)(3)(B)(vi)]

Example: T creates an irrevocable trust that pays income to C, T's child, for life, and the remainder to C's children per stirpes. The trust provides that 30% of the trust corpus be distributed to C when C reaches the age of 30. Since more than 25% of the trust corpus is to be withdrawn before C reaches 46 years of age the trust is not a GST trust. [IRC § 2632(c)(3)(B)(i)] Unless T makes an affirmative election, the GST exemption automatic allocation rules will not apply. [IRC § 2632(c)(3)(B); (c)(5)(A)(ii)]

(b) Trusts to be Included in the Gross Estate of a Non–Skip Person

If any portion of the trust would be included in a non-skip person's gross estate if that non-skip person died immediately after the transfer, it does not qualify as a GST trust. [IRC § 2632(c)(3)(B)(iv)]

Example: T creates an irrevocable trust that pays income to C, T's child, for life, and the remainder to GC, T's grandchild. C possesses a general power of appointment over 1% of the trust corpus. Since 1% of the value of the trust will be included in C's gross estate at C's death [IRC § 2041(a)(2)], the trust is not a GST trust and, unless an election is made to treat it as such, will not qualify for the deemed allocation of GST exemption. [IRC § 2632(c)(3)(B)(iv)]

If all or a significant portion of a trust will be included in non-skip person's gross estate it is not treated as a GST trust. If more than 25% of the trust corpus is to be distributed to a non-skip person's estate if such person dies before the age of 46 or before someone ten years their senior dies, the trust is not a GST trust. [IRC § 2632(c)(3)(B)(iii)]

Example: T creates an irrevocable trust that pays income to C, T's child, for life, and the remainder to GC, T's grandchild. The trust provides that if C dies before C's forty-sixth birthday, 30% of the trust corpus is to be distributed to C's estate. The trust is not a GST trust and, unless an election is made to treat it as such, will not qualify for the deemed allocation of GST exemption. [IRC § 2632(c)(3)(B)(iii)]

(2)   Elections for Deemed Allocations

If no election is made, and a GST trust is present, any unused GST exemption is allocated automatically to reduce or eliminate the GST tax. [IRC § 2632(c)(1)] Three different elections may be made under IRC § 2632(c)(5) to change this result. The transferor may elect: (1) not to have the deemed allocation apply to the current or a deemed transfer within the estate tax inclusion period [IRC § 2632(c)(5)(A)(i)(I)], (2) to have the deemed allocation never apply to the trust for any current or future transfers [IRC § 2632(c)(5)(A)(i)(II)], or (3) to have the deemed allocations apply to non-GST trusts. [IRC § 2632(c)(5)(A)(ii)] Therefore, the transferor may elect out of the deemed allocations for GST trusts or into the deemed allocation for non-GST trusts.

The time period to make the election depends on the type of election sought. An election not to apply the deemed allocation to the current transfer, but not to the trust forever, must be made on a timely filed gift tax return for the period in which the transfer was made. If the transfer was one made during the estate tax inclusion period, the election may be made on a timely return filed for the year in which the ETIP ends. [IRC § 2632(c)(5)(B)(i)]-

The election to exclude a trust permanently from the deemed allocation or to apply the deemed allocation to a non-GST trust may be made on a timely filed gift tax return for the calendar year the transferor wants the election to be effective. [IRC § 2632(c)(5)(B)(ii)] Since the election is not required in the year of transfer, it may be made any time before the earlier of when the GST tax is due or the estate tax return is required to be filed.

ii) Elective Allocation

As stated above in III. D. 2. b) (2) (a) iii) (1) (b) ii) (for the election out of the deemed allocation), a transferor may elect out of having any GST exemption allocated to a trust. [IRC § 2632(c)(5)(A)(i)] If the transferor makes such an election, then a transferor will either have a zero allocation to the trust or may allocate as much of the transferor's GST exemption as desired up to the amount of T's unused GST exemption at that time. [IRC § 2631(a)] The allocation may be made by a formula, except for charitable lead annuity trusts if the value is not dependent on the amount determined for the gift tax. [Reg. § 26.2632–1(b)(4)(i)]

In two instances an allocation of GST exemption is not effective, both benefitting the transferor. First, if the transferor allocates an exemption amount to the trust greater than that required to receive a zero inclusion ratio (i.e., an amount greater than the FMV of the property transferred), the GST exemption amount is limited to the amount required to provide a zero inclusion ratio. The second situation is where the trust has no (not just a negligible) potential to be taxed under Chapter 13. [Reg. § 26.2632–1(b)(4)(i)]

Example: T creates a trust with C, T's child, and GC, T's grandchild, as beneficiaries. C holds the right to income from the trust and also possesses a general power of appointment over the trust property. GC has the remainder interest. Any GST exemption allocation by T will be void since the trust will never incur any GST tax consequences because on C's death or exercise of the power, C becomes the Chapter 13 transferor with no generation-skipping transfers possible at that time or later. [Reg. § 26.2632–1(b)(4)(i)]

A transferor may elect out of automatic allocations for future transfers, regardless if the trust is currently in existence. The election out can be made for transfers to a trust (or trusts) for the current year, a certain time period, or all future transfers. [Reg. § 26.2632–1(b)(2)(iii)(A)] To elect out the transferor must attach a statement to timely filed Form 709 identifying the trust and specifically providing the transferor is electing out of the automatic GST exemption. [Reg. § 26.2632–1(b)(2)(iii)(B)]

Example (1): On August 4, Year 1, T transfers $100,000 to Trust XYZ, a GST trust under IRC § 2632(c)(3)(B). Later, on August 25 of the same year, T transfers $75,000 to the trust. Attached to T's timely filed Form 709 is a statement that reads "T hereby elects that the automatic allocation rules will not apply to the $100,000 transferred to Trust XYZ on August 4, Year 1." The automatic allocation will not apply to the $100,000 transfer, but will apply to the $75,000 transfer on August 25. [Reg. § 26.2632–1(b)(4)(iv)(ex. 1(i))]

Example (2): Same facts as Example (1), but T's statement reads "T hereby elects that the automatic allocation rules will not apply to any transfers to Trust XYZ in Year 1." The automatic allocation will not apply to any of the transfers made in Year 1. [Reg. § 26.2632–1(b)(4)(iv)(ex. 1(ii))]

Example (3): Same facts as Example (1), but T's statement reads "T hereby elects that the automatic allocation rules will not apply to any transfers T has made or will make to Trust XYZ in the Years 1, 2 or 3." The automatic allocation will not apply to any of the transfers made to the trust in those years. T may terminate the election for Year 2 or 3 before the gift tax filing date of the respective years. [Reg. § 26.2632–1(b)(4)(iv)(ex. 1(iv))]

Example (4): Same facts as Example (1), but T's statement reads "T hereby elects that the automatic allocation rules will not apply to any current or future transfer that T may make to any trust." The automatic allocation will not apply to any of the transfers T makes to any trust until T terminates such election. [Reg. § 26.2632–1(b)(4)(iv)(ex. 1(v))]

The primary issue for elective allocations is how much to allocate, which in turn is generally driven by the value of the property involved in the transfer and/or already in the trust. The value of the property is discussed in greater detail *infra* in III. D. 2. b) (2) (b) i) (discussing the property valuation for the applicable fraction). However, the valuation time is controlled by whether a timely gift tax return was filed or not.

(1) Timely Filing

A timely filed GST exemption allocation election is effective as of the date of the transfer. An election is timely if made on a gift tax return before the due date under IRC § 6075(b) (April 15 of the year following the transfer), including any extensions granted. The return is deemed filed on the postmark date. Modifications of the allocated amount may be made until the due date of the return. [Reg. § 26.2632–1(b)(4)(ii)(A)(1)] After the filing date however, any GST exemption allocation is irrevocable. [IRC § 2631(b)] For a timely filing, the property is valued as of its fair market value at the time of transfer. [IRC § 2642(b)(1); *see infra* III. D. 2. b) 2) (b) i).]

Example (1): On November 1, Year 1, T transfers $100,000 to an irrevocable trust in a transfer that is not a direct skip. At some time in the future the trust will either be subject to a taxable termination or taxable distribution generation-skipping transfer. On February 10, Year 2, when the property in the trust is worth $150,000, T files a gift tax return (IRS Form 709) electing out of the deemed allocation and allocating $50,000 GST exemption to the trust. Later, on April 10, Year 2, T files an amended gift tax return allocating a total of $100,000 of GST exemption to the trust. The $100,000 allocation will relate back to the time of transfer on November 1, Year 1. Since the value of the trust was $100,000 at that time the applicable fraction of the trust will be "1" and the inclusion ratio will be zero (1–1). [Reg. § 26.2632–1(b)(4)(iii)(ex. 1)]

Example (2): Same facts as Example (1), except that T files another amended return on July 10, Year 2, in an attempt to reduce the amount of GST exemption. Since T had already filed a timely return and the last amended return was filed after the due date of April 15, Year 2, no modification in the GST exemption amount is allowed. [IRC § 2631(b)] The last GST exemption amount of $100,000 controls for the allocation to the trust and is irrevocable after the due date for the gift tax return. [Reg. § 26.2632–1(b)(4)(iii)(ex. 2)]

(2) Election After Filing Date

An election made after the due date for filing a timely return is effective as of the filing date for the return, assuming no return was timely filed. [Reg. § 26.2632–1(b)(4)(ii)(A)(1)] This is different than for a timely filed return that relates back to the time of transfer. [*See supra* III. D. 2. b) (2) (a) (iii) (1) (b) ii) (1) discussing timely filing] The return is deemed filed on the postmark date. [*Id.*] For the valuation of property related to an untimely allocation of GST exemption *see infra* III. D. 2. b) (2) (b) i) (1) (b).

As a practical matter, the GST exemption is deemed allocated if no election is made, and a late election will most likely occur only if the trust corpus depreciates in value from the time of transfer. If the trust has depreciated in value, then making a late election (as opposed to using the automatic allocation at the time of transfer) may save some GST exemption. In other words, less exemption would be necessary to receive an inclusion ratio of zero if the later election is made.

Example: On November 1, Year 1, T transfers $100,000 to an irrevocable trust in a transfer that is not a direct skip. At some time in the future, the trust will generate either a taxable termination or taxable distribution generation-skipping transfer. On July 10, Year 2, with the trust property worth $75,000, T files a gift tax return (IRS Form 709) electing out of the deemed allocation and allocating $50,000 GST exemption to the trust. The allocation occurs on a late return and is effective as of July 10, Year 2. The applicable fraction is 0.667 ($50,000 ÷ $75,000), which gives an inclusion ratio of 0.333 (1–0.667). [Reg. § 26.2632–1(b)(4)(iii)(ex. 3)]

As in the election for direct skips, if an allocation does not create a zero inclusion ratio and unused GST exemption is present, a transferor's demonstrated intent to "have the lowest possible inclusion ratio" allows for more GST exemption to be deemed allocated. [IRC § 2642(g)(2)] An examination of the trust instrument, transfer documents, or any other factors the Service deems relevant can be used to demonstrate intent. [IRC § 2642(g)(2)(last sentence)]

(c) Retroactive Allocation [IRC § 2632(d)]

On a chronological basis, a transferor may retroactively allocate unused GST exemption as if he or she had done so at the time of the original transfer. The retroactive allocation is available in certain cases where a lineal descendant of a grandparent of the transferor predeceases the transferor. [IRC § 2632(d)] The rationale for this provision is to provide relief for a transferor when an "unnatural order of death" occurs (i.e., T's child dies before T) and no GST exemption was allocated to reduce the GST tax consequences. [H.R. Rep., No. 107–37, 37]

This rule should not be confused with the predeceased parent rule of IRC § 2651(e)(1), which changes the generational assignment of a lineal descendent (generally making the descendant a non-skip person). [*See supra* III. B. 4. c) (1), for a complete discussion of the predeceased parent rule.] The predeceased parent rule applies if the death of the descendent occurs *before* the generation-skipping transfer, [IRC § 2651(e)(1)(B)], whereas the retroactive allocation of GST exemption is allowed only if the death occurs *after* the transfer. [IRC § 2632(d)(1)(A), (C)]

(i)   Elements for Retroactive Allocation

Several elements must be satisfied in order for the retroactive allocation rule to apply. First, a non-skip person [IRC § 2613(b)] must have a current or future interest in a trust to which the transferor has made a transfer. [IRC § 2632(d)(1)(A)] Any right to income or corpus from the trust at a future date is deemed a future interest. [IRC § 2632(d)(3)] Second, the non-skip person must predecease the transferor. [IRC § 2632(d)(1)(C)] Third, only non-skip persons who are in both a lower generation than the transferor and who are also lineal descendants of the grandparent of the transferor (or the transferor's spouse or former spouse) qualify. [IRC § 2632(d)(1)(B)] This includes children, nieces and nephews, and grandchildren if the predeceased parent rule of IRC § 2651(e) does not apply. Finally, the allocation must be made on a timely filed gift tax return made for the year of the non-skip person's death. [IRC § 2632(d)(2)(intro.)]

The legislative history states that the retroactive allocation is applicable for any trust where the non-skip person dies after the year

2000. The formation date of the trust does not control. [H.R. Rep. No. 107–37, 37]

(ii) Effect of Retroactive Allocation

If the above elements for retroactive allocation are satisfied, the transferor may allocate the transferor's unused GST exemption retroactively to any transfer(s) to a trust on a chronological basis. [IRC § 2632(d)(1)(flush)] As its name implies, the retroactive allocation is deemed made at the time of the original transfer(s). [IRC § 2632(d)(2)] This is important for two reasons. First, the value of the property is determined as of the time of the original transfer, not at the later time of the non-skip person's death or the filing of the gift tax return. [IRC § 2632(d)(2)(A)] Second, the retroactive allocation is deemed effective before the non-skip person's death, thereby protecting the trust assets from GST taxation. [IRC § 2632(d)(2)(B)] The amount of unused GST exemption allocable is determined on the date of the non-skip person's death so any increases in the GST exemption limit may be utilized. [IRC § 2632(d)(2)(C)]

Example: T transferred $100,000 to an irrevocable trust in 1995. The trust pays income to C, T's child, for life and the remainder to GC, T's grandchild. In 1997 and 1999, T transferred an additional $100,000 (making the total amount of transfers to the trust $300,000). Since C is a non-skip person with an interest in the trust, the transfers were not generation-skipping transfers. Also, the deemed allocation rules of IRC § 2632(c) were not applicable since they only apply to trusts created after 2001. T never made any elective GST exemption allocation. C died on January 1, 2001, at a time when the trust has a total value of $1 million. Under IRC § 2632(d), T may elect to use any of T's unused GST exemption ($1,030,000 if T had made no past allocations) to the trust. If T filed a timely gift tax return for 2001, T may allocate the GST exemption of $100,000 to the transfers that occurred in 1995, 1997 and 1999, making the property value determined as of the time of the original transfer. This gives the trust a zero inclusion ratio and no GST tax consequences.

(2) Testamentary Transfers

Any unused GST exemption at T's death may be used to protect testamentary or inter vivos transfers made by the decedent from the GST tax. The executor may do this before the estate tax return is due (with extensions). If no allocations are made, the GST exemption is allocated automatically. [IRC §§ 2631(a), 2632(a), (d)(1)] Regardless of whether a return is required for the estate, the last day for the executor to make an election is on the date the estate tax return is due. [Reg. § 26.2632–1(d)(1)]

(a) Executor Election

i) General Rule

An executor may allocate any unused GST exemption among the various transfers occurring at the decedent's death or those made inter vivos. The allocation may be made by formula, but is void if made to a trust that has no (not just a remote) potential of having a generation-skipping transfer (i.e., a taxable termination or direct skip) or to the extent it does not result in the reduction in the amount of Chapter 13 tax. [Reg. § 26.2632–1(d)(1)]

ii) Effective Dates of Allocations

The effective date for an elective GST allocation depends on whether the transfer is allocated to property included in the decedent's gross estate and transferred at death and/or whether it is allocated to an inter vivos transfer.

(1) Allocations of GST Exemption to items included in Decedent's Gross Estate

The allocation is effective at the date of the decedent's death for direct skips from a decedent's gross estate. [Reg. § 26.2632–1(d)(1)]

(2) Allocations of GST Exemption to Inter Vivos Transfers

GST exemption may be allocated at death to trusts or other property transferred by the decedent inter vivos. If not done in a timely manner for the transfer, but before the filing date for the estate tax return, the allocation is effective when the return is filed. [Reg. § 26.2632–1(d)(1)]

(b) Deemed Allocation

If the executor fails to make a timely allocation of the GST exemption then the unused GST exemption is used automatically in order to minimize the GST tax consequences. The unused GST exemption is first used to lower the inclusion ratio of direct skips due to decedent's death. [IRC § 2632(e)(1)(A)] Any remaining amounts are utilized for trusts to which the decedent made inter vivos transfers that also have the possibility of a later taxable termination or taxable distributions. [IRC § 2632(e)(1)(B)]

Deemed allocations of GST exemption are distributed in proportion to the relative nonexempt portion of the trust. [IRC § 2632(e)(2)(A)] The nonexempt portion represents the value of the property at the time of the allocation (generally the estate tax value or fair market value of property not included in the gross estate) multiplied by the inclusion ratio. [IRC § 2632(e)(2)(B)] For property not given any previous allocation of GST exemption this is just the fair market value since the inclusion ratio is one (1 − 0 (applicable fraction)).

(b) The Denominator of the Applicable Fraction

To determine the applicable rate, the inclusion ratio is multiplied by the maximum Federal estate tax rate. [IRC § 2641(a)] The inclusion ratio is 1 minus the applicable fraction, computed to the nearest one-thousandth (.001). [IRC § 2642(a)(1); Reg. § 26.2642–1(a)] The numerator of the applicable fraction is the amount of GST exemption allocated to property in a direct skip, or the amount allocated to the trust in the case of a taxable termination or taxable distribution. [IRC §§ 2642(a)(2)(A), 2631, 2632] The denominator of the applicable fraction is the value of the property less the sum of any applicable federal estate and state death taxes and any charitable deductions. [IRC § 2642(a)(2)(B)] This section of the outline discusses the denominator of the applicable fraction, specifically how and when to value the property, the effective date, and the reductions allowed.

i) Valuation and Effective Date

Generally, IRC § 2642(b) provides the rules for both valuing property and determining the effective date for any allocation of GST exemption. The rules were modified in 2001 to "clarify the valuation rules relating to timely and automatic allocations of generation-skipping transfer tax exemption." [H.R. Rep. No. 107–37, Act § 563] Except for a few specific instances, the valuation of the property is the same as in the relevant gift or estate tax sections.

(1) Inter Vivos Transfers

Depending on the timely filing of a gift tax return or the estate tax inclusion period, three different times for property valuation and effective dates exist for inter vivos transfers. The time periods range from the time of transfer to the end of the estate tax inclusion period.

(a) Timely Filed Gift Tax Return [IRC § 2642(b)(1)]

If a timely gift tax return is filed [*see infra* III. E. 2. for a discussion of the filing rules], the value of the property is taken from the gift tax return (the fair market value of the property on the date of the gift). [IRC § 2642(b)(1)(A)] Any GST exemption is effective as of the date of the transfer. [IRC § 2642(b)(1)(B)]

(b) Gift Tax Return Not Timely Filed [IRC § 2642(b)(3)]

If a transferor files a late gift tax return and elects out of the automatic allocation under IRC § 2632(b), valuation of the property can occur at one of two different time periods. If no election is made, the property is valued at the time the late gift tax return is filed (which is the postmark date if mailed). [IRC § 2642(b)(3)(A); Reg. § 26.2632–1(b)(4)(ii)] The transferor can also elect to value the property as of the first day of the month during which the late allocation is made. [Reg. § 26.2642–2(a)(2)] Regardless of when the property is valued, the effective date for any allocation is the date that the gift tax return is filed. [IRC § 2642(b)(3)(B)]

Example (1): On December 15, 2000, T created an irrevocable trust with property valued at $100,000. The trust provides that the trust's income shall be paid to C, T's child, for ten years, after which the corpus is to be distributed to GC, T's grandchild. T fails to allocate any GST exemption to the trust on the gift tax return reporting the transaction and no automatic allocation to non-direct skip transfers applied to trusts before 2002. On November 15, 2001, T filed a gift tax return allocating $50,000 of GST exemption to the trust. The trust property at the time of filing was worth $150,000. The property is valued and the GST exemption is effective on November 15, 2001. The applicable fraction of the trust is 0.333 computed by taking the $50,000 GST exemption allocated and dividing it by the $150,000 value of trust property on November 15, 2001. The inclusion ratio is 0.667 (1 minus the applicable fraction of 0.333). [Reg. § 26.2642–2(c)(ex. 1)]

Example (2): Same facts as Example (1), except the trust's value on November 15, 2001, was $50,000. Now the applicable fraction is 1, determined by taking the $50,000 GST exemption allocated and dividing it by the $50,000 value of trust property on November 15, 2001. The inclusion ratio is zero (1 minus the applicable fraction of 1). [Reg. § 26.2642–2(c)(ex. 2)]

Example (3): On February 1, Year 1, T transfers $100,000 of property to a trust in a transfer that is not a direct skip. T fails to allocate any GST exemption to the trust on the timely gift tax return reporting the transaction and elects out of the automatic allocation. On August 4, Year 2, the trust makes a taxable distribution of $30,000. At that time, the trust's property value has appreciated to $150,000. On the same day as the distribution, T files a gift tax return allocating $50,000 of GST exemption. The allocation of GST exemption is effective on the day of transfer and is deemed to precede the taxable distribution. The applicable fraction of the trust is 0.333 computed by taking the $50,000 GST exemption allocated and dividing it by the $150,000 value of trust property on August 4, Year 2. The inclusion ratio is 0.667 (1 minus the applicable fraction of 0.333). [Reg. § 26.2632–1(b)(4)(iii)(ex. 4)]

(c) Estate Tax Inclusion Period [IRC § 2642(f)(2)]

See infra III. D. 2. b) (3) (b) for a full discussion of the ETIP and when the property is valued.

(d) Valuation Planning

A certain amount of GST tax planning can take place after inter vivos gifts since valuation can take place at various times. If the property value increases, it is best to file a timely gift tax return and value the property at the date of transfer. [IRC § 2642(b)(1)] If the property depreciates in value, it is best to file a late gift tax return and value the property at the time of filing to receive the benefit of a lower property value and less GST exemption required to receive a zero inclusion ratio. [IRC § 2642(b)(3)] This review period can be extended by a timely filed extension request.

(2) Transfers at Death

With one exception, the valuation of the property transferred at death is the estate tax value determined with any elections under IRC §§ 2032 or 2032A. [IRC § 2642(b)(2)(A)] Without any elections made, the estate tax valuation is the fair market value of the property on the date of death. [IRC § 2031(a)] The effective date is the death of the transferor. [IRC § 2642(b)(2)(A)]

In order to prevent the executor from selecting all appreciated or depreciated property to fulfill a pecuniary request, however, estate tax valuation is not used to value distributions of property that satisfy pecuniary bequests unless the executor evenly distributes property that has either decreased or increased in value since the valuation of the property for estate tax purposes. [IRC § 2642(b)(2)(A); Reg. § 26.2642–2(b)(2)(i)] If the property is not equally distributed to account for the appreciation and depreciation in the value of the estate's assets, the property is valued at the time of distribution for purposes of computing the applicable fraction.

Example: T dies and makes a bequest of $1,000 to GC, T's grandchild. T's estate consists of two assets, both valued at $1,000 at the time of T's death. However, at the time of distribution one piece of property has a value of $500, while the other is worth $2,000. T's will provides that the executor may satisfy the bequest by distributing either piece of property at its estate tax value. If the executor distributes the $2,000 piece of property, valuation for determining the applicable fraction occurs at the time of distribution. [IRC § 2642(b)(2)(A)(after the semi-colon)] Therefore, to get an inclusion ratio of zero, a like sum of GST exemption is required. If the executor decides to distribute one-half of each asset, the estate tax value of $1,000 is used and only that amount of GST exemption is required to receive a zero inclusion ratio.

(3) Qualified Terminable Interest Property [IRC § 2642(b)(4)]

When the executor or donor elects to treat terminable interest property transferred to a spouse as qualified terminable interest property ("QTIP"), then a marital deduction is permitted. [IRC §§ 2056(b)(7), 2523(f)] The "cost" of making this election is the inclusion of the property in the receiving spouse's gross estate, so long as it is held until death [IRC § 2044(a)].

If a reverse QTIP election is not made (*see supra* III. B. 2. c) discussing IRC § 2652(a)(3)), the spouse receiving the terminable interest property becomes the "transferor" for Chapter 13 purposes. [IRC § 2652(a)(1)] The value of the property is the estate tax value of property for the spouse who received the terminable interest property. [IRC § 2642(b)(4)] However, if the reverse QTIP election is made, then the value of the property is the value at the time the spouse benefiting from the marital deduction transferred the property.

ii) Reductions for Death Taxes and Charitable Contributions

Federal estate or state death taxes paid, as well as any charitable deductions under IRC §§ 2055 or 2522, reduce the value of the property when computing the denominator of the applicable fraction. [IRC § 2642(a)(2)(B)(ii)] These reductions only apply to property transferred to trusts, since a direct skip cannot be subject to either of the allowable reductions. Since the amount received by the transferee constitutes the taxable amount in a direct skip, it already takes into account any tax paid. Also, since a charity cannot be a skip person [IRC § 2651(f)(3)], a transfer directly to a charity cannot be a generation-skipping transfer.

(1) Federal Estate or State Death Tax Paid

A reduction is allowed for federal estate or state death taxes "actually recovered from the trust attributable to such property." [IRC § 2642(a)(2)(B)(ii)(I); Reg. § 26.2642–1(c)(1)(i)] The rationale for the reduction for taxes paid is that any tax payments made on the transfer from one generation to another would reduce the total amount available for transfer. The reduction allows for the same results when the property is only subject to the generation-skipping tax.

> *Example:*   T dies with an estate valued at $3 million. T's will leaves all of T's property in trust with the income payable to C, T's child, for ten years. At the end of the term, the property is to be transferred to GC, T's grandchild. If the federal estate and state death taxes total $1.4 million, the denominator of the applicable fraction would be $1.6 million ($3 million value of property less the $1.4 million death taxes paid).

(2) Charitable Contributions

The value of an interest in property transferred to a charitable remainder trust (i.e., where the charity receives the remainder interest) or a charitable lead unitrust reduces the value of property in the denominator of the applicable fraction. [IRC § 2642(a)(2)(B)(ii)(II); Reg. § 26.2642–1(c)(1)(ii)] The amounts transferred to a charitable lead annuity trust do not reduce the applicable fraction and the inclusion ratio is determined under IRC § 2642(e) (*see infra* III. D. 2. b) (3) (a) discussing the applicable fraction for charitable lead annuity trusts).

(3) Exceptions to the General Rules for Computing the Applicable Fraction and Inclusion Ratio

For certain trusts or after certain events, the applicable fraction is redetermined to accurately reflect the original use of the GST exemption. The "nontax" portion reflects the amount of the trust protected from GST tax by the GST exemption. Generally, the nontax portion is computed by applying the old applicable fraction to the current value of the property. This effectively protects the same percentage of the trust's current value from the GST tax as was originally protected.

(a) Charitable Lead Annuity Trust [IRC § 2642(e)]

Although not the only charitable deduction, a taxpayer may deduct the present value of the charitable lead interest from his or her federal estate and gift taxes when the lead interest is a guaranteed annuity (e.g., the charity receives $10,000 from the trust each year). [IRC §§ 2055(e)(2)(B), 2522((c)(2)(B)] Congress felt this allowed for leveraging of the exemption amount when the trust assets received a higher rate of return than the factor used in computing the present value of the charitable assets. [S. Rep. No. 445, 100th Cong., 2d Sess. 368 (1988)] To prevent this type of leveraging, both the numerator and denominator of the applicable fraction are determined when the lead charitable annuity interest terminates. [IRC § 2642(e)(1)]

The delay in determining the applicable fraction only applies to charitable lead annuity trusts. [IRC § 2642(e)(1)] A charitable lead annuity trust is any trust that contains a guaranteed annuity interest for which the transferor receives an estate or gift charitable tax deduction. [IRC § 2642(e)(3)] It is important to contrast this exception to trusts that have charitable remainder interests or no non-charitable interests. The applicable fraction for charitable remainder trusts (where the charitable interest is at the end, as opposed to the beginning of the trusts term) is determined at the time of the transfer and the denominator is reduced by the value of the charitable remainder interest. [IRC § 2642(a)(2)(B)(ii)(II); *see supra* III. D. 2. b) (2) (b) ii) covering the deduction for charitable interests.] Trusts with no non-charitable interests cannot have GST tax consequences since charitable organizations are assigned to the transferor's generation and therefore cannot be skip persons. [IRC §§ 2651(f)(3), 2613(a)(1)]

i) Amount of GST Exemption (Numerator of Applicable Fraction)

The numerator of the applicable fraction for charitable lead annuity trusts is the "adjusted GST exemption" amount. [IRC § 2642(e)(1)(A)] The adjusted GST exemption amount is the GST exemption assigned to the trust multiplied by the present value rate used to compute the deduction for the charitable lead annuity and the period of the lead interest. [IRC § 2642(e)(2)] In other words, the GST exemption for charitable lead trusts is the allocated GST exemption increased by the interest it would accrue if invested at the rate used for, and for the time period of, the charitable lead annuity. If the GST exemption allocation occurs after the transfer of property creating the charitable lead trust, the interest starts to accrue from that time. [Reg. § 26.2642–3(b)]

Unlike other GST transfers, the amount of GST exemption assigned to the trust is not limited to the property value in the trust at the time the GST exemption is allocated. [Reg. § 26.2632–1(b)(4)(i)] However, if ultimately the amount of GST exemption is greater than the value of the property, there is no refund. [Reg. § 26.2642–3(b)]

ii) Valuation of Property (Denominator of Applicable Fraction)

The property is valued at its fair market value immediately after the termination of the charitable lead interest. [IRC § 2642(e)(1)(A)]

iii) Examples of Computing the Applicable Fraction for Charitable Lead Trusts

Example (1): T transfers money to an irrevocable trust that is to pay a certain charity $20,000 each year for 20 years. After the 20 years is complete, the corpus of the trust is divided between T's grandchildren per stirpes. T transfers $100,000 of T's GST exemption to the trust. T receives a charitable deduction for the gift and, since this is a charitable lead trust, the applicable fraction is not determined until the charitable lead interest (here 20 years) terminates. [IRC § 2642(e)(1)] If the discount rate to determine the charitable gift tax deduction is 5% semi-annually, and the corpus of the trust is worth $500,000 after 20 years, the GST exemption amount (the numerator of the applicable fraction) is $268,506, computed by calculating the future value of $100,000 in 20 years at 5% compounded semi-annually. [IRC § 2642(e)(2)] The denominator of the applicable fraction is the value of the property at the end of charitable lead interest, $500,000. [IRC § 2642(e)(1)(B)] The applicable fraction is 0.537 ($268,506/$500,000) giving an inclusion ratio of 0.463 (1 – 0.5370). [IRC § 2642(a)] The applicable rate is the product of the maximum estate tax and the inclusion ratio. [IRC § 2641(a)]

Example (2):   Same facts as Example (1), except that at the termination of the charitable lead interest, the trust property declines in value to $200,000. Only $200,000 of the GST exemption (out of the $268,506 possible) is utilized. The applicable fraction is 1 ($200,000/$200,000) and the inclusion ratio is zero (1 – 1). Even though the trust did not use all the allocated GST exemption T does not receive a refund. [Reg. §§ 26.2642–3(b),–3(c)(example)]

(b)   Estate Tax Inclusion Period [IRC § 2642(f)]

Property transferred by an inter vivos transfer that is includable in the transferor's gross estate immediately after the transfer (e.g., T creates a trust giving T the income interest and the remainder to GC, T's grandchild) is subject to the **estate tax inclusion period** ("ETIP"). [IRC § 2642(f)(1)] The application of the ETIP affects three aspects of the computation of the GST tax. First, any allocation of the GST exemption is not effective until the close of the ETIP. [IRC § 2642(f)(1)(flush)] Second, IRC § 2642(f)(2) determines the value of the property. Third, direct skip transfers are treated as occurring at the close of the ETIP. [IRC § 2642(f)(1)(flush)(second sentence)]

Example: T purchases a piece of property and gives a one-half interest in the property interest to GC, T's grandchild. T and GC hold the property as joint tenants with right of survivorship. If T died immediately after the transfer, the property would be included in T's gross estate under IRC § 2040. [*See supra* I. A. 3. b) discussing IRC § 2040] Since this transaction creates an inter vivos direct skip transfer included in T's gross estate immediately after transfer, it is subject to the ETIP rules. [IRC § 2642(f)(1)] The direct skip is treated as occurring at the close of the ETIP and both the GST exemption allocation and the valuation of the property occur at that time. [IRC § 2642(f)(1)(flush)]

The rationale for the ETIP rules is that qualifying transfers are testamentary in nature and, therefore, the GST tax consequences should be delayed until both the estate and gift tax consequences are determined. This limits a transferor's ability to maximize his or her GST exemption by giving lifetime gifts (assuming they have a lower value due to the appreciating nature of the property) while at the same time having some control or enjoyment over the property leading to inclusion in the transferor's gross estate. In many cases, by delaying the determination of GST tax consequences until the end of the ETIP, the appreciation in the value of the property is subject to GST tax.

i)   Property Included in the Estate Tax Inclusion Period

(1)   General Rule

As stated above, the ETIP rules apply to an (1) inter vivos transfer of property, (2) if some or all of the property is includable in the transferor's (or transferor's spouse's) gross estate if the transferor died immediately after the transfer, (3) unless inclusion in the gross estate is caused by IRC § 2035 (re-inclusion of gift transfers made within three years of death under IRC §§ 2036–2038 and 2042). [IRC § 2042(f)(1)(A)–(B), (f)(4); Reg. § 26.2632–1(c)(2)(i)] The estate tax sections that could force inclusion into the transferor's gross estate are: IRC §§ 2036–38 (the re-inclusion provisions), 2039 (annuities), 2040 (joint interests), 2041 (general powers of appointment), and 2042 (proceeds of life insurance).

[*See supra* I. A. 2. to I. A. 3. d) for a detailed explanation of the preceding Code sections.]

If the possibility that the property is included in the gross estate of the transferor or transferor's spouse is "so remote as to be negligible," then the ETIP rules do not apply. A probability of inclusion is so remote as to be negligible if there is less than a five percent probability of inclusion using actuarial standards. [Reg. § 26.2632–1(c)(2)(ii)(A)]

(2) Treatment of Transfer by Spouse

    (a) General ETIP Spousal Transfer Rule

        It is important to note that unless the Regulations provide otherwise, references in IRC § 2642(f) to "individual" or "transferor" include the spouse of the individual/transferor. [IRC § 2642(f)(4)] This means split gifts under IRC § 2513 are possibly subject to the ETIP. In addition, any property allowed a marital deduction due to a QTIP election is covered by the ETIP, unless an exception applies (see directly below). The inclusion is a result of the QTIP property's inclusion in the gross estate of the spouse [under IRC § 2044], which satisfies the second element for application of the ETIP. [*See* Reg. § 26.2632–1(c)(2)(i)(B)]

        Example: T transfers property to an irrevocable trust, retaining the right to income for life, and leaving the remainder interest to GC, T's grandchild. T's spouse, TS, consents to split the gift with T. [IRC § 2513] TS is treated as being the transferor of one-half of the property for purposes of Chapter 13. [IRC § 2652(a)(1)] Since this is an inter vivos transfer that would be included in T's (or T's spouse, TS's) gross estate (under IRC § 2036), the property is subject to the ETIP. [IRC § 2642(f)(1); Reg. § 26.2632–1(c)(2)(i)]

Since TS is the transferor of one-half of the property, TS may allocate GST exemption of up to one-half value of the trust at the time of transfer. [IRC § 2631(a)] However, the allocation will not be effective until the close of the ETIP (until T either transfers the property or dies). [IRC § 2642(f)(3); Reg. § 26.2632–1(c)(5)(ex. 3)]

(b) Exceptions to the ETIP's Application to Spouse

IRC § 2642(f)(4) states that "individual" or "transferor" includes the spouse of such individual or transferor "[e]xcept as provided in regulations." [IRC § 2642(f)(4)] The regulations do provide two exceptions exempting the spouse's portion of the transfer from application of the ETIP. [*See* Reg. § 26.2632–1(c)(2)(ii)(A)–(C)]

i) Spouse Holds a "5 by 5" Power in Trust [Reg. § 26.2632–1(c)(2)(ii)(B)]

A spouse's property interest is not treated as includible in the gross estate (and is therefore not subject to the ETIP rules) if the spouse has the right to withdraw for no more than 60 days after a transfer to a trust the greater of $5,000 or 5% of the trust corpus (known as a "5 by 5 power"). [Reg. § 26.2632–1(c)(2)(ii)(B)] Therefore, a transferor and spouse may avoid estate and gift taxation and application of the ETIP rules through the strategic use of a 5 by 5 power. [*See* IRC § 2041(b)(2), 2514(e); Reg. § 26.2632–1(c)(2)(ii)(B)]

ii) Reverse QTIP Election Made

The ETIP rules do not apply to qualified terminable interest property (QTIP) if a reverse QTIP election is made under IRC § 2652(a)(3). [Reg. § 26.2632–1(c)(2)(ii)(C)] Without this exception QTIP trusts created inter vivos would always be subject to IRC § 2652(f), since the property is included in the transferor's spouse's gross estate under IRC § 2044. This regulatory exception allows a transferor's GST exemption to apply immediately and protects the trust's assets from GST tax.

Example: T creates an irrevocable trust giving TS, T's spouse, a qualifying income interest for life and GC, T's grandchild, the remainder. T elects to treat the income interest as qualified terminable interest property and validly claims a marital deduction for the value of the qualifying income interest. [IRC § 2523(a), (f)] T also makes a reverse QTIP election under IRC § 2652(a)(3). Even though the trust corpus would be included in TS's gross estate if TS died immediately after the transfer, the Regulations permit an exception for this type of transfer under IRC § 2642(f)(4). [Reg. § 26.2632–1(c)(2)(ii)(C)] Any GST exemption T utilizes on the trust takes effect immediately, and the property's value is determined at the time of transfer (unless some valuation exception applies, *see supra* III. D. 2. b) (3) for the exceptions to valuation). If the ETIP rules applied here, any GST exemption would not be effective and the property would not be valued until the close of the ETIP, generally when TS died.

ii) The Estate Tax Inclusion Period [IRC § 2642(f)(3)]

The ETIP is defined as the period starting with the transfer of property includible in the transferor's gross estate and ending at the earlier of one of three events: (1) when the property is no longer potentially includible in the transferor's gross estate [IRC § 2642(f)(3)(intro.); Reg. § 26.2632–1(c)(3)(ii)]; (2) when the property is subject to a generation-skipping transfer (but only for such portion of the property) [IRC § 2642(f)(3)(A)]; or (3) when the transferor dies [IRC § 2642(f)(3)(B)]. The significance of the termination of the ETIP is that it determines (1) the GST exemption allocation, (2) when the property is valued in calculating the inclusion ratio, and (3) when covered direct skips occur. [IRC § 2642(f)(1)(flush)]

(1) Property Ceases to be Includible in Transferor's Gross Estate

The ETIP is defined as the period "during which the value of the property involved in such transfer would be includible in the gross estate of the transferor." [IRC § 2642(f)(3)(intro.)] Therefore, by definition, if none of the property is includible in the gross estate of the transferor, the estate tax inclusion period ends. The property must be includible in the gross estate by an estate tax provision other than IRC § 2035 (Inclusion of certain gifts made within three years of death). [Reg. § 26.2632–1(c)(3)(ii)] If the ETIP applies to a spouse as a result of an election to split gifts (IRC § 2513), the ETIP ends when the property can no longer be included in the gross estate of the spouse (again, other than by IRC § 2035). [Reg. § 26.2632–1(c)(3)(ii)]

Example: T creates an irrevocable trust, retaining the right to income for a period terminating at the earlier of nine years after the date of transfer or T's death. The trust gives GC, T's grandchild, the remainder interest. Due to T's retained income interest, the trust corpus is includible in T's gross estate under IRC § 2036 if T dies immediately after the transfer of property to the trust. This provision subjects the trust to the ETIP rules (there was an inter vivos transfer of property includible in T's gross estate). [IRC § 2642(f)(1)] Four years after the transfer, T gifts the income interest to R, T's unrelated friend. The ETIP ends on the transfer of the income interest to R since after the transfer none of the trust is includible in T's gross estate (except by IRC § 2035). [Reg. § 26.2632–1(c)(5)(ex. 4)]

(2) Property Subject to a Generation–Skipping Transfer [IRC § 2642(f)(3)(A)]

The ETIP ends when property is subject to a taxable termination or taxable distribution. [IRC § 2642(f)(3)(A)] However, the ETIP terminates only with respect to the property involved in the generation-skipping transfer, and any other trust property is still within the ETIP. [Reg. § 26.2632–1(c)(3)(iii)]

While covered in greater depth below (in the section covering the valuation of the property included in the ETIP), the inclusion ratio is determined when the ETIP terminates. For property subject to a taxable termination or taxable distribution, a separate inclusion ratio must be determined for the generation-skipping transfer. For the first generation-skipping transfer, the computation of the inclusion ratio is relatively simple. The numerator is the sum of the GST exemption previously allocated to the trust plus the amount of GST exemption allocated on a timely gift tax return. The denominator is the value of the trust at the time of the generation-skipping transfer. [Reg. § 26.2642–1(b)(2)]

Example: T creates an irrevocable trust, retaining the right to income for a period ending at the earlier of nine years from the date of transfer or T's death. The trust gives GC,

T's grandchild, the remainder interest. The trust corpus is includible in T's gross estate under IRC § 2036 if T dies immediately after the transfer of property to the trust. The property is therefore subject to the ETIP rules since it involves an inter vivos transfer of property that would be includible in T's gross estate. [IRC § 2642(f)(1)] Additionally, the trustee has the power to distribute income to GC during the period of T's income interest. In Year 1, T allocates $100,000 of T's GST exemption to the trust. In Year 3, when the trust has a value of $300,000, the trustee distributes $30,000 to GC in a taxable distribution. [IRC § 2612(b)] The ETIP terminates for $30,000 due to the taxable distribution. [IRC § 2642(f)(3)(A)] The applicable fraction is 0.333. The numerator of the applicable fraction is $100,000, the amount of GST exemption previously allocated by T. [Reg. §§ 26.2632–1(c)(1)(i), 26.2642–1(b)(1)] The denominator is $300,000, the value of the entire trust at the termination of ETIP for the property involved in the taxable distribution. The inclusion ratio is 0.667 (1 – 0.333 (applicable fraction)). [Reg. § 26.2632–1(c)(5)(ex. 2); Reg. § 26.2642–4(b)(ex. 5)]

The applicable fraction must be re-determined for any subsequent generation-skipping transfers ending the ETIP for such transfers (with regard to taxable distributions) or for the entire trust (with regard to taxable terminations). The numerator of the trust starts out the same as before: the sum of the GST exemption previously allocated to the trust, plus the amount of GST exemption allocated on a timely gift tax return. However, the numerator is reduced by the amount of GST exemption used in protecting any former transfers from GST tax. The reduction is called the "nontax amount of any prior GSTs with respect to the trust." [Reg. § 26.2642–

1(b)(2)(i)(A)] It is computed by multiplying the GST exemption utilized previously by the applicable fraction of the trust utilized previously. The denominator of the fraction is the value of the trust at the time of the generation-skipping transfer.

Example: Same facts as the prior Example, except that in Year 4, when the trust assets are worth $400,000, the trustee distributes an additional $50,000 to GC in a taxable distribution. Assume T allocates no additional GST exemption to the trust. The numerator of the applicable fraction is $100,000 less the portion of GST exemption used to protect the Year 3 transfer ($10,000, determined by multiplying the previous transfer amount ($30,000) by the previous applicable fraction (0.333)). [Reg. § 26.2642–1(b)(2)(i)(A)] The numerator is therefore $90,000 ($100,000 – $10,000). The denominator is $400,000, the present value of the trust. The applicable fraction is 0.225 ($90,000 ÷ $400,000). [IRC § 2642(a)(2)] The inclusion ratio is 0.775 (1 – 0.225). [IRC § 2642(a)(1)] The nontax portion of any subsequent transfer from the trust is $21,250 ($10,000 from the first transfer plus $11,250 ($50,000 × 0.225)).

In Year 5, when the trust has a total fair market value of $450,000, T transfers the income interest to X, an unrelated friend, making the trust subject to a taxable termination [IRC § 2612(a)(1)] and thereby ending the ETIP. [IRC § 2642(f)(3)(A)] Assuming no additional allocation of GST exemption, the applicable fraction is 0.175. The numerator is $78,750 (the $100,000 original GST exemption less the nontax portion of $21,250 from the transfer in Year 4, which includes the $10,000 nontax portion from the transfer in Year 3). The denominator is $450,000 (the fair market value of the trust at the time of termination). Any future distributions will not be generation-skipping transfers because the generational assignment of GC changes under IRC § 2653(a). [*See supra* IV. B. 4. d) discussing the taxation of multiple skips.]

(3) Death [IRC § 2642(f)(3)(B)]

The ETIP terminates when the transferor dies. [IRC § 2642(f)(3)(B); Reg. § 26.2632–1(c)(3)(i)] If the ETIP applies to the transferor's spouse due to a split gift election, the death of the transferor's spouse terminates the ETIP. [Reg. § 26.2632–1(c)(3)(iv)(A)]

iii) Effects of Applying the ETIP Rules

The ETIP rules potentially affect two factors in the determination of the GST tax. First, they delay the timing of direct skips until the end of the ETIP. [IRC § 2642(f)(1)] Second, computation of the inclusion ratio for any direct skips or trusts included in the ETIP is also delayed until the end of the ETIP. [IRC § 2642(f)(1)(flush)]

(1) Application of the ETIP Rules to Direct Skips

Direct skips of property includible in the transferor's gross estate (except under IRC § 2035 for certain gifts made within three years of death) are treated as made when the ETIP terminates, not at the time of the actual transfer. [IRC § 2642(f)(1)(flush)(second sentence); Reg. § 26.2632–1(c)(4)] When the ETIP terminates, the taxable amount [IRC § 2623] and inclusion ratio [IRC § 2642(a)] are determined. Additional GST exemption can be allocated to the direct skip on the termination of the ETIP.

Example: In Year 1, T transfers T's vacation house to GC, T's grandchild, retaining the right to live in the house until T's death. The house is includible in T's gross estate since T retains a right of enjoyment for the property for T's life. [IRC § 2036(a)] The transfer is also a direct skip (a transfer to a skip person (GC) subject to the gift tax). [IRC § 2612(c)(1)] T dies in Year 5. The fair market value of the house increased from $100,000 at the time of transfer to $300,000 in Year 5, when the ETIP terminates at T's death. The direct skip is treated as occurring in Year 5 and the amount of transfer is $300,000. The inclusion ratio and GST tax are computed in Year 5. [*See* 2009 Instructions for IRS Form 709, p. 3]

(2) Effects of ETIP Rule on the Inclusion Ratio

For all transfers of property subject to IRC § 2642(f), the inclusion ratio is determined at the termination of the ETIP. [IRC § 2642(f)(1)(flush)] Whether the ETIP terminated during the transferor's lifetime or at the transferor's death affects both the GST exemption and the valuation of the property. [IRC § 2642(f)(2)]

(a) GST Exemption Amount

i) Allocations Before Termination of the ETIP

Any GST exemption amount allocated at transfer (either by election or automatically) or before the termination of the ETIP does not take effect until the close of the ETIP and may not be revoked. [IRC § 2642(f)(1)(flush); Reg. § 26.2632–1(c)(1)(ii)] The ETIP creates assurances that the GST exemption may not be leveraged on transfers possessing both gift and estate tax characteristics.

Example: T creates an irrevocable trust, retaining the right to income interest for a term ending on the earlier of nine years from the date of transfer or T's death. T gives GC, T's grandchild, the remainder interest. T initially transfers property worth $100,000 to the trust and allocates a like amount of GST exemption to the trust. Since the trust property would be includible in T's gross estate if T died immediately after transfer (IRC § 2036), the trust is subject to the ETIP. [IRC § 2642(f)(1)] The allocation of GST exemption is not effective until the ETIP terminates for some or all of the property and may not be revoked. [Reg. § 26.2632–1(c)(1)(ii)] Assuming T does not allocate any additional GST exemption, if the ETIP terminates at T's death when the trust is valued at $400,000, the applicable fraction is 0.250 ($100,000 (GST exemption) ÷ $400,000 (value of property at time of death)). [Reg. § 26.2632–1(c)(5)(ex. 1)]

The allocated (elected or automatic) GST exemption decreases if used to protect any taxable distributions from the trust. The GST decrease is the "nontax amount" of the generation-skipping transfer, computed by multiplying the taxable distribution by the applicable fraction at the time of transfer. [Reg. § 26.2642–1(b)(2)] *See supra* III. D. 2. b) (3) (b) ii) (2) covering the termination of the ETIP when property is subject to a generation-skipping transfer, for a more detailed explanation.

ii)   Allocations After Transferor's Death

The normal rules for GST exemption allocation apply when the ETIP terminates by death of the transferor. [Reg. § 26.2632–1(c)(1)(ii); *see supra* III. D. 2. b) (3) (b) ii) (1) covering the GST exemption rules at death of the transferor]

(b) Valuation of Property Included in the Estate Tax Inclusion Period [IRC § 2642(f)(2)]

The ETIP rules do not follow the general rules for valuation. [IRC § 2642(b); *see supra* III. D. 2. b) (2) (b) i) discussing the general valuation rules] Instead, the exact timing of valuation depends on whether the property is included in the gross estate of the transferor or whether a timely gift tax return is filed if the property is not included in the transferor's gross estate.

i) Property Included in the Transferor's Gross Estate [IRC § 2642(f)(2)(A)]

If the ETIP ends and the property is included in the transferor's gross estate by any Code section other than IRC § 2035 (for certain gifts made within three years of decedent's death discussed *supra* at I. A. 2. d)), the applicable fraction is computed using the estate tax value. [IRC § 2642(f)(2)(A)] Generally the estate tax value equals the fair market value of the property at the time of death of the transferor, unless some other election is made as to date or method. [IRC §§ 2032, 2032A; *see supra* I. A. 4. a)–b) discussing alternate valuation date and special use valuation.]

ii) Property Not Includible in Transferor's Gross Estate, Timely Gift Tax Return Filed [IRC § 2642(f)(2)(B)]

If the ETIP terminates for any reason besides the transferor's death and a timely gift tax return is filed, the property is valued on the date when the ETIP terminates. [IRC

§ 2642(f)(2)(B)] The return is timely if it is filed on or before the due date for gift tax returns for the year in which the ETIP terminates. [*See supra* II. G. discussing the time of filing for gift tax returns.]

iii) Property Not Includible in Transferor's Gross Estate, Timely Gift Tax Return Not Timely Filed [IRC § 2642(f)(2)(B)]

If a gift tax return is not timely filed for the year in which the ETIP terminates, the property is valued as of the date the gift tax return is filed. [IRC § 2642(f)(2)(B)(parenthetical)] The transferor may elect to value the property as of the first day of the month the gift tax return is filed or on the actual date the return is filed. [Reg. § 26.2642–2(a)(2)]

(c) Trust Consolidation [Reg. § 26.2642–4(a)(2)]

If a transferor creates separate trusts that the transferor then wants to consolidate, a new applicable fraction must be computed for the consolidated trust. The numerator (which consisted of GST exemption in the separate trusts) is the sum of the nontax portions of the separate trusts. The nontax portion is the product of the applicable fraction and the value of the separate trust just before consolidation. [Reg. § 26.2642–4(a)(2)] The denominator is the sum of the separate trusts' fair market values at that same time.

Example: T has two trusts T wants to consolidate, Trust A and Trust B. Trust A has an applicable fraction of 0.250 and a value of $100,000. Trust B has an applicable fraction of 0.500 and a value of $300,000. The new consolidated trust (Trust AB) has an applicable fraction with a numerator of $175,000, the sum of $25,000 from Trust A (0.250 * $100,000) and $150,000 from Trust B (0.500 * $300,000). The denominator of Trust AB's applicable fraction is $400,000, the total fair market value of the property in Trust A and Trust B. The applicable fraction for

Trust AB is 0.438 ($175,000 ÷ $400,000) and the inclusion ratio is 0.562 (1 – 0.438). [Reg. § 26.2642–4(a)(2)]

(d) **Additional Transfers of Property or GST Exemption to a Trust [IRC § 2642(d)]**

The applicable fraction is recomputed if additional property or GST exemption is allocated to an existing trust. [IRC § 2642(d)] This is because the trust's applicable fraction was determined using other property values, so merely adding GST exemption or property to the applicable fraction would not accurately reflect the protected amount.

To remedy this problem, the applicable fraction is redetermined when additional property or GST exemption is transferred to an existing trust. [IRC § 2642(d)(1)] This is done by treating the amount of the trust protected from GST tax by the old GST exemption (called the "nontax portion" in the Code) as GST exemption for the new applicable fraction. [IRC § 2642(d)(2)]

i) **Numerator of New Applicable Fraction**

The numerator of the new applicable fraction is the sum of two numbers: first, the amount of any additional GST exemption allocated to the trust [IRC § 2642(d)(2)(A)(i)], and second, the "nontax portion" of the trust, computed by multiplying the fair market value of the trust immediately before the transfer by the old applicable fraction. [IRC § 2642(d)(2)(A)(ii), (d)(3); Reg. § 26.2642–4(a)] If the GST exemption is allocated on a late gift tax return, the property is valued at the time of the allocation; otherwise the property is valued at the time of transfer. [IRC § 2642(d)(4); *see also* IRC § 2642(b)(3); Reg. § 26.2642–2(a)(2)]

Example: T created an irrevocable trust that had an applicable fraction of 0.400 and an inclusion ratio of 0.600 (1 – .0400). When the trust was worth $100,000, T assigned the trust an additional $30,000 of GST exemption. The nontax portion of the trust is $60,000 (the inclusion ratio of 0.600 multiplied by the $100,000 value of the trust). [IRC § 2642(d)(3)] The new numerator is $90,000, the $30,000 new allocation of GST exemption plus the nontax portion of $60,000. [IRC § 2642(d)(2)(A)] The new applicable fraction is 0.9 ($90,000 divided by $100,000 value of the trust). [IRC § 2642(d)(2); Reg. § 26.2642–4(b)(ex. 1)]

ii)   Denominator of the New Applicable Fraction

The denominator of the new applicable fraction is determined by adding the amount of the property transferred (if any) to the value of the property in the trust immediately before the event triggering the reevaluation of the applicable fraction. [IRC § 2642(d)(2)(B)] Any new property that is transferred may receive the same deductions as for property to a new trust, the sum of federal estate and state death tax paid on the property and charitable deductions related to the property. [IRC § 2642(d)(2)(B)(i)(I, II); *see supra* III. D. 2. b) (2) (b) ii) discussing the reductions for tax paid and charitable contributions made.]

Example: T transferred an additional $100,000 to an existing trust, the income of which was distributed to GC, T's grandchild. The trust has a value of $900,000 before the transfer. The denominator of the new applicable fraction is $1 million, the $100,000 transferred plus the current $900,000 value of the trust. [IRC § 2642(d)(2)(B)]

iii)   Recomputation of Applicable Fraction

Having determined the new numerator and denominator, the application of the new applicable fraction is easily illustrated.

Example: T transfers $5 million to an inter vivos trust. Assume the GST exemption amount remains constant at $1 million and T allocates T's entire GST exemption to the trust. Upon creation, the trust's applicable fraction is 0.20 ($1 million GST exemption divided by $5 million value of the trust). T transfers an additional $2 million to the trust at a time when the trust corpus is valued at $10 million. Under IRC § 2642(d)(1) the applicable fraction must be recomputed.

The numerator of the trust is the sum of the additional GST exemption allocated (here, zero) plus the nontax portion of the trust. [IRC § 2642(d)(2)(A)] The nontax portion is $2 million (the applicable fraction of the trust (0.20) multiplied by the value of the trust immediately before the transfer ($10 million)). Note that the percentage of property protected by the original GST exemption (20%) is the same even though the property increased in value.

The denominator of the applicable fraction is $12 million. This is the sum of the value of the property transferred (here $2 million) plus the trust's $10 million value before the additional transfer. [IRC § 2642(d)(2)(B)]

The new applicable fraction for the trust is 0.167 ($2 million divided by $12 million) and will be used in computing the inclusion ratio and applicable rate for future GST tax.

(e) Pour–Over Trusts [IRC § 2653(b)(2)]

The generational assignment of the transferor can change due to multi-generational skips from a trust. [*See supra* III. B. 4. d) for how the generational assignment of the transferor can change due to multi-generational skips from a trust.] Trusts subject to this rule experienced (1) a generation-skipping transfer of property, and (2) immediately after such transfer, the property was held in trust. [IRC § 2653(a)] If the property is transferred to another trust (a "pour-over trust"), a portion of the transferring trust's GST exemption is allocated to the pour-over trust. [IRC § 2653(b)(2)(A)] This is done regardless of whether the transferring and pour-over have the same transferor. However, if the trusts do have the same transferor, the applicable fraction of the pour-over trust must be recomputed under

IRC § 2642(d) (discussed immediately above) since there has been an additional transfer of property and GST exemption to a trust.

As in the other recomputation sections, the GST exemption for the pour-over trust is the nontax portion of the transferring trust. [IRC § 2653(b)(2)(A)] The nontax portion here is the product of the applicable fraction for the distribution and the pour-over amount before any GST tax is paid. [IRC § 2653(b)(2)(B)]

Example: T creates two irrevocable trusts, each containing property valued at $1 million. Trust 1 pays its income to C for life, remainder to Trust 2 (making Trust 2 a pour-over trust). Trust 2 pays income to GC, T's grandchild, with the remainder to GGC, T's great-grandchild. T assigns $300,000 of GST exemption to Trust 1 and zero to Trust 2. The applicable fraction for Trust 1 is 0.300 ($300,000 GST exemption divided by $1 million value). [IRC § 2642(a)(2)]

On C's death a taxable termination is present. [IRC § 2612(a)(1)] At C's death, Trust 1 is valued at $3 million, Trust 2 is valued at $2 million, and the highest estate tax rate is 35%. The taxable amount is $3 million, the value of property involved in the taxable termination. [IRC § 2622(a)(1)] The applicable rate is 24.5%, determined by multiplying the maximum federal estate tax rate (35%) by the inclusion ratio of 0.700 (1 − 0.300 (applicable fraction) = 0.7). [IRC § 2641(a)] The GST tax amount is $735,000, the applicable rate of 24.5% times the taxable amount ($3 million). [IRC § 2602] The trustee for Trust 1 bears the responsibility for the GST tax, leaving $2,265,000 to distribute to Trust 2. [IRC § 2603(a)(2)]

The applicable fraction of Trust 2 must be recomputed. [IRC § 2642(d)] Some of the GST exemption T assigned to Trust 1 will flow to Trust 2, the pour-over trust, determined by computing the nontax portion of Trust 1. [IRC § 2653(b)(2)] The nontax portion for this transaction is $900,000, the product of the applicable fraction for Trust 1 (0.300) multiplied by the pre-GST tax distribution amount of $3 million. [IRC § 2653(b)(2)(B)] Trust 2's new applicable fraction then is 0.397 (the new GST exemption amount ($900,000 from Trust 1 plus zero for Trust 2) divided by the value of property in Trust 2 at the time of transfer ($2,265,000)). [IRC § 2642(d)]

(f) Recomputation of Applicable Fraction After Taxable Terminations [IRC § 2653(b)(1)]

Generally, generation-skipping transfers from trusts do not affect the applicable fraction or inclusion ratio for the distributing trust. [IRC § 2653(b)(1)(first sentence)] However, if a trust (1) has an inclusion ratio of less than 100 percent, (2) a taxable termination occurs, and (3) the trust does not terminate and the transferor remains the same after the taxable termination, the applicable fraction is recomputed to reflect a "proper adjustment." [IRC § 2653(b)(1)(second sentence); *see* RICHARD STEPHENS ET. AL., FEDERAL ESTATE AND GIFT TAXATION 17–47 (8th ed. 2002)]

While regulations still have to be enacted, it is understood that a "proper adjustment" allows for the nontax portion of the trust property to represent the new GST exemption amount for a trust stated in the above paragraph. This protects the GST exemption amount from being used to pay the GST tax. If this were not the case a portion of the transferor's GST exemption would be lost due to the payment of GST tax by the trust on the taxable termination. The denominator of the properly adjusted applicable fraction is the value of the trust less any GST tax paid.

Example: T creates an irrevocable trust that pays income to C, T's child, for life, then to GC, T's grandchild, for life. At GC's death, the remainder will be paid to GGC, T's great-grandchild. The trust assets are worth $5 million at the time of transfer and T allocates $1.5 million of GST exemption to the trust on a timely filed gift tax return. [IRC §§ 2631, 2632] The applicable fraction for the trust is 0.300 ($1.5 million GST exemption divided by the $5 million value at time of transfer). [IRC § 2642(a)(2)]

Several years later, C dies when the trust's value has increased to $10 million and the maximum estate tax rate is 35%. A taxable termination occurs on C's death, even though the trust does not terminate and T remains the transferor. [IRC § 2612(a)(1)] The applicable rate is 24.5% (computed by multiplying the inclusion ratio of 0.700 (1 − 0.300 (applicable fraction) = 0.7) by the maximum estate tax rate of 35%). [IRC § 2641] The taxable amount is $10 million, the value of the property at the time of the termination. [IRC § 2622(a)] The GST tax due is $2.45 million ($10 million (taxable amount) × 24.5% (applicable rate)). [IRC § 2602]

After the GST tax is paid, the trust has $7.55 million ($10 million less the $2.45 million GST tax paid). If the old applicable fraction of 0.30 were used, only $2,265,000 of the trust would be protected from future GST tax consequences (30% of $7.55 million). A "proper adjustment" must be made to reflect the increase in the property's value protected by the GST exemption and payment of the GST tax. [IRC § 2653(b)(1)(second sentence)] The Regulations should provide a new GST exemption amount equaling the nontax portion before the taxable termination. This is $3 million, the original applicable fraction of 0.30 times the $10 million valuation. The new applicable fraction is then 0.397 (the $3 million GST exemption divided by the $7.55 million remaining value in the trust). The properly adjusted applicable fraction (and, therefore, the inclusion ratio too) protects the original GST exemption amount from being subject to the GST tax on any subsequent transfers from the trust.

(g) Qualified Severance [IRC § 2642(a)(3)]

The Economic Growth and Tax Relief Reconciliation Act of 2001 added a provision allowing under certain circumstances for the severance of trusts into taxed and non-taxed portions. [IRC § 2642(a)(3)] The stated reason for the change was to reduce complexity, but it also allows for planning opportunities. Before the new legislation, the Regulations allowed for severance only under limited circumstances and the inclusion ratio of the severed trusts could not be changed to make a taxed and non-tax trust. [*See, e.g.,* Reg. § 26.2654–1(a)(3),–1(b)]

Trusts severed in a "qualified severance" are treated as separate trusts for purposes of Chapter 13. [IRC § 2642(a)(3)(A)] A severance is qualified if (1) the division is allowed under the governing instrument or local law, (2) the trust is divided on a fractional basis, and (3) in the aggregate, the new trusts provide for the same succession of interests in benefits as the severed trust. [IRC § 2642(a)(3)(B)(i)] Trusts with inclusion ratios of 0 (where the GST exemption equaled the value of the property on the effective date) or 1 (where no GST exemption is allocated) are severed if they meet the three elements. For trusts with inclusion ratios between 0 and 1 an additional step for severance is required. The old trust must be divided to create two trusts, one with an inclusion ratio of 0 and the other with an inclusion ratio of 1. [IRC § 2642(a)(3)(B)(ii)]

For trusts that do not have a 0 or 1 inclusion ratio the severance is into a nontaxed portion and a taxed portion. The trust with the 0 inclusion ratio is one with property equal to the applicable fraction multiplied by the value of the trust before severance. The trust with "1" for an inclusion ratio contains what remains after the nontax portion is severed.

The rule applies to trusts severed at any time after the effective date of December 31, 2000.

Example: T creates an irrevocable trust. The trust is to accumulate income for five years, then distribute income annually to GC, T's grandchild, at the trustee's discretion. After GC's death the remainder interest will be paid to GGC, T's great-grandchild. The applicable fraction of the trust is 0.250, giving an inclusion ratio of 0.750 (1 – 0.25 (applicable fraction)). [IRC § 2642(a)(1)] State law permits the trust to be severed.

Assume the maximum federal estate tax rate is 35% and the trust is worth $2 million. The trustee severs the trust into two separate trusts (Trust A and Trust B), leaving the succession of interests to the beneficiaries unchanged. Trust A has $500,000 of assets (computed by taking the applicable fraction of the original trust (0.250) times $2 million). Trust B has the rest of the original $2 million trust, a $1.5 million balance. The severance is a qualified severance and Trust A and Trust B are treated as separate trusts. [IRC § 2642(a)(3)(A)–(B)]

Due to the severance of the original trust, GC may now receive income from Trust A without GST tax consequences. Before severance, any income GC received was a taxable distribution subject to an applicable rate of 26.25% (35% estate tax rate * 0.750 inclusion ratio). [IRC § 2641(a)] Now, if GC receives distributions from Trust A there are no GST tax consequences since the applicable rate for Trust A is zero (the applicable fraction for Trust A is 1 giving an inclusion ratio of zero).

(h) Recapture of Estate Tax Savings from Special Use Valuation [Reg. § 26.2642–4(a)(4)]

As discussed more fully in I. A. 4. b), IRC § 2032A allows for property to be valued based on its actual use instead of the fair market value for its highest and best use. [IRC § 2032A(a), (b)(2)] This permits estate tax savings due to the lower valuation of the property. If the property is disposed of, or used in a nonqualifying manner, any decrease in estate tax attributable to the IRC § 2032A valuation is recaptured. [IRC § 2032A(c)]

Since the value of the property increases when valued at its highest and best use, the applicable fraction computed using property valued under IRC § 2032A must be recomputed upon a recapture of the IRC § 2032A benefit. [Reg. § 26.2642–4(a)(4)(i)] The recomputed applicable fraction applies to all generation-skipping transfers from the trust made since the transferor's death, and any additional GST tax is due within six months of the event causing the revaluation of the property. [Reg. § 26.2642–4(a)(4)(ii)]

i) Numerator of Applicable Fraction

Any unused GST exemption not allocated at the transferor's death is allocated to the trust when computing the new applicable fraction due to the IRC § 2032A recapture. [Reg. § 26.2642–4(a)(4)(i)]

ii) Denominator of Applicable Fraction

The denominator of the applicable fraction is the fair market value of the property at the time of the transferor's death. [Reg. § 26.2642–4(a)(4)(i)] Although not provided for in the Regulations, if the estate elected to use the alternate valuation date this will most likely control for the redetermination of the applicable fraction. The value is reduced by the amount of federal estate or state death tax paid (including any GST tax paid by the trust). [Reg. § 26.2642–4(a)(4)(i)]

3. Credit for State Death Taxes [IRC § 2604]

Before 2005, GST tax due could be reduced by up to five percent of the GST tax liability for payment of state tax due on generation-skipping transfers. [IRC § 2604(a)–(b)] The credit was only allowed for state taxes due to the death of an individual and not for direct skips. [IRC § 2604(a)] As of 2005, the credit is no longer available, but will be resurrected starting in 2013 when the provisions sunset of their own accord. [Economic Growth and Tax Relief Reconciliation Act of 2001, Pub. L. No. 107–16, 115 Stat 38, § 901 as modified by P.L. 111–312, § 101(a)(1) (2010)]

E. Collateral Issues

1. Effect on Adjusted Basis of Property

The basis for property subject to the GST is computed under either IRC § 1014 (for property acquired from a decedent) or IRC § 1015 (for property acquired by gifts and transfers in trust). The basis is used to determine a variety of income tax consequences (depreciation, gain, loss, etc.). The GST tax impacts the property's basis under IRC § 2654(a), depending on whether the property passed by the death of an individual or through an inter vivos transfer.

a) Gift Transfers

Gift transfers generally receive a transferred basis under IRC § 1015, meaning the donee of the property receives the same basis as the donor.

[IRC § 1015(a)] Two exceptions exist. The first exception concerns loss property (i.e., the adjusted basis of the property is greater than the fair market value at the time of transfer) later sold at a loss. In this case, the fair market value of the property at the time of transfer is used to calculate the basis. [IRC § 1015(a)(after "except that")] The second exception allows for an increase in basis to reflect gift tax paid. [IRC § 1015(d)(1)(A), (d)(6)] Under IRC § 1015(d), the adjusted basis of the property increases (but not above the fair market value of the property) by the proportion of the gift tax paid on the net appreciation of the gift. [IRC § 1015(d)(6)(A)] This is computed by multiplying the gift tax paid by the fair market value of the property less the adjusted basis of the property divided by the amount of the gift [gift tax paid × ((fair market value − AB) ÷ amount of gift)]. The increase is allowed in order to represent the portion potentially facing double taxation under both the gift tax (which taxes a property's fair market value) and income tax (which only taxes the gain).

The increase in basis for GST tax paid parallels the increase under IRC § 1015(d)(6). An increase is allowed (but again, not over the fair market value of the property) for the portion of the GST tax imposed on the appreciation of the property. [IRC § 2654(a)(1)] Any GST tax imposed is taken into account without regard for any credits allowed for state generation-skipping transfer taxes paid under IRC § 2604. [IRC § 2654(a)(1)(second parenthetical)] The increase in basis is computed in the same manner as for the gift tax: the product of the GST tax imposed, multiplied by the fair market value of the property less the adjusted basis of the property, all divided by the fair market value of the property [GST tax paid × ((fair market value of property − AB) ÷ fair market value of property)].

The basis used in computing the appreciation is determined after any increase under IRC § 1015(d). Therefore, the basis for the gift tax must be computed before any additions for the GST tax. [IRC § 2654(a)(1)(last sentence)]

Example: T gives property to GC with a fair market value of $100 and an adjusted basis (AB) to T of $20. Assume the transfer creates a $50 gift tax and a $40 GST tax liability. The property is a gift to GC, so IRC § 1015 is used to compute the basis. Under IRC § 1015(a) the AB is $20, T's transferred AB. The increase allowed for gift tax paid is $40, the $50 gift tax paid multiplied by the net appreciation of the property ($80) divided by the amount of the gift ($100) [$50 × (($100 − $20) ÷ $100)]. The total AB after the application of IRC § 1015 is $60 ($20 transferred + $40 adjustment). [IRC § 1015(d)(1), (6)] The increase for GST tax liability is $16. The GST tax liability of $40 is multiplied by the appreciation of the property computed after the application of IRC § 1015 ($40) divided by the value of the property ($100) [$40 × (($100 − $60) ÷ $100)]. [IRC § 2654(a)(1)] GC's basis in the property is $76 ($20 transferred AB under IRC § 1015(a) + $40 under IRC § 1015(d) + $16 under IRC § 2654(a)(1)).

b) Testamentary Transfers

(1) Direct Skip Testamentary Transfers

The basis increase for GST tax paid does not apply to direct skip testamentary transfers. The increase in basis is limited to the "fair market value of such property" and the property receives a fair market value basis under IRC § 1014(a).

(2) Taxable Distributions

If property is transferred at death to a trust that is later the subject of a taxable distribution, the property's basis may be increased in the same manner as property transferred by gift. The increase for the GST tax is proportionate to the net appreciation of the property (FMV at time of distribution − AB of the property) over its fair market value. [IRC § 2654(a)(1)]

Example: T creates a trust that pays income to C, T's child, or to GC, T's grandchild, at the independent trustee's discretion. The trustee transfers GC property with a fair market value of $200 and an adjusted basis to the trust of $50. The transfer is a taxable distribution. [IRC § 2612(b)] Assuming the trust's GST tax liability is $40, GC's basis in the property is $80. This is the total of the trust's basis in the property ($50) plus the $30 increase for GST tax liability on the net appreciation [$40 GST tax x (($200 − $50) ÷ $200)].

(3) Taxable Terminations at Death

Two different rules apply to determine the adjustments to basis allowed for the GST tax paid on property transferred in a taxable termination occurring upon the death of an individual. [IRC § 2654(a)(2)] Under IRC § 2654(a)(2), one rule exists for trusts with inclusion ratios of "1," and the other rule applies to trusts with inclusion ratios less than "1."

(a) Trusts with Inclusion Ratios of "1"

If a trust has an inclusion ratio of "1" (possible only if no GST exemption is allocated to the trust or the trust was subject to a qualified severance (*see supra* III. D. 2. b) (3) (g) covering qualified severance)) the basis of the property is "adjusted in a manner similar to the manner provided under [IRC § 1014(a)]." [IRC § 2654(a)(2)] This means the property receives a basis equal to the fair market value at the individual's time of death.

(b) Trusts with Inclusion Ratios Less Than "1"

If GST exemption was assigned to the trust, no basis increase (or decrease) is allowed for the proportion of the property's appreciation sheltered from GST tax due to the GST exemption. The basis of the property increases (or decreases) by the difference between the basis of the property before death and the IRC § 1014 basis multiplied by the inclusion ratio. [IRC § 2654(a)(2)(after "except")]

Example: A taxable termination occurs at T's death. Assume that the trust has a 60% inclusion ratio and the sole piece of property in the trust has a fair market value of $100,000 and a basis of $28,000. The increase in the adjusted basis allowed under IRC § 2654 is $43,200. This is computed by subtracting the basis of the property ($28,000) from the basis of the property if IRC § 1014(a) gave the basis ($100,000), multiplied by the inclusion ratio (0.600) [($100,000 – $28,000) × 0.600]. The property's basis to the skip person is $71,200 ($28,000 + $43,200). [IRC § 2654(a)(2)]

2. Generation–Skipping Transfer Tax Procedural Rules

Besides payment and filing requirements, all other procedure rules are covered by IRC § 2661, which incorporates the procedural rules of the gift and estate tax. If the generation-skipping transfer does not occur at the same time, and as the result of, a death, the procedure rules pertaining to the gift tax of Subchapter F apply. [IRC § 2661(1)] If the GST does occur at the same time, and as result of, a death, the procedure rules pertaining to the estate tax of Subchapter F apply. [IRC § 2661(2)] Therefore the rules of administration and procedure for the GST stem from the same rules applicable to either the gift or estate tax.

Liability of payment of the GST tax, any tax returns due (who must file and when it must be filed), and general procedure rules are covered below. In order to determine liability and filing requirements the specific type of generation-skipping transfer must first be determined.

No specific rules in the Code establish who must file, what return must be filed, or when any required return must be filed to account for any generation-skipping transfer. IRC § 2662 states that the Secretary is to promulgate regulations to give guidance "to the extent practicable" that the person who is liable for the tax must file the return and suggestions for the filing date. [IRC § 2662(a)(1)] Responsibility and return requirements for the GST tax depends on which generation-skipping transfer occurred (direct skip, taxable termination, taxable distribution). The following sections explain the procedural requirements for the various types of generation-skipping transfers.

a) Direct Skip

(1) Liability for Payment of GST Tax

Unless the transfer is from a trust, any GST tax due on direct skips must be paid by the transferor. [IRC § 2603(a)(3); *see supra* III. B. 2. discussing IRC § 2652(a) defining "transferor" for Chapter 13.] For transfers from a trust, the tax liability falls on the trustee. [IRC § 2603(a)(2)] The GST tax is charged directly to the property involved in the direct skip unless the governing instrument (i.e., trust document or will) specifically directs the GST tax be paid from another source. [IRC § 2603(b)] If the direct skip is from an inter vivos gift, the payment of the tax by the transferor results in an additional gift transfer. [IRC § 2515; *see supra* II. C. 5. discussing IRC § 2515]

Example: T gifts Blackacre to GC, T's grandchild, when the property is worth $2 million. T's transfer is subject to both the gift and GST (a direct skip) tax. Assuming the gift and estate tax rate are 50%, T pays $1 million GST tax (50% of the $2 million transfer). Therefore, the amount of gifts by T to GC totals $3 million ($2 million for Blackacre, $1 million from the payment by T of the GST under IRC § 2515). T's gift tax liability will be $1.5 million (again, assuming a 50% gift tax rate). The total amount of transfer taxes for T from the transfer is $2.5 million, or 125% of the value of the property transferred.

(2) Tax Returns

(a) Who Must File

The Code suggests that the person liable to pay the GST tax should file the return. [IRC § 2662(a)(1)] For non-trust direct skips, the transferor is liable to pay the GST tax. [IRC § 2603(a)(3)] For transfers from a trust, the tax liability is on the trustee of the trust. [IRC § 2603(a)(2)] Therefore, a return is required from the transferor (for inter vivos direct skip not from a trust), the trustee (for inter vivos direct skip from a trust), or executor (for testamentary direct skip). [Reg. § 26.2662–1(c)(1)(iii–v)]

(b) Date and Type of Return to be Filed

i) Inter Vivos Direct Skips

For inter vivos direct skips, Form 709 (pertaining to gift and generation-skipping transfers) must be filed before April 15 of the year following the transfer, unless an extension of time is granted. [IRC § 2662(a)(2)(A); Reg. § 26.2662–1(b)(3)(i), (d)(1)(i)] The time may be extended in the same manner as for the gift tax. [*See supra* II. G. 2. covering extensions of time to file a gift tax return.]

ii) Testamentary Direct Skips

Direct skips following an individual's death must be reported on Form 706 (estate tax return) or Form 706NA (estate tax return for non-resident aliens). [Reg. § 26.2662–1(b)(3)(ii)(A)] If a trust is involved, Schedule R–1 must also accompany the return. [Reg. § 26.2662–1(b)(3)(ii)(B)] All forms must be filed by the estate tax return date, which is nine months after the testator's death, unless an extension of time is granted. [IRC § 2662(a)(2)(A); Reg. § 26.2662–

1(d)(1)(i)] The Service grants the trustee an automatic two-month extension of time to file Schedule R–1. [Form 706, Revised September 2009, p. 37]

b) Taxable Termination

(1) Liability for Payment of GST Tax

The trustee of a trust assumes liability for the GST tax on any taxable terminations. [IRC § 2603(a)(2)] Just like direct skips, the GST tax is charged directly to the property involved in the taxable termination, unless the governing instruments (i.e., trust document or will) directly specifies payment of the GST tax from another source. [IRC § 2603(b)]

(2) Tax Returns

(a) Who Must File

The trustee of the trust must file a return for taxable termination generation-skipping transfers. [IRC § 2662(a)(1); Reg. § 26.2662–1(c)(1)(ii)]

(b) Date and Type of Return to be Filed

The trustee must file Form 706GS(T) by the 15th day of the fourth month after the close of the taxable year of the trust, unless an extension is granted. [IRC § 2662(a)(2)(B); Reg. § 26.2662–1(b)(2)] If the trust is on the calendar year accounting period, this means April 15. If the date falls on a Saturday, Sunday, or legal holiday, the next business day is the filing date. [IRC § 7503] If the election to use an alternative valuation under IRC § 2032 is selected under IRC § 2624(c), the return is to be filed by the later of the 15th day of the fourth month after the termination of the taxable year, or 10 months following the date of the death leading to the taxable termination. [Reg. § 26.2662–1(d)(2)]

c) Taxable Distributions

(1) Liability for Payment of GST Tax

The transferee is liable for any GST tax on taxable distributions. [IRC § 2603(a)(1)] Just like direct skips and taxable terminations, the GST tax is charged directly to the property involved in the taxable distribution, unless the governing instruments (i.e., trust document or will) specifically directs payment of the GST tax from another source. [IRC § 2603(b)]

(2) Tax Return

Initially, the trustee must file an informational Form 706GS(D) for the trust and provide a copy of Form 706GS(D–1) to each distributee. [Reg. § 26.2662–1(b)(1)] The transferee must fill out and file the form received by the 15th day of the fourth month after the close of the taxable year of the taxable distribution. [IRC § 2662(a)(2)(B); Reg. § 26.2662–1(c)(1)(i)] For calendar year taxpayers, this is April 15.

F. Review Questions

1. Answer true or false, are the following individuals skip persons in relation to Tom?

    a. Greta, Tom's grandchild. Greta's parents, Chris (Tom's child) and Spouse, are both living.

    b. Greta, if at the time of transfer Chris is not living.

    c. Greta's child Evie (Tom's great-grandchild), if Chris is not living at the time of transfer.

    d. Greta, if Chris is living at the time of transfer, but Spouse (Greta's mother) is not.

    e. Chris

    f. Dora, who is unrelated and was born 38 years after Tom.

    g. Maggie, the grandchild of Bart. Bart is Tom's cousin (the son of Tom's Uncle Homer). Bart is dead at the time of transfer.

2. Teruo makes the following transfers in the current year:

    1. A transfer of $30,000 directly to his son Brit.

    2. A transfer of $50,000 to an irrevocable trust, the income of which goes to Teruo's grandchild, Kaia (Brit's son), and the remainder to his great-grandchild, Kelley.

3.   A transfer of $100,000 to a corporation whose shares are split equally between Brit and Kaia.

Which, if any, of the above are generation-skipping transfers?

3.   Todd creates an irrevocable trust with the income interest going to Gertie, Todd's grandchild, and the remainder to Helen, Todd's great-grandchild. Todd gives his friend, Xavier, the power to distribute the income of the trust to Charlie, Todd's child. What generation-skipping transfer occurs, if any, when Xavier relinquishes the non-general power to give income to Charlie?

4.   Terri creates an irrevocable trust with the income to be distributed to Clara, Terri's daughter, for life. After Clara's death the corpus is to be distributed equally between Doug, Terri's second child, and Gaia, Terri's grandchild. What, if any, generation-skipping transfers occur at Clara's death?

5.   Thelma transfers a piece of property worth $500,000 to her grandson Jack. Both of Jack's parents are alive at the time of transfer. Assuming that both the gift and GST tax rates are 40%, what is the amount of tax due? In computing your answer, disregard the IRC § 2503(b) exclusion, the gift tax credit under IRC § 2505, and assume an inclusion ratio of one (IRC § 2642).

6.   Trevor gives $50,000 as a gift to his grandson Richard. Both of Richard's parents are alive at the time of transfer. Which of the below statements on the generation-skipping transfer tax consequences is correct?

   A.   The transfer is not subject to both the gift and generation-skipping transfer taxes.

   B.   The transfer is subject to both the gift tax and generation-skipping transfer tax.

   C.   Richard is not a skip person since both his parents are living at the time of transfer.

   D.   If Trevor had placed the money in an irrevocable trust with income to Richard, the transfer would not be subject to the generation-skipping transfer tax.

APPENDIX A

Answers to Review Questions

PERSPECTIVE

Q1. Politics aside, is it inaccurate to refer to the "federal death tax?" Explain your answer.

A1. To the extent the term "death tax" implies that a levy is imposed upon the death of an individual, it is misleading. The federal estate tax is a levy imposed upon the transfer of wealth at death. Only those estates with a "taxable estate" in excess of the applicable exclusion amount face the potential for estate tax liability. True, the federal estate tax is imposed only upon the death of an individual, but it is not a tax imposed on the occasion of death. Like the federal gift tax and the federal generation-skipping transfer tax, the federal estate tax is a tax imposed on wealth transfers.

Q2. In 2005, a national newspaper reported that "[b]eginning in 2006, the unified credit for estates will be $2 million." Is this statement entirely correct? Explain your answer.

A2. No. The unified credit is an amount equal to the tax imposed on a taxable estate equal to the applicable exclusion amount. The applicable exclusion amount in 2006 was $2 million, but the amount of the unified credit that year was $780,800 (the tax imposed under IRC § 2001(c) on a $2 million taxable estate at that time). In 2011 the applicable exclusion amount is $5 million, and the unified credit $1,730,800.

Q3. Flanders owns three parcels of real estate: Blackacre, Whiteacre, and Redacre. Each is worth $5 million. Flanders is contemplating a gift of one of these parcels to his son, Rod. Flanders acquired Blackacre several years ago for $100,000. Because Blackacre is located in a major metropolitan area, Flanders reasonably expects that its value will continue to grow over time. The same cannot be said of Redacre. Flanders bought it five years ago for $5.3 million, but the recent addition of a factory on adjoining acreage has made the property far less suitable for development. Flanders recently purchased Whiteacre for $5 million. While Flanders hopes the property will appreciate like Blackacre has, it is too early to know whether neighboring development will occur and, if so, how it will affect the value of Whiteacre. How would you advise Flanders with respect to his proposed gift to Rod?

A3. No matter which property Flanders gives Rod, Flanders will nearly exhaust his applicable exclusion amount for federal gift tax purposes (limited to $5 million in 2011). [IRC § 2505(a)(1)] The gift will qualify for the annual exclusion [IRC § 2503(b)], yet because each property is worth $5 million, only about $13,000 (the annual exclusion amount in 2011) of the unified credit for gift tax purposes will be left. Because he is making such a substantial gift, Flanders will want to leverage his applicable exclusion amount as much as possible. By giving away property that is likely to appreciate in value, Flanders would maximize the benefit of the gift. Any subsequent appreciation in the value of the gifted property will not subject Flanders to federal wealth transfer tax consequences. Given its history of appreciation and reasonable expectation of future growth, Blackacre looks to be a good candidate for the gift. One drawback to gifting Blackacre is that Rod will take Flanders' $100,000 basis in the property. [IRC § 1015(a)] That means when Rod sells Blackacre, he will pay a 15% tax on the $4.9 million of appreciation that accrued while the property was held by Flanders, in addition to any appreciation in value that accrues after the gift. [IRC § 1(h)] Had Flanders devised Blackacre to Rod in his will, Rod would have taken Blackacre with a fair market value basis [IRC § 1014], eliminating any income tax liability on the pre-transfer appreciation in value. The estate tax rates, however, are currently higher than the income tax rates applicable to capital gains, so even though there is an income tax cost, the transfer tax benefit may outweigh. Whiteacre might be a fine candidate for the gift to Rod, too, for at least Rod would take the property with a relatively high basis that compares favorably to the income tax exposure attached to Blackacre. The drawback with Whiteacre is that Flanders is less sure about the property's chance to maximize the use of Flanders' applicable exclusion amount. For certain, however, Flanders should not give Redacre to Rod. Redacre is "loss property" (its value is less than Flanders' basis in the property), and there is a chance that the property may further decline in value. If it does, Flanders would be wasting a portion of the unified credit amount allocated to the gift—there is no mechanism for recapturing wasted credit if gifted property declines in value. Furthermore, Rod would take Redacre with a basis equal to the property's value at the date of the gift [IRC § 1015(a)] In effect, any pre-gift loss on the property does not carry over to the donee. From an income tax and transfer tax standpoint, Flanders would be better off to sell Redacre and transfer the cash proceeds to Rod.

CHAPTER 1: THE FEDERAL ESTATE TAX

Q1. Diagnosed with a terminal sinus infection early in Year 1, Sneezy began some aggressive estate planning. Sneezy formed two trusts in Year 1, creatively named "Trust A" and "Trust B." Sneezy contributed property worth $1 million to Trust A, which gave an income interest to Dopey for life and a remainder to Doc. If Doc does not survive Dopey, the remainder is to revert to Sneezy or Sneezy's estate. Assume that the value of Sneezy's contingent remainder interest in Trust A at all times is greater than 5% of the value of the Trust A corpus.

Sneezy transferred an additional $1 million in assets to Trust B, which gave an income interest to Bashful for life and the remainder to Happy or Happy's estate. Shortly after the formation of Trust B, Happy, flattered but unwilling to accept a gift from Sneezy, purchased the remainder interest for its fair market value ($700,000) immediately after formation of Trust B. Sneezy promptly (still in Year 1) transferred the purchase price proceeds to ACME Insurance Company in exchange for an annuity contract. Under the terms of the annuity contract, Sneezy was to receive fixed payments monthly for life. A lump sum benefit of $500,000 would then be paid to Sneezy's designated beneficiary, Grumpy. When he appointed Grumpy beneficiary, Sneezy renounced any rights to change the identity of the beneficiary.

If Sneezy dies in Year 2 survived by all other parties named in this question, what will be included in Sneezy's gross estate?

A1. Sneezy's gross estate will include the value of Sneezy's contingent remainder interest in Trust A and the $500,000 benefit payable to Grumpy, but no portion of the corpus of Trust B. IRC § 2037 does not apply to Trust A since neither Dopey nor Doc's interests are contingent on surviving Sneezy. However, IRC § 2033 would apply to include the value of Sneezy's contingent remainder interest. No portion of the Trust B corpus is includible in Sneezy's gross estate since Sneezy has no retained interest in (or power over) the trust corpus. IRC § 2043 does not apply to the payment received by Sneezy from Happy since the remainder interest purchased would not have caused inclusion in Sneezy's gross estate under IRC §§ 2035–2038. The value of the death benefit payable to Grumpy is clearly included under IRC § 2039.

Q2. Hank and Peggy, residents of a separate property state, have been married for over 20 years. Eighteen years ago, Hank purchased a home in Portland for $100,000. Hank and Peggy owned the house as "joint tenants with rights of survivorship." Five years later, when the home was worth $150,000, Peggy paid for the construction of a swimming pool, deck, and an extra bedroom for the home. The total cost of the improvements was $50,000. In the current year, when the value of the home was $400,000, Peggy died. Based on these facts, how much will be included in Peggy's gross estate?

A2. The correct answer is $200,000. Because Hank and Peggy are married and own the property as joint tenants with rights of survivorship, IRC § 2040(b) requires Peggy to include one-half of the value of the residence in her gross estate. One might be tempted to argue that the correct answer is $100,000, based upon the fact that Peggy furnished one-fourth of the total consideration used to purchase and/or improve the residence. IRC § 2040(b) trumps this rule, however.

Q3. Decedent's will directed the personal representative to transfer Decedent's entire estate (with a date of death value of $3,000,000) to a trust. No other assets are included in Decedent's gross estate for federal estate tax purposes. Under the terms of the trust, the trustee is to pay $50,000 each year to Decedent's spouse, Spouse, for Spouse's life. If the trust does not have $50,000 of income during any year in which payments to Spouse are required, the trustee is directed to distribute principal to the extent required to satisfy the $50,000 annual distribution obligation. No other payments may be made to Spouse for any reason. Upon Spouse's death, the trust will terminate and the remainder of the trust estate will pass to the American Heart Association, an organization described in §§ 170(c), 2055(a) and 2522(a). The trust makes no provision for any other beneficiary. The value of Spouse's interest in the trust is $900,000, and the value of the American Heart Association's remainder interest is $2,100,000. What is the amount of Decedent's taxable estate?

A3. Decedent's taxable estate is zero. This is a very vanilla example of an IRC § 2056(b)(8) trust that qualifies as an exception to the terminable interest rule. Thus Spouse's interest qualifies for the marital deduction. [IRC § 2056(a)] In addition, the terms of the trust satisfy the requirements of a "charitable remainder annuity trust," so Decedent's estate will get a deduction under

IRC § 2055(a) for the value of the charity's interest. Between the IRC § 2055 charitable deduction and the IRC § 2056 marital deduction, the taxable estate is reduced to zero.

Q4. Marcia created a trust on January 1, Year 1. The trust gives her sister, Jan, an income interest for life. Upon Jan's death, the remainder will pass to Marcia's other sister, Cindy, or Cindy's estate. The trust also gives Alice, an individual unrelated to Marcia, Jan, or Cindy, a power to invade income or corpus of the trust up to a total $20,000 each year for the benefit of Jan and/or Cindy. Under the trust instrument, Alice has the discretion to apportion between Jan and Cindy any amounts withdrawn through the exercise of the annual invasion power. The trust only allowed Alice to exercise her annual invasion power during the month of December. At all times from the creation of the trust through the end of Year 3, the value of the trust corpus was $100,000. Alice never exercised her invasion power at any time. In Year 4, the value of the trust corpus grew to $200,000. Alice died in September of Year 4. How much of the trust corpus will be included in Alice's gross estate?

A4. The correct answer is zero. Alice held a power of appointment, which is not an interest in property for purposes of the estate tax. If Alice held a general power of appointment, however, there would be potential for inclusion under IRC § 2041(a)(2); however, in order to be a general power of appointment, Alice must be able to exercise her power for her own benefit (or to her creditors, her estate, or the creditors of her estate). Since Alice lacks the power to appoint to herself (or to her creditors, her estate, or the creditors of her estate), she does not hold a general power of appointment and thus there is no inclusion in her estate.

Q5. Three years prior to D's death, D purchased an annuity contract that will provide monthly payments to D for ten years. The contract provided that if D died before the expiration of the ten-year term, payments would be made to D's spouse, S, for the balance of the term. At the same time, X, D's uncle, created a trust that gives D an income interest for D's life. Upon D's death, the remainder will pass to D's cousin, Z, or to Z's estate if Z is not then living. Seven months prior to D's death, D assigned D's income interest under the trust to S. At the same time, D created a trust that provides an income interest to S for life and a remainder to D's child, C. D named Bank as trustee but retained the power to remove Bank as Trustee and name Trust Company as Bank's successor at any time for any reason. Based only on these facts, what will be included in D's gross estate?

A5. The value of the annuity contract will be included in D's gross estate under IRC § 2036—D dies holding a prescribed interest (right to enjoy the property or income therefrom) in transferred property (the funds used to buy the contract) for a prescribed period (a period that does not in fact end before D's death). No portion of the trust created by X will be included in D's gross estate. D only has an income interest in this trust and there is nothing to transfer at D's death. D's transfer of the income interest to S does not trigger inclusion under IRC § 2035(a) because that provision will only capture transfers made within three years of death of property which, if held by D until death, would cause inclusion under IRC §§ 2036, 2037, 2038, or 2042. As mentioned above, there would be no inclusion in D's estate if D simply held onto the income interest until death; thus, there is no inclusion in D's gross estate if D gives away the income interest within three years of death. Finally, none of the assets from the trust created by D will be included in D's gross estate. Although D has the power to substitute corporate trustees, D does not have the power to name D as trustee, so there is no argument that D still holds a power to alter or amend the terms of the transfer (IRC § 2038) or a prescribed interest (IRC § 2036).

CHAPTER 2: GIFT TAX

Q1. Bill gives $1 million to the Green Party. Is that amount a gift?

A1. No. Gift to political parties are not gifts. [IRC § 2501(a)(4); *see infra* discussion at II. B. 1. b)]

Q2. Jason owes Laura $15,000. Without any business purpose, Laura forgives the debt. Has Laura made a gift to Jason?

A2. Yes. Laura has made a gift to Jason of $15,000. *See supra* discussion at II. B. 3. a).

Q3. By contract Jack owes Jill $10,000 which is due on April 15, Year 1. The payment date passes with no payment. Jill does not seek payment and lets the statute of limitations run out on the collection of the debt. Has Jill made a transfer of property to Jack?

A3. Yes. By allowing the statute of limitations to run Jill transferred control of payment of the debt to Jack, who now may either pay, or not pay, the $10,000, as he chooses. *See* Estate of Lang, 613 F.2d 770 (9th Cir. 1980).

Q3. Bill transfers to Steve several state bonds that are exempt from taxation under IRC § 103. Has Bill made a gift to Steve that can be subject to the gift tax?

A4. Yes. The gift tax is an excise tax on the transfer of property, not a tax on the actual property transferred. Therefore, no statutory provision that exempts property from income taxation will prohibit the taxation under Chapter 12 (gift tax).

Q5. Douglas creates a trust that pays income to Nancy for her life and the remainder to Bruce. Nancy and Bruce are unrelated to Douglas. Douglas retains the right to change the remainder interest, but only with the consent of Nancy. Douglas does not maintain the power to change the income interest. Is there a completed transfer of any interest in property?

A5. Yes, but only of the income interest. Douglas has no dominion and control over the income interest and that is a completed gift. Even though Douglas may only change the remainder interest with Nancy's consent, since she does not have an adverse interest it is disregarded for determining Douglas' dominion and control over the property. *See* Reg. § 25.2511–2(e); discussion *supra* at II. B. 3. b) (4) (a).

Q6. David's father promises to pay David $20,000 if he stops chewing tobacco. David quits and receives $20,000. Has a gift transfer been made?

A6. Yes. Under IRC § 2512(b), a gift occurs when property is transferred for less than "adequate and full consideration in money or money's worth." Although the consideration (quitting a habit) is enough to support a contract, it is disregarded for gift tax purposes because it is not capable of being monetarily valued. [Reg. § 25.2512–8]

Q7. Kitty pays for ice-skating lessons and rink time for her minor daughter at a cost of $20,000 per year. Has Kitty made a gift?

A7. Probably not. Most likely these payments will not be considered gifts since they are in satisfaction of Kitty's support obligations. However, if the lessons were not treated as support under state law, they would be treated as a gift from Kitty to her daughter. *See* Rev. Rul. 68–379, 1968–2 C.B. 414; discussion *supra* at II. B. 4. b) (1).

Q8. Kitty transfers $20,000 to Whatsamatta University Law School for her 35–year–old son's law school tuition. State law provides Kitty does not have any support obligations to her son. Has Kitty made a gift?

A8. No. Even though Kitty has no support obligation, tuition payments made directly to educational organizations are "qualified transfers" and therefore are not treated as a transfer of property by gift. [IRC § 2503(e); discussion *supra* at II. B. 4. b) (2)]

Q9. Wally has a general power of appointment over $20,000 per year from a trust created by Theodore. The trust provides income to Wally, and the remainder interest to Wally's son, Beaver. If Wally does not exercise the power it will lapse. What are the gift tax consequences, if any, if Wally fails to exercise the power in a year when the trust corpus is $300,000?

A9. Wally is treated as transferring a $5,000 gift to Beaver in each year the power lapses. Under IRC § 2514(e), a lapse occurs only to the extent that the property that could have been appointed ($20,000) exceeds the greater of $5,000 or 5% of the trust ($15,000). Generally, since Wally has the income interest, the amount of the gift would be the value of the remainder interest of $5,000. However, since Beaver is a related party, IRC § 2702(a) values Wally's income interest at zero and the gift transfer is the entire $5,000.

Q10. In the current year Donor gives Mary an income interest in a trust for life, with the right to demand the corpus of the trust after 10 years. Donor's initial transfer to the trust is $20,000 and Mary's life estate interest, disregarding the right to demand the corpus, has a value of $17,280. What is the amount of taxable gifts from Donor to Mary from this transfer assuming the annual exclusion under IRC § 2503(b) is $10,000?

A10. $7,280. Even though Mary has the right to withdrawal, the right is disregarded under the second sentence of IRC § 2503(b)(1). After the power is disregarded Mary's interest may be valued ($17,280) and the IRC § 2503(b) exclusion taken (reducing the $17,280 by $10,000).

Q11. Using his separate property, Husband purchases a $100,000 annuity for his wife. The annuity provides annual payments to Wife for her life. If the total amounts of payments made before Wife's death are less than $100,000, additional payments are to be made to Son. Does the transfer of the annuity from Husband to Wife qualify for the marital deduction under IRC § 2523(a)?

A11. No. Here IRC § 2523(b)(1) applies and no marital deduction is allowed. Husband transferred an interest in property to Son that he might enjoy after the termination of Wife's life interest in the annuity. If the annuity had no payments to be made after Wife's death, or any additional payments to be made to Wife's estate, this would not be terminable interest property and a marital deduction is permitted. *See* Reg. § 25.2523(b)–1(b)(6)(ex. 3).

Q12. Husband transfers an apartment building to Alan, an unrelated third-party, reserving a right to the rental income from the property for the next 10 years. The next year, Husband transfers his remaining income interest in the property to Wife for no consideration. What are the tax consequences of the transfer to Wife?

A12. Husband has made a gift of property to Wife. There has been a transfer of a property interest and Husband received no consideration. [IRC § 2512(b)] Even though Husband makes the transfer of the income interest to Wife, no marital deduction is allowed here under IRC § 2523(a). Since Husband transferred an interest to Alan, and Alan receives the property after Wife's interest in the property terminates, this is a non-deductible terminable interest. [IRC § 2523(b)(1)] It is immaterial that the transfer of the interest to Alan was not completed in the same transaction as the transfer to Wife. *See* Reg. §§ 25.2523(b)–1(b)(2), 25.2523(b)–1(b)(6)(ex. 5).

Q13. Generally, under which of the following circumstances (if any) is a gift tax return required to be filed? Assume the IRC § 2503(b) annual exclusion amount is $10,000.

    A. A donor gives gifts to someone (other than a spouse) totaling more than $10,000.

    B. A donor gives a gift of a future interest in property less than $10,000.

    C. A donor gives a gift to an individual and splits the gift with donor's spouse.

    D. All of the above.

A13. All of the above. Gifts to any individual more than the IRC § 2503(b) exclusion amount requires a gift tax return. [IRC § 6019] Future interests do not qualify for the annual exclusion under IRC § 2503(b) so this transfer requires a gift tax return. Finally, split gifts require a gift tax return be filed showing consent to such treatment. While under certain circumstances both spouses may consent on one gift tax return, there are no joint gift tax returns. *See* II. C. 4. a).

Q14. Tom gifts a vase with a fair market value of $50,000 to his friend, Katie. Tom's adjusted basis in the vase is $10,000. What is the gross amount of the gift to Katie (without any reduction from IRC § 2503(b))?

    A. $10,000

B. $29,000

C. $40,000

D. $50,000

A14. D. Gifts are valued at there fair market value less any consideration received. The basis of the property is not relevant for computation of the gift tax. [IRC § 2512]

Q15. True or false: All gifts over $10,000 to an unrelated individual 38 years younger than the donor are subject to both the gift and generation-skipping tax. Assume the IRC § 2503(b) exclusion amount is $10,000.

A15. True. All "transfers of property by gift" are subject to the gift tax unless excluded. All generation-skipping transfers are subject to the GST tax. Unrelated individuals more than 37.5 years younger than the transferor are "skip persons" and therefore the transfer is a "direct skip." *See* IRC §§ 2601, 2612(c)(1), 2651(d)(3).

Q16. Bill transferred the following gifts to individuals during the current year. Which, if any, are "taxable gifts"?

1. $15,000 transferred to Bill's mother to offset medical expenses.

2. A $20,000 state bond exempt from Federal taxation under IRC § 103.

3. 500 shares of Macrohard stock transferred to Bill's sister, Tina. The stock had a basis of $3,000 and a fair market value of $20,000.

4. $17,000 paid to Whatsamatta University (a qualified educational organization) for his son's room and board.

A. All of the above

B. 2 and 3 only

C. 2, 3, 4, but not 1

D. 1, 2 and 3, but not 4

A16. A, all of the above. The payments made for medical expenses not paid directly to the medical provider are not excluded under IRC § 2503(e). [Reg.

§ 25.2503–6(c)(ex. 4)] The gift tax is imposed on all "transfers of property by gift" unless excluded by a provision in Chapter 12. [IRC § 2501(a)(1)] The fact the state bond is exempt from Federal income taxation is irrelevant to the application of the gift tax. The stock is valued at its fair market value at the time of transfer and is therefore not under the annual exclusion amount of $10,000 (not adjusted for inflation). [IRC §§ 2503(b), 2512] Only amounts paid for tuition are possibly excluded under IRC § 2503(e); room and board does not qualify. [Reg. § 25.2503–6(b)(2)]

Q17. Jimmy transfers several assets in the current year.

- Transfer of his business to his son for $50,000. The fair market value of the business at the time of transfer was $125,000.

- Transfer of $20,000 to the Republican National Committee.

- Transfer of stock worth $20,000 to the University of Florida, where he got his LL.M. in taxation. The basis of the stock was $3,000.

- Payment directly to the school of $17,000 for the college tuition of his niece.

What is the total amount of taxable gift transfers, before any IRC § 2503(b) or unified credits, given by Jimmy?

A. $50,000

B. $75,000

C. $95,000

D. $132,000

E. None of the above

A17. $75,000. Jimmy gave a gift to his son of the value of the business ($125,000) less any consideration paid ($50,000). [IRC § 2512(b)] The other transfers are excluded from taxable gifts since they are either: 1) a transfer to a political organizations (excluded under IRC § 2501(a)(4)), 2) a charitable contribution (deductible under IRC § 2522(a)), 3) or a qualified transfer for tuition costs (excluded under IRC § 2503(e)(1)).

Q18. Dennis transfers a life insurance policy on his life valued at $100,000 to a trust. After Dennis dies, the insurance proceeds are to be held in trust with the income going to Steve, remainder to Trevor, Steve's son. Dennis transfers $10,000 to the trust each year to pay the premiums on the insurance policy. Steve has the non-cumulative yearly right to withdraw $10,000 from the corpus of the trust. What are the estate and gift tax results of the $10,000 yearly transfer? What are some ways to avoid any negative consequences? Assume the IRC § 2503(b) exclusion amount is $10,000.

A18.

Dennis: Steve's right to withdraw $10,000 from the trust each year is a present interest in the trust. Therefore Dennis receives an IRC § 2503(b) exclusion of $10,000 and the transfer of the premiums creates no taxable gifts for Dennis.

Steve:

Gift tax consequences: Steve has a general power of appointment over $10,000 each year. The power lapses under IRC § 2514(e) for the amount that is the greater of $5,000 or 5% of the trust ($5,000 here since the trust is worth $100,000). This means the amount by which the transfer of $10,000 is greater than $5,000 (that is $5,000) is treated as being "released" and therefore "transferred" by Steve each year under IRC § 2514(a). The transfer is not a present interest since no beneficiaries have a current right to the income from the trust. The transfer is to both Steve and Trevor since it is a transfer to the trust. However, Steve's life estate interest will be valued at $0 after the application of IRC § 2702. Steve has made a $5,000 gift to Trevor.

Estate tax consequences: Again, Steve has a general power of appointment that has lapsed. Under IRC § 2041(a)(2), since IRC § 2036 would include the amount in Steve's gross estate at death (Steve has made a transfer, and has an income interest in the trust that is measured by his life), Steve must include a fractional share of the transfer in his gross estate.

Planning provision: The negative consequences of IRC § 2041 and IRC § 2514 could have been avoided by either decreasing the withdrawal right (to $5,000), increasing the amount in the trust (to $200,000 in this instance, since 5% of $200,000 is $10,000), or giving what is called a "hanging *Crummey power.*" If the *Crummey* power was hanging, Steve would retain the power over the amount of the withdrawal right which exceeded the 5 by 5 power. In this way the power would not have gift or estate tax consequences unless Steve died while holding the power.

CHAPTER 3: GENERATION–SKIPPING TRANSFER TAX

Q1. Answer true or false, are the following individuals skip persons in relation to Tom?

    a.   Greta, Tom's grandchild. Greta's parents, Chris (Tom's child) and Spouse, are both living.

    b.   Greta, if at the time of transfer Chris is not living.

    c.   Greta's child Evie (Tom's great-grandchild), if Chris is not living at the time of transfer.

    d.   Greta, if Chris is living at the time of transfer, but Spouse (Greta's mother) is not.

    e.   Chris

    f.   Dora, who is unrelated and was born 38 years after Tom.

    g.   Maggie, the grandchild of Bart. Bart is Tom's cousin (the son of Tom's Uncle Homer). Bart is dead at the time of transfer.

A1:

    a.   True. Greta has a generational assignment of three (Tom's grandparent→Tom's parent→Tom→Chris (Tom's child)→Greta (Tom's grandchild). Tom has a generational assignment of one. (Tom's grandparent→Tom's parent→Tom) [IRC § 2651(b)(1)] Greta is a skip person since she has a generational assignment two below Tom. [IRC § 2613(a)(1)]

    b.   False. Under the deceased parent rule, if Chris is dead at the time of transfer Greta moves up one generational assignment (from three to two). [IRC § 2651(e)(1)] Since Greta's changed generational assignment is not two below Tom's she is not a skip person. [IRC § 2613(b)]

    c.   True. Even though the deceased parent rule applies, Evie's generational assignment is three (instead of four) and will be two below Tom's. [IRC § 2651(b)(1), (e)(1)] Evie is a skip person. [IRC § 2613(a)(1)]

    d.   True. The deceased parent rule only applies to the "individual's parent who is a lineal descendant of the parent of the transferor." [IRC § 2651(e)(1)] The rule only applies to the descendants of Tom's parent, of which Spouse is not.

e.   False. Chris has a generational assignment of two (Tom's grandparent→Tom's parent→Tom→Chris) and is therefore not a skip person. [IRC §§ 2613(a), 2651(b)(1)]

f.   True. Dora's generational assignment is determined under IRC § 2651(d). Since Dora is 38 years younger than Tom, her generational assignment is 3. [IRC § 2651(d)(3)] Dora is a skip person since she has a generational assignment two below Tom. [IRC § 2613(a)(1)]

g.   True. Maggie's generational assignment is three. Even though Bart is dead at the time of transfer, the deceased parent rule does not apply since the rule only applies to "a lineal descendant of the parent of the transferor [Tom]." [IRC § 2651(e)(1)(B)] Maggie is not a lineal descendant of Tom's parent so the rule does not apply to her unless Tom has no living lineal descendants. [IRC § 2651(e)(1)(flush)]

Q2. Teruo makes the following transfers in the current year:

1.   A transfer of $30,000 directly to his son Brit.

2.   A transfer of $50,000 to an irrevocable trust, the income of which goes to Teruo's grandchild, Kaia (Brit's son), and the remainder to his great-grandchild, Kelley.

3.   A transfer of $100,000 to a corporation whose shares are split equally between Brit and Kaia.

Which, if any, of the above are generation-skipping transfers?

A2.

Transfer #1 is not a generation-skipping transfer. Brit is only one generational level below Teruo [IRC § 2651(b)(1)] and is therefore not a skip person [IRC § 2613(b)].

Transfer #2 is a direct skip generation-skipping transfer. [IRC § 2612(c)] Both Kaia and Kelley are more than two generational levels below Teruo [IRC § 2651(b)(1)] and are therefore skip persons [IRC § 2613(a)(1)]. The trust is a skip person since the only Chapter 13 interest in the trust (the income interest) [IRC § 2652(c)(1)(A)] is held by a skip person (Kaia) [IRC § 2613(b)(2)(A)].

Transfer #3: 50% ($50,000) of the transfer is a direct skip. [IRC § 2612(c)] Transfers to entities require the application of the IRC § 2651(f)(2) look-through rules. Under IRC § 2651(f)(2), the transfer is treated as being made to each individual having a beneficial interest in the entity, here Kaia and Brit. Since Kaia is a skip person (see above in Transfer #2), the portion being treated as transferred as a direct skip.

Q3. Todd creates an irrevocable trust with the income interest going to Gertie, Todd's grandchild, and the remainder to Helen, Todd's great-grandchild. Todd gives his friend, Xavier, the power to distribute the income of the trust to Charlie, Todd's child. What generation-skipping transfer occurs, if any, when Xavier relinquishes the non-general power to give income to Charlie?

A3. A taxable termination occurs. Gift tax consequences are present at the creation of the trust, but no direct skip occurs, since a non-skip person, Charlie, holds a Chapter 13 interest by way of being a permissible recipient of trust income. [IRC §§ 2613(b), 2651(b)(1), 2652(c)(1)(B)] When Xavier relinquishes his power, Charlie's Chapter 13 interest terminates, leaving only skip persons, Gertie (Todd's grandchild) and Helen (Todd's great-grandchild), to receive trust proceeds. [IRC §§ 2613(a)(1), 2651(b)(1)] There are no gift tax consequences upon such termination since Xavier's power is a non-general power and not subject to gift taxation. [*See* IRC § 2514]

Q4. Terri creates an irrevocable trust with the income to be distributed to Clara, Terri's daughter, for life. After Clara's death the corpus is to be distributed equally between Doug, Terri's second child, and Gaia, Terri's grandchild. What, if any, generation-skipping transfers occur at Clara's death?

A4. There is a generation-skipping transfer at Clara's death. There is no IRC § 2612(a)(1) taxable termination since some of the property goes to a non-skip person, Doug. [IRC § 2612(a)(1)(A)] However, since the interest in property was terminated on the death of a lineal descendant of T (Clara) and the property was distributed to a skip person (Gaia), a partial taxable termination occurs under IRC § 2612(a)(2). One-half of the trust assets will be subject to a taxable termination generation-skipping transfer. [IRC § 2612(a)(2)]

Q5. Thelma transfers a piece of property worth $500,000 to her grandson Jack. Both of Jack's parents are alive at the time of transfer. Assuming that both the gift and GST tax rates are 40%, what is the amount of tax due? In computing your answer, disregard the IRC § 2503(b) exclusion, the gift tax credit under IRC § 2505, and assume an inclusion ratio of one (IRC § 2642).

A5.

- Chapter 13 (GST) tax due: Jack generational assignment is "3" [IRC § 2651(b)(1)] and is therefore two generational assignments below

Thelma and a skip person [IRC § 2613(a)(1)]. The transfer is a direct skip. [IRC § 2612(c)(1)] The taxable amount is the "value of property received by the transferee [Jack]," or $500,000. [IRC § 2623] The applicable rate is 40% since the inclusion ratio is "1" and the assumed tax rate is 40%. [IRC § 2641(a)] The amount of GST tax due is $200,000 (40% of $500,000). [IRC § 2602]

- Chapter 12 (gift) tax due: Thelma has made a "transfer of property by gift" that is subject to the gift tax. [IRC § 2501(a)(1)] The total amount of gifts present is $700,000; $500,000 fair market value of the property [IRC §§ 2511(a), 2512(b)] plus the $200,000 of Chapter 13 tax due [IRC § 2515]. The gift tax liability is $280,000 (40% of $700,000) since the gift tax rate is an assumed 40%. [IRC § 2501(a)]

- An additional issue of the basis of the property to Jack is present, but Thelma's basis is not given. Jack's basis will be determined under IRC § 1015 as a transferred basis (assuming the property has appreciated while in Thelma's possession), with increases for the gift and GST tax paid under IRC §§ 1015(d) and 2654(a).

Q6. Trevor gives $50,000 as a gift to his grandson Richard. Both of Richard's parents are alive at the time of transfer. Which of the below statements on the generation-skipping transfer tax consequences is correct?

A. The transfer is not subject to both the gift and generation-skipping transfer taxes.

B. The transfer is subject to both the gift tax and generation-skipping transfer tax.

C. Richard is not a skip person since both his parents are living at the time of transfer.

D. If Trevor had placed the money in an irrevocable trust with income to Richard, the transfer would not be subject to the generation-skipping transfer tax.

A6. B.

APPENDIX B

Practice Examination

SUGGESTED TIME LIMIT: 2 HOURS

This practice examination consists of six (6) essay questions. If you want to simulate actual exam conditions, write out answers to each question and stick to the suggested time allocated to each question. Alternatively, you may want to outline answers to the essay questions and compare your outline with the sample answers provided.

This practice examination was actually administered as a final examination. The sample answers are the actual answers written by a student. They may be incomplete or contain errors. Some notes to the sample answers are given in italic print.

ESSAY QUESTIONS

All six (6) of the essay questions are based upon the following facts:

Robin, a United States citizen, has never made taxable gifts. Robin's spouse, Terry, died in Year 1.

In October, Year 7, Robin transferred a policy of insurance on Robin's life to an irrevocable trust. The trust instrument provided that upon the death of Robin, the trust corpus (the death benefits from the life insurance policy) would be distributed in equal shares to Robin's children, Alex and Lou (both United States citizens), or to the survivor if one child predeceased Robin. The trust instrument specifically provided that no distributions were to be made from the trust to any beneficiary until after Robin's death. Robin was named trustee of the trust, but otherwise Robin retained no interest in the trust corpus. The value of the life insurance policy at the time of Robin's transfer to the trust (and at all times prior to Robin's death in Year 9) was $50,000. The policy pays a death benefit of $500,000 at Robin's death.

In July, Year 8, Robin contributed $20,000 to the trust. The trustee then used these funds to pay the premium on the life insurance policy owned by the trust.

In September, Year 8, Alex died. At Alex's death, Alex owned stocks and bonds (fair market value $2 million) and investment real estate (fair market value $2 million). Alex's will provided that Alex's entire estate would pass in trust for the benefit of Alex's spouse, Pat (a United States citizen). Under the terms of the trust, the trustee (Pat) was allowed distribute income and/or principal to Pat only as needed for Pat's maintenance, education, support, and health. At Pat's death, the remaining trust corpus was to be distributed to the American Cancer Society. Alex had never made any taxable gifts.

In March, Year 9, Robin died. At Robin's death, Robin owned a residence (fair market value $1.5 million) and a substantial bank account (date of death balance $1.5 million). As provided in Robin's will, the entire estate was distributed to Lou, Robin's surviving child.

[END OF FACT PATTERN]

Question 1 (20 minutes).

Discuss the federal gift tax consequences to Robin upon the formation of the irrevocable trust in Year 7.

Question 2 (10 minutes).

Discuss the federal gift tax consequences to Robin from the cash contribution to the irrevocable trust in Year 8.

Question 3 (10 minutes).

Assuming Robin had been your client, what changes to the trust instrument, if any, would you have recommended?

Question 4 (40 minutes).

Discuss the federal estate tax consequences to Alex's estate upon Alex's death in Year 8. Compute Alex's "taxable estate" as defined in IRC § 2051, but do not attempt any specific tax calculations.

Question 5 (20 minutes).

Assuming Alex had been your client, what changes to Alex's will, if any, would you have recommended?

Question 6 (20 minutes).

Discuss the federal estate tax consequences to Robin' estate upon Robin' death in Year 9. Compute Robin' "taxable estate" as defined in IRC § 2051 and the amount under IRC § 2001(b)(1) upon which a "tentative tax" will be computed, but do not attempt any specific tax calculations.

SAMPLE ANSWERS TO PRACTICE EXAMINATION

Answer to Question 1

This transaction is a completed gift to the extent Robin has given up dominion and control over the property. Under § 2511, transfers in trust are considered gifts. Because this trust was irrevocable there has been a completed gift. The value of the gift is the value of the insurance policy at the time of the transfer. This is generally the replacement cost of $50,000 in this case. Therefore, Robin has made a taxable gift of $50,000 to each of his 2 children.

The next question is whether Robin is allowed two annual exclusions. The answer in this case is No. In order to receive an annual exclusion under § 2503(b), the gift must be of a present interest. This is not a gift of a present interest because Alex & Lou did not have any right to the immediate use and enjoyment of the property. No distributions could be made until Robin's death. Therefore, the "total amount of gifts" made by Robin in Year 7 was $50,000. This amount will be taxable and Robin must file a gift tax return. Robin will owe no tax because there will be a sufficient unified credit available as Robin has made no previous taxable gifts.

Answer to Question 2

This payment also represented a completed gift to Alex and Lou of $20,000. No annual exclusions are available because there is no present right to the immediate use and enjoyment of the property. It does not appear that Robin, as trustee, can affect the use and enjoyment of this property. Therefore, Robin has taxable gifts of $20,000 and must file a return. Again, the unified credit amount will be sufficient, such that Robin will owe no tax.

Answer to Question 3

First, I would have given each of the beneficiaries a *Crummey* withdrawal power. This would allow for at least some use of the annual exclusion. I would have either limited the power to $5,000 or used a "hanging power" to avoid lapse problems. I would probably have recommended the use of contingent beneficiaries to take more advantage of the annual exclusions. Finally, I probably would have recommended a different trustee simply to avoid all incidents of ownership by Robin in the policy. However, this was probably OK because of limited trustee powers.

Answer to Question 4

The "taxable estate" is defined as the gross estate reduced by the deductions allowed for in §§ 2053, 2054, 2055 & 2056. The gross estate here is $4 million. This is the $2 million of stocks & bonds and the $2 million in investment real estate which are included under § 2033. The first issue is whether Alex's interest in the trust is included under § 2033 as well. It is not because he did not survive Robin.

The next issue is whether any deductions are allowed. The first possibility is the marital deduction available under § 2056. This seems logical because the property goes initially to Alex's spouse, Pat. However, because of a poorly drafted will, no marital deduction will be allowed. Under § 2056 a bequest to a spouse is allowed as a deduction unless it is a terminable interest under § 2056(b). Because this interest will terminate on Pat's death and the ACS will then receive the property and enjoy its benefits, this is a terminable interest. Absent some exception to the terminable interest rule, no marital deduction will be allowed.

The first possible exception which comes to mind is the QTIP election under (b)(7). This will not work however, because Pat does not receive a qualifying income interest. Pat must have the right to all of the income at least annually. Here, Pat's interest is limited by an ascertainable standard, which could be less than all of the income. The charitable remainder trust exception under (b)(8) also fails because this is not a qualified CRT, which will be discussed below. Therefore, no marital deduction is allowed.

We must then examine whether a charitable deduction is allowed. Under § 2055(e), a charitable deduction is not allowed for any bequest to a charity in trust where part of the trust goes to a non-charity. This applies unless the trust qualifies under § 664 as a CRAT or CRUT. This trust has a remainder going to charity, but it fails the requirement that either a fixed annuity or a fixed percentage of the trust corpus be payable to the income beneficiary. The other requirements are met, but the trust still does not qualify as either a CRUT or a CRAT. Because of this no charitable deduction is allowed.

Absent a marital and charitable deduction, the "taxable estate" is equal to $4 million minus any administrative expenses under § 2053.

Note: This was a very good answer, even though the description of the terminable interest rule was not entirely accurate or complete. In addition, it would have been helpful if the requirements for a charitable remainder annuity trust or charitable remainder unitrust were laid out with more specificity. Still, the answer focused on what was important and came to the correct answer.

Answer to Question 5

There are a couple of different routes which could have been utilized in this situation. First, this trust could have been drafted such that it qualified as a CRUT or a CRAT. This would involve giving Pat only a fixed annuity or a fixed percentage of the trust. This would have qualified the entire interest for deductions, both the marital and charitable.

The second avenue is probably more in keeping with Alex's objective of supporting Pat during his/her life. This would involve qualifying the interest as an interest with respect to which an election under § 2056(b)(7) could be made. The trustee would be required to pay all of the income to Pat at least annually. In addition, the trustee could have been given a power to invade the corpus as necessary for Pat's support, maintenance, education, or health. This is OK because no property can be appointed to anyone else. A remainder interest could then be given in the trust to the ACS. These provisions would allow the election to be made and marital deduction to be used.

Note: Sadly, the student who wrote this answer did not get many points. There is no mention of a "credit shelter trust," which could utilize Alex's remaining exemption amount. If everything qualifies for a deduction, Alex's taxable estate would be zero and Alex's exemption amount would be wasted. The answer should have recommended a credit shelter trust and set forth the basic features of a credit shelter trust (distributions to the spouse for maintenance, education, support or heath, remainder to another party). In addition, the description of an IRC § 2056(b)(8) trust was somewhat lacking—no explanation of why the use of a charitable remainder trust would have qualified Pat's interest for the marital deduction (i.e., no reference to IRC § 2056(b)(8) itself). The discussion of the QTIP option was good, however.

Answer to Question 6

Robin's gross estate will include the $1.5 million residence and the $1.5 million bank account for a total of $3 million. Robin's gross estate will also include the proceeds of the insurance policy on his life because of § 2035. § 2035 includes in the gross estate the value of property transferred within the last 3 yrs which would have been included under §§ 2036, 2037, 2038, and § 2042. § 2042 includes in the gross estate the proceeds of all insurance policies on the decedent life (sic) receivable by other beneficiaries, if the decedent possesses any incidents of ownership.

Although Robin is Trustee and has legal title, if his powers are limited to normal fiduciary powers, this does not qualify as incidents of ownership. However, Robin did have ownership & incidents of ownership of the policy when it was transferred to the trust in 1996. Because this transfer took place within 3 yrs, the $500,000 proceeds are included in Robin's gross estate under § 2035. Therefore, Robin's taxable estate is $3.5 million minus any administrative expenses under § 2053. No marital or charitable deductions are allowed.

APPENDIX C

Text Correlation Chart

Topic in Outline	Bittker, Clark and McCouch (9th ed. 2005)	Bloom, Boyle, Gaubartz and Solomon (3d ed. 2002)	Campfield, Dickinson, and Turnier (2d ed. 2002)	McDaniel, Repetti, and Caron (5th ed. 2003)	Pennell (4th ed. 2003)	Stephens, Maxfield, Lind, Calfee, and Smith (8th ed. 2002)	Willbanks (2004)
1. Perspective	1-43	1-13, 26-56	2-24	2-64	1-11	¶1.01-¶1.06	
2. Property Held at Death [IRC §2033]	181-205	59-65, 365-366	276-297	100-123	41-63	¶4.05	211-217, 219-233
3. Transfers with a Retained Life Estate [IRC § 2036]	268-331	322-355, 389-396, 400-404, 409-419, 430-433	345-417	204-254, 279-298	188-250, 266-314	¶4.08	236-238, 241-260
4. Transfers Taking Effect at Death [IRC § 2037]	331-348	369-375	450-461	269-275, 279-298	250-266	¶4.09	238, 301-305
5. Revocable Transfers [IRC § 2038]	238-267	378-380, 390, 400-405, 409-419, 430-437, 451, 472	419-448	255-268, 279-298	266-346	¶4.10	238-241, 260-300
6. Certain Transfers within Three Years of Death [IRC § 2035]	220-238	305-313, 405, 476-484	411-415, 526-546	418-433	153-180, 243-248	¶4.07	235-236, 305-318
7. Consideration Paid by the Recipient [IRC § 2043]	109-121	116, 338-346	548-569	178-199, 294-298	353-389	¶4.15	
8. Annuities [IRC § 2039]	349-364	491-521	463-487	320-337	519-561	¶4.11	319-351
9. Jointly Owned Property [IRC § 2040]	209-219	563-572, 575-579	299-311	338-354	391-432	¶4.12	219-233
10. Powers of Appointment [IRC § 2041]	401-428	67-76, 525-535, 543-544, 553-554	488-524	355-376	109-151, 248-250	¶4.13	353-378
11. Life Insurance [IRC § 2042]	364-401	460-476, 479-484	312-343	377-417	435-517	¶4.14	379-408
12. QTIP Property [IRC § 2044]	521, 530	138-139	679-680	606-610	658, 664-665	¶4.16	
13. Valuation Issues	574-632	76-103, 139-147	168-246, 248-263, 281	676-777	64-106, 927-957	¶4.02-¶4.04, ¶19.02-¶19.05	57-105
14. Certain Expenses and Debts [IRC § 2053]	429-463	103-117	571-584	491-524	563-600	¶5.03	
15. Charitable Bequests [IRC § 2055]	464-490	160-173	586-613	532-551	721-751	¶5.05	
16. Martial Bequest [IRC § 2056]	490-552	118-160	614-706	572-645	601-709	¶5.06	
17. Gift tax Introduction		185	26-31	65-67	789	¶1.03, ¶9.01	119-120
18. Imposition of Gift Tax [IRC § 2501]	44, 109-121, 132-139	185-198	26-31	124-176, 410-417	798-805, 832-838, 848-863	¶9.02	129-135, 153-154, 170-176
19. Transfers in General [IRC § 2511]	83-109	185-198, 317-322, 365, 377, 383-389, 399, 408-409, 429-430, 455-457, 559-563	70-97	124-130, 143-156, 299-319, 350-353, 410-417		¶10.01	
20. "By Gift" [IRC § 2512(b)]	55-77	205-207, 491	32-35, 57-69	165-176	838-863, 876-919	¶10.02[3]-[6]	155-159, 176-184, 185-208
21. Powers of Appointment [IRC § 2514]	427	524-534, 538-543, 550-553	98-103	355-376	919-921	¶10.04	353-378
22. Disclaimers [IRC § 2518]	165-180	242-250, 587-590	105-109	434-444	819-831	¶10.07	149-152
23. Dispositions of Certain Life Estates [IRC § 2519]	537-538	138-139, 270-271	161	661	666-671	¶10.08	
24. Gifts by Husband and Wife to Third Party [IRC § 2513]	25, 551-552	202, 208-209, 579-580	163-164	638-640	434, 924-925	¶10.03	
25. Payments of Direct Skips GST Tax [IRC § 2515]		313-314	727	660-662		¶10.05	
26. Below-Market Gift Loans [IRC § 7872]	45-53	198-205	35-45	130-143	805-813	¶10.01[2][f]	139-146
27. Special Valuation Rules [IRC § 2702]	77-83	264-266, 318-319	244-246	770-777	957-969	¶19.03	102-106, 242-244
28. Annual Exclusion [IRC § 2503(b)]	139-165	208-235, 457-459	111-162	446-490	876-919	¶9.04	
29. Gift Tax Deductions	464-552	267-272	160-162	532-551, 637-638	847-848, 921-924	¶11.02-¶11.04	
30. Computation of the Gift Tax [IRC § 2502]	17-23	28-30, 35-40	27-29	66-67, 552-559	789-798	¶9.03[3]	107-113
31. Generation-Skipping Transfer (GST) Tax Introduction	560	40-42, 275-277	726-728	69-72, 648-653	981-989	¶1.04, ¶12.01	515-517
32. GST Terminology	562-565	277-278, 294-299	728-729	654-656	989-992, 1007-1012	¶13.03, ¶17.01-¶17.04	517-523
33. Generation Skipping Transfers	565-567	41, 278-288	728-729	653-656, 658-660	992-997	¶13.01-¶13.02	523-527
34. Computation of the GST Tax	567-569	42-43, 288-293, 355-356	728-735	660-669	997-1007, 1012-1026	¶12.02, ¶14.02-¶14.05, ¶15.02-¶15.03, ¶16.01-¶16.02	528-534
35. Collateral Issues	647-	43, 295-301	731	669-674		¶18.01-¶18.05	

APPENDIX D

Glossary

This glossary is intended to provide the reader with a brief definition of some of the terms frequently encountered in federal wealth transfer taxation. Many of the terms, however, do not lend themselves to a brief definition because they are highly technical or conceptual. More detailed information can be found in the main text of the outline.

A

Adjusted Taxable Gifts: The total amount of taxable gifts made by the decedent after 1976, but not including any such gifts that are includible in determining the decedent's gross estate. [IRC § 2001(b)]

Alternate Valuation Date: The date six months after the decedent's death. Under IRC § 2032, the decedent's personal representative may elect to value assets included in the gross estate as of the alternate valuation date instead of the date of death, but only where such an election results in a reduced liability for estate tax.

Annual Exclusion: The total amount that an individual may transfer by gift to any one individual during a calendar year without creating a "taxable gift" and without having to file a gift tax

return. [IRC § 2503(b)] The annual exclusion only applies to gifts of present interests in property; no annual exclusion is available for gifts of future interests. As of 2011, the annual exclusion amount is $13,000.

Annuity: A contractual arrangement whereby one party (usually an insurance company) agrees to make a series of payments, often quarterly or annually, to the other party or the other party's assignee.

Applicable Exclusion Amount: The cumulative amount that an individual may transfer, whether during life or at death, without triggering liability for federal estate or gift tax. [IRC § 2010(c); 2505(a)] As of 2011, the applicable exclusion amount for gift tax and for estate tax purposes is the same, $5 million. For estate tax and gift tax purposes, a surviving spouse may claim an additional exclusion (called the "deceased spousal unused exclusion amount") if proper elections are made on the deceased spouse's estate tax return. The deceased spousal unused exclusion amount is generally equal to that portion of the deceased's spouse's applicable exclusion amount that was not utilized by the deceased spouse in making wealth transfers during life or at death.

Applicable Family Member: For purposes of Chapter 14, the transferor's spouse as well as the ancestors and their spouses of either the transferor or the transferor's spouse. The lineal descendants of the transferor or the transferor's spouse are not included. [IRC § 2701(e)(2)]

Applicable Fraction: A component of determining the applicable tax rate for purposes of the generation-skipping transfer tax, computed by taking the amount of GST exemption allocated (if any) to the transaction or trust, divided by the value of the property received (for direct skips or taxable distributions) or the value of the trust (for taxable terminations), less any federal or state tax paid and charitable deductions allowed on the property. Subtracting the applicable fraction from the number 1 determines the "inclusion ratio" applicable to the transaction. [IRC § 2642(a)]

Applicable Rate: Used in computing the GST tax. To compute the GST tax, the "taxable amount" is multiplied by the "applicable rate." [IRC § 2602] The applicable rate is the product of the "maximum Federal estate tax rate" multiplied by the "inclusion ratio." [IR § 2641(a)]

Applicable Restriction: Any limitation on the entity's ability to liquidate that either lapses to any extent after the transfer or can be removed after the transfer by the transferor or any member of the transferor's family. [IRC § 2704(b)(2)] Applicable restrictions are to be disregarded when valuing a transferred interest in the entity.

Ascertainable Standard: An enforceable limitation on the discretion given to a trustee or other fiduciary to distribute principal or income to a beneficiary. For example, where a trustee is authorized to distribute principal or income for the "maintenance, education, support, or health" of a beneficiary, the trustee's power to distribute principal or income to the beneficiary is limited by an ascertainable standard.

B

Below–Market Loan: A demand loan where the interest rate is less than the applicable federal short-term rate for the year in question, or a term loan where the amount loaned exceeds the discounted present value of all payments due under the loan. Certain below market loans are covered by IRC § 7872.

Blockage Discount: An adjustment made to the liquidation value of property included in the gross estate or transferred by gift (usually marketable securities) to reflect the fact that the trading volume in the applicable market may not be large enough to absorb the sale of the large block at issue. For example, if the decedent owned 40% of the stock of a publicly-traded company, the sale of the entire block at once would almost certainly reduce the trading price per share.

Buy–Sell Agreement: A contractual arrangement between two or more parties that fixes the price at which property may be transferred. Such agreements are most common in the context of closely-held businesses because owners want to restrict the class of eligible co-owners, but they can be utilized for any form of property. Where a person agrees to purchase or sell property at an agreed value, that agreement is often good evidence of the property's value.

C

Charitable Deduction: A deduction applicable to both the estate tax and the gift tax that allows for the transfer of property to a charitable organization. [IRC §§ 2055, 2522]

Charitable Lead Trust (CLT): A variation of the charitable remainder trust, except that the annual payments are made to the charitable organization with the remainder passing to one or more non-charitable beneficiaries. All other requirements applicable to charitable remainder trusts apply to charitable lead trusts.

Charitable Remainder Annuity Trust (CRAT): A variation of the charitable remainder trust where the non-charitable beneficiary receives a fixed annuity amount paid at least annually.

Charitable Remainder Trust: A trust where a fixed amount (or fixed percent- age of trust assets) ranging from 5% to 50% of the initial value of the trust's corpus is paid at least annually to the non-charitable beneficiary for his or her life or for a term not to exceed 20 years. At the end of the trust term, the remainder interest passes to one or more qualified charities. The present value of the charity's remainder interest (using annuity tables and assumed interest rates computed by the Service under the rules of IRC § 7520) must be at least 10% of the value of the property transferred to the trust. In addition, no other payments may be made to any other person.

Charitable Remainder Unitrust (CRUT): A variation of the charitable remainder trust where the non-charitable beneficiary receives a fixed percentage of the net fair market value of the trust assets, as determined annually.

Conservation Easement: A voluntary agreement with respect to real property to limit certain types of uses of the property or to prevent development of the property, while protecting the property's ecological or open-space values.

Control Premium: An adjustment made to the liquidation value of stock or other ownership interests included in the gross estate or transferred by gift to reflect the fact that the property represents a controlling interest in an entity. A willing buyer will pay more than liquidation value if the buyer is assured to have control over the entity. Often, the control premium is seen as the inverse of the minority interest discount.

Controlled Corporation: For purposes of IRC § 2036(b), a corporation in which the decedent owned or had the right to vote stock possessing at least 20% of the total combined voting power of all classes of stock at any time following the gratuitous transfer (or, if longer, the three-year period ending on the decedent's death).

Credit Shelter Trust: A common estate planning strategy fully utilizing the applicable exclusion amounts of married couples, whereby the estate of the first spouse to die is apportioned between two beneficiaries: that portion of the estate equal to the then-remaining exemption amount is allocated to the credit shelter trust and the balance passes to the marital deduction share (either outright to the surviving spouse or to a QTIP trust). The credit shelter trust typically provides the surviving spouse with access to income or principal as needed for the surviving spouse's maintenance, education, support, or health.

Crummey **Powers**: General powers of appointment given to trust beneficiaries such that transfers to the trust will qualify for the gift tax annual exclusion. Named after the Ninth Circuit case that upheld their validity.

Curtesy: A husband's right under state law to a prescribed portion of his deceased wife's estate.

D

Demand Loan: A loan either payable in full at any time on the demand of the lender or non-transferable and conditioned on the performance of substantial future services by an individual. [IRC § 7872(f)(5)]

Direct Skip: A transfer of an interest in property to a skip person that is subject to the estate or gift tax. A direct skip is one of the three types of generation-skipping transfers.

Disclaimer: If any person makes a "qualified disclaimer" under IRC § 2518, the interest in property is treated as if it was never transferred. The same rule applies for disclaimers for the estate, gift and GST tax.

Discounted Present Value: The current value of a sum of money due at a future time assuming a certain interest rate. The discounted present value can be determined by formula, accounting tables, financial calculator or spreadsheet. For example, the discounted present value of $1 million due in 10 years at an assumed rate of 10% annually is $385,543. If the $385,543 is held at 10% interest per year, after 10 years it will increase to $1 million.

Dower: A wife's right under state law to a prescribed portion of her deceased husband's estate.

E

Estate Freeze: A plan to slow or stop the appreciation in the estate tax value of an asset in the hands of the taxpayer while transferring the bulk of the asset's growth to the beneficiary at a low tax cost.

Estate Tax: An excise imposed on the gratuitous transfer of wealth at death.

Estate Tax Inclusion Period (ETIP): That period starting with the transfer of property includible in the transferor's gross estate and ending at the earlier of one of three events: (1) when the property is no longer potentially includible in the transferor's gross estate; (2) when the property is subject to a generation-skipping transfer (but only for such portion of the property); or (3) when the transferor dies. The significance of the termination of the ETIP is that it determines (1) the GST exemption allocation, (2) when the property is valued in calculating the inclusion ratio, and (3) when covered direct skips occur.

Executor Purchase Rule: No marital deduction is allowed where a terminable interest is, at the direction of the decedent, to be acquired by the personal representative for the surviving spouse.

Exemption Amount: A shorthand term for the applicable credit amount. It refers to the cumulative amount that an individual may transfer, whether during life or at death, without triggering liability for federal estate or gift tax. [IRC §§ 2010(c); 2505(a)] After 2010, the exemption amount for gift tax, generation-skipping transfer tax, and estate tax purposes is unified at $5 million and is adjusted for inflation.

F

Fair Market Value: "[T]he price at which the property would change hands between a willing buyer and a willing seller, neither being under any compulsion to buy or sell and both having

reasonable knowledge of relevant facts." [Reg. § 20.2031–1(b)]

Five-by-Five Power: A general power of appointment that can be exercised only to the extent of the greater of $5,000 or 5% of the value of the property subject to the power. Limiting the power holder's interest to a five-by-five power ensures that the power holder will not make a gift to the other trust beneficiaries, or have gross estate inclusion, when the power lapses without exercise. [IRC §§ 2041(b)(2), 2514(e)]

Fractional Interest Discount: An adjustment to the value of assets held in co-ownership to reflect the fact that a willing buyer will not pay full value for an undivided interest in an asset because of the costs to partition the property or sever the interest, not to mention the general inconveniences of co-ownership.

Future Interest: Anything other than an unrestricted right to the immediate use, possession, or enjoyment of property or the income from property. Donors may not claim an annual exclusion for gifts of future interests in property.

G

General Power of Appointment: Any power to appoint property or the income therefrom that is exercisable in favor of the decedent, the decedent's estate, or the creditor's of the decedent's estate. [IRC § 2041(b)(1)]

Generation–Skipping Transfer: A transfer of property that takes the form of a direct skip, a taxable termination, or taxable distribution. [IRC § 2611(a)]

Generation–Skipping Transfer Tax: An excise imposed on the gratuitous transfer of wealth to a recipient that is two or more generations junior to the transferor.

Generational Assignment: Defined in Chapter 13, it is used in determining whether a generation-skipping transfer has occurred. [IRC § 2651] Generational assignments are determined by comparing the individual receiving the interest with the Chapter 13 "transferor" [IRC § 2652(a)]

Gift Tax: An excise imposed on gratuitous inter vivos transfers of wealth.

Grantor–Retained Annuity Trust (GRAT): An irrevocable trust where the grantor retains the right to receive not less than once per year either a stated dollar amount or a fixed percentage of the initial fair market value of the property transferred to the trust.

Grantor Retained Income Trust (GRIT): An estate freeze technique in which the grantor transfers assets to an irrevocable trust, but retains the right to income for a term of years. The value of the gift will be the present value of the right to the remainder interest, which is often much less than the value of the property contributed to the trust.

Gross Estate: The date-of-death value of all property specifically described in IRC §§ 2031–2044. [IRC § 2031(a)] Generally, all interests in property held by the decedent at death, together with certain property transferred by the de-

cedent but over which the decedent held certain powers or control at the date of death, comprise the decedent's gross estate.

H

Hanging *Crummey* Power: A *Crummey* power that only lapses to the extent of the greater of $5,000 or 5% of the funds from which the exercise of the power could be satisfied. In this manner there will be no gift tax consequences upon the lapse of a *Crummey* power, though there will still be estate tax consequences if the power holder dies during the year since nothing has "lapsed."

I

Incidents of Ownership: With respect to a life insurance policy, any of the following: the power to change the beneficiary; the power to surrender or cancel the policy; the power to assign the policy; the power to revoke a prior assignment of the policy; the power to pledge the policy to creditors; the power to borrow against the policy; or the power to change the beneficial enjoyment of a policy owned by a trust. [Reg. § 20.2042–1(c)]

Inclusion Ratio: A component of the applicable tax rate for purposes of the generation-skipping transfer tax, computed by subtracting the applicable fraction from the number 1. The maximum estate tax rate is multiplied by the inclusion ratio to determine the applicable tax rate for Chapter 13 purposes. [IRC § 2642(a)]

Inheritance Tax: A tax imposed on the recipients of a bequest, devise or inheritance of a decedent. Contrasted with an estate tax that is imposed on the estate of the decedent.

J

Joint Tenancy with Rights of Survivorship: A form of co-ownership where each owner has an equal, undivided interest that passes directly to the surviving joint tenant(s) upon the death of any joint tenant. Property held as joint tenants with rights of survivorship does not pass through the probate process following the death of a co-tenant.

L

Lapse: The failure to exercise a power or right within the prescribed period. The lapse of a general power of appointment is considered to be a release of that power to the extent the value of the property subject to the power exceeds the greater of $5,000 or 5% of the value of the assets from which the exercise of the lapsed power could have been satisfied. [IRC §§ 2041(b)(2), 2514(e)]

M

Marital Deduction: A deduction applicable to both the estate tax and the gift tax that allows for the unlimited transfer of property from one spouse to the other. [IRC §§ 2056(a), 2523(a)]

Marketability Discount: An adjustment to the value of an asset applicable where an interest cannot be readily sold because of practical obstacles to sale, a limited market of buyers, or because of restrictions on the owner's ability to transfer the interest. The marketability discount reflects the fact that a willing buyer will consider the costs and delay involved in selling the subject property in deciding the appropriate value of the subject interest.

Minority Interest Discount: An adjustment to the value of an asset that reflects the inability both to compel a sale, distribution, or other disposition of the asset and to control its management.

N

Net Income Makeup Charitable Remainder Unitrust (NIMCRUT): A variation of the charitable remainder unitrust where the trustee pays to the non-charitable beneficiary the lesser of the trust's income or the amount normally required to be paid (a fixed percentage of the value of the trust's assets). If the income is less than the normal amount, then, in later years, when the trust's income exceeds the amount required to be paid to the non-charitable beneficiary, the excess income is paid to the non-charitable beneficiary to make up for the amount that should have been paid in the earlier year when trust income was less than the required distribution amount.

Non–Probate Assets: Assets not subject to the probate process following the decedent's death. Examples of non-probate assets include property held as joint tenants with rights of survivorship, benefits payable under retirement plans, property held in trust, and death benefits payable under a life insurance policy.

P

Pooled Income Fund: An arrangement used for obtaining a charitable deduction where two or more donors agree to contribute property to a single fund administered by the charity. The fund will pay an income interest to one or more persons and, at the end of the term, the remainder will pass to the charity.

Power of Appointment: The right to designate beneficial interests of property, for example who will enjoy the income from a trust. If the power is only over the administrative aspects of the property (such as where to invest trust property), those rights and duties are not considered powers of appointment.

Predeceased Parent Rule: For generation-skipping transfer tax purposes, an individual is moved up to the generational level of his or her predeceased parent (or higher if the individual's grandparents are also deceased) if (1) the individual is the descendant of the transferor's parent, (2) the parent died before the transfer was subject to the estate or gift tax, and (3) the individual is a lineal descendant of the transferor (i.e., child, grandchild, etc.), unless the transferor has no living descendants. The rule also applies to the descendants of the transferor's spouse or former spouse. If the transferor has no living lineal descendants at the time of transfer, the predeceased parent rule may apply to all lineal descendants of the transferor's parent. [IRC § 2651(e)]

Prescribed Interest: Any of the following with respect to property transferred by a decedent during life: the right to income; the right to possession; the right to enjoyment; the right to designate who shall receive the income; the right to designate who shall receive possession; or the right to designate who shall receive enjoyment. Under IRC § 2036, property previously gifted by the decedent may be re-included in the decedent's gross estate if the decedent retained a prescribed interest in the transferred property for a prescribed period.

Prescribed Period: Any of the following: the decedent's life; a period not ascertainable without reference to the decedent's death; or a period which does not in fact end before the decedent's death. Under IRC § 2036, property previously gifted by the decedent may be re-included in the decedent's gross estate if the decedent retained a prescribed interest in the transferred property for a prescribed period.

Present Interest: The unrestricted right to the immediate use, possession, or enjoyment of property or the income from property. Donors may claim an annual exclusion on for gifts of present interests in property.

Probate Assets: Property in which the decedent held an interest that is subject to the probate process under applicable state and local laws.

Q

Qualified Heir: In the context of special use valuation for real property under IRC § 2032A, any member of the decedent's "family" who received the real property from the decedent. The term also includes one who receives the property from a qualified heir, provided the recipient is a member of the qualified heir's family. [IRC § 2032A(e)(1)]

Qualified Payment: A right to a dividend on cumulative preferred stock payable on a periodic basis to the extent the amount of the dividend is determined at a fixed rate or bears a fixed relationship to a specified market rate. The zero-value rule of IRC § 2701 does not apply if the transferor retains the right to a qualified payment immediately after the transfer.

Qualified Real Property: Generally, land used for farming or for the operation of any other trade or business. Under IRC § 2032A, qualified real property meeting certain requirements can be valued according to the property's actual use instead of its highest and best use, the normal standard applicable in determining the fair market value of real property.

Qualified Terminable Interest Property (QTIP): An exception to the terminable interest rule that allows the marital deduction for the value of property in which the surviving spouse has a "qualifying income interest" for life and where the personal representative of the decedent makes an election on the estate tax return.

Qualified Use: A use of real property for farming or business purposes. To be eligible for special use valuation under IRC § 2032A, real property must be put to a qualified use for certain prescribed periods.

Qualifying Income Interest: A right with respect to property held by or for the benefit of a surviving spouse which entitles the spouse to all of the income from the property for life, payable at least annually. Furthermore, no one (not even the surviving spouse) may hold a power to appoint any portion of the property to anyone but the surviving spouse. If anyone does hold such a power, no part of the spouse's right to income is a qualifying income interest.

R

Reciprocal Trust Doctrine: A common law doctrine providing that where two grantors create trusts that give similar lifetime interests to each other such that the arrangement leaves the grantors in roughly "the same economic position as they would have been in had they created trusts naming themselves as life beneficiaries," each grantor will be treated as the grantor of the trust created for his or her benefit by the other transferor, meaning IRC § 2036(a) will apply.

Re–Inclusion Provisions: A reference used by the authors to describe IRC §§ 2035–2038, where assets previously transferred or consumed by the decedent are included in the decedent's gross estate.

Release: In the context of a power of appointment, the waiver of the right to exercise such power. The release of a general power of appointment is treated as the exercise of such power, because by waiving the power, the power holder is essentially choosing to let the property pass to the taker in default.

Reverse–QTIP Election: An election for generation-skipping transfer tax purposes to treat property "as if the election to be treated as qualified terminable interest property had not been made." Absent the reverse-QTIP election, there would always be a new transferor created for any qualified terminable interest property (for generation-skipping transfer tax purposes) since the property is later "subject to" either the estate or gift tax. This would result in the loss of any GST exemption amount allocated to the trust by the transferring spouse. [IRC § 2652(a)(3)]

Reversion: A power retained by a transferor to reacquire transferred property, whether by express reservation in the instrument of conveyance or by operation of law.

S

Skip Person: In the case of an individual, one with a generational assignment two or more generations below that of the transferor. A trust is a skip person when all of the current Chapter 13 interests in the trust are held by skip persons. Also, if no one has a current Chapter 13 interest in the trust, a trust is deemed a skip person if no distributions, including upon termination of the trust, can ever be made to a non-skip person. [IRC § 2613]

Special Use Valuation: An election under IRC § 2032A made on the decedent's estate tax return to value qualified real property according to its actual use instead of its highest and best use, the normal standard for measuring the

fair market value of property.

Split–Interest Transfers: A reference to any gift or bequest that is split between a charity and another, non-charitable beneficiary (typically, an individual).

State Death Taxes: Estate, inheritance, legacy and succession taxes imposed by a state government (or by the District of Columbia). State death taxes are deductible without limitation for purposes of computing a decedent's taxable estate.

Survivorship Clause: A provision in a will that conditions a beneficiary's gift upon the beneficiary surviving the decedent for a stipulated period of time. Survivorship clauses avoid back-to-back probates of the same assets where the decedent and the beneficiary die close in time.

T

Tainted Asset Rule: Where the interest passing to the surviving spouse may be satisfied out of a group of assets which includes an asset that would be nondeductible if it passed from the decedent to the surviving spouse (a "tainted asset"), the amount of the marital deduction is reduced by the value of the tainted asset.

Taxable Distribution: A distribution from a trust to a skip person that is not also a direct skip or a taxable termination. The taxable distribution is one of the three types of generation-skipping transfers.

Taxable Estate: The excess of the gross estate over the deductions allowable under IRC §§ 2053–2058. [IRC § 2051] The taxable estate is added to the decedent's adjusted taxable gifts in computing liability for estate tax.

Taxable Gifts: The total amount of gifts made during the taxable year minus any gift tax deductions allowable. The amount of "taxable gifts" is one of the primary factors used to compute the gift tax under IRC § 2502(a) for the current year (the other being the amount of taxable gifts for all preceding years).

Taxable Termination: A termination of an interest in property held in trust that does not, by itself, trigger liability for federal estate or gift tax unless, immediately after the termination, a non-skip person has a Chapter 13 interest in the trust or no future distributions (including those on termination of the trust) may be made to a skip person. This is one of the three types of generation-skipping transfers.

Tenancy by the Entirety: A form of co-ownership between married couples that operates like a joint tenancy with rights of survivorship.

Tentative Tax Liability: The amount computed by applying the rate table in IRC § 2001(c) to the sum of the decedent's taxable estate and adjusted taxable gifts, then subtracting the amount

of any gift tax that would have been payable on post–1976 gifts if the rate table in IRC § 2001(c) were in effect at the time of such gifts. Applicable credits are then subtracted from the tentative tax liability to compute the estate's final liability for tax.

Term Loan: Any loan that is not a demand loan. [IRC § 7872(f)(6)]

Terminable Interest Rule: No marital deduction is allowed where, due to the lapse of time or on the occurrence (or failure to occur) of an event or contingency, the interest in property passing from the decedent to the surviving spouse will terminate, causing the interest to pass to another (for less than an adequate and full consideration in money or money's worth) who may possess or enjoy the property after the termination of the surviving spouse's interest. [IRC § 2056(b)(1)] The terminable interest rule also applies to inter vivos transfers to a spouse. [IRC § 2523(b)(1)]

U

Unified Credit: A nonrefundable credit allowed to the estate of every decedent against the estate tax [IRC § 2010(a)] and to every United States citizen and resident against the gift tax [IRC § 2505(a)]. The unified credit is equal to the amount of tax imposed on the "applicable exclusion amount," using the rate table in IRC § 2001(c).

APPENDIX E

Table of Cases, IRC Sections, Treasury Regulations, and Rulings

Fratini, Estate of v. Commissioner, T.C. Memo. 1998-308 (U.S.Tax Ct.1998), 148

Furman v. Commissioner, T.C. Memo. 1998-157 (U.S.Tax Ct.1998), 149

Goodwin v. McGowan, 47 F.Supp. 798 (W.D.N.Y.1942), 218

Grace's Estate, United States v., 395 U.S. 316, 89 S.Ct. 1730, 23 L.Ed.2d 332 (1969), 101

Gradow v. United States, 897 F.2d 516 (Fed.Cir.1990), 98, 99

Gregory, Estate of v. Commissioner, 39 T.C. 1012 (Tax Ct.1963), 98

Hagmann, Estate of v. Commissioner, 60 T.C. 465 (U.S.Tax Ct.1973), 157

Harris v. Commissioner, 340 U.S. 106, 71 S.Ct. 181, 95 L.Ed. 111 (1950), 231

Harrison, Estate of v. Commissioner, T.C. Memo. 1987-8 (U.S.Tax Ct.1987), 295

Helmholz, Helvering v., 296 U.S. 93, 56 S.Ct. 68, 80 L.Ed. 76 (1935), 106

Helvering v. _____ (see opposing party)

Herr, Commissioner v., 303 F.2d 780 (3rd Cir.1962), 310, 310

Hogle, Commissioner v., 165 F.2d 352 (10th Cir.1947), 217

Hutchings, Helvering v., 312 U.S. 393, 61 S.Ct. 653, 85 L.Ed. 909 (1941), 298

In re (see name of party)

Jardell, Estate of v. Commissioner, 24 T.C. 652 (Tax Ct.1955), 300

Jennings v. Smith, 161 F.2d 74 (2nd Cir.1947), 97, 108

Kass v. Commissioner, T.C. Memo. 1957-227 (Tax Ct.1957), 250

Kohlsaat, Estate of v. Commissioner, T.C. Memo.

1997-212 (U.S.Tax Ct.1997), 307

La Fortune v. Commissioner, 263 F.2d 186 (10th Cir.1958), 326

League of Women Voters of United States v. U.S., 148 Ct.Cl. 561, 180 F.Supp. 379 (Ct.Cl.1960), 161

Levine, Estate of, 526 F.2d 717 (2nd Cir.1975), 311

Lober v. United States, 346 U.S. 335, 74 S.Ct. 98, 98 L.Ed. 15 (1953), 108

Magnin, Estate of v. Commissioner, 184 F.3d 1074 (9th Cir.1999), 98

Maryland Nat. Bank v. United States, 609 F.2d 1078 (4th Cir.1979), 300

Maxwell, Estate of v. Commissioner, 3 F.3d 591 (2nd Cir.1993), 98

McGuire v. Commissioner, 44 T.C. 801 (Tax Ct.1965), 89

Merrill v. Fahs, 324 U.S. 308, 65 S.Ct. 655, 89 L.Ed. 963 (1945), 227, 229

Messing v. Commissioner, 48 T.C. 502 (Tax Ct.1967), 89

Metzger v. Commissioner, 38 F.3d 118 (4th Cir.1994), 223

Moore v. Commissioner, 146 F.2d 824 (2nd Cir.1945), 228

Moss, Estate of v. Commissioner, 74 T.C. 1239 (U.S.Tax Ct.1980), 88

Noel's Estate, Commissioner v., 380 U.S. 678, 85 S.Ct. 1238, 14 L.Ed.2d 159 (1965), 131

Okerlund v. United States, 365 F.3d 1044 (Fed.Cir.2004), 147

Old Colony Trust Co. v. Commissioner, 279 U.S. 716, 49 S.Ct. 499, 73 L.Ed. 918 (1929), 379

O'Malley, United States v., 383 U.S. 627, 86 S.Ct. 1123, 16 L.Ed.2d 145 (1966), 96

Propstra v. United States, 680 F.2d 1248 (9th Cir.1982), 157

Regester, Estate of v. Commissioner, 83 T.C. No. 1, 83 T.C. 1 (U.S.Tax Ct.1984), 240, 240

Robinette v. Helvering, 318 U.S. 184, 63 S.Ct. 540, 87 L.Ed. 700 (1943), 219

Sachs (Samuel C.), Sachs (Stephen C., Sophia R.), Estate of v. Commissioner of Internal Revenue, 88 T.C. No. 43, 88 T.C. 769 (U.S.Tax Ct.1987), 229

Sanford's Estate v. Commissioner, 308 U.S. 39, 60 S.Ct. 51, 84 L.Ed. 20 (1939), 235

Self v. United States, 135 Ct.Cl. 371, 142 F.Supp. 939 (Ct.Cl.1956), 240

Sharp, Estate of v. Commissioner, T.C. Memo. 1994-636 (U.S.Tax Ct.1994), 149

Silverman's Estate, In re, 521 F.2d 574 (2nd Cir.1975), 133

Smith v. Shaughnessy, 318 U.S. 176, 63 S.Ct. 545, 87 L.Ed. 690 (1943), 87, 218

Spruance v. Commissioner, 60 T.C. 141 (U.S.Tax Ct.1973), 230

Spruill (Euil S.), Miers (Kathleen Spruill), Spruill (Weyman E.), Estate of v. Commissioner, 88 T.C. No. 68, 88 T.C. 1197 (U.S.Tax Ct.1987), 89

Stark v. United States, 477 F.2d 131 (8th Cir.1973), 301

Stinson Estate v. United States, 214 F.3d 846 (7th Cir.2000), 299

Thebaut, Commissioner v., 361 F.2d 428 (5th Cir.1966), 310

Trenchard, Estate of v. Commissioner, T.C. Memo. 1995-121 (U.S.Tax Ct.1995), 147

United States v. _____ (see opposing party)

Wemyss, Commissioner v., 324 U.S. 303, 65 S.Ct. 652, 89 L.Ed. 958 (1945), 225, 226

TABLE OF INTERNAL REVENUE CODE SECTIONS

TABLE OF TREASURY REGULATIONS

Table of Rulings

APPENDIX F

Index of Key Terms